THE SE

THE SEA ANGLER
Afloat and Ashore

DESMOND BRENNAN

ADAM & CHARLES BLACK · LONDON

REISSUED 1982

FIRST PUBLISHED 1965

BY A & C BLACK (PUBLISHERS) LIMITED

35 BEDFORD ROW, LONDON WC1R 4JH

© 1965 DESMOND BRENNAN

ISBN 0 7136 2246 6

PRINTED IN GREAT BRITAIN BY

MANSELL BOOKBINDERS LTD, WITHAM, ESSEX

CONTENTS

		PAGE
ILLUSTRATIONS		vii
ACKNOWLEDGMENTS		xi
INTRODUCTION		xiii

CHAPTER

1	THE SEA	1
2	THE FISHES OF THE SEA	25
3	NATURAL BAITS	73
4	TACKLE	87
5	TECHNIQUES	103
6	THE ANGLER AFLOAT	129
7	DO'S AND DON'TS	150
8	BASS	154
9	MULLET	177
10	POLLACK, COALFISH, MACKEREL AND SCAD	194
11	COD, LING, HAKE	211
12	WHITING, HADDOCK, POUTING AND POOR COD	222
13	CONGER	229
14	THE FLATFISHES	238
15	THE WRASSES, GURNARDS AND SEA BREAMS	249
16	THE SHADS AND THE SEA TROUT	260
17	TOPE	269
18	THE DOGFISHES, MONKFISH AND ANGLER FISH	287

19 THE SKATES AND RAYS   297

20 SHARKS   312

21 BIG GAME FISHES   332

INDEX   344

ILLUSTRATIONS

Page

THE AUTHOR FISHING A LIVELY SURF FOR BASS ON AN
ATLANTIC STORM BEACH. Frontispiece

EFFECT OF WIND ON MOVEMENTS OF FISH 13

DEPTH SCALE IN FATHOMS 17

PROFILE OF A LONG ESTUARY 22

EXTERNAL FEATURES OF FISH 26

SCAD 31

SEA BREAM AND WRASSES 37

GREY MULLETS 39

THE GURNARDS 41

THE THREE COMMONEST FLATFISHES 44

COD FAMILY (I) 51

COD FAMILY (II) 54

THE GREATER AND LESSER SPOTTED DOGFISHES 62

SHARKS 63

THRESHER SHARK 65

SMOOTH HOUND SHARK 66

DISCS OF THREE SKATES AND THEIR FUNDAMENTAL GEOMETRIC
SHAPES 68

BLOOD KNOT "FAMILY," BASIC KNOTS IN TACKLE MAKING 102

TERMINAL LOOP IN MONOFILAMENT, AND ITS USES 102

BASIC TERMINAL RIGS FOR BOTTOM FISHING 104

FLOAT GEAR 113

TRACE FOR SPINNING 116

PORTION OF A CHART 131

FOUR POINT AND COMPASS BEARINGS 133

ALLOWING FOR TIDE   135

VENOMOUS FISHES   153

GILL RAKERS OF THE SHADS   261

BROADBILL SWORDFISH   340

TUNNY, ALBACORE AND BONITOS   342

To
My Wife

ACKNOWLEDGMENTS

IN THE WRITING OF THIS BOOK I AM INDEBTED TO A GREAT many people, particularly to Dr Michael Kennedy, without whose active encouragement I would not have undertaken the task, and for his continued encouragement, advice and assistance in proof reading, so generously given, I am deeply grateful. I am also greatly indebted to him for the many fine line drawings which illustrate the text. My thanks also to the many anglers, too numerous to mention here with whom I have fished over the years and from whom I have learnt so much about the sport of sea angling and whose friendship and comradeship I have been fortunate to enjoy.

Sea Angling is a sport of considerable variety and not a little complexity. There are many different branches of sea angling, and there are specialists in each branch. Local knowledge too counts for a lot in sea fishing. Marine biology, navigation, meteorology and other sciences enter into sea angling to a greater or lesser degree. In this book it has been possible to deal only in a general way with certain aspects of sea angling on which very much more could and should be said. The writer has, in compiling the book, consulted the works of many other writers who are specialists in various fields ; and for more information than can be given in this volume about sea angling in all its aspects, the reader is referred to these works, namely :—The Sea Anglers Fishes by Michael Kennedy (Hutchinson and Co. Ltd., London), The Fishes of the British Isles by J. Travis Jenkins (Frederick Warne & Co. Ltd., London), The Open Sea, Vols. I and II. by Sir Alister Hardy (Collins, London), Collins Pocket Guide to the Sea Shore by John Barrett and C. M. Yonge (Collins, London), The Sea Shore by C. M. Yonge (Collins, London), The Seas by F. S. Russell and C. M. Yonge, (Frederick Warne & Co. Ltd., London), Saltwater Angling by Michael Kennedy (Hutchinson & Co. Ltd., London), Shore Fishing by Clive Gammon (MacGibbon & Kee, London), Tope, How to catch them, by Bruce McMillen (Herbert Jenkins, London), Grey Mullet, How to catch them, by Alan Mitchell (Herbert Jenkins, London), Tunny Fishing by L. Mitchell Henry (Rich & Cowan Ltd., London), Big Game Angling by J. H. Bennett (Faber & Faber, London), Shark Angling in Great Britain by Brigadier J. A. L. Caunter (George Allen & Unwin, Ltd., London), Motor Boating for the Novice by Mary Hervey Murray and Percy Woodcock (Frederick

Mullen Ltd., London), Teach Yourself Motor Boating by Dudley Noble and A. J. Shimmin (The English Universities Press Ltd., London), Hank Bowman's Boat Owners Handbook by Hank Bowman (Fawcett Publications, Connecticut, U.S.A.), Understanding Weather by O. G. Sutton (Penguin Books Ltd., Middlesex). My thanks are also due to Mr Johannes Hamre, Directorat of Fisheries, Bergen, Norway, for the information on the movements and migration of Tunny.

The cover photograph and frontispiece are both by Brian Lynch and are reproduced by the kind permission of Bord Failte (The Irish Tourist Board).

INTRODUCTION

ANGLING AS A SPORT AND A RECREATION HAS ENJOYED A tremendous increase in popularity since the last war. Game fishing, coarse fishing and sea angling have all been affected as literally thousands take up the sport each year. Today the number of anglers in these islands alone is not far off the four million mark and while this has its drawbacks as is evidenced by overcrowded waters in many areas it has also conferred great benefits. Fresh minds have been brought to bear on old problems, new techniques discovered and new materials developed.

Sea Angling has been affected probably more than any other form of the art. Progress has been great not alone in the numbers participating in the sport but in new methods, techniques, tackle and in actual knowledge gained about sea fishing in general. Out of the melting pot of this great influx of anglers, many of them freshwater fishermen who have brought freshwater tackle and methods to the game have been born new ideas.

It is only natural that where such a great upsurge of interest takes place in a sport that there should be some conflict of opinion between seasoned anglers loyal to traditional methods and the new school of anglers who have brought a fresh outlook to the sport. There is something to be learned both from the old and the new, some ideas and practices can be accepted, others must be discarded. Newcomers and indeed anglers of long standing may find this confusing and the purpose of this book is to help them understand the fundamental principles of angling and to show them the way to better and more sporting fishing. It is intended to be a guide rather than a textbook on tackle, traces and gears. Much, indeed too much, has been written on this subject already, and has led to over-complication and a tendency towards gadgetry, where the simple straightforward approach is often the key to success. There is little use in possessing good equipment and knowing how to make up complicated rigs if you do not know what you are fishing for or how, where and when to fish for it.

Angling like any other sport requires proper equipment and acquired skills but it requires more than that alone. It calls for a knowledge of the ways of fish, their life history, their habits, haunts and foods. You must know your fish if you want to catch them. You must even learn to think like them. There is no easy way of becoming a good sea angler, no "rule of thumb" method to ensure success. The more you learn the more you come to realise how little you really know. This is not meant to be discouraging but to emphasise the absolute necessity of keeping an open mind at all times and always to be willing to learn. The Sea Angler should always be willing to experiment, to try something new, to accept what is good, to reject what is bad and not to be hidebound in either his outlook or methods.

The fundamental elements of all Angling are *Tackle*, *Technique* and "*Know How*". All of the three elements involved are important but of the three the last mentioned is by far the most important. The good angler will of course have good tackle, but he would still catch fish even if he had to use inferior equipment, because he knows his job. Even the best equipped angler, however, will not be successful if he does not "know how".

The secret of successful angling is to fish in the *right place*, at the *right time*, with the *right lure* and the *right tackle*. The right place is where the fish are most likely to feed under the prevailing conditions of season and weather. The right time is the state of tide or weather or the time of day when the fish are most likely to feed. The right bait or lure is their natural food at the time or an acceptable alternative. The right tackle is that which will most easily and effectively present the bait in an acceptable manner to the fish, hook the fish when it takes, and handle the fish when hooked. Where there are a variety of suitable methods the one which gives the most sport to the angler is the one which should be used.

There is a common fallacy among those who have little experience of sea angling that all one has to do is bait a hook and drop it into the sea and you will catch fish. While I have seen complete novices make good catches and even break records on their first day's fishing, nothing could be further from the truth. The sea is a vast place and fish are not everywhere in it. In many ways the sea is like the land on which we live. Some areas are very fertile and rich in food and consequently carry a big population of fish.

Others, like our deserts are completely barren and devoid of fish. Large areas are not very rich in food and can only support a sparse fish population. Fish will be found where their food is. This fact is of paramount importance. For this reason the angler must study the natural food of the fish he seeks and he must know where that food is found. Then he knows the right place to fish.

It is not enough to know the fish's food but you must also be conversant with its feeding habits. The topography of the sea-bed is as varied as that of the land. In the sea, too, are vast plains, high mountain ranges, deep valleys and broken ground, each with its distinctive fish populations. Pollack and wrasse are fish of rough and rocky ground, while flounders, plaice and turbot find their living on soft bottoms of mud, sand and gravel. Some fish, like the cod, range freely over smooth and rough ground in search of food. Others again, like the sharks, are pelagic and feed mainly in the upper layers of the sea. Some, like the ling, prefer deep water but more, like the bass, are found mainly in shallow water. Some fish are specially adapted to a particular kind of feeding, i.e. the herring on plankton, while some feed mainly on other fishes. Such predator species usually have big mouths and depend on their speed to catch their prey, e.g. tunny and mackerel, or they can be sluggish creatures, e.g. angler fish, John Dory, depending on guile and disguise to conceal their presence from their victims until it is too late.

Most species are not so highly specialised as the herring as to be restricted to a limited range of food and most are adapted to feed on a variety of foods. Nevertheless, even in the most omniverous species there are usually well marked food preferences and it is important to learn what these preferences are. A lot can be learned from books as to the food of a particular species but this can vary from place to place depending on the type of food available and there is nothing like finding out first hand for yourself. Anglers should make it their business to become familiar with aquatic creatures by searching for them at every opportunity among weed and stones or on the sands when the tide is out. They should make it a practice to examine the stomach contents of the fish they catch. Not just a few stomachs but *all* of them. After all the seagull found in the stomach of one blue shark may not prove to be the staple diet of all sharks. This is the only way to become familiar with the feeding pattern of a particular species not alone on different types of ground but at different times of the year. In this way you will learn more about fish and their habits.

The importance of food is obvious yet it is so often seemingly overlooked by anglers. Frequently I have watched anglers spend fishless hours at the end of a long pier fishing in deep water while the fish they sought were feeding closer to the shore. Either the anglers found the end of the pier more convenient to fish from or else suffered from the delusion that fish can only be caught in deep water. The same applies to shore anglers who insist on casting as far as they possibly can when a short cast of 20 yards or less would put them amongst the fish. It leads one to think that some anglers are more concerned with the distance they can cast than with catching fish. Remember fish will be where their food is and not where you think they should be or where it is convenient for you to fish. Fish are not concerned with your convenience but with their own stomachs. So find the food and you will find the fish.

The feeding habits of fish are affected by a variety of factors, temperature, light, tide, currents, weather, wind and the seasons. Every fish has a preferred range of temperatures and becomes most active towards the upper middle of that range. Towards the lower limits it becomes torpid and seeks warmer conditions and towards the upper limit it seeks cooler conditions. Thus cod and whiting which prefer cold water keep to the cooler deeps in summer but move inshore in winter when the shallow inshore water has cooled and become colder than the deep water. On the other hand bass and mullet prefer warm water and are found in the shallows in summer along beaches and in estuaries and creeks. In autumn or early winter as the shallows rapidly cool they move out into deeper water which retains the heat accumulated during the summer or they may migrate southwards to where temperatures are more to their liking.

Light affects many species of fish. Conger, although they can be caught during the day, are essentially nocturnal and become more active after dark. Pollack tend to rise up to the surface at dawn and dusk and while they can be taken during the day, bright hot days are not good for them. Some species seem unaffected by light but others are indirectly affected through their food, i.e. hake, which rise up after herring at night, which in turn have followed the upward movement of plankton after dark. Apart from the migration of certain species from cold to warmer waters and vice versa there are also seasonal migrations for spawning, i.e. flounders move offshore in winter.

The twice daily movement of the tides is of the greatest importance to the angler. Fish usually feed best when the tide is making or falling but this is not constant for every place. Some places fish best on the flood tide, some on the ebb tide or for only portion of the tides. Others may fish well only on the slack of the tides, i.e. near high or low water. The action of the tide sweeps food and fish along with it and fish may travel along one route on the flood but the ebb tide may take them back another way. Some species, i.e. bass, travel long distances with the tides, along beaches and into estuaries feeding over ground not available to them when the tide is out. Others, like turbot, may let the tide take food to them, lying in ambush on the bottom and pouncing when some tasty morsel is swept within their reach. Tidal currents, particularly where they are swift, or are compressed by headlands, islands, shoal ground or underwater obstructions, sweep along large quantities of bait fish which may become concentrated in a small area. Many predator species, such as mackerel and bass, may be found in such circumstances feeding on small fry, whilst they in turn may be preyed upon by larger predators, such as tope and shark.

Wind and weather must also be taken into consideration by the angler. Small bait fishes, such as herring fry or sand-eels, dislike rough water and sink deep in rough conditions. They tend to swim against the wind, i.e. inshore when the wind is blowing from the land and offshore when the wind is blowing into the land. This affects the behaviour of such fish as mackerel which prey on the fry and in turn the fish which feed on the mackerel. Bass feed along beaches in the surf in onshore winds but in calm conditions they often follow shoals of fry. Mullet take best in calm warm weather but sink deep when the sea is rough.

These are but a few examples of the ways that the habits and movements of fish can be affected by different conditions. The angler must get to know how any particular species he seeks will behave under varying circumstances and conditions and to be able to adjust his fishing accordingly. Otherwise he will often be only wasting his time.

Once you know where the fish are and when they are likely to be feeding the next step is to offer them the right bait or lure.   This varies considerably not alone with the species but with conditions prevailing at the time of fishing.   Plaice and sole feed mainly on bivalves and worms whilst turbot are almost exclusively fish eaters. Bass when fry are plentiful may take little interest in bottom food. Different types of bottom provide different types of food and the food organisms present in shallow water are different from those found in deep water.   The anglers' aim should be to present to the fish the food they are feeding on or a suitable alternative and to present it in as natural a way as is possible.

Outside of the spawning season fish are actuated by two main urges—hunger and fear.   The angler is concerned with both.   Fish sometimes seize a bait through anger or curiosity but mostly, however, they do so because they want to eat it.   Fish are creatures of limited intelligence and their behaviour is a combination of simple instincts and acquired reflexes (automatic reactions to certain stimuli).   A fish cannot outthink the angler.   In fact it cannot think at all.   If it refuses to accept a lure or bait it is not because it recognises it as a fraud but because it fails to recognise it as a desirable food.   Or the fish simply may not be hungry.   Or the fish may be frightened.

Few sea anglers pay much attention to this last point.   I have fished with keen anglers who will make use of every scrap of cover, creep on their stomachs and keep down off the skyline when pursuing the wily trout.   Yet when they turn to the sea they will gaily splash through the shallows, stand up on prominent rocks and bang about in boats.   How often have you come down on the shore, seen a fish swirl in alarm in the shallows and watched the bow wave arrowing out into deeper water.   That fish had seen you and you had seen it.   How many fish have seen you and slipped quietly away without you ever having been aware of their presence?

Fish do not hear in the same way as we do but make no mistake they can hear quite well.   Sounds created in the air do not pass readily into water and consequently fish pay little attention to them. However, they are very sensitive to vibrations, and noises which can be passed on through the ground or through the keel of a boat as vibrations are quickly detected.   The heavy "knock" of a diesel engine may affect fishing but little (although I must confess that I always prefer to have the engine switched off when fishing) in deep water but in shallow water it is definitely detrimental to fishing.

The angler's primary concern, therefore, is to present to the fish something that it will accept as or mistake for food and to do so in the way most likely to attract the fish's attention at a time that it is likely to be feeding. His secondary concern is to avoid frightening the fish. This in many instances is just as much of importance as a frightened fish will not take.

The last of our fundamental principles is the use of the right tackle and the right method for the particular type of fishing you intend to do. Most fishing rods are designed for a specific purpose, be it shark fishing or surf fishing. There is no such thing as an all purpose rod and although some rods can be used quite well for purposes other than that which they were designed for, a rod is a hundred per cent efficient only when doing its own job. It seems ridiculous to use a heavy shark rod and line for flounder fishing from a pier or a light spinning rod when bottom fishing for heavy fish in 30 fathoms but I have seen this happen. In between these two extremes you will see a variety of unsuitable rods and mismatched tackle that not alone makes efficient angling difficult but also makes fishing a penance instead of a pleasure. Not alone should the rod, reel and line match but they should also match the species of fish which is being sought. Thus one will use light tackle for smaller species such as flounder and strong tackle for powerful heavy fish such as big skate which must be lifted up from deep water. The angler's aim should be to use the tackle which will give him the maximum amount of sport from the species which he seeks and under the conditions he must fish.

The right method is the one which will enable the angler to present his bait or lure in the most natural way or in a manner likely to deceive the fish. Thus, spinning with artificial lures may be the best method to take shoaling bass, whilst a bottom bait fished just behind the surf would be the answer on a beach. The methods used will vary with the species and with the conditions under which the fishing is done. The angler must be familiar with all the different methods and techniques used and to be able to adapt his methods to suit conditions. If one method fails he should try another; he should be willing to experiment and to learn. He should always think about his fishing and he should never fish by rule of thumb. Fish may not be intelligent but there is no reason why the angler should not be.

Every angler should keep a fishing diary. Not just for a season or two, but always. In it he should enter the fish caught, date, precise place, tackle, bait, lure, weather and water conditions, natural foods noted as present at the time, the food present in the fish and any other relevant data. He should do this every time he goes fishing not just for the good days but for the poor or blank days as well. It is amazing what one can learn from the frequent study of a well kept fishing diary. Memory is a strange thing and cannot always be trusted. We remember the good days and many important things are forgotten or escape unnoticed. If you keep a diary and study it frequently facts begin to add up and a clearer overall picture is obtained. It will help you know your fish better, to improve your fishing and perhaps prevent you from jumping to hasty conclusions on insufficient evidence. Properly kept and properly used it can be one of the greatest aids to fishing.

Tackle, Technique and "Know How": the three fundamentals of any form of angling. It is these that make the good angler stand out from the rest. Whilst there is often a lot of luck in sea angling it is the man who thinks about his fishing, studies the habits of the fish he seeks, who has the right tackle and is proficient in its use, he is the man who is consistently successful. It is not a matter of luck with him.

The object of angling is to catch fish, but there is more to it than just that, otherwise easier and more efficient methods than rod and line would be used. It is a question of catching fish by certain methods and in accordance with certain rules formulated by the anglers themselves over many generations. They are much less rigid and more elastic than the rules governing most sports and they are, moreover, unwritten rules. Anglers should never lose sight of the fact that angling is a sport pursued as a sport rather than for its results no matter how acceptable they may be on the breakfast table. The aim of the angler should be the maximum of sport rather than the maximum of catches and his conscience should be his guide as to what is fair and sporting. Most anglers when they first take up the sport want to catch as many fish as possible but later their ambitions change from bigger catches to bigger and better fish. Gradually they begin to concentrate on those species which give them the most pleasure and eventually graduate to catching them on the tackle and by the methods which provide them with the greatest sport. It is then that they are getting the most out of angling.

Sea Angling has long been considered by those not participating in it, a crude and perhaps a rather unsporting type of fishing. Crude it may have been in the past but make no mistake about it not being a sport. There are gamer and more sporting fish in the sea than there are in fresh water and when taken on the right tackle they provide some of the finest fishing of all. Sea angling requires as much finesse and skill as any other form of angling, and if it is crude, the fault lies with the angler and not with the sport. In the past, due to the materials available, sea angling was "thick-eared" and on the heavy side but with present day tackle, technique and methods there is no excuse for unsporting fishing. Provided the angler has the right approach to Sea Angling and uses the right type of tackle he will find that he is enjoying the greatest sport of all.

CHAPTER I

THE SEA

IF WE ARE PROPERLY TO APPRECIATE THE HABITS, MOVEMENTS and reactions of fish it is essential that we first know something of the element in which they live and in which we must fish if we are to catch them. There is more to the sea than meets the eye. Actually we can see very little of it, just a small portion of the surface and a very short distance into it and this gives us little indication of the teeming and complex life which exists beneath the waves. Science has gradually lifted the lid, so to speak, off the sea and unfolded a fantastic picture of the millions of organisms, fishes and animals that are born, live out their lives and die beneath the surface. We are still far from knowing the whole story but what we do know, apart from making fascinating reading is important to the angler. It will help him to a better understanding of the ways of his quarry and fit him better to seek them out and catch them.

We know that the sea is big but its very vastness is seldom fully comprehended. More than two-thirds of the surface area of the earth is covered by the seas and hidden from our eyes are the enormous depths which are found in all the oceans. The greatest depth recorded so far is an incredible $6\frac{1}{4}$ miles near the Phillipines in the Pacific Ocean. There are great depths found in all the oceans for the sea floor is far from being flat. In the Atlantic, for example, there are huge mountain ranges rising from the bottom, four miles beneath the surface, to heights ranging from $2\frac{1}{4}$ miles to $3\frac{1}{2}$ miles. The seas are shallowest near the land, shelving gradually from the tidal zones on the shore to a depth of approximately 100 fathoms (600 feet) then dropping quite abruptly to 1000 fathoms before gradually easing off into deeper water. The comparatively shallow and narrow zone stretching out to the 100 fathom line is known as the Continental Shelf and is an extension of the land mass which has gradually been submerged or it may have been built up by material washed off the land and carried by the rivers to be deposited on the sea bed. The angler is concerned with the inner portion of this shelf, out to approximately the 40 fathom line unless he is fishing for pelagic species such as shark when he may fish farther out. The limit of effective fishing with rod and line for bottom living species is about 40 fathoms, indeed bottom fishing in depths greater than 30 fathoms often ceases to be a pleasure and becomes hard work.

The most striking thing about sea water is its saltiness. This salt has been derived from the land and is due to the accumulation of minute quantities of salt washed down in our rivers over countless ages. Sea salt is composed mainly of over 75% sodium chloride with smaller amounts of other salts. The actual composition of the salt is practically the same in all the seas but the actual amount present in the water varies from place to place and from time to time. The salinity of the open Atlantic off our coasts varies from 35 to 35·5 parts per thousand. In the North Sea and in the Irish Sea where the salt water has been diluted by the influx of fresh water from large rivers it varies from 34 to 34·8 parts per thousand. Where there is little or no dilution by fresh water and where evaporation from heat is great the salinity can be very high, as in the Red Sea where the proportion is 40 parts per thousand. On the other hand in the Baltic Sea, which is partially enclosed and which receives large quantities of fresh water, the salinity is very low, 29 parts per thousand, and varies with the distance from its connection with the open sea. In places in the Baltic it is not uncommon to catch both freshwater and saltwater species in the same area. It is obvious that the salinity will be lower in the proximity of land than in the open sea, especially near the mouths of large rivers.

Sea fish are adapted to living in salt water, and while they can become acclimatised gradually to living in waters of varying salinity, any sudden change will cause them distress and may in fact kill them. The blood of fishes is a salt solution in physical character and so is the water in which they live, so consequently osmosis enters into the picture. Where two solutions of different concentrations are separated by a semipermeable surface, fluid passes from the weaker to the stronger until the concentration of the solutions is equalised. The blood of bony fishes, for example, is less saline than the sea so they lose water and must compensate for this by drinking. If they were transferred suddenly to fresh water their blood being a stronger solution they would absorb large amounts of water and being unable to get rid of it they would quickly become waterlogged and die. Few fish possess the necessary physical requirements to live in both fresh and salt water, the salmon and sea trout being good examples of species that can successfully cross the barrier. Other species, like mullet and bass, have varying degrees of tolerance and can become accustomed to living in brackish waters. While the salinity in the open sea varies but little and probably does not affect the distribution of different species the change of salinity in certain sea areas due to seasonal changes in ocean currents, and the amount of fresh water present may affect the habits of certain species of fish in those areas.

In the sea there is present in solution traces of all the known chemical elements washed down from the land in the same way as the salt. The most important of these are the phosphates and nitrates, the principal elements in all natural and artificial manures, and which are as essential to the sea as they are to the land. On them depends the whole cycle of life in the sea. Also present, dissolved in the water, are various gases. No animal can live without oxygen and no plant without carbon dioxide. All living creatures in the sea have specialised apparatus for extracting oxygen from the water, e.g. the gills in fishes, and having used the oxygen they release carbon dioxide, which is utilised by the plants which restore oxygen back into the water again. Oxygen is also absorbed into the sea by the action of wind and waves.

While salinity throughout the seas varies but little and has no great effect on the distribution of fish, the temperature of the water does vary considerably and has a very definite limiting effect on the distribution of the different species. Fish are cold blooded creatures and unlike warm blooded animals have no way of controlling their own body temperature so they must take up their heat from the surrounding water. Every fish has a preferred range of temperature within which it must live. They are most active towards the upper middle of their temperature range and must avoid water which is either too cold or too warm for them. Even a small increase of a few degrees in water temperature can have a distressing effect on their metabolism, increasing their chemical reactions and if the increase is too great, causing death. The effect of water temperature on fish distribution is very evident in the species caught around these islands. Owing to our geographical position we are fortunate to be situated where two major fish distribution areas meet and overlap. In many ways we enjoy the best of both worlds. Our southern waters are comparatively warm and hold such characteristic warm water species as blue shark, bass, mullet and pilchard. Our more northerly waters are colder and more suited for such typical cold water fish as cod, herring and coalfish. While these species overlap in places around our coasts many, e.g. the bass, are nearing their temperature limit and fade out along the coast.

The sea receives its heat from the sun and most of this heat is absorbed in the surface layers and does not penetrate to any great depth. The sea warms up very slowly and does not reach its maximum temperature until August, well after the warmest part of our summer is past. It also loses its heat very slowly and for this reason is warmer in winter than the land. The inshore shallows absorb heat and also lose it more quickly than the deeper water offshore and this has an effect on the movements of several species of fish. Cod and whiting prefer cold water and stay in the cooler deeps during the summer, moving inshore in winter when the shallows have lost their heat and have become colder than the deeper water outside. Bass and mullet, on the other hand, revel in the warm shallows in summer but seek deeper water in winter when the shallows have become too cold for their liking.

As the summer sun warms the surface layers, heat, due to the bad conductivity of water, is passed only very slowly downwards. Warm water is lighter than cold water and they do not mix readily. Consequently, in summer you find a layer of warm water above a mass of cold water and in between you have a layer of water where the temperature drops sharply. This layer known as the Thermocline, makes it very difficult for the upper and lower layers to mix. It is only in winter when surface temperatures drop to as low as or lower than those of the deeper water or when severe gales violently agitate the water as happens during the autumn, that the two layers mix.

Our summer sun is not the only source of heat to the waters off our coasts. The sea is far from being a stagnant mass and ocean currents have a great effect on the life in the sea. The sea is like a huge boiler receiving heat from the blazing tropic sun and losing it in the icy waters of the Arctic. The warmer lighter water flows northwards on the surface whilst the cold water from the pole flows southwards on the bottom, setting up the great ocean currents. The most important of these currents to us is the Gulf Stream or North Atlantic Drift as it is more correctly known. It originates in the Gulf of Mexico and flows out of the Straits of Florida as a mighty river 50 miles wide and over 300 fathoms deep and at a speed of 3½ knots. This warm current widens as it travels, losing heat on its way, and by the time it reaches our coasts it is no longer a definite stream but a drift of warm surface water. It bathes the south and west coasts of Ireland, flows around the north of Scotland and into the North Sea and also in variable amounts into the English Channel. It is responsible in no small way not alone for our equitable climate but also for the variety and quantity of fish life around our shores.

The sun not alone provides heat but it also provides the light which is so essential to all plant life. The sea has depth as well as surface and while the whole of the surface will be illuminated, the rays of the sun can only penetrate a short distance into the water. The amount of light which penetrates the water depends on the altitude of the sun, its strength, the turbidity of the water (i.e. on the amount of sand or silt suspended in it) and the condition of its surface. More light is reflected from the surface when there is wave action than when the sea is calm and even on the calmest day about two-thirds of the light is absorbed in the first three feet of water. At 10 fathoms on many parts of our coast there is no more than a murky twilight and at 100 fathoms there is perpetual darkness. This has a very important effect on life in the sea as plant life can only exist in the upper illuminated layers and of course it also has an effect on the distribution of fish. Those species which are adapted to find their food by sight are more at home in the brighter waters whilst bottom living fish in deep water used to seeking their food in complete darkness would find bright light both blinding and frightening.

Even though the land and the sea are two very different elements the basis of life in both is very similar. Fundamentally all life on the land is dependent on plants. They are eaten by herbivorous animals which in turn are eaten by carnivorous animals. The

nutrient salts, principally the phosphates, nitrates and iron com-
pounds, the gases, oxygen and carbon dioxide, are the basic raw
materials of all living matter. Only the plants under the stimulus
of light on their chlorophyll cells can turn these inorganic substances
into living plant material which can then be used as food by the
animals. The sea supports a multitude of life far exceeding in
variety and numbers that which exists on the land. An immense
quantity of plant food is required to support them. Where are
these plants? The seaweeds are unimportant as food, being browsed
upon by only a few small animals and providing shelter for others.
Needing both light and attachment to grow they are found only in
shallow water in a relatively narrow strip around the coast.

We have seen that the essential salts and gases are present in the
sea and as light is a necessary factor the plants must be found in the
surface layers where the rays of the sun can stimulate their growth.
They bear little resemblance to plants as we know them, most of
them being so tiny as to need a microscope to see them. Yet they
exist in their countless billions, being browsed upon by a myriad of
tiny animals. Although microscopic in size these plants make up
an enormous mass of vegetable matter, as much as ten tons per acre
of water at certain times of the year. Collectively both the plants
and animals at the surface waters of the sea are known as the plankton
(meaning to wander or drift). Although some of the tiny animals
are quite active they are, unlike fish, unable to swim against the
tide or currents and are swept along by them. The plant plankton
is known as the phytoplankton and consists of a variety of single
celled plants, diatoms and dinoflagellates being the most common.
The animals are known as the zooplankton, among which small
crustaceans predominate and of course also included in the plankton
are the eggs and larvae of fish and many bottom living invertebrates
which spend their early stages in the surface water.

The phytoplankton are browsed upon by the zooplankton, some
of which eat each other, and feeding directly on the plankton are a
number of fish including the mackerel, herring, pilchards and sprats,
which themselves form the food of many larger fish such as shark and
tope. The huge basking shark so common around our coasts during
the summer feeds exclusively on the tiny plankton, as indeed do
some of the giant whales, the largest animals that have ever existed
on the earth. While the plants are confined to the surface layers

the animals are not as there is a continuous rain of dead and dying material gradually sinking towards the bottom, feeding zooplankton living in the deeper layers. On the seabed are a great variety of creatures equipped to gather this falling food and these in turn are preyed upon by crustaceans, worms, molluscs and other creatures which in their turn are the food of such fish as cod and plaice. Such is the chain of life in the sea, each link interdependent on the other and all ultimately dependent on the plants.

The amount of plankton present in the sea is not constant but depends on many factors. Although there is an immense amount of nutrient salts in solution in the sea the supply is not inexhaustible and, of course, the intensity of light received from the sun varies with the seasons and has a big bearing on planktonic life. The manurial salts are present in greatest quantities during the winter months but cannot be utilised by the plants as the sun is low in the sky and little light penetrates the water as most of it is reflected from the surface. In spring as the sun rises higher in the sky and its rays increase in strength the plants can once again make use of its energy and they multiply at a tremendous rate. However, in a short time (about one month) almost all the salts have been used up and the plants die down. At the same time there is a great outburst of animal plankton to feed on the bountiful supply of plant food. Born in time to enjoy this great crop are the young of many fishes and the larval stages of a host of creatures such as crustaceans, worms and molluscs which form part of the temporary plankton. By early summer the phytoplankton has almost disappeared, some of it cropped by the animals, the rest of it sunk to the bottom forming food for the bottom living creatures. The zooplankton is now growing up, feeding upon one another and reproducing their species.

Although the manurial salts in the surface layers have been exhausted a new supply has gradually been building up in the deeper layers, converted back mainly by bacterial action from the dead animals and other organic remains. During the summer due to the Thermocline caused by the heating of the surface waters the upper and lower layers cannot mix and the manurial salts are not available to the plants in the surface layers where alone they can be used. It is only in the autumn when the surface waters begin to cool down that the Thermocline can be broken and the waters thoroughly mixed by the autumnal gales.   A new upsurge of plant life then takes place, not as vigorous or as great, however, as the spring outburst, for the sun is sinking lower in the sky with the onset of winter and its rays are becoming weaker.   The plants soon die down again and remain quiescent until the following spring.

The importance of the plankton is obvious.   It is the foundation on which the whole cycle of life in the sea is based.   On its abundance or scarcity the quality of our fishing depends.   It will affect the growth of fish which in our waters naturally make most of their growth during the summer months when food is plentiful. Its distribution will affect the location of such fish as herring, pilchard and sprat which feed directly on the plankton and this will affect the fish such as sharks which in turn prey on them.   It also affects the quantity of fish available, for should the plankton fail in a spawning area for different species of fish, food will not be available for the larval stages and the mature fish will not be there for the angler to catch in future years.

Now that we have an idea of the general background of life in the sea let us take a look at some other aspects which are of great importance to the angler.   Paramount among these is the phenomena of the tides.   They govern not alone the movements and feeding habits of many species of fish but also the often tedious business of collecting bait.   They must be taken into account in planning any sea fishing trip.   On the shore some places fish well on the flood, some on the ebb, others at high or low water while some good fishing spots may be accessible only at low water.   When boat-fishing the same applies.   Different marks may fish well at different stages of the tide, others, on account of the strength of the tides, may be fishable only at slack water, i.e. high or low tide.   A knowledge of tides may also save you considerable time in getting to and from your fishing grounds as you can use the ebb tide to take you out and the flood tide to take you back.   Many anglers fish by the tides without ever really understanding them, so perhaps a brief word of explanation may not be out of place here.

The tides are caused by the gravitational pull of the moon and to a lesser degree by that of the sun.   This pull is not strong enough to raise the water vertically when the moon is directly overhead but it is strong enough to exert a horizontal pull as the moon passes by and the water is more or less pulled after it.   This causes the water to pile up beneath the moon and a similar piling up takes place on the other side of the earth, opposite the point where the moon is situated. In between, as the water is drawn away the level is lowered, so that at two points on the earth's surface where this simultaneous piling up takes place you have high tides and at two other points where the water level has dropped you have low tides. The moon is not stationary in the heavens but circles the earth once every twenty-eight days, while the earth revolves on its axis once every twenty-four hours, thus the attraction of the moon on the water and the daily revolution of the earth causes a movement of water known as the tidal wave. This should not be confused with the huge destructive and wrongly named "tidal wave" which is caused by submarine earthquake and has nothing whatsoever to do with the tides. In the open ocean this tidal wave is not noticeable, being only about 2 feet high, but as it reaches the Continental Shelf and shallow coastal waters its speed is reduced by friction and its height increases as the water piles up. It is this piling up that causes the big variation in water level which we experience between high and low tide. Water will always seek to find its own level and this massing of water on the comparatively shallow shelf near the land and in the inshore waters causes a horizontal as well as a vertical movement of water as is demonstrated by the familiar forward movement of tide over our beaches and up our estuaries. In addition it causes the tidal streams or currents which in places can be very strong, as is experienced at Portland Bill and at the Splaugh Rock near Rosslare.

The tidal wave in the open Atlantic flows east and strikes the west and south coasts of Ireland and the coast of Cornwall at approximately the same time causing almost simultaneous high and low tides along these coasts. The southern portion of the tidal wave is divided by the Cornish coast, portion of it flowing up the Channel and portion into the Irish Sea. As the wave progresses past the north-west coast of Ireland it sends a branch down the North Channel into the Irish Sea while the main body flows round the tip of Scotland and down the east coast of England merging at last with the stream which flows up the English Channel. While the time of high water at ports along the west coast of Ireland is roughly the same, it varies considerably around the rest of these islands for it takes the tidal wave a further seven hours to reach the

Straits of Dover and almost twenty hours to reach the mouth of the Thames via the north of Scotland.

We have two high tides daily, one when the moon is overhead, the other when it is on the opposite side of the earth. During the twenty-four hours that it takes the earth to make one complete revolution the moon has travelled a portion of its twenty-eight day orbit around us and consequently at any given point on the earth's surface it arrives overhead later each day until in twenty-eight days it has gone the full circle. The daily difference in arrival time is fifty minutes and of course this progressive time lag affects the tides. This difference, however, is not constant, varying from about thirty minutes on spring tides to about seventy-five minutes on neap tides, and is due to the fact that the sun (which also exerts a gravitational pull) and the moon are not always pulling in the same direction. When both the sun and moon are exerting their power in a straight line we have the greatest rise and conversely the greatest fall in the tides and these are known as spring tides. This happens about two days after each new and each full moon. At the new moon both sun and moon are on the same side of the earth and at full moon though at opposite sides of the earth they are still exerting their pull in a straight line. The range of tides is least at the periods of half moon as the sun and moon are then at right angles to each other and these are known as the neap tides.

Apart from the monthly rhythm of the tides there is also an annual rhythm. As we approach the equinoxes (around 21st March and 21st September), at which time the pull of sun and moon is directly in line, the spring tides become progressively bigger. The highest spring tides of the year occur after the equinoxes, and the smallest spring tides occur around midsummer and midwinter, but they are, of course, the biggest tides of their fortnightly cycle.

Remember that the tide flows farthest up the beach and ebbs farthest down the beach on the springs. The smallest advance and retreat of the tides occurs on the neaps. After the highest fortnightly spring tides for a period of seven days as the angle between the pull of the moon and the sun increases so do the tides weaken and for a similar period after the lowest neap tide as the angle of pull decreases once more so do the tides strengthen until the spring tides are reached again.

The vertical range of tides around our coasts on springs is on the average from 12 feet to 15 feet. However, where the forward movement of the tidal force is constricted by the land or bottled up by narrow channels the rise of tide can be much greater as happens in the Bristol Channel where at Chepstow there is a rise of almost 50 feet on the springs and 20 feet on the neaps. The strength of the tidal streams varies, being strongest where the water is shallow, where the main current is set off by projecting headlands or where its movement is constricted as between islands and the mainland or in estuaries. The strength of these streams is important for in places they can attain a speed of 6 knots or even more. This may mean that the angler may be able to fish them only when the tide is slack, i.e. at high tide or low tide. He may even find it impossible to fish in certain places at slack water except on the neaps as the tides no not "stand" for very long on the springs. Wind also has an effect on the range of the tides. Strong winds blowing on to the shore help the tide rise higher while winds blowing off the land help reduce the tide and causes it to ebb farther.

The time of high water at full and new moon is always the same at any given port and from this the times of high and low water can be calculated for all the intermediate tides. Most Port Authorities and many other bodies issue tide tables giving these times, usually for a period of twelve months. They give not only the times of high and low water but also the vertical range of the tide above datum, and are an invaluable aid to the angler. They enable him to plan his fishing trips and also his bait collecting even months in advance if he so desires. These tables usually give a list of tidal constants for a number of other ports as well. As the time of high water at full and new moon is constant at any given port it follows that if this high water takes place, for example, at Dublin at 12 noon and at London Bridge at 2.21 p.m., and provided that you know the difference in timing (i.e. tidal constant) you can calculate the times of high water at either port from either tide table. The value of this information is obvious for any angler planning a fishing holiday or trip away from home.

The heights given in the tables are heights above datum, that is, above a fixed mark in each port, and the heights and timings of the tides are for that port only and may not necessarily be the same for places a short distance away. Ports of approximately the same longitude and facing the main tidal stream have high tide at approximately the same time. For example, there is only a difference of fifteen minutes between high water at Schull on the south coast of Ireland and the mouth of Lough Swilly on the north coast, two places hundreds of miles apart. Yet there is a difference of ninety minutes between high water in Wexford Bay and at Wexford Quays, only a short distance away up the estuary. In estuaries the tide must first overcome and turn back the outpouring flow of water before it can start to "make" in the estuary. This may be a considerable time after the tide has started to flood on the open coast outside. This is often particularly noticeable in small estuaries where a sandbar builds up at the estuary mouth. The water will continue to flow outwards not alone until the tide has risen as high as the sandbar but until it is strong enough to stop the outflow and push back up the channel again. This may be as long as two hours or more after the tide has started to flood outside. As many species of fish ascend estuaries with the tide this information is important to the angler and usually can only be obtained locally or through experience.

The rate of the rise and fall of the tides and the speed of the tidal streams is not constant. Usually the tides will stand for a longer or shorter period at high and low water depending on whether they are spring or neap tides. Gradually they begin to flow faster until about half tide and then gradually ease off again. Usually a quarter of the rise takes place in the first two hours, half in the next two hours and a quarter in the last two hours. The pattern on the ebb is the same. The speed of the tidal currents varies with the stage of the tide, being fastest about half flood and half ebb and, of course, is stronger on spring tides than on neaps. Where tidal streams are very strong as at the Tuskar Rock on the south-east coast of Ireland the flood tide may continue to make long after it has started to ebb on the coast inside.

Most fish seem to feed better when there is some movement in the tide. Many species use the tides to take them to their feeding grounds, others let the tides bring their food to them. Bass, mullet and flounders swim up beaches and into estuaries on the flood tide, retreating again as the water begins to ebb. Turbot prefer to wait on gravelly or sandy bottoms where there is a good run of tide, feeding on whatever smaller fish are swept their way. Dabs and plaice seem to feed best when the tide is fairly slack, i.e. at high and low water. The tide sweeps along with it shoals of small fry, herring fry, sprat, sandeels, etc., and where large quantities of fry are concentrated by fast tidal streams the fish that prey on them will be found. Tides may set in one direction on the flood, in another on the ebb carrying fish over different ground on each tide. If you can discover the different routes taken on both tides you will enjoy fishing on both the ebb and flood. The strength of the tides will affect the movements of fish as they will travel farther on springs than on neaps.

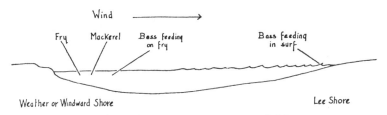

Effect of wind on movements of fish

Wind and weather apart from making it impossible at times to go fishing, affect the movements of fish to quite a considerable extent. How often have we heard "you will catch nothing in this wind" or been advised "it's no use trying, the day is too bright and the water too clear". Sometimes it's true, at others it is not. What holds good for one locality may not apply to another. For that reason let us consider why and how fish are affected by conditions.

In fine weather small fry, such as the young of herring and pilchard, sprats, sandeels and other small fish, swim near the surface in large shoals. On these feed a variety of bigger fish such as mackerel, bass and pollack while larger predators like tope and shark in turn feed on them. In lightish winds fry tend to swim against the wind, towards the shore when the wind is off the land and out to sea when the wind is onshore. They prefer smooth and untroubled waters and in offshore winds will be found in the lee of the land, on the sheltered side of bays and even on the downwind side of jetties and piers. When the weather is rough the shoals scatter and the fry sink deeper in the water. In the absence of fry the concentrations of fish feeding on them also break up, to reassemble again when conditions are right.

During periods of calm bright weather bass may be difficult to
tempt ground fishing from the shore during daylight but fishing
usually improves after the sun has gone below the horizon. On
the other hand, these are ideal conditions for mullet fishing and in
places for taking tope from the shore. Pollack are no lovers of
these conditions, staying deep during the day but rising to the
surface as darkness descends and in the dusk or "pollack light" often
dimpling the water and taking a bait readily. For daylight fishing
for pollack a dull dark day with a fair amount of surface movement
is best. Strong onshore winds causing heavy surf on the beaches
makes surf fishing difficult and if conditions are very rough both
bass and flatfish will seek calmer conditions in deeper water. A nice
lively surf caused by a moderate onshore breeze makes ideal surf
fishing conditions for bass but if it persists for too long a period bass
may become satiated with bottom food. The first few days after a
storm when the water is clearing are also good for bass.

Really stormy weather scatters fish in water shallow enough to
be affected by wave action. Pollack will desert the rocks and reefs
seeking shelter in the deeper and less affected water. In prolonged
spells of calm weather the bigger pollack and coalfish may leave the
rocks and travel far after fry. Flatfish take better in calm conditions
and clear water while eels are more active when the water is dirty.
Rough seas will tear weeds from the rocks and deposit them on the
shore making fishing virtually impossible in places. Even when
the weed has decayed a horrible "soup" is often left making fishing
a nightmare. Prolonged spells of mild weather may in spring
bring bass and mullet inshore earlier than usual and in autumn may
delay their departure. In the far south in Cornwall and in Cork
and Kerry, in a mild winter, bass may never leave the shore. In
late autumn and winter onshore gales draw cod and codling inshore
into the shallows whilst offshore winds attract whiting.

While fish may be caught in the sea throughout the whole year,
some seasons are better than others for fishing generally and some
for a particular species of fish. Spring is probably the leanest
period, as the fish that gave us sport during the long winter months
are gradually moving out and those that delight us in summer have
not yet arrived. There are seasonal migrations in the sea, some for
the purpose of spawning, others influenced by temperature changes.
In the spring many species of seafish migrate to spawn, and cod,

whiting, pollack and flatfish are usually outside the range of the angler. Towards the end of April pollack begin to show up on the inshore reefs, a few at first but during early May they are there in great numbers. The flatfish will have started to move back, too, and in reasonable weather both bass and mullet will be plentiful again in the south but will take longer to reach the more northerly limit of their range. Tope, too, begin to make their appearance and as we get deeper into the summer a great variety of fish are within the angler's range. The mackerel usually appear inshore in July followed by the sharks. Cod and ling are by now almost recovered and can be caught in deep water and all through the summer and autumn the sea is at its most bountiful. It is during this period that we have our best fishing. The sea is full of fish, all growing apace and most of them in their best condition.

As the colder weather approaches the temperature migration commences. The warm water fishes slowly seek conditions that are more to their liking. The mackerel disappear, followed by the sharks. Bass and mullet are gradually thinning out as the inshore waters cool, either moving into deeper water or slowly making their way southwards. The autumnal gales have swept the pollack from the reefs and they are now out of reach of the angler. The flatfish are moving out into deeper water but the tope may still linger on, feeding on the first inshore migration of whiting but soon, too, they are gone.

Now that the inshore shallows have chilled the cold water fishes come within the reach of even the shore angler. The first sharp frosts usher in the advance guard of the whiting which will continue to give us sport until well into January. Haddock and coalfish are now no great distance off and the November gales usually herald the opening of the winter cod season while the skates and rays are usually within our reach for most of the year. Thus month follows month each with its share of fish to fill the angler's bag.

Many sea fish, although within the angler's reach after spawning, are not fit to catch, providing neither sport nor food for the angler. There is nothing more ugly than a badly spent cod and they are seldom properly mended by the end of June. Bass and Mullet, on the other hand, which spawn over a protracted period although they grow leaner are seldom so out of condition that they are not worth catching. Most of the shark family (which includes tope, dogfish

and the skates) which either give birth to live young or else lay egg
capsules over an extended period are nearly always in good condition when caught.

Depth is an important factor in the distribution of fishes. The
pressure of water increases with depth, the rate of increase being
approximately 1 lb. pressure per square inch for every 2 feet in
depth, and at 5 fathoms it is roughly 30 lbs. per square inch, i.e.
double than at the surface, where the pressure is that of the atmos-
phere. As can be easily appreciated, the pressure at the bottom of
the oceans is tremendous and may amount to two or more tons
per square inch. Yet even in these great depths and under such
great pressures there is life. While most sea fish can bear a great
amount of pressure they vary in the range of pressures they can
endure, in the pressure to which they are best suited and this has a
limiting effect on their distribution. Many species of fish are
adapted to living on the bottom and these are known as demersal
fish. Others are adapted to living in the upper layers of the water
and these are known as pelagic fishes. The Skates, rays and flatfishes are typical of the former group and the mackerel and shark
are typical of the latter. While many species find all their food and
spend all or most of their lives either on the bottom or near the
surface others like the hake may feed partly in both. Some demersal
fish, the cod for example, may rise from the bottom to feed on
small shoal fish in the upper layers whilst a pelagic fish like the
shark may be found feeding on the bottom when surface food is scarce.

Depth in itself naturally enough has little effect on the distribution
of pelagic species, but it does limit to a greater or lesser extent the
distribution of many demersal fishes. The following figures for
landings of commercial catches at British ports given by Howell
(Ocean Research and the Great Fisheries) will serve to illustrate this.
43% of the turbot landed were taken in depths under 20 fathoms,
56% in depths ranging from 20 to 55 fathoms and only 1% in
depths over 55 fathoms. The bulk of the cod catch was taken in
20 to 55 fathoms (71%), 21% under 20 fathoms and only 8% over
55 fathoms. On the other hand, hake were taken in depths ranging
from 15 to 600 fathoms, 6% came from less than 20 fathoms,
24% from 20 to 55 fathoms and 70% from over 55 fathoms. It
was found that ling though taken in depths ranging from 15 to 150
fathoms were most plentiful in the 20 to 50 fathom range of depths.

Some species can adapt themselves to a wide range of depths; others, particularly those which live in the shallows around our coast, are very limited in the amount of pressure that they can tolerate. Most bony fishes possess an air bladder which is filled with gases and can be inflated or deflated at will. It enables the fish to adjust its specific gravity to that of the surrounding water so that it can rest on the bottom or rise through the depths as it wishes. This swim bladder is familiar to anglers who have caught cod, ling

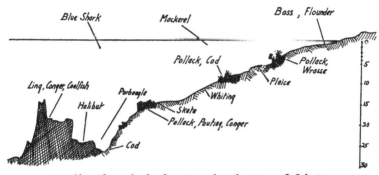

Profile of sea bed, showing distribution of fish in
summer

Depth scale in fathoms. Vertical scale exaggerated.
Rocks cross-hatched.

or pouting in deep water and is on landing often seen protruding from the fish's mouth. When a fish is raised too quickly from deep water, its swim bladder cannot adjust itself fast enough to the varying pressures through which it is being pulled. When it has been hoisted up a certain distance and the water pressure decreases, its swim bladder expands like a balloon, forcing the fish to float to the surface. For this reason many species taken in deep water which put up a strong fight in the first 5 or 6 fathoms suddenly come easily to the angler for they cannot help themselves once their internal pressure exceeds that of the water outside.

Like the land, the bed of the sea consists of hills and valleys, sandy and muddy plains, strewn with boulders and rocks in places, a steep hill or a deep hole here or perhaps a jagged ledge of rock there. The type of bottom has a great bearing on the species of fish which you will find over them. Different species have a distinct preference for particular types of bottom and will generally be found on them.   Pollack and coalfish are lovers of the high wild rock in fairly deep water.   Other fish that display a preference for rocky bottoms are wrasse, ling, pouting, bream and conger, though the latter will often range far over clean bottoms.   The flatfishes are found on clean or soft bottoms, the plaice on sandy or shelly bottoms, the turbot on gravelly or sandy bottoms often where there is a run of tide, the flounder on bottoms of mud and sand. Even the pelagic species have preferences.   In most areas around the coast there are certain well known spots where mackerel are more plentiful than in others.   Many species like the cod roam freely over smooth and rough ground, even big skate usually associated with sandy or muddy bottoms will be found over patchy and low rough ground or in the gulleys and ravines found in very rough ground.

We will deal in greater detail with types of fish found on the different kinds of bottom in later chapters.   However, it is worth stressing here that the angler should know what type of bottom he is fishing over, the species of fish he expects to catch on that kind of bottom and he should specifically fish with suitable tackle and baits and use the best methods to catch these fish   There is little sport in catching dabs or plaice on tackle best suited for big conger or skate and the opposite is also true.   Not only will you have far less chance of success but neither will you have sport.

Remember that angling is a sport and the real pleasure in angling is in fishing for and deceiving the particular species you seek, using tackle and methods which will allow the fish to show its true mettle.

Of particular interest to the angler is the frontier where sea and land meet.   The shore is the eternal battleground between the sea and the land.   It is the result of the ceaseless action of the water, in one place wearing away the land, in another building it up again. On exposed coasts, subject to heavy wave and tidal action, the sea first eats away the softer strata, undermining the harder rock until it collapses and is then broken down into boulders, rocks, shingle, stones, sand and mud.   The action of the tides and tidal streams carry these away varying distances.   The heavier shingle or stones travel least and are often seen built up into banks or spits off rocky headlands or estuary mouths.   The coarser gravelly sand is carried farther and often makes up the storm or surf beaches on exposed coasts.   The fine sand and mud is carried farthest and deposited well offshore or in sheltered waters where it is precipitated and allowed to settle. The character of the shore or bottom be it rock, sand or mud to a large extent controls the type of fish and fish food found on it.

Rocky shores vary greatly depending on the type of rock, i.e. hard or soft and the slope of the strata. Hard rock which weathers smoothly offers little means of attachment for weeds or marine animals. However, where the slope is inclined, pools, crevices and gulleys may be left exposed by the receding tide and may harbour many marine animals. Here may be gathered a variety of small creatures, rocklings, blennies, gobies, prawns, limpets, mussels, periwinkles and crabs, to name a few. The water off rocky coasts is usually deep and offers a variety of fishing to the angler. Pollack, coalfish, wrasse and conger are typical fish of this type of shore while in places there may be good fishing for such species as codling, tope and mackerel.

Beaches vary greatly in their nature and extent but break down roughly into three main types, shingle beaches, beaches of small gravel and coarse sand, and flat firm beaches of muddy sand. Beaches are often a mixture of these main types but the predominant character of a mixed type of beach determines what food and what fish are likely to be present on it.

Shingle beaches are usually very exposed and subject to heavy surf or wave action which builds up steep banks of shingle. They are usually found along a rugged coastline but can also be formed as spits in estuaries, or bays or near headlands where strong tidal currents build them up. The shingle may be composed of small pebbles, or rounded stones as big as 6 inches across and usually has a very steep slope. Owing to the constant movement of the pebbles caused by wave action it is the most unstable of shores. On account of this and also because it cannot hold water, nothing either plant or animal can live on or within the shingle. The fact that there is no food on this type of shore does not mean it is not worth fishing. These types of beaches usually drop off steeply into deep water or are washed by fast tides or strong currents. Small fry or sandeels are often plentiful off these beaches either having swum in against continued offshore winds or having been channelled along it by strong tides or fast currents. In these conditions there is often very good fishing for mackerel, bass, sea trout and tope and in

winter time cod.   On the whole, however, this is the least productive type of beach.

The second type of beach is also an exposed one, subject to surf
and to the surges of the open sea.   They are often extensive,
backed by rolling sand dunes and in places by banks of shingle.
Near low water mark these beaches are often comparatively shallow,
sloping gradually up towards high water mark, then rising quite
steeply.   The coarse gravelly sand high up on the beach is not fully
stable, being subject to heavy surf, but it is much more stable than
shingle, it retains water and contains abundant if specialised life,
e.g. sand hoppers.   This loose coarse textured type of sand is often
the home of sandeels, a very important food for many fishes, while
lower down on the strand and below low water mark the sand
may be more stable and more productive of life.   Smelt may also
be present on these beaches and in summer small fry.   This type of
beach can provide excellent surf fishing for bass which are often
plentiful and at times shoal after sandeels and fry along these
beaches.   Flounders are usually plentiful and sometimes small
turbot, plaice and other flatfish.   If there is a fair depth of water
close in, tope can often be taken; and in winter the rough water
along the beaches may prove attractive to cod.

The first two types of beaches are usually called storm or surf
beaches and differ greatly from the last type of beach which is only
found in sheltered conditions where it is not exposed to heavy wave
action.   These are flat or gently sloping beaches composed of firm
muddy sand, corrugated and rippled on the surface by gentle wave
action.   On account of their small slope they are extensive beaches
where tides advance and retreat a long way and there is no great
depth over these beaches when the tide is in.   They are the most stable
of beaches and very rich in food.   There are usually extensive beds
of lugworm and cockles, whilst the pools and channels left by the
receding tide are full of shrimps, gobies, baby flatfish, mullet, fry,
small crabs and other creatures.   Down near low water mark there
may be beds of razorfish.   As would be expected, such a rich larder
of food would not be ignored by hungry fish and on the tide, bass,
mullet, seatrout, gurnards and flatfish swim in over these beaches
seeking a variety of food organisms.   This type of beach provides
excellent fishing provided that you know where, how and when to
fish it.

The foregoing is a very general classification of beaches. No two beaches are the same. A beach is often a combination of two and sometimes even of the three types. The angler must get to know the characteristics of each, to figure out the species of fish he is likely to catch, the most favourable spots and state of tide, and the best methods, tackle and baits to use.

Fish are taken occasionally all along a beach but some portions are more productive than others. Some stretches may be completely barren of fish and it is a waste of time to fish them. Fish will be found where there is plenty of natural food for them so *never* fish blindly, but *think* about your fishing before you start. Study your beaches. Walk along them at low water, noting the likely places. You will find that if you make a point of studying your beaches at low water you will be well repaid by better fishing.

There is one last type of shore to mention and that is the *muddy shore*. This type of shore also has its distinctive fauna and distinctive location. It is the typical bottom of harbours, creeks and estuaries and of the three the creeks and estuaries usually provide the more interesting fishing. Estuaries vary in size from small creeks into which little streams flow, to large harbours which are the tidal mouths of major rivers and may be many miles wide and a score or more miles in length. These large harbours, really arms of the sea, may be difficult to recognise as estuaries, possessing as they do in many cases large amounts of rocky and sandy shores.

This type of shore is found in the lower part of large estuaries and is entirely marine in character. It differs from the open sea in that on the ebb tide the water may be brackish and discoloured and the bottoms vary from sand and gravel to mud depending on the swiftness or sluggishness of the tides and currents. Bass, mullet, flatfish and codling are typical fish of the lower estuary and tope, skate, rays, mackerel, and many other marine species may be caught.

Farther up the estuary the water is brackish, thick with silt and the bottom muddy. This is the middle estuary and the limit of the respective ranges of both freshwater and marine organisms and fishes. Typical fish of the middle estuary are freshwater eels, flounders, slob trout and perhaps mullet and bass.

The upper estuary is entirely fresh in character although still influenced by the movement of the tides which twice daily stop and reverse the seaward flow of the river causing the water level to rise. The sea is still represented here for flounders are quite at home in fresh water and even mullet may ascend this far and linger awhile. Such migratory sea fishes as salmon and sea trout will pass through the upper estuary and it is here at the limit of the tidal influence that shad in some rivers will spawn.

The three major zones, e.g. the upper, middle and lower estuary are readily discernable in the larger estuaries but in the smaller ones their extent will naturally be less and one, i.e. the marine, may predominate. It is the lower estuary that provides the sea angler

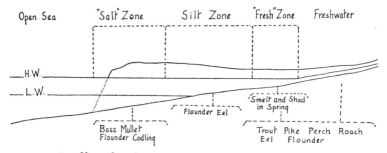

Profile of a long estuary, showing characteristic
fishes of different zones

H.W. and L.W indicate high tide and low tide levels

with bait but all the reaches of an estuary can provide him with fishing.

No summary of the shore would be complete without reference to the effect that the tides have not alone on the fish which live in the shallow waters but also on the creatures which live in the "no man's land" between tide marks and which are an important part of the food of these fishes.

The daily and lunar cycles of the tides were described earlier in this chapter and their effect is nowhere more evident than on the shore. Anyone who has spent a holiday by the sea will be familiar with both the vertical and horizontal movements of the tides on our beaches and in our estuaries, but the range of the tides over the lunar cycle from neaps to springs and its effect on the distribution of life on the shore is not immediately apparent. The tides ebb and flow over the shore twice daily and their range is greatest on the spring tides. It is then that the tides cover the greatest area of the shore on the flood tide and expose the greatest area on the ebb.

At the other extreme are the neap tides when the sea makes its smallest advance up the shore but also uncovers the least on the ebb. In between these two extremes is the average range of tides which weaken and strengthen through the monthly cycle.

The animals which live on the shore have adapted themselves to being covered and uncovered twice daily as the tides ebb and flow. The amount of exposure, however, which the different species can tolerate varies considerably and affects their vertical distribution on the shore. The inhabitants of the shore are marine in origin but through evolution have become adapted to life in the intertidal zone and many are well on their way to becoming land animals. Five different zones are readily recognisable on the shore each with its distinct plant life and population of animals.

The lowest division is the Sublittoral Zone which lies below the extreme low water level of the springs and where the bottom is never uncovered. Here the plants and animals though living in shallow water are truly marine. Typical plants of this zone are the tangled mass of kelps and oarweeds.

Extending from the sublittoral zone to the average low tide level is the lower shore which is only exposed on the spring tides. It is on this portion of the shore that the razorfish, a very useful bait, is found.

The most interesting and most extensive division is the Middle Shore which extends from the average low tide level to the average high tide level and is exposed twice a day every day to the air. This region is extensively colonised by many creatures useful to the angler, i.e. lugworms, cockles and ragworms.

The Upper Shore is that region above average high tide level and is only covered on the spring tides. This is a difficult zone for marine animals to colonise and it is sparsely populated. The sandhopper is typical of this zone.

The last zone, the Splash Zone, is of little interest to the angler as it holds little in the way of useful baits. It is the area affected by spray above high water springs and is not part of the true shore. Typical of it are the sea slater (*Ligia oceanica*) which is useful bait for some species of fish.

Many species of fish which live in our inshore waters travel in over the sands and up the estuaries as the rising tide covers the shore and opens up feeding grounds not available to them when the tide

is out.   Their movements will naturally tend to be more nomadic
on springs than on neaps as a greater feeding area is available to
them.   Different species have different feeding habits and the angler
must get to know how the tides affect their habits and movements.
He must also know where on the shore the bait he wishes to use is
available and at what stage of the tide it is obtainable.   The importance of the tides and the location of baits in the different zones is
obvious.   There is little joy in arriving on a beach to find the tide
just right for catching fish but too far gone to collect the bait with
which to catch them.

CHAPTER 2

THE FISHES OF THE SEA

WE IN THESE ISLANDS ARE FORTUNATE TO LIVE IN A REGION where two major fish distribution areas meet and overlap. This affords us a much wider choice of species than would otherwise be our lot. It also poses the problem of the correct identification of the different fishes which we may catch. Most species differ greatly in appearance but a number are difficult to tell apart, i.e. the spotted dogfishes, and this causes a certain amount of confusion among anglers. In this chapter is given a brief description and biography of each species likely to be encountered by the angler; but first a few words about the external anatomy of fishes in general.

Fish as the angler knows them break down into two main groups i.e. the bony-skeletoned fishes (which are the true fishes) and the Selachians or cartilaginous fishes. These two groups differ in that the backbone is true bone in the former whilst in the latter it is made up of cartilage or tough gristle. Bass and cod are typical bony fish whilst the sharks, rays and skates are cartilaginous. They also differ in the method of reproduction of the species. The bony fishes usually produce eggs which are shed by the female and fertilised by the male in the water outside the body. The eggs in the cartilaginous fishes are fertilised internally and the young brought forth either alive or in the form of eggs enclosed in a tough horny capsule. They also differ in that the gills by which fish breathe, present in the bony fishes, a single opening covered by a movable gill cover. In the cartilaginous fishes the gills, usually five in number, open directly to the outer surface in the form of gill slits. The cartilaginous fishes usually also possess spiracles, which they use as accessory gills.

The external surface of a fish can be divided into the upper or *dorsal* surface, the lower or *ventral* surface and the two sides or *lateral* surfaces.   The surface can be further subdivided into the *head* region, the *trunk* region and the *tail* region.   The fins situated on the dorsal and ventral surfaces are known as *median* fins, e.g. those along the centre line of the body, to differentiate them from the *paired* fins found on the lateral surfaces.   The median fins on the back are called dorsal fins and that on the underside the *anal* fin, which is situated behind the *vent* or anus.   The paired fins are the

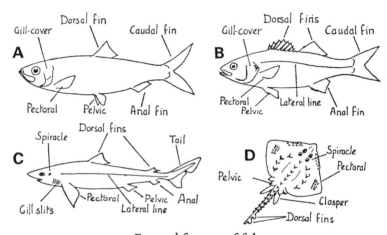

External features of fish

A Herring.   B Bass.   C female Tope.   D male Thornback Ray.

pectoral fins just behind the head and the *pelvic* fins which are situated lower down and which may be under, in front of or farther back than the pectorals but which are always in front of the vent.

The fins of bony fishes are composed of soft rays or sharp spines or a combination of both.   The number, shape and position of the fins, and the number of rays and spines in each fin, are all important aids to identification and can be written in formula form.   This formula will be used in describing the different species so a few words of explanation are called for.

The number of rays and spines which make up a fin varies slightly with individual fish within a species.   For example, the bass has two dorsal fins, the first which may have 8 or 9 spines and the second 1 spine and 12 or 13 soft rays.   This is the variation for the dorsal fins of the species so the fin ray formula is written as follows:—

D8-9/$\frac{1}{12\text{-}13}$. The pectoral fins have no sharp spines but 16 soft rays and is written PECT 16. The pelvic fins possess 1 spine and 5 soft rays and is written PELV $\frac{1}{5}$. The *Caudal* or tail fin has 17 soft rays, i.e. C.17 and the anal fin has 3 spines and 10 soft rays, i.e. A$\frac{3}{10}$.

Fish, like any other animal, possess a number of senses. Fish are of a very low order of intelligence and their behaviour is largely reflexive, that is, consists of automatic reactions to stimulii or conditions affecting these senses. They possess a sense of smell, sight, taste, touch, hearing and balance, and in addition a special sense peculiar to fish and associated with the *lateral line*. Some of these senses are very important to the angler. Fish have a very highly developed sense of smell, some indeed, i.e. the lesser spotted dogfish, depending on it almost entirely to find their food. Most fish can see quite well and those which hunt by sight, i.e. the mackerel, are very keen sighted. They possess a sense of both taste and touch to enable them to identify food and some species have developed external organs of taste as is evidenced by the barbels of such fish as cod and the taste buds on the elongated fins of the gurnards.

The ear of a fish is an organ of both balance and hearing but of far greater importance for detecting movement and vibration is the sense associated with the lateral line. In most species this is visible as a conspicuous line or seam running along both sides of the fish although in some it may not be so obvious and may be represented by a series of punctures or minute holes in the skin. It is a highly efficient organ, extremely sensitive to vibrations and enables fish not only to detect movements of other fish be they friend, foe or food but to swim safely and at speed past obstacles in the dark by picking up the echoed vibrations of the fish's own movements.

The following biography is intended as a brief guide to the identification of the different species. Only those fish commonly caught or met with in the waters around these islands and that are of angling interest are included. The species described are dealt with in accordance with their natural relationships. Features common to related species are given first for each family or genus; the special distinguishing features of each fish are given in the description of the individual species.

THE SEA PERCHES

(*Serranidae*)

A large and very widely distributed family found throughout the world in the tropic and temperate seas.   This family includes species found in the deep sea, in the shallow coastal waters and a few fresh-water or partly freshwater species.   Many are noted for their sporting qualities and are much sought after by anglers, e.g. the striped bass the the sea bass of the American coasts, the snook, the groupers and the spotted jewfish.   Four species have been recorded from our waters, the Common Bass (*Dicentrarchus labrax*), the Stone Basse (*Polyprion Americanus*), the Dusky Perch (*Epinephelus gigas*) and the Comber or Gaper (*Serranus cabrilla*). All but the Common Bass are rare and therefore of little interest to the angler and will not be described here.

BASS (*Dicentrarchus labrax*)

The bass is a silvery somewhat salmonlike fish with two dorsal fins close together, the first with 8–9 spines, second dorsal and anal short.   Fin ray formula:—$D8–9/\dfrac{1}{12–13}$; $A\dfrac{3}{10–11}$; C17; PECT 16; PELV $\frac{1}{5}$.   The preopercular bone (between cheek and gill cover) has a serrated edge and there are flat spiny points at the angle of the gill cover.   The back is coloured blue-grey or greenish-grey, sides silver, underside white.   Lateral line black and slanted upwards from tail to head.   Scales ctenoid and rather small.   Eye dark with golden rim around pupil.

Bass of well over 20 lb. have been recorded but these are very old fish and the average size is from 3 to 6 lb.   A fish of 10 lb. or over is considered a specimen whilst small fish (under 2/2$\frac{1}{2}$ lb.) are known as "school bass".   A warm water species, bass extend from the Mediterranean to the British Isles.   In our waters they are nearing the limit of their range and are most plentiful on the south and south-west coasts.   They become rare in the North Sea and although caught in the Irish Sea their numbers have thinned out considerably and they are very rare on the north coasts of Ireland, England and on the coast of Scotland.

Their favourite haunts are estuaries, lagoons, tidal creeks and open beaches. They have a liking for brackish waters and will travel long distances up estuaries on the tide. Their chief food is mainly crustaceans, e.g. crabs, prawns, shrimps, etc., and small fish, e.g. sandeels, baby flatfish, sprats and herring or mackerel fry. They are very catholic in their tastes and worms, e.g. lugworm, ragworm, and molluscs, e.g. razorfish also figure in their diet. Bass eggs have been taken in a number of places on the Irish coast and the indications are that Bass spawn inshore in areas of fast tides over a protracted period extending approximately from the end of April to early June. They first appear inshore about the end of April on the south coast and leave again around October depending on the season. Further north they arrive progressively later and leave earlier whilst in the far south of these islands in winter they never go far from the shore and in mild winters may provide good fishing all year round. As a species they are slow growing, a fish weighing 1 lb. may be 5 years old, a 5 or 6 lb. fish may be 10 to 14 years old and a 10 lb. fish 15 to 20 years of age.

Bass can be caught from the shore by a variety of methods: i.e. spinning with artificial lures, light or heavy (surf fishing) bottom fishing with natural or fish baits, float fishing, driftlining and trolling. Baits are many and varied and include soft or peeler crab, hermit crab, lugworm, ragworm, prawns, razorfish, mussel, slipper limpet and a variety of fish baits, e.g. sandeels, mackerel, squid and small fishes.

	British Record	Irish Record	Specimen Weight
Bass	18 lb. 6 oz.	17 lb. 1¼ oz.	10 lb.

SEA BREAMS

(Sparidae)

Fishes with a long dorsal fin with spines in front portion, hard scales, narrow pointed pectoral fins, forked tails, special dentition. They are a widely distributed family found in the tropical and sub-tropical seas. Of the ten species recorded from our waters only two, e.g. the Common or Red Bream (*Pagellus bogaraveo*) and the Black Bream (*Spondyliosoma cantharus (Gmelin)*) are taken commonly by anglers. None of the breams attain any great size and there is a strong family resemblance amongst all the species. They are deep, laterally compressed fish with a single long dorsal fin, both the body and head are covered with scales and their teeth are characteristic and highly developed.

THE COMMON SEA BREAM OR RED SEA BREAM (*Pagellus bogaraveo*)

A handsome, colourful fish, body deep, laterally compressed, shoulder high and curved, single long dorsal fin.   Fin ray formula:—
$D\dfrac{12}{12-13}$; $A\dfrac{3}{12-13}$; PECT 16–17; C19.   Colour orange/scarlet or red on the back, becoming lighter and giving way to silver on the sides and underneath the fish.   Conspicuous black spot on the shoulder at origin of curved lateral line.   Pointed curved teeth in the front and at the sides of the mouth and three or four lines of blunt molar teeth at the rear.   No canine teeth present.

Average size 1 to 3 lb. but fish of up to 9 lb. have been taken. Small fish (6 to 7 inches in length) are known as chad and they lack the dark shoulder spot of the adult.   Red Sea Bream are migratory fish found in the Mediterranean and from the Canaries to Scandinavia.   They are summer visitors to our shores first appearing about June and departing about the end of September.   They swim in shoals, usually near the bottom and are taken over or in the vicinity of rough and rocky ground.   Their food is varied and crustaceans, bivalves, molluscs, starfish and small fishes have been found in their stomachs.   Little is known about their spawning which probably takes place during their offshore migration.

Small Sea Bream may be taken bottom fishing or float fishing where deep water washes the shore but the bigger fish are taken bottom fishing from a boat in depths from 10 to 40 fathoms.   They will take fish baits, mussel, worm and artificial feather lures readily.

	British Record	Irish Record	Specimen Weight
Red Sea Bream	9 lb. 8 oz. 12 dr.	9 lb. 6 oz.	4½ lb.

THE BLACK SEA BREAM (*Spondyliosoma cantharus* (*Gmelin*))

Locally known as Black Bream or Old Wife and much sought after by light tackle anglers.   Similar in appearance to the Red Sea Bream but the body is more laterally compressed and there is no black spot at the origin of the lateral line.   Fin ray formula:—
$D\dfrac{10-11}{12-14}$; $A\dfrac{3}{10-11}$.   Coloration variable but usually blue or purple

grey on the back and silvery grey or reddish grey on the sides. Sometimes dark vertical bands on the sides with dark spots in bands on dorsal and anal fins. Conical teeth in bands in the jaws the outer row being the largest and slightly compressed.

Usual size ranges from 1 to 3 lb. but fish over 6 lb. have been taken. Found in the Mediterranean and Atlantic. Distribution very localised and they are most numerous in the Channel, particularly near the Sussex coast. A migratory species, they appear inshore towards the end of April or early May, departing again about the end of June. Little is known of its spawning habits but fish taken inshore usually have well developed gonads. They are found over rough ground, often in midwater and seem to feed mainly on worms, shrimps and small bivalves.

Black Bream fishing is a specialised form of fishing with very light tackle either paternostering or driftlining with lightly leaded trace using lugworm or ragworm as bait.

	British Record	*Irish Record*
Black Sea Bream	6 lb. 14 oz. 4 dr.	None

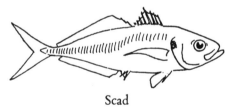

Scad

SCAD (*Trachurus trachurus*)

The Scad or Horse-Mackerel resembles the mackerel in appearance but is deeper and more compressed. It is easily recognised by its distinctive lateral line which begins high up at the gill cover and dips sharply between the first and second dorsal fins. The lateral line is covered by large plate-like scales which on the straight portion between the "dip" and the tail are keeled with backward facing spurs. There are two sharp spines just in front of the anal fin. This species is abundant in most temperate and tropical seas and is found as far north as Norway. It averages 1 to $2\frac{1}{2}$ lb. in size but grows to 3 lb. or more. It is common on our south and south-west coast but relatively rare in the Irish Sea and in the North Sea north of Norfolk.

The scad migrates inshore to spawn, first appearing on our coast about April and the spawning period is from June to August. Mainly a surface living species, its food consists chiefly of small fry and sprats. A strong fighter, it swims in shoals and scad are also found among the mackerel shoals. Tackle, methods and baits as used in mackerel fishing.

	British Record	Irish Record	Specimen Weight
Scad	3 lb. 5 oz. 3 dr.	None	2 lb.

THE RED MULLET (*Mullus surmeletus*)

The Red Mullet (not closely related to the grey mullets) is the only member of its family to reach our waters. There are two colour varieties of the Red Mullet, one the Plain Red Mullet, the other red on the back and sides with three to five yellow bands extending along the sides. The latter is the more common in our waters and is found mainly on the south and south-west coast and on parts of the west coast of Ireland. The body is low, compressed and covered with large thin scales. It has two dorsal fins with the pectorals situated under the first dorsal and pelvics immediately beneath the pectorals. Fin ray formula:—$D7$–$8/\frac{1}{8}$; $A\frac{2}{6}$. The forehead is steep, the eyes high up and underneath the chin are two long stiff barbels which can be laid back in grooves under the lower jaw.

A southern species, it is abundant in the Mediterranean but ranges as far north as Norway and is found mainly on soft, muddy and gravelly bottoms, its food consisting mainly of shrimps, molluscs and worms. It is a small fish rarely exceeding 17 inches in length and migrates inshore from May to September, spawning during June and July. It is of little angling interest (apart from being a table delicacy) and is usually taken by anglers ground fishing for other species.

THE WEEVERS

(*Family Trachinidae*)

Fishes with eyes close together high up on head, body and head compressed, two dorsal fins, close together, first dorsal small and coloured brown or black, upward angled mouth. The two species of weever found around our coasts are of little angling interest but they are important in that they are among the few really venomous fishes in our waters, being equipped with poison glands and *capable of inflicting a very dangerous and painful wound.* It is important that the angler be able to recognise both of these fish and he should handle them with the utmost caution.

THE LESSER WEEVER (*Trachinus vipera*)

This is the more common of the two species and possesses two dorsal fins. *The first, which contains six sharp and poisonous spines, is coloured black* and is a readily recognisable danger signal. *It also has a sharp spine at the corner of the gill cover.* Fin ray formula:— D6/21 24; A25–26. The back is grey or greyish brown and there are dark diagonal streaks on the sides. The eyes are high up on the head and the mouth points obliquely upwards.

Its distribution is wide, ranging from the Mediterranean to the North Sea and it is found all around our coasts. It is found on sandy bottoms in shallow water, being particularly fond of soft gravelly sand on beaches and estuaries where it lies partly buried in the sand—a dangerous hazard to angler and bather alike. Its food consists mainly of shrimps, mysids and small fishes and in some localities it can be particularly abundant. A small fish rarely exceeding 7 inches, it spawns from May to September.

THE GREATER WEEVER (*Trachinus draco*)

Resembles the Lesser Weever in appearance except that it is bigger (growing to about 18 inches) and its body is a deeper yellow with several dark oblique streaks on its sides. Fin ray formula:— D5–6/29–31; A31. It frequents deeper water and is rarely taken from the shore. Its breeding habits are similar to the lesser weever and its food consists mainly of small fishes and crustaceans.

	British Record	Irish Record
The Greater Weever	2 lb. 4 oz.	None

THE MACKERELS

(*Scombridae*)

Highly streamlined fishes with slender tail columns, two dorsals (first dorsal spiny) row of small finlets extending from behind the second dorsal and the anal fin to the tail. Two or three keels on tail column at junction with caudal fin; curved tails, pelvic fins set under pectorals.   The mackerel family and its allies, the swordfishes and spearfishes, are a large and important family, highly prized as food and including in its members some of the finest game fishes in the sea.   The Common Mackerel (*Scomber scombrus*) is the most common representative in our waters.   Occasional visitors to our shores are Colias Mackerel (*Pneumatophorus colias* (*Gmelin*)), otherwise known as the Spanish Mackerel, the Plain Bonito (*Auxis rochei*), the Oceanic Bonito (*Katsuwonsus pelamis*), the Belted Bonito or Pelamid (*Sarda sarda*) and the Long Finned Tunny or Albacore (*Germo alalunga*).   The giants of the family, i.e. the Tunny (*Thunnus thynnus* (*Linn*)) and the Broadbill Swordfish (*Xiphias gladius*) may be more common in our waters than is commonly thought.

THE MACKEREL (*Scombur scombrus*)

One of the most beautiful fish in the sea, round in cross-section, narrow tail section, two dorsals (set wide apart, the first triangular), five finlets between the tail fin and the anal and second dorsal fins, pectorals set high up and in advance of pelvics.   No swim bladder present and only two keels on tail column.   Small sharp spine behind the vent and in advance of the anal fin.   Fin ray formula:—

$$D10\text{-}14/\frac{I}{10\text{-}11}; \quad A\frac{I}{11}.$$

Colour metallic or enamel like, varying from blue to green with pattern of dark wavy or zigzag bands on back and sides giving way to silver below undulating lateral line.   Colour variations of the common mackerel are the Scribbled Mackerel (scribbled narrow lines instead of usual wavy pattern on the back) and the Spotted Mackerel (spots on the back instead of usual pattern).

A pelagic species, it ranges from the Canaries to Southern Norway, feeding on plankton in spring and in summer almost entirely on small fry, i.e. the young of herring, pilchards, sandeels, etc. Spawning takes place about April/May in deep water some distance from the land and the fish begin to move inshore about mid June and stay until the end of September or early October before migrating into deeper water.   Mainly a surface feeding species, they can be found over every type of bottom.   The average size in summer ranges from 11 to 15 inches, a fish of 2 lb. being considered a good one, and mackerel of over 4 lb. have been recorded.   They

take greedily and can be caught by spinning with artificial lures, by
feathering, or with fish baits.

	British Record	Irish Record	Specimen Weight
Mackerel	5 lb. 6 oz. 8 dr.	4 lb. 2 oz.	2½ lb.

THE TUNNY (*Thunnus thynnus*)

A giant version of the mackerel, with two dorsal fins (set closely
together), moderate sized pectoral, anal and second dorsal fins.
Fin ray formula:—$D13-14\dfrac{1-2}{13} + VIII-IX$; $A\dfrac{2}{12} + VII-VIII$. In
addition to the two small keels the tunny has a *prominent median keel*
on the free portion of the tail. Colour is dark blue on back,
shading to silver on the sides and white underneath. A migratory
species, it spawns in the Mediterranean and Atlantic coast of North
Africa near the Straits of Gibraltar in early spring and migrates
northward as far as the Norwegian coast in summer. Occasionally
seen on the west coast of Ireland, off Scotland and in the North Sea.
Has been taken on rod and line off Yorkshire. Food consists of
pelagic fishes, such as flying fishes, herrings, mackerel, etc., and it
can attain a weight of 1500 lb. or more. Average size in these
waters 400 to 800 lb. Captured on heavy tackle using whole fish
as bait, usually in the vicinity of herring or mackerel drifters.

	British Record	Irish Record	Specimen Weight
Tunny	851 lb.	None	100 lb.

THE BROADBILL SWORDFISH (*Xiphias gladius*)

An unmistakable fish. The upper jaw is elongated to form a
rectangular sword, first dorsal (crescentic in shape) in adult fish is
widely separated from the second, pelvic fins absent and a single
long lateral keel on each side of the tail column. Colour is dark
purple or blue on back, silver on sides. It can reach a weight of
1000 lb. or more and is not uncommon off our coasts from July to
November, especially in the south and south-west.

THE WRASSES

(*Labridae*)

Brilliantly coloured thick-set fish with thick fleshy lips which can
be curled back to reveal powerful, conical teeth. Tails broad,

rounded or square edged, single long dorsal, front spiny portion more developed than the soft rayed part, as is also the case in the anal fin. A very diverse and widely distributed family through the tropical and temperate seas, they are fish of rough and rocky ground. Seven species are represented in our waters, of which the Ballan Wrasse (*Labrus bergylta*) is the commonest. The Cuckoo Wrasse (*Labrus mixtus*) and the Corkwing Wrasse (*Crenilabrus melops*) are often taken by anglers whilst the other species are either rare or of no angling interest. The wrasses are unusual in that several species build nests for their eggs.

BALLAN WRASSE (*Labrus bergylta*)

Thick, fairly deep body, single row of powerful, conical teeth, two beds above and one below of rounded molar-like pharyngeal teeth, fins spotted, broad rather rounded tail fin, pectorals broad, rounded and paddle-like. Fin ray formula:—$D\dfrac{20-21}{9-11}$; $A\dfrac{3}{8-10}$. Colour very variable and unreliable for identification. Back and sides usually green, brown or blue, scales on head and body usually have a bluish or whitish spot. Lovers of rough and rocky ground the bigger fish are usually taken in 5 to 10 fathoms, smaller fish along rocky shores. Grows to 10 lb. or more, average size 1 to 3 lb. Found all around our coast on rocky and weedy bottoms feeding on crabs, prawns, mussels and other bivalves, and will also eat small fish. Spawns May to July, making nests of seaweed in the rocks between tide levels. The wrasse is found inshore from May to November but migrates offshore in winter. Will take crab, prawn, ragworm, lugworm, mussel or fish bait float fished or bottom fished over rocks and kelp.

The **Cuckoo Wrasse** (*Labrus mixtus*) is another nest builder, spawning from May to August. A common species, it is more plentiful in southern waters and has a longer snout and a more elongated and not so deep body as the Ballan Wrasse. Fin ray formula:—$D\dfrac{16-18}{(11)12-14}$; $A\dfrac{3}{10-12}$. Colour very variable and differ-ent in the sexes. Males usually yellow or orange tinged with red with five or six blue bands radiating backwards from the eye, corners of tail fin dark blue. Female red or reddish, no radiating bands but with two or three large dark spots under and behind the soft rayed portion of the dorsal fin.   A smaller fish than the Ballan Wrasse, its habits are similar.

The **Corkwing Wrasse** (*Crenilabrus melops*) is a small species and easily recognised by the serrated edge to the preopercular bone. Coloration is very variable and there may be a number (about

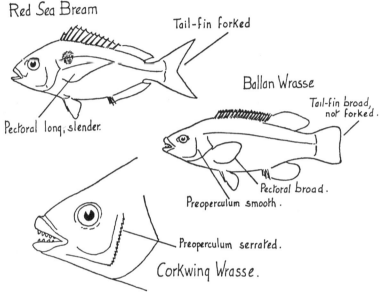

Red Sea Bream

Tail-fin forked

Pectoral long, slender.

Ballan Wrasse

Tail-fin broad, not forked.

Pectoral broad.

Preoperculum smooth.

Preoperculum serrated.

Corkwing Wrasse.

Sea Bream and Wrasses

eight) of vertical bands extending down each side and usually longitudinal bands on the dorsal.   Fin ray formula:—$D\dfrac{14-17}{8-9}$; $A\dfrac{3}{9-10}$.

A small fish not infrequently taken by boat anglers is the **Rainbow Wrasse** (*Coris julis*).   It differs from the other wrasses in that it has no scales on head or gill cover, in having pointed pectorals, and the spinous portion of the dorsal fin is no longer than the soft rayed portion.   Fin ray formula:—$D\dfrac{9}{12-13}$; $A\dfrac{3}{11-12}$.   The sexes are differently coloured, the female being purplish on the back, blue or grey on the sides, with a light yellow stripe running from eye to tail.   The male is the more colourful, being green or greenish purple on the back and upper sides, silver on the lower sides, with a

pale yellow indented band running from head to tail. It seldom
exceeds 7 or 8 inches in length.

	British Record	Irish Record	Specimen Weight
Ballan Wrasse	8 lb. 6 oz. 6 dr.	7lb. 6 oz.	4 lb. 8 oz.

THE GREY MULLETS

(Family Mugilidae)

Broadheaded, blunt snouted, thick lipped bass-like fishes of the
shallow coastal waters.   Scales large, no lateral line, dorsal fins well
separated, mouth small, teeth feeble and poorly developed, eye dark
with golden ring around the pupil.   A very successful and widely
distributed group of fishes found in all the oceans of the world.
Due to their peculiar feeding habits they are difficult to catch on rod
and line, but the commonest species in our waters, i.e. the Thick
Lipped or Grey Mullet (*Crenimugil labrosus*) is one of the gamest
Sea fish we have. The other two representatives of the species in
our waters are the Thin Lipped Grey Mullet (*Liza ramada*) and the
Golden Mullet (*Liza aurata*).   All three species closely resemble
each other.

THE THICK LIPPED GREY MULLET (*Crenimugil labrosus*)

A well proportioned bass-like fish (often mistaken for bass) with
a short blunt but broad head, broad across the back, large ctenoid
scales easily shed, forked tail, triangular pectorals, dorsals well
separated, mouth triangular, upper lip thick and fleshy possessing
taste buds, can be protruded slightly and is separated from the
forehead by a thin loose skin; eye dark with golden ring around the
pupil, no lateral line but scaling gives the illusion of several dark
lines or streaks running along the sides.   First dorsal triangular with
four spines, second dorsal has one or two spines followed by soft
rays.   Space between dorsals equals or only slightly exceeds length
of base of first dorsal; pectoral fin at least three-quarters length of
the head but not exceeding length of pelvic fin by more than one-
third; greatest thickness of upper lip more than half the diameter
of the eye.

The Grey Mullet looks dark on top, i.e. a brownish or bluish
grey, merging into silver on the sides.   The average size is 2 to 5 lb.,

but mullet of well over 10 lb. have been recorded. Its range extends from the Canaries to Norway, it is found all around our coast but is more plentiful in the south. A gregarious species, it swims in shoals of anything from two or three fish to several

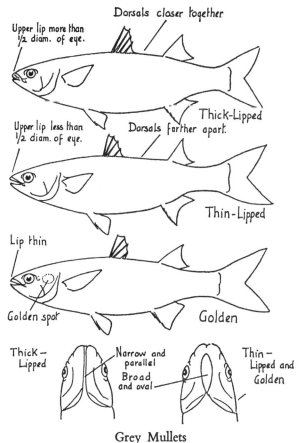

Dorsals closer together

Upper lip more than ½ diam. of eye.

Thick-Lipped

Upper lip less than ½ diam. of eye.

Dorsals farther apart.

Thin-Lipped

Lip thin

Golden spot

Golden

Thick—Lipped

Narrow and parallel

Broad and oval

Thin—Lipped and Golden

Grey Mullets
Below : underside of heads

thousand, and haunts our beaches, estuaries, creeks, harbours and tidal lagoons. Mullet have a liking of brackish water and can live for a time in water that is entirely fresh. Their natural food consists of minute marine organisms and small molluscs and crustaceans sifted from the sand and mud, but in places they can become accustomed to feeding on refuse and offal. Little is known of their spawning habits but indications are that it takes place inshore in May and June. They first appear towards the end of April, migrating into deeper water offshore around October. They are caught by float fishing, legering, and on paternosters using a great variety of baits including fish flesh, ham fat, cheese, red rag-worms, mussel, bread, peas and cabbage stumps.

	British Record	*Irish Record*	*Specimen Weight*
Grey Mullet	14 lb. 2 oz. 12 dr.	7 lb. 12 oz.	5 lb.

THE THIN LIPPED GREY MULLET (*Liza ramada*)

This species closely resembles in appearance and habits the thick lipped grey mullet but is a more southerly species. It differs from the latter in that the space between the two dorsals is one and two-thirds to two times the length of the base of the first dorsal; the pectoral fin is not more than two-thirds the length of the head and does not exceed the length of the pelvic fin by more than one-quarter. The greatest thickness of the upper lip is less than half the diameter of the eye and the taste buds are absent or poorly developed. There is no scaling or only slight scaling at the base of the second dorsal and anal fins.

THE GOLDEN MULLET (*Liza aurata*)

The rarest and smallest of the three species attaining only about half the size of the other two. A more southerly species, it is reported mainly from our southern coasts. It possesses long pectoral fins and distinctive gold spots, a large one on the gill cover and a smaller one on the cheek behind the eye. The other mullets sometimes have a hint of gold on both cheek and gill covers but are not spotted. The thickness of the upper lip is less than half the diameter of the eye; the space between the dorsals is about one and a half times the length of the base of the first dorsal and the pectoral fin at least three-quarters the length of the head and at least two-fifths longer than the pelvic fin. Taste buds in upper lip absent or poorly developed.

THE GURNARDS

(*Triglidae*)

Very distinctive fishes with large wedge-shaped bony heads heavily armed with spines; two dorsal fins set in grooves which usually have sharp spiny margins; thin tapering bodies, forked tails and large pectorals, the lower rays of which are modified into fleshy finger-like appendages.   There are six representatives of this family in our waters but only three are commonly taken by anglers, the others being rare.

THE GREY GURNARD (*Eutrigla gurnardus*)

As the name implies, the colour though variable is usually greyish with purple or green tints and there are distinctive white spots on

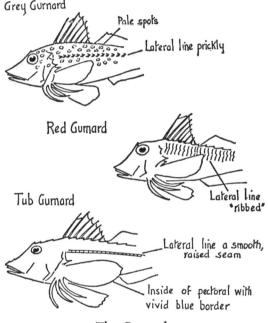

Grey Gurnard

Pale spots

Lateral line prickly

Red Gurnard

Lateral line "ribbed"

Tub Gurnard

Lateral line a smooth, raised seam

Inside of pectoral with vivid blue border

The Gurnards

the sides (yellow spots on head).   The head is bone with no scales, as in all the species.   The grooves in which the dorsals are set are prickly.   The lateral lines (a diagnostic character in the three species) is distinctive, being a series of raised, backward facing spiny plates.   The scales are ctenoid.   The Grey Gurnard is found from the Mediterranean to the Arctic and is the commonest of our gurnards.   The smallest of our gurnards, rarely exceeding 18 inches in length, it is found on clean bottoms (usually of sand) feeding on crustaceans and small fishes, such as sandeels and herring fry. Spawning time is April to August.   Can be caught bottom fishing with paternoster or leger using fish baits, crabs, prawns, etc. Can also be taken on a baited spoon.

	British Record	Irish Record	Specimen Weight
Grey Gurnard	2 lb. 7 oz.	3 lb. 1 oz.	1½ lb.

THE TUB GURNARD (*Trigla lucerna*)

The largest and least common of our gurnards, it is of stouter build than the others, the chief diagnostic pointers being: (1) the lateral line is a smooth raised ridge without spines and not crossed by plates; (2) the large colourful pectoral fins have a distinctive bright blue border at the tip on the inner side. The scales are cycloid and the margins of the grooves in which the dorsals are set are armed with spiny plates. The colour, which can be very red (it is often mistaken for the Red Gurnard), is usually red with brown or orange overtones. There are no white spots.

It ranges from the Mediterranean to Norway and is found all around our coasts but is more plentiful in the south than in the north. It is found on sandy and also on mixed bottoms feeding on crustaceans, molluscs and fish. Spawning takes place over an extended period through the summer and into the autumn. It may attain a length of as much as over 2 feet and a weight of 11 lb. Baits and fishing methods as for the Grey Gurnard.

	British Record	Irish Record	Specimen Weight
Tub Gurnard	12 lb. 3 oz.	12 lb. 3½ oz.	5 lb.

THE RED GURNARD (*Aspitrigla cuculus*)

A very red gurnard which differs from the Tub Gurnard in it being a very much more brilliant red and in not possessing a blue border on the pectorals. It has spiny plates on the margin of the groove in which the dorsals are set; possesses no white spots, and the scales are ctenoid. The lateral line is again diagnostic, having no spines but being crossed by narrow vertical plates which give a ribbed or V-shaped effect. It ranges from the Mediterranean to Norway (scarce in the North Sea), is found all around our coasts but can be abundant locally. More common than the Tub Gurnard but less common than the Grey Gurnard, it prefers hard bottoms of low rock or coral and feeds on crustaceans and small fish. Spawning time is April to June and it can grow to a weight of 3 lb. but the

average weight is much less.   Baits and methods similar to the
other gurnards.

	British Record	Irish Record	Specimen Weight
Red Gurnard	5 lb.	3 lb. 9¼ oz.	2 lb.

THE JOHN DORY (*Zeus faber* (*Linn*))

A very odd looking fish with a deep but very narrow body
similar to a flatfish but it swims upright in the normal manner.   It
has a big head and a large protrusible mouth which can be extended
suddenly to catch passing fish.   There are two dorsal fins not completely separated from each other.   The first dorsal is spinous, as is
the first portion of the anal and both the second dorsal and the
posterior portion of the anal fin are rounded.   Both the first dorsal
and the pectorals are elongated into straggling filaments and there is
a row of spines on either side along the base of the dorsal and the
anal fins.   The underside edge from throat to vent is serrated with
backward facing spines and there is a conspicuous black spot on the
sides.   The scales are small, spineless and the skin smooth.   The
colour is olive or brown.   A southern species, it is fairly common
on our southern and western coast, but is rare in the northern
North Sea.   It moves inshore in summer, feeding almost entirely
on fish such as sandeels, herrings and pilchards.   A poor swimmer,
it depends on disguise to get within striking distance of its prey.   It
can reach a weight of 18 lb. but the average weight is 2 to 5 lb.   A
solitary fish it is of no great angling interest, its capture on rod and
line for the most part being accidental.

	British Record	Irish Record	Specimen Weight
John Dory	11 lb. 14 oz.	7 lb. 1 oz.	4 lb.

THE FLATFISHES

(*Heterosomata*)

A large and important group, much sought after commercially as
food, and many members of which are the quarry of the angler.
As their name implies, they are flat with their bodies strongly compressed laterally.   Unlike other fishes, they swim on their sides.
The flatfishes have both eyes on the upper side, which is coloured,
the underside being colourless.   The group is divided into several
families, e.g. *The Bothidae*, which have their eyes on the left side

(they swim with the right side downwards) and large mouths with teeth and jaws equal on both sides. This group includes the turbot, brill, megrim, scaldfish and top-knots. The second family, the *Pleuronectidae*, can be further subdivided into two groups, i.e. *Hippoglossinae*, which includes the halibut and the Long Rough Dab, and the *Pleuronectinae*, which include the plaice, dab and flounder. Finally there are the *Soleoidea*, the sole group.

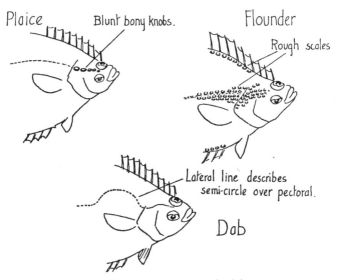

The Three Commonest Flatfishes

Many of the flatfishes, due either to their habits or habitat, are seldom taken by the angler and are not therefore described. The others for convenience of identification can be divided into two groups, i.e. those that have their eyes on their right side and those that have their eyes on the left side (in some species it is not uncommon to have "reversed" examples in which the eyes are on the opposite side to the rest of the species). To avoid confusion in deciding which side the eyes are on, the fish should be held in the hands, eyed side uppermost and the head facing away from the body. First we will deal with the *dextral* or right-sided species.

THE PLAICE (*Pleuronectes platessa*)

Eyes and colour on the right side, scales small and embedded in the skin, mouth at end of snout, the teeth are more developed and the mouth extends farther back on the under or "blind" side, lateral line almost straight except for slight undulation at pectoral fin, *bony knobs on the head extending backwards from between the eyes*, spine in front of anal fin. Colour typically brown on upper or eyed side with red or orange spots on the body and fins. Underside an opaque white with a tendency to translucence.

Plaice range from the Mediterranean to Iceland and are found all around our coast on shelly, sandy or gravelly bottoms feeding mainly on bivalves and shellfish. They also feed on crustaceans (shrimps, small crabs), marine worms and occasionally on fish, but the latter is not an important part of their food. Can be caught from the shore in places (mostly small fish) but are found mostly in depths of 10 to 40 fathoms. Spawning takes place from January to March in deep water, they move inshore again in late spring and summer. Have been taken up to 15 lb. in weight but average weight is approximately 2 to 4 lb. Will take razorfish, cockle, mussel, lugworm and ragworm fished on a leger or paternoster trot.

	British Record	Irish Record	Specimen Weight
Plaice	10 lb. 3 oz. 8 dr.	7 lb. 7 oz. 13 dr.	4 lb.

THE FLOUNDER (*Platichthys flesus*)

Similar in shape to the plaice; eyes on right side, lateral line slightly curved near head, biggish mouth, strong conical teeth, mouth extends farther back on blind side; *patch of rough tubercles on head behind the eyes and also rough tubercles extending along the base of both the anal and dorsal fins*; strong sharp spine in front of anal fin. Colour varies from very dark brown to greenish grey, sometimes with plaice-like spots; underside a distinctive opaque marble white. This species is found from the Mediterranean to Norway and is very common all around our coasts. It frequents muddy and sandy bottoms, has a liking for brackish water and is found in creeks, estuaries, harbours, and will even ascend considerable distances into freshwater (mostly young fish). It feeds on crustaceans (crabs, shrimps), worms (lugworm, white ragworm) and fish (sandeels, herring fry, sprats).

A smaller fish than the plaice, it averages $\frac{1}{2}$ to 2 lb. in weight. An inshore species, it spawns in the open sea from February to May. It begins to return inshore towards the end of April, remaining inshore until winter, when it begins to gradually migrate into deeper water for spawning. It will take peeler or soft crab, lugworm, ragworm, or fish bait fished leger or paternoster fashion and will also take a baited spoon.

	British Record	Irish Record	Specimen Weight
Flounder	5 lb. 11 oz. 8 dr.	4 lb. 6½ oz.	2½ lb.

THE DAB (*Limanda limanda*)

A smaller fish than the flounder or plaice, body thinner, more rounded; *ridge behind the eye smooth*; *lateral line strongly curved around pectoral fin*; *skin rough when rubbed against the grain and covered with small tooth edged scales*; eyes on the right side; mouth small and extended further on the blind side; spine in front of anal fin. The blind side has smooth scales and is a translucent bluish-white colour. The eyed side is a light sandy brown, sometimes covered with orange and black spots.

The dab ranges from the Bay of Biscay to the Arctic and is distributed all around our coasts. It favours bottoms of sand or muddy sand, often in the vicinity of a strong run of tide, and is found from the shore out to depths of 50 fathoms. A small species, it seldom exceeds 16 inches in length. It feeds on a wider variety of food than the plaice—crustaceans (hermit crabs, swimming crabs, amphipods), echinoderms (sand stars, brittle stars), bivalves (cockles, razorfish), various marine worms and small fry (the young of sandeels and herrings). Spawning time is mainly March to May in depths of 10 to 20 fathoms, the fish moving inshore from May onwards, but gradually migrating to deeper water as winter sets in. Light tackle fishing (leger, paternoster, paternoster-trot) using mussel, cockle, razorfish, ragworm, lugworm or shrimp as bait.

	British Record	Irish Record	Specimen Weight
Dab	2 lb. 12 oz. 4 dr.	1 lb. 13½ oz.	1½ lb.

LEMON DAB (*Microstomus kitt*)

More often called the *Lemon Sole*, this species *has a very distinctive oval shape*, which is in itself sufficient identification. The head and mouth are small, the tail column short and thick; eyes on the right side; mouth extends farther back on the blind side; scales small and smooth on both sides; lateral line only slightly curved over pectoral fin; no "knobs" or tubercles on head region. The colour of the blind side is similar to the dab and it is a rich brownish yellow on the eyed side with darker marbling effects but no spots. Extends from the Bay of Biscay to the Arctic, it is found all around our coasts on bottoms of sand, muddy sand and gravel in depths of 10 fathoms upwards, feeding on crustaceans and shellfish. A small species, seldom exceeding 18 inches, it spawns over a protracted period from January to September (the actual spawning time depending on geographical location) in deep water. Baits and methods are similar to those used for plaice.

THE SOLE (*Solea solea (Linn)*)

One of the true soles and the only one commonly taken by anglers. The soles differ from other flatfish in that they have longer, more flexible bodies, with a rounded snout projecting beyond the downward-curved mouth. The body is a narrow oval not unlike a footprint in shape. They possess tufts of filaments or "beards" on the front of the head on the blind side and teeth only in the jaws on the blind side.

The species of the sole family are very similar in appearance, but the Common or Black Sole (*Solea solea*) can be distinguished from the others by its larger pectoral fins and that the nostril on the underside is small and not dilated. Fin ray formula:—D73–90; A61–74. After death the colour on the eyed side is usually dark brown or grey, but in living fish it is variegated with lighter and darker markings depending on the type of bottom on which it was taken. There is a dark tip to the pectoral on the eyed side and the dorsal, caudal and anal fins have a narrow white border.

The sole is most plentiful in depths of 5 to 40 fathoms and is common in the Irish Sea, on the south and west coasts of Ireland, in the Channel and the North Sea, preferring bottoms of sand, muddy sand, mud and gravel in areas of mixed ground, i.e. interspersed with rocks, reefs and ledges. It feeds mainly on various burrowing marine worms, sand stars, brittle stars, sand shrimps, small razorfish and other bivalves. It has been recorded up to a weight of 9 lb. but the average size is 12 to 18 inches. Spawning takes place from February to August, and as the sole is noctural in habit it is usually caught by anglers when fishing after dark. It will take razorfish, ragworm or lugworm, fished on the bottom using leger or pater-noster-trot tackle.

	British Record	Irish Record	Specimen Weight
Sole	5 lb. 7 oz. 1 dr.	4 lb. 4 oz. 10 dr.	2 lb.

THE HALIBUT (*Hippoglossus hippoglossus* (*Linn*))

The largest of the flatfishes, it has a less-compressed, narrower, more rounded body than other species, with a very large mouth and sharp teeth. Eyes on the right side separated by a flat space no wider than the eye; origin of the dorsal fin level with or in front of the pupil of the upper eye; lateral line strongly curved over pectoral fin, body covered with smooth scales. Eyed side coloured medium to dark brown or olive, lower surface pearl white. The halibut is a veritable giant among flatfishes, having been recorded to a weight of over 600 lb. Notable fish taken by rod and line in our waters ranged from 50 to 150 lb.

A northern deep water species, it has been taken as far south as the Channel and the south coast of Ireland but is more plentiful farther north. An active predator feeding mainly on other fishes (crustaceans have been found in smaller fish), it has a liking for mixed and rough ground from 20 fathoms upwards. It spawns in deep water from January to June. Halibut have been taken on large fish baits, both bottom fishing to an anchor and drifting using heavy boat tackle.

	British Record	Irish Record	Specimen Weight
Halibut	234 lb.	156 lb.	50 lb.

THE BOTHIDAE

The sinistral or left-sided flatfishes include the megrim, scaldfish and the top-knots, but only two, both of which are similar in appearance, e.g. the turbot and the brill, are of interest to the angler. Both are excellent food fishes.

THE TURBOT (*Scopthalmus maximus* (*Linn*))

A thick, broad, diamond-shaped fish, covered with blunt bony tubercles or spines on the eyed side. The mouth is large, equal on both sides with numerous sharp teeth. The lateral line is strongly curved over the pectoral and the body has no scales. The dorsal fin extends on to the head. Fin ray formula:—D61–72; A45–56.

The colour on the eyed side is usually brownish (can be greyish) speckled with lighter and darker markings, blind side opaque white.

Of more southerly distribution than the plaice, it is found from the Mediterranean to the southern North Sea, but is most plentiful off our south and west coasts. The turbot is an inshore species (can be taken in places from the shore) and the best fishing is found in depths of 10 to 20 fathoms. It prefers bottoms of sand or gravel preferably sandbanks or tideways where small fish are plentiful. The turbot is almost entirely a fish eater and will eat almost any small fish but is particularly partial to sandeels and sprats. Spawning takes place offshore from April to July. Turbot weighing upwards of 30 lb. have been recorded, but the average size of fish taken is from 10 to 15 lb. except in the case of small fish taken from or near the shore. The best baits are live sandeels, mackerel lashes, sprats or small fish, using leger or paternoster-trot terminal tackle anchor fishing or drifting.

	British Record	Irish Record	Specimen Weight
Turbot	33 lb. 12 oz.	32 lb. 8 oz.	18 lb.

THE BRILL (*Scopthalmus rhombus (Linn)*)

The brill differs from the turbot in that it is more oval in shape, i.e. narrower in proportion to its length, the eyed surface is smooth, bearing no tubercles as does the turbot; both sides of the body are covered with smooth cycloid scales. Fin ray formula:—D76-85; A53-65. Coloration is similar to the turbot but may tend to be more greenish and with more marbled or mottled effects. Its distribution, haunts and feeding habits are the same as the turbots, indeed they are often taken on the same grounds. Spawning takes place offshore from March to August. A smaller species than the turbot, it grows to about half its size. Fishing methods and baits as for turbot.

	British Record	Irish Record	Specimen Weight
Brill	16 lb.	None	8 lb.

THE COD FAMILY

(*Gadidae*)

A family which includes several important food fishes, some of which are the quarry of the angler. The species of this family have extensive soft rayed fins; the dorsals, one to three in number, occupying most of the length of the back and the anal fins, one or two in number, occupying much of the length of the ventral surface. The pelvic fins, long and sinuous in some species, very small in others, are in advance of the pectorals, more or less on the throat. The scales are smooth and small. Many species have a beard or barbel under the chin.

THE COD (*Gadus morrhua* (*Linn*))

The cod has three dorsal fins and two anal fins. The head is large and broad, the shoulders high and the body tapers off abruptly towards the tail. The upper jaw is longer than the lower and there is a conspicuous fleshy barbel beneath the chin. The teeth are sharp, the stomach protruberant, the lateral line is white and curves shallowly over the pectoral fin. The colour varies and is usually greenish or brownish or greyish green (fish taken on rocky ground are red) and covered with brown or yellowish spots.

The cod is a northern cold water species seldom found below Latitude 40′ and is caught all around our coasts. It is most plentiful in the Irish Sea, the North Sea, off Scotland and the north coast of Ireland. A demersal species, it is found over every type of bottom feeding on a very wide variety of food. It has been aptly described as "all head and gut". Crustaceans form a large part of its diet, followed by molluscs (squids, whelks, etc.), starfish and fish. It spawns from January to June, spending the summer months in the deeper cooler water (good fish are usually found in depths over 15 fathoms), migrating inshore in winter when they can in places be caught from the shore. The cod attains a weight well in excess of 100 lb., but in our waters the average run of fish is 10 to 30 lb. Will take mussel, lugworm, crab and fish baits fished paternoster or leger style on or near the bottom.

	British Record	Irish Record	Specimen Weight
Cod	53 lb.	42 lb.	25 lb.

THE HADDOCK (*Melanogrammus aeglifinus*)

A smaller species than the cod, which it closely resembles. It differs in having a much smaller barbel than the cod; the lateral line is black and has a much straighter curve and there is a conspicuous black spot or patch on the shoulder just above the pectorals. It has three dorsal fins (the first somewhat pointed), two anal fins and a somewhat forked tail fin. The back is greyish brown shading to white underneath and it is not spotted like the cod.

Distribution is similar to the cod, but due to very heavy commercial fishing is not as abundant around our coasts as it once was. It is more plentiful in our northern waters, especially off the coast of Scotland. It is found on soft bottoms, mainly in depths of over 15 fathoms, feeding on molluscs (razorfish, whelks, squid, etc.),

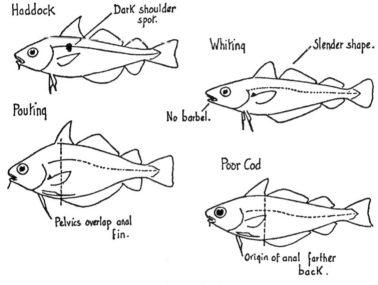

Cod Family (I)

crustaceans (shrimps, crabs, etc.), bivalves and various marine worms. Fish are not an important part of its diet. Spawning takes place in deep water offshore from January to June and from November to February it enters comparatively shallow water before migrating offshore again. Although a fish weighing 24 lb. has been recorded the average weight of haddock is in the region of 2 to 4 lb. Usually taken bottom fishing using lugworm, mussel or crab.

	British Record	Irish Record	Specimen Weight
Haddock	13 lb. 11 oz. 4 dr.	10 lb. 13½ oz.	7 lb.

THE WHITING (*Merlangius merlangus*)

A more slender fish than the cod or haddock, it has a longer, narrower head, silvery sides, no barbel, and there is a conspicuous black spot on the upper side of the root of the pectoral fin. The three dorsals are set close together; the vent is very far forward; the tail fin square edged, the pelvics long and sinuous; the long sharp teeth are conspicuous, as also are the mucous pores on the head. The curved lateral line is brown in colour. The whiting is brownish coloured on the back and large fish may have traces of golden brown on the lower sides.

The whiting is a more southerly species than the cod and haddock and is found from the Mediterranean to the Arctic. It is plentiful all around our coast, preferring clean bottoms of sand and mud. It is a small species but has been recorded to a weight of 8 lb. The average weight, however, is 1 to 2 lb., a 3 lb. whiting being considered a good fish. It is more of a fish eater than either the cod or haddock, preying on small fishes (even its own young), and it also feeds on crustaceans and various marine worms. Like the cod, it prefers deeper, colder water in summer, migrating into the inshore shallows in winter. Spawning takes place from February to June. It is usually caught by paternoster fishing with fish baits, mussel, lugworm and ragworm.

	British Record	Irish Record	Specimen Weight
Whiting	6 lb. 12 oz.	4 lb. 14½ oz.	3 lb.

THE POUTING (*Trisopterus lusus*)

The pouting is a short, deep-bodied fish possessing a barbel under the chin; the upper jaw is slightly longer than the lower; the first dorsal very pointed; the pelvics long and sinuous, stretching back beyond the origin of the anal fin; square edged tail fin. There is a dark spot at the base of the pectoral fin and the lateral line is a narrow curved brownish seam. Freshly caught pouting are an iridescent copper or bronzy colour with dark vertical bands on the sides.

A more southerly species that the rest of the cod family, it ranges as far south as the Mediterranean. It is plentiful on rocky ground or in the vicinity of rocks and on wrecks all around our coast, but is more abundant in our southern waters. Feeding mainly on crustaceans and small fishes, it spawns from January to April in deep water offshore. A small species, seldom exceeding a weight of 5 lb., fair sized pouting run from 1 to 3 lb. in weight. Will take small fish baits, mussel, ragworm, lugworm, prawns, shrimps and squid fished on or near the bottom.

	British Record	Irish Record	Specimen Weight
Pouting	5 lb. 8 oz.	4 lb. 10 oz.	3 lb.

THE POOR COD (*Trisopterus minutus*)

The smallest and most widely distributed member of the cod family. Closely resembles the pouting but differs in being more slender and less deep than it; the pelvic fins are not as long, reaching only to the vent, which is farther back. There are no vertical bands and the colour varies from pinkish brown to brownish yellow on the back. Distribution, habits and haunts are similar to the poutings except that it ranges widely over clean bottoms as well as over rough ground. Seldom exceeds 8 inches in size and the average length is considerably less.

THE POLLACK (*Pollachius pollachius*)

A handsome fish with a narrow, somewhat angular body. The head is narrower and more pointed than in most other gadoids. There is no barbel under the chin; the lower jaw is longer than the upper, the teeth are small, sharp and in bands in the jaw, and the inner edges of the gill arches are toothed. The eye is large; the pores in the sensory canals on the head are conspicuous; the pelvic fins are very small and situated in advance of the pectorals; the lateral line is dark and strongly curved over the pectoral fin. The colour is variable, usually dark green or reddish brown on the back, olive on the sides, which are speckled reddish gold at times and the belly is white.

The pollack is a more southerly species than the cod and ranges from the Mediterranean to Norway and is found all around our coasts, but is much more plentiful in our southern waters being most abundant on our south and south-west coasts. Spawning time is February to May, the first pollack appearing inshore towards the end of April where they stay until about the end of September or early October before beginning their offshore migration. Lovers of the high wild rock and rough bottoms, they prefer relatively shallow water and are found mostly in depths out to 20 fathoms.

In summer they feed mainly on other fishes, i.e. sandeels, sprats, herring, pilchard and small fry.   Strong fighting fish, they grow to over 20 lb., but the average size depending on the locality varies from 2 to 8 lb.   They can be caught by spinning, trolling, drift-lining, float fishing, feathering or paternostering, using fish baits, sandeels, ragworms, peeler crab and artificial lures.

	British Record	Irish Record	Specimen Weight
Pollack	25 lb. 12 dr.	19 lb. 3 oz.	12 lb.

THE COALFISH (*Pollachius virens*)

The coalfish so closely resembles the pollack in general appearance that it is often confused with it.   It differs in that the lateral line is an almost straight narrow white line;   the tail fin is forked (in

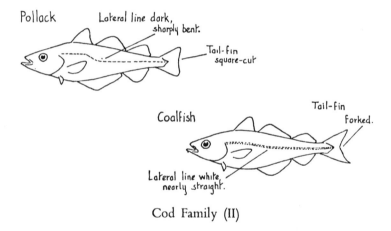

Cod Family (II)

pollack it is square edged);   the lower jaw though longer than the upper does not protrude as far as in the pollack;   there is a rudimentary and hardly distinguishable barbel folded back under the chin.   A rounder fish than the pollack, its pelvics though relatively small are bigger, and the coalfish is very dark in colour being a dark green (almost black) on the back while the underside is white.

Its distribution, habits, haunts and food are similar to the pollack's but it is a more northerly species, being more plentiful on our northern coasts whilst the pollack are more prolific in the south.   A larger species than the pollack, it grows to over 30 lb. but the average weight depends on the locality.   While small fish are plentiful inshore the larger fish prefer much deeper water than pollack and are more nomadic.

	British Record	Irish Record	Specimen Weight
Coalfish	33 lb. 7 oz.	24 lb. 7 oz.	15 lb.

THE LING (*Molva molva* (*Linn*))

The ling has two dorsal fins and one anal fin. The first dorsal is short and rounded with a black blotch on the rear portion, the second dorsal is long and uniform in height and the tail fin is rounded. The body is long, slimy and rather eel-like, the head and back are broad; the mouth large with sharp teeth in the jaws and on the roof of the mouth; there is a barbel under the chin. The colour on the back varies from drab grey to brown or olive with indistinct marbled effects on the sides. The dorsal, anal and tail fins are edged with white and there are dark bands on the tail fin.

A northerly species, ling are found from the Bay of Biscay to Iceland. A deep water species, they are found all around our coasts, usually on rough or rocky bottoms. They can attain a length of 6 to 7 feet and a weight of over 100 lb. In our waters a good fish would weigh from 12 to 25 lb. and fish of this size are usually taken in depths of over 15 fathoms. A demersal species, feeding almost entirely on other fishes, they spawn in deep water offshore from April to June. They are taken on fish baits, fished on or near the bottom over rough ground.

	British Record	Irish Record	Specimen Weight
Ling	57 lb. 2 oz. 8 dr.	46 lb. 8 oz.	25 lb.

Note:—Small or "baby" ling are often taken in relatively shallow water inshore and are often confused by anglers with the *Rocklings*. The rocklings differ from the ling in that there is no separate front dorsal, the front portion being a fine vibratory membrane sunk in a longitudinal groove. There are three common species: the Three-Bearded Rockling (*Gaidrosarus vulgaris*) has two barbels on the upper lip and one under the chin; the Four-Bearded Rockling (*Rhinonemus cimbrius*) has an additional barbel on the upper lip in front of the other pair as well as one under the chin; the Five-Bearded Rockling (*Ciliata mustela*) has a pair of barbels on the lips, another pair on the anterior nostrils and one under the chin.

THE HAKES

(*Merluccidae*)

THE HAKE (*Merluccius merluccius* (*Linn*))

Not unlike the ling in general appearance, it has a deeper and less round body; the first dorsal is triangular, the tail fin square edged; the long second dorsal and anal fins wider towards the tail; the lateral line is a conspicuous straight dark line; the mouth is large, teeth long and sharp, the lower jaw slightly longer than the upper, the inside of the mouth is black and there is no barbel under the chin. Scales thin, round and easily detached. The colour on the back is a grey or slate colour, underside white, overall appearance silvery grey.

The hake is found from the Mediterranean to Iceland and Norway but is no longer as plentiful around our coasts as it once was, due to intensive commercial fishing. A deep water species, it moves into shallower water in summer and autumn within reach of the angler. Spawning takes place over a very long period from January to November. Nocturnal in its feeding habits, it lives almost entirely on other fishes, feeding in midwater or near the surface after dark and resting on the bottom during the day. It has been recorded to a weight of over 20 lb. but the average weight where taken on rod and line these days is small. Sometimes taken on fish baits on the bottom during the day but more likely to be taken in midwater or near the surface after dark when they are feeding on shoal fish, e.g. mackerel, herring, pilchard, whiting.

	British Record	Irish Record	Specimen Weight
Hake	25 lb. 5 oz. 8 dr.	25 lb. 5½ oz.	10 lb.

THE BELONIDAE

THE GARFISH (*Belone belone* (*Linn*))

A very distinctive species, easily recognised by its long sandeel-like body and its long slender toothed bill or beak. There is one dorsal fin set very far back over the anal and the tail fin is forked, the lower lobe being longer than the upper. The pelvic fins are set far back at the middle of the belly and the lateral line is straight, running very low down almost on the belly. The colour is green on the back and brilliant silver on the sides.

A pelagic and nomadic species, like the mackerel, it is found from the Mediterranean to Norway. Spawning takes place from May to July in shallow water. Garfish migrate inshore about May, feeding mainly on small bait fishes though crustaceans also figure in their diet. A small species, the garfish seldom exceeds 3 feet in length and is usually taken by anglers spinning or feathering for mackerel. It will also take small fish baits.

The garfish is often confused with the Saury Pike (*Scombresox saurus* (*Walbaum*)), which it resembles very closely. The Saury Pike, however, is a smaller species seldom exceeding 18 inches and differs in that its dorsal and anal fins are separated from the tail fin by a series of finlets similar to those found in mackerel. The bill-like mouth is shorter and the teeth smaller than in the garfish.

	British Record	Irish Record	Specimen Weight
Garfish	2 lb. 15 oz. 9 dr.	3 lb. 10¼ oz.	2½ lb.

THE CONGRIDAE

THE CONGER (*Conger conger* (*Linn*))

The conger possess the familiar eel or snake-like appearance and a stout muscular slimy body. The head is flat, the jaws powerful and set with razor-sharp teeth; the upper jaw is longer than the lower; the dorsal fin commences over or very nearly over the tip of the pectoral and extends right to the tip of the tail. There are no pelvic fins and no scales apparent on the skin. The colour varies with habitat and is usually dark green or a bluey black above and a dead white underneath.

The conger is found all around our coasts mostly on or near rough or rocky ground, in piers and harbour walls and on wrecks. Inshore it is mainly nocturnal in habit, feeding mostly on fishes, but it will also eat crustaceans. It grows to a weight of 100 lb. or more and the average size is 8 to 20 lb. Spawning takes place in the depths of the ocean and the conger spawns but once before death. Very strong tackle and a short wire trace are essential in fishing for conger. Fresh fish baits (mackerel, herring, squid, pilchard, etc.), fished leger fashion or paternoster fashion on very rough ground.

	British Record	Irish Record	Specimen Weight
Conger	109 lb. 6 oz.	72 lb.	40 lb.

Note.—Small congers and large freshwater eels are often confused with one another. The freshwater eel (*Anguilla anguilla* (*Linn*)) differs in that the head and eye are small, the lower jaw protrudes and the dorsal fin begins a considerable distance behind the pectoral fins.

THE SALMON AND THE SEA-TROUT

(*Salmonidae*)

Members of this family possess one short soft rayed dorsal fin and a very distinctive small fleshy rayless fin (the adipose fin) behind the dorsal and near the tail fin. The pelvic fins are set near the middle of the body and the scales are small and cycloid. There are no scales on the cheeks or gill cover.

The typical salmon and trout shape is familiar to us all and the only difficulty likely to face the angler is in distinguishing between a small salmon (*Salmo salar*) and a large sea trout (*Salmo trutta*). The distinguishing features are: (a) If a line is drawn from the snout to the farthest extremity of the gill cover, the eye in the salmon is bisected by this line while the eye in the sea trout is situated above this line; (b) If the anal fin be folded back, the longest anterior ray in the sea trout extends beyond the posterior rays but does not in the salmon; (c) In the salmon there are 10 to 13 (usually 11) scales in a row from the rear edge of the adipose fin to the lateral line while there are 13 to 16 (usual 14) in the sea trout; (d) There is a definite "thickening" at the end of the tail where it joins the tail fin in the salmon allowing the fish to be grasped and held when wet.

Both species are anadromous, ascending into fresh water to spawn. The salmon feeds far out at sea and rarely takes food in our inshore waters on its spawning migration. It is occasionally taken on artificial baits (though very rarely) in salt or brackish water. The sea trout, however, feeds mostly in the shallow coastal waters, along beaches and in estuaries and will take suitable baits or lures. It feeds mainly on small fishes and various marine worms and

crustaceans.   The sea trout grows to over 30 lb. but the average size
is 1 to 3 lb.   It will take small artificial lures and natural baits, such
as sandeels and small fry.

THE HERRING FAMILY

(Clupeidae)

The herring is the typical fish of this family.   They are fish which
possess no spiny fin rays;   have a single short dorsal fin near the
middle of the back;   a short anal fin situated towards the tail;
pelvics under or nearly under the dorsal;   big mouths and poorly
developed teeth.   Some members of the family are important
commercial food fish, a few are of angling interest either for sport
or for bait.

THE HERRING (Clupea herengus (Linn))

A very familiar fish that anglers have no difficulty in recognising.
Feeding almost entirely on plankton, it can at times be caught on
small fresh water size flies but it is of no great angling interest apart
from its usefulness as bait.   It is easily confused with its near
relative the pilchard (Sardinia pilchardus (Walbaum)), another excellent bait fish.

The herring is usually bluish green on the back and brilliant
silver on the sides, while the pilchard is more olive on the back and
less brilliant silver on the sides.   In the herring the dorsal is set in
the middle of the back and the pelvics are directly under it and a
little behind its origin.   In the pilchard the dorsal is a little forward
of the middle of the back with the pelvics underneath.   The pilchard
has radiating streaks on the cheeks and gill cover (absent in the
herring), its belly is more rounded and armed with weak spines,
whilst the herring's belly is knife-edged and without spines.   The
pilchard is the smaller species and has larger scales.   Both are very
oily fish and make excellent bait.

THE TWAITE SHAD (Alosa fallax)

A bigger edition of the herring with a deeper body, a saw-edged
belly, a very forked tail (the tips of which are dark and at the base
of which there is a dark V-shaped bar).   There are radiating streaks

on the gill cover, the scales are large and easily detached and there is a dark blotch or patch behind the gill cover, followed by a row of dark spots which extend along the upper side of the body. The gill rakers (not to be confused with the gill filaments) are rather coarse and short and there are not more than 28 on the lower portion of the gill arch. A beautifully coloured fish, it is a dusky blue on the back and silver on the sides with opalescent reflections.

An anadromous fish, found from the Mediterranean to the Baltic, it ascends many of our rivers to spawn in fresh water (at the top of the influence of the tide) from late April to early June. A much larger fish than the herring, the average size is from $\frac{1}{2}$ to 2 lb. During the summer it feeds mainly on small fry and will strike freely at any small spinning lure.

	British Record	Irish Record	Specimen Weight
Twaite Shad	3 lb. 2 oz.	2 lb. 1½ oz.	2¼ lb.

THE ALLIS SHAD (*Alosa alosa* (*Linn*))

Closely resembles the Twaite Shad but is a much larger fish, growing to 8 lb. or more. It differs in that its gill rakers are finer and more numerous, there being 60 or more on the lower portion of the first gill arch. The row of spots distinctive of the Twaite Shad is not present in adult Allis Shad but the dark blotch behind the gill cover is present.

Its habits, distribution, food and spawning are similar to the Twaite Shad except that it ascends much further into fresh water, even as far as the salmon, to spawn.

THE CARTILAGINOUS FISHES

(*Selachii*)

A very large, diverse and widely distributed group of fishes which includes the sharks, dogfishes, rays and skates. They differ from the true or bony fishes in that their skeleton consists entirely of gristle or cartilage and not true bone. The gills, too, are different, presenting several different openings or gill slits to the outside, whereas in the true fishes the gills present a single opening covered by a gill cover. They possess no scales but the skin is usually covered by denticles (minute sharp spines) which give the skin a rough texture when rubbed against the grain. The mouth is usually on the underside and the males have claspers (intromittent organs) attached to their pelvic fins.

For convenience the selachians can be divided into two groups: (a) Round fish with the snout produced longitudinally or laterally, mouth crescentic in shape and situated on the underside, two dorsal fins, e.g. the dogfishes and sharks; (b) Body broad, depressed from above, disc round, circular or rhomboid and formed by the enormously developed pectoral fins. Two small dorsal fins usually situated near the extremity of the tail, e.g. the skates and rays. We will deal with the former group first.

THE LESSER SPOTTED DOGFISH (*Scyliorhinus caniculus* (*Linn*))

A long slim rough-skinned fish covered with small dark round spots. The two dorsal fins are set far back towards the tail, the nostrils are large and in front of the crescentic-shaped mouth; the spiracles are conspicuous and close behind the eyes. Colour is usually brownish on the back with numerous dark spots and white underneath. Dogfish taken over rocky ground may be very dark (almost black) on the back. The diagnostic characters in this species are: (a) *The base of the anal fin ends under or slightly in advance of the origin of the second dorsal fin*; (b) *The nasal flaps are large and continuous (not divided) and their lower margins are in line with the mouth.*

This species is found all around our coasts on every type of bottom, feeding on all kinds of small life, i.e. crustaceans, molluscs, starfish, and small fishes. A small species, it grows to about 3 feet in length and the average weight is 2 to 3½ lb. There is no particular spawning time, internally fertilised eggs being produced in horny capsules at intervals throughout the year. It will take almost all bottom baits used by anglers and the difficulty is not how to catch it but usually how to avoid catching it.

	British Record	Irish Record	Specimen Weight
Lesser Spotted Dogfish	4 lb. 8 oz.	4 lb. 3 oz.	3 lb.

THE GREATER SPOTTED DOGFISH (*Scyliorhinus stellaris* (*Linn*))

A larger and more robust looking fish than the Lesser Spotted Dogfish, with which it is often confused. It differs in that (a) *the end of the base of the anal fin is well behind the origin of the second dorsal i.e. they overlap*; (b) *the nasal flaps are smaller, separate from each other and from the mouth, and each flap has a small gristly rib–like point projecting from the centre of the flap.* The spots are usually larger and less regular but should not be used as a guide to the species as they are not diagnostic in character.

It is found all around the coast but is less plentiful than the Lesser Spotted Dogfish, prefers deeper water and rougher ground. Food and habits are similar to the Lesser Spotted Dogfish but it is a more

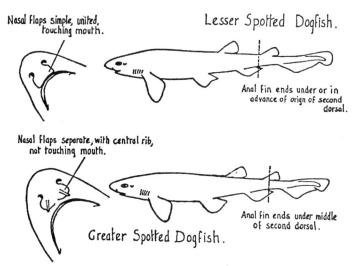

The Greater and Lesser Spotted Dogfishes

active fish and fish bulks more largely in its diet. It grows to over 20 lb. in weight and the average size is 8 to 12 lb. Usually taken on fish baits, legering or paternostering over rough or broken ground from a boat or from the shore where there is deep water.

	British Record	Irish Record	Specimen Weight
Greater Spotted Dogfish	21 lb. 3 oz.	21 lb. 4 oz.	16 lb.

THE SPURDOG (*Squalus acanthias (Linn)*)

This species is more typically shark-like in shape and is immediately distinguished by the single sharp spine in front of each of the two dorsal fins and by the absence of the anal fin. The colour on top is usually bluish or brownish grey, white underneath, with some small pale spots on the back.

A pelagic species, it is found in all the temperate waters of the northern hemisphere. This very destructive fish swims in shoals, is found all around our coasts and tends to be very abundant locally at times, feeding mainly on shoaling fish such as mackerel, whiting, etc.   The Spurdog is viviparous, producing its young alive during the spring in our inshore waters.   It attains a weight of over 14 lb. and averages about 4 to 8 lb.   It will take any fish bait readily.

	British Record	Irish Record	Specimen Weight
Spurdog fish	21 lb. 3 oz. 7 dr.	18 lb. 12 oz.	12 lb.

THE BLUE SHARK (*Prionace glauca*)

A long slim shark with a raked-back tail which has a long shallow notch; there is no lateral keel on either side of the tail column. Long slender pointed and sickle-like pectorals; the gill slits are

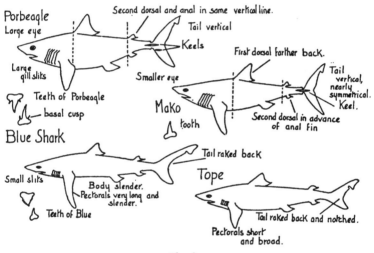

Sharks

small and there are no spiracles.   It has razor-sharp, triangular teeth with a serrated cutting edge.   The colour in life is usually dark blue or marine blue shading to white underneath.

A pelagic species feeding mainly on shoal fish such as mackerel and pilchard, it arrives on our south and south-west coasts in June or July and migrates offshore around September.   Fish of well over 200 lb. have been recorded from our waters and the average size is from 40 to 70 lb.   Usually taken on whole fish baits, float fished from a boat.

	British Record	Irish Record	Specimen Weight
Blue Shark	218 lb.	206 lb.	100 lb.

THE PORBEAGLE SHARK (*Lamna nasus*)

A more portly fish than the Blue Shark, it has a thick high body in front narrowing towards the tail. It has large gill slits, and the upper lobe of the vertically-set tail is much larger than the lower. *Below the strengthening lateral keel on the tail column there is a small secondary keel.* The first dorsal is much larger than in the blue shark and its origin is well in advance of the upper hind corner of the pectoral. The origin of the second dorsal and the anal fin are in the same vertical line. The teeth are pointed and have small additional basal cusps in the adult. The colour is usually greyish or brownish shading to white underneath.

The porbeagle is a big fish and has been recorded up to about 400 lb. in our waters. It is viviparous and is found in our inshore waters in summer and autumn. It feeds mainly on mackerel, herring, whiting and pollack, but will also eat most other fish. It may be found harrying shoals of smaller fish or on good pollack reefs. It may be more plentiful around our coasts than is realised. Usually taken on large whole fish baits, float fishing, bottom fishing, driftlining or trolling from a boat.

	British Record	Irish Record	Specimen Weight
Porbeagle Shark	465 lb.	365 lb.	150 lb.

THE MAKO SHARK (*Isurus oxyrhynchus*)

A very large shark and one of the real big game fishes. A much slimmer and more symmetrical looking fish than the porbeagle, it can be distinguished from it by the fact that the origin of the first dorsal is behind the upper hind corner of the pectoral, while the origin of the second dorsal is well in advance of the origin of the anal. The tail is more or less symmetrical, i.e. the upper lobe is not noticeably larger than the lower and there is no secondary keel present on the tail column nor are there any small basal cusps present on the teeth. Colour is blue or bluish grey.

Not much is known about the habits and distribution of this species but Mako Shark have been caught off the Cornish coast and the Channel Islands. They have been hooked but only one has so far been landed off the south coast of Ireland.

	British Record	Irish Record	Specimen Weight
Mako Shark	500 lb.	None	200 lb.

THE THRESHER SHARK (*Alopias vulpinus*)

A very distinctive and easily recognised shark with an extremely long tail (making up about half the fish's total length) which has a pit at its root. The pectoral fins and the first dorsal are long, whilst the second dorsal and the anal fin are very small. The tail has no lateral keel. The teeth are small, triangular and unserrated. The colour can be bluish grey or dark grey above and white underneath.

A summer visitor to our coasts, it is quite often seen rounding up shoals of mackerel or pilchard using its tail as a flail to drive the

Thresher Shark

shoal into a huddled mass. Specimens up to 16 feet long have been recorded in our waters. A pelagic species, feeding mainly on shoal fish, it is viviparous.

	British Record	Irish Record	Specimen Weight
Thresher Shark	295 lb.	None	120 lb.

THE TOPE (*Galeorhinus galeus*)

The Tope is not unlike the Blue Shark in shape but is a much smaller species possessing a small spiracle behind the eye which is absent in the Blue Shark. Its pectoral fins are much shorter and more proportionate to its size. It has two dorsal fins, the first some distance behind the pectorals and the origin of the second dorsal is a little in advance of the anal fin. It has small, sharp, flat, triangular teeth which are both notched and serrated and there is a short deep notch at the lower margin of the tail fin. The colour on the back is brownish or greyish.

A fine fighting fish, it grows to over 80 lb. and the average size is 20 to 35 lb. It is found all around our coasts on both clean and rough ground and can be quite plentiful locally. The Tope is viviparous, migrating inshore in late spring or early summer to spawn in quite shallow water and remains until the autumn. It feeds almost entirely on other fishes, both pelagic and demersal species. Taken on fish baits legered or float fished from the shore or from boats.

	British Record	Irish Record	Specimen Weight
Tope	74 lb. 11 oz.	66 lb. 8 oz.	40 lb.

THE SMOOTH HOUND (*Mustelus mustelus (Linn)*)

Not unlike the Tope but much more clumsily built with larger fins. Its teeth are very distinctive, being flat and adapted for crushing as in the rays. There is a long shallow notch in the tail fin and the first dorsal is set far forward (almost over the pectorals). The colour on the back is usually greyish; white underneath and with rows of pale white spots along the upper sides.

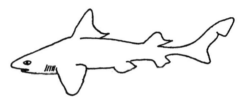

Smooth Hound Shark

A smaller species than the Tope, it has been recorded up to 6 feet in length but usually averages about 3 to 4 feet in length. It is found all around our coasts, preferring rougher ground than the Tope. It feeds mainly on crustaceans and molluscs, for the crushing of which its teeth are well adapted. It is viviparous and migrates inshore around the same time as the Tope to spawn and leaves again about the same time. It is not specially fished for by anglers and is caught in the course of general bottom fishing.

THE MONKFISH (*Squatina squatina (Linn)*)

A species which appears to have been unable to decide whether it should be a shark or a skate. The body is depressed or flattened from above downwards, as in the rays and skates, but the very enlarged pectorals are separate from the flat broad head and from the enlarged pelvics. The gill slits are on the sides between the pelvics and the pectorals, the two dorsal fins are on the tail column, and there is no anal fin. The mouth is almost at the tip of the snout, the sharp teeth conical, and far apart, the nostrils (above and near the mouth) are covered by frilled nasal flaps. The large crescentic spiracles are situated some distance behind the eyes on top of the head. The colour is usually a dirty brownish grey with darker and lighter variegated blotches and lines. The fish is not unlike a big bass fiddle in appearance.

This species has been recorded to over 60 lb. in weight and averages 20 to 40 lb. It is found all around our coasts on sandy or muddy bottoms in shallow water (often exceedingly shallow water), preying on small fishes, particularly on flatfishes, but crustaceans and molluscs are also eaten. The monkfish is viviparous, moving inshore in summer to spawn and remaining in the shallows until late autumn or early winter before migrating into deep water. It is taken on fish baits, leger or paternoster fished from a boat but is also caught from the shore.

	British Record	Irish Record	Specimen Weight
Monkfish	66 lb.	73 lb.	50 lb.

THE RAYS AND SKATES

A very distinctive group of fishes which are flattened from above downwards and which lie on their bellies and not on their sides as the flatfishes do. Their pectoral fins are enormously developed and continuous with the head and body, forming the typical heart or diamond shape disc. The tail is long, ox-like and armed with rows of strong spines. The two dorsal fins are small, placed near the extremity of the tail and there is no anal fin. The mouth and gills are on the underside, whilst the eyes and spiracles are on the upper.

In adult males (not in the female) there is always a rectangular patch of closely packed spines near the tip of each wing on the upper side and the males also possess claspers attached to the pelvic fins, which are set at the junction of the tail and the disc. The upper surface of the disc is free from large spines (apart from the patch present in all males), except in The Thornback and Starry Rays. The young in most species have a conspicuous "eye spot" on the upper surface of each wing which disappears or becomes less conspicuous with age except in the Cuckoo Ray.

The skates are a *long snouted* species, i.e. a line drawn from the tip of the snout to the wing tip does not cross or intersect the leading edge of the wing, while in the rays, which are *short snouted*, the same line is intersected by the leading edge of the wing. We will deal with the long snouted species or skates first.

THE COMMON SKATE (*Raja batis (Linn)*)

Underside usually grey with dark stippling or streaks and liberally covered with small black pores. On specimens taken from muddy bottoms the anterior portion of the underside may be very black

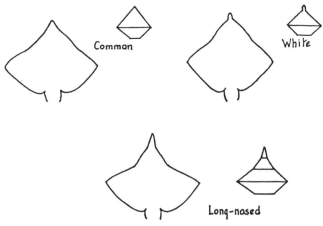

Discs of three skates and their fundamental geometric shapes

but the central region is always grey. The length from the tip of the snout to the mouth does not exceed one-fifth of the total length of the fish. The colour on the upper side is usually greyish or brownish but may be very colourful and variegated.

The Common Skate is found all around our coasts on clean and mixed bottoms, both in deep water and in shallow water inshore. It attains a weight exceeding 400 lb., and big fish of 100 lb. or over are plentiful on the south and west coasts of Ireland. Big fish feed mainly on a great variety of other fishes whilst the smaller fish also eat crustaceans and marine worms. The spawning is prolonged, the female producing large eggs encased in horny capsules. Usually taken on heavy leger or paternoster tackle, bottom fishing from a boat, using fish baits.

Note.—The so-called Flapper Skate is not a different species but only a colour variety of the Common Skate. It is very white on the undersurface but always possesses the black pores, which are sufficient to distinguish it from the White Skate for which it is often mistaken.

	British Record	Irish Record
Common Skate	226 lb. 8 oz.	221 lb.

THE WHITE SKATE (*Raja alba*)

Underside white, *without dark spots* but with a greyish border to the pectoral fins (young fish have a black border). The snout is prominent and parallel sided for an appreciable part of its length, giving the fish a bottle-nosed appearance. Upper surface grey or bluish grey but young fish tend towards reddish brown.

The White Skate grows to over 500 lb. in weight, is of more southerly distribution than the Common Skate and prefers much deeper water. Consequently it is not as plentiful, but a number of specimens have been taken at Westport and Galway on the west coast of Ireland. Its feeding and spawning habits are similar to the Common Skate. Not specially angled for, it is taken in the course of general bottom fishing.

	British Record	Irish Record	Specimen Weight
White Skate	76 lb.	165 lb.	120 lb.

THE LONG NOSED SKATE (*Raja oxyrhynchus (Linn)*)

This skate has a very distinctive long nose and the disc between the wing tip and the tip of the snout has a very definite inward curve which emphasises the "long nose". The length from the tip of the snout to the mouth is a quarter or more of the total length of the fish. The underside is covered with dark dots and/or streaks, as in the Common Skate, and the ground tint is grey, either all over or at least in the central body region. The upper surface is usually greyish or dark brownish with pale spots and dark stipplings. Probably the rarest of our big skates, it attains a length of 5 feet or over and prefers deeper water than the others.

	British Record	Irish Record	Specimen Weight
Long Nosed Skate	None	None	80 lb.

THE SHAGREEN RAY (*Raja fullonica*)

This species belongs to the long nosed group but has a rather short and triangular snout and the underside is white. A more southerly species and a summer visitor to our coasts, it is a deepwater fish not often taken by anglers.

THE THORNBACK RAY (*Raja clavata (Linn)*)

Apart from the rare Starry Ray this is the only ray which possesses large thornlike spines scattered over the general surface of the disc (the males, as in all the rays and skates, have the usual patch of spines on the wings), and in addition it has small spines around the eyes, along the middle of the back, and there are large spines in rows on the tail. The teeth in the females are large and flat but the males have pointed teeth. The disc is more angular than in the other rays. The dorsal surface is usually greyish or brownish, marbled with lighter coloured spots with darker rings which throw them into relief. The underside is white.

It ranges from the Mediterranean to Norway and is by far the commonest ray in our waters. It is found on clean bottoms in moderate or shallow water feeding on crustaceans, molluscs and small fishes. It has been recorded to 40 lb. in weight in our waters, but the average is 5 to 12 lb. It migrates inshore in summer, seeking deeper water in winter. It will take small fish baits, peeler crab, prawns or ragworm legered from boat, pier or beach.

	British Record	Irish Record	Specimen Weight
Thornback Ray	38 lb.	37 lb.	20 lb.

BLONDE RAY (*Raja brachyura (Lafont)*)

A larger species than the Thornback, the upper surface is very heavily spotted with small dark spots which extend right out to the margin of the wings. There are an equal number of symmetrically arranged light spots on each wing and the upper surface of the wings are smooth and free from spines (except for the usual patch in the males). The underside is white and bears a border of small spines on the rear margin of the disc. It is found all around our coast but appears to be scarce in the North Sea. It frequents moderate depths and is not fished for specially by anglers who sometimes catch it when fishing for other bottom species.

	British Record	Irish Record	Specimen Weight
Blonde Ray	37 lb. 12 oz.	36 lb. 8 oz.	25 lb.

THE HOMELYN RAY (*Raja montagui (Fowler)*)

Very similar to and easily confused with the Blonde Ray. There are, however, fewer though larger spots on the upper surface, which do not extend to the wing margins. There is no border of spines on the white underside and the upper surface is a darker brown than the Blonde Ray. Its distribution and habits are similar to the Blonde Ray and both species are often taken on the same ground.

A number of other rays are taken by anglers in the course of general boat fishing and a very brief description of the principal distinguishing marks may be useful. The CUCKOO RAY (*Raja naevus (Muller and Henle)*) is a yellowish brown fish with a very distinctive single black spot on each wing, with yellow markings overlying the black in the rings. The SANDY RAY (*Raja circularis (Couch)*) is sandy brown in colour with eight or more cream or yellow spots circled by a dark border symmetrically arranged on the disc and pelvic fins. The PAINTED RAY (*Raja microcellata*) is light grey in colour with pale broken bands forming rows more or less parallel with the margin of the wings and it also has pale spots. The UNDULATE RAY (*Raja undulata*) has yellowish brown or orange leopard-like markings with dark undulating stripes bordered by pale spots and with larger spots scattered over the disc.

THE STING RAY (*Dasyatis pastinaca*)

This ray is easily recognised by its long whiplike tail armed with a sharp jagged spine or spear near the base of the tail. It has a thicker and more elevated body than the other rays and the anterior margins of the wings are straighter. There are no dorsal fins, the upper surface is brownish in colour and free from spines.

A warm water species, it is a summer migrant to our south coasts, arriving in late summer and early autumn. It is viviparous, giving birth to its young alive, and frequents very shallow water and is often taken from the shore. It feeds mainly on crustaceans and molluscs and has been recorded to a weight in excess of 60 lb. in our waters.

	British Record	Irish Record	Specimen Weight
Sting Ray	61 lb. 8 oz.	51 lb.	30 lb.

THE ANGLER FISH (*Lophius piscatorius*)

A truly remarkable looking fish with a huge broad head tapering to a short rounded tail column.   The head is broader than it is long, with a wide cavernous mouth lined with two rows of sharp, movable and backward facing teeth.   The first dorsal fin has evolved into a "rod, line and bait" and is an elongated ray with a fleshy off-white coloured flap of skin which it can dangle in front of its mouth to simulate a small fish.

It is found from the Mediterranean to the north of Scotland, usually on clean bottoms, but because of its habit of half burying itself in the sea-bed waiting for a victim to be lured within reach of its jaws it is not a fish taken commonly by anglers.   It has been recorded to over 60 lb. from our waters.

The Angler Fish is included here for the purpose of convenience. It is in fact a bony fish of a highly specialised group of which there is no other representative in shallow water.

	British Record	Irish Record	Specimen Weight
Angler Fish	82 lb. 12 oz.	71 lb. 8 oz.	40 lb.

CHAPTER 3

NATURAL BAITS

WE HAVE SEEN THAT IN THE SEA THERE IS A GREAT VARIETY of fish and to feed these fish there is an even greater variety of food. The chief foods of sea fishes are:—

(1) PLANKTON ORGANISMS.

(2) CRUSTACEANS—crabs, prawns, shrimps, etc.

(3) MOLLUSCS—bivalves (razorfish, etc.), gastropods (whelks, etc.) and squids.

(4) ECHINODERMS—sand stars, brittle stars, etc.

(5) WORMS—ragworms, lugworms, etc.

(6) SMALL FISH—sprats, sandeels, mackerel, herring fry, etc.

(7) LARGER FISH—pilchard, herring, mackerel, etc.

Though some fish are specially adapted to feeding on a particular kind of food, e.g. the herring on plankton, most species are not so restricted and some, indeed, are very catholic in their tastes. This, of course, is a great advantage to the angler, as many of the fish food organisms are seldom, if ever, available to him. It is obvious that the natural baits can be divided into those which can be collected by the angler himself from the shore and those which must be obtained from the sea.

On the physical nature of the shore and its zonation depends the type of bait which it provides. For example, on the middle shore on beaches of firm muddy sand you would expect to find lugworm and cockles, whilst razorfish are a possibility on a similar bottom on the lower shore. On beaches of loose coarse gravelly sand you might find sandeels, but the lower shore is the place to seek them out. Not only must you get to know the type of bait found on a particular kind of shore but you must know where and when to find it. Whilst a great variety of shore creatures can be used for bait some are far better all-round baits than others. Then again, certain baits are very attractive to some kinds of fish but are not so good for other species.

The Lugworm

This worm is probably the commonest and most easily obtained marine worm used by anglers. It consists of a rather soft sausage-shaped head and a much thinner and firmer tail portion usually filled with sand. In colour it can be reddish, brownish, greenish or black, depending on the type of sand in which it is found. It grows to 12 inches or so in length, but an average sized lug or lugworm is about 6 to 8 inches long. It is found in sandy bays, beaches and tidal flats where there is some shelter from wave action. The lugworm does not like exposed beaches and is found between tide marks on the middle shore on bottoms of wet muddy sand.

Lugworms can be very numerous in places, their familiar castings littering and speckling the sand, whilst in others they may be sparse and quite far apart. They make U-shaped burrows in the sand, the extremities of which are represented by the typical and well known spiral castings at one end and by a small hole or depression at the other. The lugworm is usually found midway between the two extremities, i.e. at the bend of the U, and always faces the hole. It is important to remember this when digging lugworm and to be able to line up the right casting with the appropriate hole, otherwise you will have little success. The depth at which they lie varies, being usually about a foot below the surface, but they may be shallower or deeper.

There is an art in digging lugworm and a good strong spade or fork is essential. The first spadeful should be dug from the hole end and a little to one side to avoid cutting the lugworm in two, while the second spadeful should come from the cast end. This clears the top sand and the third spadeful angled in from the side, midway between hole and casting, should bring up the lugworm. Where lugworm are plentiful and the castings close together many anglers prefer to excavate an area of sand instead of digging each worm out separately. This method will produce worms and is excellent exercise but you will miss far more worms than you get.

A good bait for bass, flounders, dabs and plaice, lug will also take cod, codling, wrasse, sea bream, whiting and gurnards. Small lugworms are best for flatfish, the larger ones for bass, and they should be threaded up the hook, and the barb left exposed. As lug is a soft bait, beginners may have some difficulty putting it on a hook; but if the head of the worm is tapped on a hard object it will stiffen up and can then be easily threaded on the hook. A nice juicy bait, it is easily scented by fish and is excellent for night fishing.

Lugworm go off quickly if kept in metal containers, especially in warm weather, and the smell of liquid lugworm is not easily forgotten. The best method that I have found of keeping them is to lay them on newspapers or a damp sack. The worms should be cleaned and laid out in a row on the newspaper, making sure that they do not touch each other. Fold the paper over once and then spread out another row and fold once more. Continue doing this until all your bait has been accommodated and then store in a cool place or in the shade. Lugworm treated in this manner will keep for several days and save you a daily trip to the bait grounds.

The Ragworms

These make excellent baits for many species of fish but are not as abundant as lugworm and are of more localised distribution. The Common Bronze Ragworm is a wriggly active worm averaging 3 to 7 inches in length and resembles a centipede with its rows of closely spaced legs running down each side. It possesses a pair of hard pincer-like nippers in its mouth which in the larger specimens can inflict quite a painful bite on the fingers if incautiously handled. There is no need to be afraid of them, however, just grip them firmly behind the head as one would grasp a nettle and thread them on the hook. Long worms should be threaded up on to the line so that little is left dangling free at the end, as they have a habit of breaking easily. Secondly, as in the case of the lugworm, very little of the bait should be left trailing behind the hook, as flatfish tend to take the free end and escape being hooked.

Ragworm is an excellent all-round bait, either for bottom fishing, float fishing, driftlining or spinning. Bass, pollack, gurnard, wrasse, flatfish and small rays and skates take it readily. It is found only a short distance below the surface at low tide in harbours on bottoms of mixed stones and mud, under beds of mussels and on the surface under flat stones or boulders.

The King Ragworm, as its name implies, is a huge ragworm,

attaining a length of up to 18 inches. It is more localised in distribution than the other ragworms and is found on the lower shore on the spring tides, principally under boulders or large stones or in gravelly mud. A big worm, it is usually cut into pieces for shore fishing but can be used whole on a large hook when fishing for big fish from a boat and it is an excellent bait for pollack.

The commonest and most plentiful member of the family found on the shore is the Small Red Ragworm. A very thin, soft and fragile worm found in muddy harbours, creeks, lagoons, estuaries and, indeed, in most places where there is thick mud fairly high up on the middle shore. Their presence is marked by hundreds of tiny pinholes in the mud and they are usually present in great numbers. Sometimes there is no need to dig for them. A few handfuls of mud and you will probably have all that you require. They are quite a good bait for small bass and flatfish, while in places they are a useful bait for mullet. They should be baited on a very fine wire hook and the usual method is to thread one worm up the hook and on to the line and one or more worms are then hooked through the head and left dangle free.

The White Ragworm or Herringbone is a very attractive and active white worm, usually 3 to 6 inches in length, found on beaches of firm muddy sand, usually in the same locality as lugworm. It does not, however, burrow as deep as the lugworm and is seldom found more than 6 inches below the surface. A thin brittle worm, it should be mounted on a fine wire hook, and it is an excellent bait for small bass, flounders, plaice, dabs, sole, gurnard, sea trout and a variety of fishes, including mackerel.

Ragworm can be kept for quite a long time if handled carefully. They should be placed in a box, preferably made of wood, and never in any sort of metal container. Spread them out on a layer of damp seaweed, giving them a fair amount of room, then cover with a layer of damp weed. On top of this you can place another layer of ragworm, followed by another layer of weed, and so on. They must be kept cool and out of the sun, otherwise they will perish. They should be examined daily, the seaweed renewed or cleaned and the dead or weakly worms removed, otherwise they will very quickly contaminate and ruin the healthy ones. They will stay alive and active for long periods if treated in this manner, and I have kept them for as long as eleven days in warm weather. The important points to remember are: give them plenty of room, keep them cool, pick out the dead ones daily and renew the damp weed.

The Crab

There is no greater pest when bottom fishing in shallow water than the ordinary common shore crab. Where crabs are plentiful they will tear and strip the bait off your hooks as fast as you can replenish them. However, where there are crabs there are fish and these selfsame crabs are probably the finest baits of all for bass, and excellent baits for flounders, codling, cod, gurnards, wrasse, rays and small skate.

Encased in a hard inflexible shell, the crab cannot grow, so at regular intervals it casts off its suit of armour, under which a new shell has been developing as a sort of tough skin. After the crab has moulted it puts on a fast spurt of growth before the new shell hardens up and once again restricts its expansion. The crab which is nearly ready to moult is known to anglers as a "Pill" or "Peeler" crab because the old shell can be stripped off, revealing the new soft skin beneath and in this condition it is most attractive to fish. The newly moulted crab is known as a Soft Crab and is also an excellent bait, though not as attractive to fish as a "Peeler". Gradually as the crab grows its skin first becomes leathery (leatherbacks), then crackly hard, until eventually the shell is as hard as ever. Although fish will take leatherbacks or crinkly backs and even small hard backs it is the Peeler or Soft Back that are the most useful baits.

The crab which is about ready to shed its shell hides itself under dense weed or stones, in piers or tin cans, in fact under anything that will give it shelter for in its moulted condition it is defenceless and fair prey for any fish and even for other crabs. It will be usually found well down on the shore near low watermark hiding under weeds, flat stones, in pools at the base of rocks and in clefts and crevices in the rocks. It will be found in sheltered spots where there is little wave action in sandy bays near rocks and weeds, and in estuaries, creeks or slobs. It prefers soft sand or mud in which it can partly burrow to conceal itself. Where crabs are plentiful but Peeler or Soft Crabs are hard to come by it is possible to trap them. Any object which will provide shelter, i.e. a section of old gutter pipe placed upside down near low water mark will attract its quota of crabs.   So also will a covered box (an old fish box is ideal) with the centre plank knocked out, weighed with stones to keep it on the bottom.

The Soft Crab is easily recognised for what it is but the Peeler often presents difficulty to the uninitiated.   However, if you find two crabs together, one shielding the other or holding it in one claw you may be sure that the one so held is a Peeler.   Peelers, too, are duller in colour than the ordinary crab and tend to cower away, drawing their legs up under them, in contrast to the hardback, which is a very pugnacious individual and full of fight.   The softback or leatherback which is hardening up often puts up a bluff of ferocity, but the pressure of your finger on its·back will proclaim it for what it is.   If in doubt as to whether a crab is a Peeler or not, grasp it firmly with thumb and forefinger across its back behind the claws so that it is unable to reach you with its nippers.   Thus held the crab is helpless and can do you no harm.   Break off one of its legs near a joint and if the shell comes away with pieces of flesh and tendons adhering to it then it is a hardback.   However, if only the shell breaks and comes away revealing the limb clothed in its new skin then it is a peeler.

Small crabs should be used whole, but big specimens can be divided up to make two or more baits depending on how short of bait you are.   Most anglers strip off both legs and claws before mounting the crab on the hook but when bass fishing I prefer to use the whole crab, removing only the claws because it looks more natural. The claws and legs should not be thrown away in case you run short of bait, and furthermore they make excellent baits for flatfish. The hook size will depend on the size of the bait and the species of fish that you are seeking.   The hook should be inserted through one of the leg sockets and brought out the back.   The leg socket is the toughest part of the crab and ensures that the hook will not tear out when casting.   A useful dodge is to wind some thin elastic crimping thread around the hook shank and then back and forth across the crab.   The elastic thread eliminates knots, as it will bind on itself and secures your bait firmly on the hook.   It also ensures that if a fish wants the bait it must also take the hook, and in fact more than one fish can often be landed on the same bait for it may be used again if not too badly damaged.

Crabs can be easily kept alive for days in a perforated wooden box which possesses a lid. A lid is essential for crabs can escape from an open container simply by climbing on top of one another's backs. The bottom of the box should be lined with damp seaweed and the crabs covered by another layer of damp seaweed. Renew the seaweed daily or else give the crabs a "drink" by washing out the seaweed in salt water and then replacing it. They should be kept in a cool place out of the sun. Remember that Peelers will moult and softbacks harden up in a short time, so don't try to keep your crabs indefinitely. Use them.

On low water spring tides, when the lower shore is fully exposed you can often find moulting or soft specimens of the Edible Crab. These also make excellent baits, and owing to their size can be cut in several portions. Remember, too, that the soft insides or "the works" of the hardback edible or eating crab makes a very useful bait for wrasse.

Prawns

A very useful bait for many species of sea fish but one not used as frequently by anglers as it should be. The two most common species are the Common Prawn (*Leander Serratus*) whose body length is usually 1 to 4 inches, and the smaller Dwarf Prawn (*Leander Squilla*) which averages about 2 inches in length.

Prawns are found in rock pools, especially near low water mark, around weedy and kelpy rocks at low tide, and along the faces of quays and piers. They are most easily gathered by working a stout, wide-mouthed hand net quickly and thoroughly through the submerged weeds attached to rocks, quay walls and piers. Where they are plentiful a baited dropnet of fine-mesh netting or cloth lowered into the water and left for a while before being carefully raised again will account for its quota of prawns as well as a host of avaricious hardback crabs. The selfsame crabs or pieces of smelly fish will make suitable baits for the net.

Prawns are difficult to keep alive for any length of time and should be used as soon as possible after capture. If placed in metal containers filled with sea water they seem to expire quickly, especially if a goodly number has been caught. If placed in wet weed inside a cloth or canvas bag they will last for several hours at least, and if not for immediate use the bag (duly closed and tied) should be submerged in salt water. They should, however, be used as soon as possible, for though fresh dead prawns are quite good as bait, live prawns are infinitely better.

They are an excellent bait for bass, pollack, whiting, gurnard, flounders and wrasse and can be used for float fishing, driftlining, light spinning and paternostering from boat or pier. A small fine wire hook, size 1 or 2, is best and the hook should be inserted through the second segment of the tail with the point exposed and facing upwards. A large prawn is best for bass and pollack, smaller ones for flatfish and if necessary two small prawns can be mounted back to back on the same hook.

The smaller Shrimp of sandy beaches, so familiar to bathers paddling through the shallows, is quite a good bait for flounders, gurnards and whiting. Though well camouflaged it reveals its presence by the little spurt of sand it makes when disturbed and can easily be gathered with a hand net. Sand shrimps can be kept in the same way as prawns.

Mussels

Decent sized mussels are one of the most useful all-round baits available on the shore and where plentiful are easily gathered. They need something firm to which they can attach themselves, i.e. quay walls, piers, rocks, bridges, piles, or firm stable gravel along beaches, in estuaries or harbours and can be gathered at low tide. The small seed mussel found high up on the shore is too small to use as bait but broken up or pounded into mush it makes excellent ground bait. The bigger mussels are found on the lower shore and can be gathered easily by hand. Be careful when pulling them off for the edges of their shells are quite sharp and can leave a series of razor blade like cuts on the fingers of the careless or unwary.

The mussel is best opened by holding it in the palm of the hand (pointed end upwards and the outwardly curved portion facing inwards) and inserting a sharply pointed knife between the two valves about midway along its length. The knife should be angled upwards and worked towards the lower edge of the mussel to cut the tough muscle which keeps the shell closed. Remove the knife, reverse it and then work it up to the other end and the shell should now open revealing the mussel lying intact on the lower half. It is then an easy matter to scrape under it and cut the lower muscle.

Mussels are an excellent bait for codling and cod and are taken by whiting, gurnard, plaice, dabs, wrasse, pouting, haddock, flounders and bass. A soft bait, which is easily torn, it should be mounted on fine wire hooks which do not have "slices" cut in the shanks. The hook point is best inserted through the "foot" and out the back of the mussel, which is then twisted around and the hook put through once again.

Mussels are quite easily kept for a considerable length of time if they are placed in a sack and suspended in the water. They will also keep for quite a long time in a sack or bucket in which they are covered with damp weed but they must be kept cool and out of the sun.

Cockles

This is another bait that is easy to collect. It is found on the lower middle shore on flat beaches of firm muddy sand. When cockles are present they are usually plentiful, and as they only burrow an inch or so under the surface they can be easily routed out by inserting your finger into the two small holes made by the siphons and feeling about for them. To open, place two cockles back to back, interlocking their hinges, and twist. At least one cockle will then open. They are good baits for dabs, plaice, wrasse and whiting and two or three should be used at a time on small hooks.

Razorfish

This excellent bait inhabits the lower shore and is only available to the bait gatherer on the spring tides. Consequently, not alone are there only a few days each fortnight that it is within reach but there is also very little "stand" in the tide on springs, so one cannot dawdle when gathering razorfish. However, where it is plentiful fair numbers can quickly be gathered by using a thin flat metal spear about 3 to 4 feet long and $\frac{1}{4}$ inch wide. The point should be beaten out into a triangular shape about $\frac{1}{2}$ inch wide at the base. The razorfish burrows are readily recognised by their "keyhole" shape about $\frac{1}{2}$ inch in length. Insert the point of the spear in the hole and ease it gently into the burrow. It should pass through the long shell of the razorfish, and when the sand at the bottom of the burrow is felt twist the spear through 90 degrees and draw it out of the hole. The twisting of the spear should engage the flanges of

the spear head in the shell of the razorfish which can then be withdrawn without difficulty. Another method is to sprinkle salt in
the holes, which will cause the razorfish to rise to the surface where
it can be secured by sticking a fork or spade quickly into the sand
to lever it out. It is an excellent bait for bass, dabs, plaice, flounders,
gurnards and small skate and rays. It can be used whole or cut into
pieces to make several baits.

Sandeels

Sandeels are an excellent though elusive bait, somewhat localised
in distribution. There are two common species, the Greater
Sandeel, which grows to over 1 foot in length, and the Lesser Sandeel,
which attains a length of 5 to 7 inches. The former has a distinctive
wedge-shaped lower jaw which protrudes considerably beyond the
upper and its long dorsal fin commences some distance behind the
pectoral fins. In the Lesser Sandeel the origin of the dorsal is
approximately over the tip of the pectorals, whilst the lower jaw
protrudes very much less.

Sandeels are most easily gathered when they bury themselves in
the loose coarse gravelly sand found on certain beaches and estuaries
down near and below low water mark. A long pronged fork, or
better still an old blunt reaping hook or sickle with several V-shaped
notches cut along its length will simplify the work. NEVER
burrow with your hands for them as the poisonous Lesser Weever
also buries itself in the same kind of sand and it is foolish to run the
risk of injury.

The sickle or fork is swept through the loose sand and the buried
sandeels are thrown out. An agile assistant is a great help as the
sandeels are like quicksilver and one must pounce and secure them
immediately. If the notched reaping hook is used the sandeel
usually slides into the V-shaped notches on the upward stroke and
with practice can be pinned there by your free hand as it emerges
from the sand.

Live sandeels are a wonderful bait for bass, pollack and sea trout
float fished, driftlined, bottom fished or mounted for spinning.
Large sandeels are really first class for turbot in deep water and
most fish, even tope, will take them. Live sandeels should be
hooked in the back a little behind the pectorals or else the hook
should be inserted through the mouth, out the gills and lightly put

through the skin of the belly just behind the pectorals. The fish must be handled carefully and as little damage as possible done to it so that it may swim freely and actively on the hook. For that reason small fine wire hooks only should be used, the size depending on the size of the eel being used as bait. Fished dead they are a good bait but not comparable to the live bait.

A very difficult bait to keep alive, they should be put in a "courge", which is a boat-shaped perforated wooden or plastic box which can be kept submerged in the water or towed behind a boat. In this they will stay alive and should only be removed from it as they are needed for hook bait. If placed in tin cans, buckets or metal containers of any kind they die in a very short time.

Clams, Limpets, Piddocks

Various clams burrow in sand or muddy sand between tide marks, their rather large round holes denoting their presence. They are easily dug out and with their shells removed make tough durable baits. They may be used whole or cut into pieces. They are quite good bait for deep water ground feeding fish and for beachfishing for bass.

The limpet, so common on our rocky shores, is not a particularly good bait but will take wrasse. Shaped rather like a Chinese coolie's hat, they adhere very strongly to the rock but can be dislodged with a single sharp blow with a hard instrument or stone.

Piddocks are rock boring shellfish, growing to about 3 inches in length and are found in stiff clay or soft rocks, such as chalk, shale or sandstone. Their small neat holes, about $\frac{1}{2}$ inch in diameter, often pepper the rock strata and they can be dug out with a hammer and chisel. They are quite a good bait for bass and other species.

Other Baits gathered on the Shore

There are a number of other useful baits which can be picked up from time to time when one is searching for crabs under weeds and stones. The most common is the Butterfish, a most distinctive little fish 4 to 6 inches long, covered with 10 to 13 white ringed dark spots running along the back and overlapping the long dorsal fin. This is a useful bait for pollack, as is also the small freshwater eel of 4 to 8 inches in length which is found in similar places.

Baby flatfish, i.e. flounders, turbot or plaice, found in shallow pools and channels left on the beaches by the receding tide, are also a first class bait for bass.   Larger specimens, about 4 to 8 inches in length, are very good conger baits.

A great variety of shore organisms are found from time to time in fishes' stomachs.   If you make a practice of examining each fish that you catch you may see over a period a feeding pattern for a particular place, and this will help you choose the correct bait for that place.   Although it is a lot less bother to purchase bait from a tackle dealer and it may be very convenient to do so at times, it is worth remembering that the fresher the bait the better the results normally and the bait you gather yourself you can be sure is fresh. Furthermore, the angler who gathers his own bait learns more about the ground over which he is fishing and this is of great importance to the shore angler.

Fish Baits

Whole fish or pieces of fish are the most commonly used baits in boat fishing and make the best baits for some species, such as conger and tope, which can be caught from the shore.   A variety of species may be used for bait but the oily fishes, e.g. mackerel, herring and pilchard, are by far the best.

Whole fish are used when fishing for shark, tope and big skate and long lashes or small pieces cut from the sides of the fish for other species.   The bait should be as fresh as possible and a *very sharp* knife should be used to prepare the baits.   Fish will take chunks or even cutlets cut from the side of bait fishes but it is far better to make your bait look as like a small fish as possible.   Hence the necessity of a sharp knife, so that your bait is neat and not ragged in appearance.

Cut the mackerel, herring or pilchard just behind the pectoral fin and along the backbone to the tail.   This will give a long lash which is excellent for large skate, tope, cod, ling and other large species.   This lash can be cut again along the centre giving two long baits or, if a smaller bait is required, a cut can be taken from the tail portion about a quarter of the length of the fish from the tail.   If used on a long flowing trace in a bit of tide these baits will fish with a very nice action if the hook is inserted in the narrow end.   The long lashes, if fished on the bottom, are best mounted from the narrow end, the hook put through the bait twice and the narrow end run up the line for a short distance and secured there by a length of elastic crimping thread. A long thin lash cut from the silvery underbelly of the mackerel is excellent either driftlined or paternoster fished for big pollack.

The heads are first class bait for conger, while the front half of the fish, including the head, is a good skate bait and the second half, i.e. the tail portion is good for tope. Big turbot like a good chunky bait and the thick portion of the side of a mackerel, i.e. the first half of a long lask, is very suitable. So also is a long strip cut to represent a sandeel. For smaller species, like whiting, pouting, gurnard, red sea bream, etc., thin strips about $\frac{1}{2}$ to $\frac{3}{4}$ inch wide should be used. The strips are best cut at a slight diagonal slant from the back to the belly. The bones apart, all of these oily fishes can be used as bait, for even the guts will catch fish. Fish baits will last longer on the hook and become less messed up if the point of the hook is always brought out through the skin. If the hook is brought out on the fleshy side the bait becomes ragged in a short while. The hook size used will depend on the size of the bait and of the species for which you are fishing.

Fish baits are also excellent when used in shore fishing. They will take tope, conger, bass, small skate, rays, gurnard and even flounders and dabs. A lash of mackerel is a very good bait for bass, especially big bass. Although the use of fresh bait is always advocated, it is surprising how at times bass will take a really "high" fish bait.

Small bait fishes, i.e. herring fry and sparts, are good baits for bass, pollack, coalfish, cod, sea trout, whiting, turbot, brill, gurnard and conger. They can be fished on the bottom, driftlined, trolled or mounted for spinning. Most small fish make good hook baits either fished dead or as live baits. Fish like conger or tope will take medium sized pouting, wrasse or sea bream, whilst a whole whiting is a recognised bait for tope. Pollack flesh is not a good fish bait but a whole large pollack is an excellent bait for big sharks.

Squid is another very useful bait. The flesh is firm and it is a tough, long-lasting bait. It keeps quite well in the deep freeze and, like frozen mackerel, herring or pilchard, it is very useful as an "iron ration" when fresh bait is scarce. On the whole I do not care for frozen baits, always preferring to fish with fresh bait. However, frozen bait is better than no bait at all and if anglers went to the trouble of providing themselves with an iron ration of frozen bait they would save themselves a lot of frustration and lost time when fishing. Whole small squid or pieces of a large one are good for cod, conger and tope whilst smaller pieces will take bass, haddock, pollack and many other species. Octopus is not an easily obtained bait and, unfortunately, a very soft one to use. The tentacles will hold firmly on the hook but the soft body is easily torn off the hook by fish. It is an excellent bait and one which always produced bites when I have used it.

Hermit Crabs and Whelks

Hermit crabs and whelks I have left until last, for though they can be found on the shore they are more usually obtained from commercial fishermen. The Hermit Crab is unusual in that it has no hard shell of its own. It has a very soft body and it seeks shelter in empty whelk shells, leaving the shell only to exchange it for a larger one as it grows in size. It is a very good bait eagerly taken by bass, cod, codling, pollack, whiting, haddock, gurnard, wrasse and flatfish. A species of ragworm is often found sharing the same home as the Hermit Crab and this, too, is an excellent bait for many species. The whelk, although a very tough and durable bait, is not a particularly good one. It is a better bait for commercial longlining than for angling, where it is left for a considerable length of time before the lines are taken in again.

I have tried preserved baits without much success. The fault may be mine for I have no great faith in them. I have been successful with salted mussel but have found generally that baits preserved in any other way are far from satisfactory.

CHAPTER 4

TACKLE

SEA ANGLING IS A SPORT AND THE USE OF PROPER EQUIPMENT or tackle is an essential part of that sport. There is more to angling than just the catching of fish, otherwise we would use far more efficient means than rod, reel and line to capture them. The use of the correct tackle enables us to present our bait in the most suitable way to the fish, to hook it when it takes, to play and land it and to derive the greatest amount of sport or pleasure from so doing.

This last point, i.e. the question of sport or sporting fishing, is one that has given sea angling the reputation of being a heavy or crude form of fishing and one that was to a certain extent justified in the past. This was to a great extent due to the unsuitable materials and tackle available at the time but in the last twenty years enormous strides have been made in this respect and there is no reason now why sea angling should not be as sporting as any other form of angling. There are many species of fish in the sea that are of little sporting value though excellent for the table, but there are many others, such as bass, tope, mullet and pollack, that rank among the finest of game fish if taken on suitable tackle.

Suitable tackle is the real crux of the matter. The tackle should be balanced and designed for the type of fishing you wish to do. There is little point and no sport in fishing for dabs with tackle capable of landing a 200 lb. skate, or in fishing for shark with a mullet rod. These are extremes, I know, but walk down any pier or beach where there are numbers of anglers or go to a deep sea angling competition and you will be amazed at the amount of unsuitable and mismatched tackle that you will see. We have the materials and we have the "know-how". Why do we not put them to proper use? There are several reasons. The fault is partly the angler's and partly the manufacturer's and retailer's.

As in many other aspects of life tradition dies hard. Many

anglers who started fishing in the days of heavy tackle are reluctant to try new fangled ideas and equipment.   Those who are taking up the sport for the first time may through ignorance or bad advice purchase unsuitable gear.   Then again they may not have the choice of suitable tackle and in this respect the retailers and manufacturers of sea fishing tackle must shoulder a great deal of the blame.   I have often been attracted into a shop by an imposing display of rods and tackle.   The rods looked attractive, well furnished and finished but on closer examination I have often wondered just what type of fishing they could be used for.   Spinning rods that were more suitable for boat fishing, surf rods that would handle three-quarters of a pound of lead and that would require a shark at the end of the line to put a bend in them.

Many manufacturers produce excellent and sporting freshwater tackle but fail to understand or appreciate the requirements of sea angling and continue to produce tackle in excess of or equal in power to the heavy gear used when sea angling was young and the equipment of necessity heavy.   A number of firms are, however, at last designing and producing tackle specifically to suit the requirements of the sea angler and I feel sure that the rest will in time follow their lead.   Tackle shops, no matter how good they are, that have little knowledge of sea angling or experience in catering for the sea angler are also at fault in providing beginners with unsuitable tackle.   It is not that they are only concerned with making a sale but that they are in no position to advise on the correct tackle for the particular type of fishing the angler wishes to do.   For that reason it is best to deal with a firm that specialises in catering for the sea angler and, if possible, the beginner should seek the advice of some experienced angler before purchasing.

A fishing outfit is composed of a rod, reel, line and terminal tackle.   Each of the four items must match and balance each other and must be suited to the type of fish you wish to catch and the type of ground over which you will fish.   You will use one type of rod, reel and line for spinning, another for surf fishing and still another for boat fishing.   There is no single rod that will do for all types of sea angling as a rod will be only most efficient doing the job for which it was designed.   Many rods are fairly versatile and can be used for methods of fishing other than that for which they were designed but they can never be as satisfactory as rods specifically designed for those methods. There are combination rods on the market, some of which are quite good but others are terrible and a combination rod at best is only a compromise.

The reel should match the rod, balance it and be suitable for the type of fishing for which it will be used. The line should have the correct breaking strain and be made of suitable material. Thus for light spinning you would use a light flexible rod, freshwater type multiplier or fixed spool reel, 5 to 10 lb. breaking strain line and ¼ to ¾ oz. lures. A large surf fishing type multiplier or fixed spool reel would not match the rod as it would be too heavy and throw it out of balance, thus lessening its efficiency. The use of heavy line of 25 to 30 lb. breaking strain on the freshwater type reel would reduce its line capacity and because of the thickness of the line it would also seriously reduce the casting distance. The use of lures of a greater weight than the rod was designed to cast would reduce its efficiency and seriously overload and perhaps damage it.

This principle applies to all forms of sea angling whether it be bass fishing, conger fishing or shark fishing. Matched and balanced tackle is more pleasant to use, makes for more efficient angling and gives the angler the greatest amount of pleasure. Do not, however, get the idea that I am advocating light tackle just for the sake of it. Nothing could be further from the truth. The angler who uses tackle so light that a fish must be fought for an unduly long period before being landed may prove his ability to play and land a fish but does little to prove his sportsmanship. Your tackle should be light enough to allow the fish to show its true mettle but it should at the same time be strong enough to give you a reasonable chance of landing the fish in a reasonable length of time. It should be borne in mind at all times that angling is a sport pursued for the pleasure it gives and not just a means to filling the larder.

Not alone should your tackle be balanced and suitable for the fish you seek but it should also suit the type of ground over which you will fish. Anglers fishing for cod from the beaches at Dungeness can use very much lighter tackle than those who fish over the very rough ground on the Yorkshire coast. All these factors must be taken into consideration when purchasing tackle and the angler should first consider what species he intends fishing for and the type of shore or bottom on which he must fish. He may be limited by what is available to him in the locality in which he can fish but it is these factors which will decide the type of tackle with which he must equip himself.

Modern rods are usually made from split cane, fibre glass or carbon fibre. Each material has its advantages and disadvantages and we will discuss them briefly in turn.

Good split cane rods are excellent for shore fishing, spinning and boat fishing.   They are strong, light, and possess a very nice action. They are, however, expensive and unless the greatest care is taken in their maintenance their life is short.   Salt water is very destructive and should the rod varnish become chipped and allow salt water to penetrate between the sections of cane the results are disastrous. Sea rods, because of the element in which they are used and the conditions under which we often fish, must take a great deal of abuse and hardship.   It is impossible to avoid this and for that reason split cane has almost entirely been supplanted as a rod making material by glass fibre.

Most sea fishing rods today are manufactured from fibre glass, and what a wonderful material it is. Light, supple and possessing amazing power and strength, it has in many ways revolutionised sea angling.   It is durable, long lived, little affected by salt water and as sweet in action as split cane.   There are two kinds of fibre glass, i.e. hollow and solid.   The hollow glass is both light and strong and is suitable for most types of sea rods.   The solid glass is heavier and is mainly suitable for short rods.   In long lengths it is too heavy and sloppy in action.   It makes excellent spinning rods and short boat rods though these latter tend to be on the heavy side and are very powerful.   It is frequently used as the top joint in long surfcasting rods where a fast tip is required.   Glass rods, though not unbreakable, will stand up to a tremendous amount of hard work and require a minimum of maintenance.

Carbon fibre is a very new and exciting rod building material. Rods made from carbon fibre combine great strength with ultra lightness. This power and lightness are a particular boon to the surfcaster and there is no doubt that it is the rod building material of the future. At present, carbon fibre rods are very expensive but with developments and increased production, they should eventually come within the reach of most anglers.

Most anglers these days purchase fibre glass rods. They are reasonably cheap, the glass is almost universally good but in the cheaper rods the fittings may be poor and they should be examined carefully. Though incredibly strong, fibre glass is not unbreakable, as many anglers have found to their cost. One of the major causes of breakages is the ferrules. Ideally a rod should be all one piece but this creates difficulties in transport, especially ·in very long rods. For that reason rods are made in reasonably short lengths which can be fitted together by means of ferrules. When the rod is bent the ferrules, being made of metal, cannot yield with the strain and interrupt the even curve of the rod. In the cheaper rods these ferrules are just plain tubes into which the sections of the rod have been fitted and the edges tend to cut into the rod when it is under tension, weakening the material and eventually causing it to break. Hard edges in ferrules should be avoided and ferrules whose extremities are prolonged in a series of serrations which are secured to the rod by whipping, spread the strain from rod to ferrule more smoothly. This type of ferrule is usually tempered as well, allowing it to flex a little but in general the less ferrules on a rod the better. In boat rods the ferrule should always be where the butt and tip are joined and never well up the rod near the tip. Ferrules should always be a tight fit but not so tight that they are very difficult to take apart. They should always be kept clean and when through wear they become loose they should be immediately replaced.

Another weak point in many rods is the ferrule joining the rod butt to the tip. If this ferrule is too short or the rod butt material not strong enough to carry the strain where it is joined to the ferrule it often breaks when casting or under tension from a heavy fish. The rod butt or rod handle is usually made of plain wood, or covered in cork or sometimes with a rubber or plastic material. Wooden handles tend to become slippery when wet and rubber handles a trifle tacky. Cork is usually the most satisfactory material though a wrapping of strong twine or tape gives the most secure grip. Make sure that the handle is comfortable to grip for too thin or too thick a handle becomes very tiring and uncomfortable on the hands after a short time.

The reel fitting is often another cause of trouble. In cheap rods they may be made of very light metal which warps, twists or breaks under strain. In boat rods or surf rods they should be the screw-up type, i.e. with a locking nut and made of stainless steel or brass. The ordinary slide up ring fitting is quite good on spinning rods but the rings have a tendency to slip and are not really suitable for use with a multiplying type reel.

Rod rings are very important. They should be so spaced on the rod that when strain is applied the rod takes a nice even curve which distributes the strain gradually over the whole rod. They should be of some very hard smooth material, such as stainless steel, agate or agatine and as corrosion proof as possible. Line friction will wear grooves in rings made of softer material causing excessive line wear and in extreme cases may even cut the line. Rings lined with agatine, agate, porcelain of other similar smooth materials should be of the "buttressed" or protected type to guard against breakage from hard knocks. They should be examined frequently for cracks which could easily cause line breakage. Spinning rods used in conjunction with fixed spool reels should have large "stand off". butt rings to allow the line to spiral off the spool but rods used with a multiplier type reel are best fitted with smaller rings which will obviate line flap and flutter in casting. Top rings must take the greatest strain and should be of the nonfouling type. Many roller type top rings which can be fished "over or under", i.e. with the reel on top or underneath the butt, have a dangerous tendency to foul the line in fishing. In this respect tulip type rings are excellent. Finally rod butts should be fitted with rubber buttons so that they may be rested comfortably against the body when required.

Rods and their fittings should always be kept clean and the reel fittings and ferrules lubricated from time to time. It is a good practice to carry a cloth with you when fishing to rub your rod down as soon as you are finished. They should be washed in fresh water after use and never stored away in wet or damp rod bags. Ring whippings should be examined frequently for wear and if necessary rewhipped. The varnish should be examined for cracks or chipping and even fibre glass rods should bear a protective coat of varnish or cellulose as otherwise the material may suffer slightly from oxidation. When storing rods away for the winter always hang them vertically in their bags or suspend them from a hook by attaching a loop of line to the top ring. Never lay them flat or rest them on other objects lest they take a permanent set. Buy a good rod to start with. If cared for properly it will last you a lifetime.

A question which often crops up when rods are discussed is the test curve of a rod. Briefly the test curve of a rod is the amount of pull or strain that it exerts on a fish being played. It is determined by fixing the rod and reel at an angle of approximately 60 degrees (which is about the position in which a rod is normally held in playing a fish) and exerting a pull on the rod until the angle between the line and the rod tip disappears. Thus if it requires a pull of 2½ lb. to bend the rod to the position where the angle between the line and the tip disappears the rod is said to have a test curve of 2½ lb. The test curve of a rod is important in deciding its suitability for the type of fishing you intend to do: e.g., if you must fish under conditions in which 1½ lb. of lead is needed to keep your bait on the bottom a rod with a test cuve of 1 lb. would be entirely unsuitable. Similarly, you would require a rod with a bigger test curve for big skate and conger than you would for tope or blue shark. Where rods used for shore fishing or casting are concerned the test curve of the rod will decide the weight of the lure or sinker which can effectively be cast.

Reels used in sea fishing are of three main types: fixed spool reels, multiplier type reels and centre-pin or Nottingham type reels. The freshwater type fixed spool reels, as used for salmon fishing, are ideal for light spinning, light bottom fishing and float fishing in salt water. They are excellent for casting light weights or lures and with proper care will give long service. The big saltwater type fixed spool reel with a large line capacity is a good surf fishing reel. It is relatively trouble free in casting and is of particular value in night fishing as one is not liable to suffer from overruns, as is the case with a multiplier. On the whole the fixed spool reel is more suitable for casting light weights—up to 1 oz. in the freshwater type and about 3 oz. in the saltwater type. The multiplier type reel is definitely better than the fixed spool when heavier weights are used. The reel should have a reasonably large capacity, a spare spool for a different breaking strain line if possible, should be of rugged construction and made of materials that will resist corrosion by salt water. There are many excellent makes on the market and provided they are kept clean and washed in fresh water after use in the sea even the freshwater type reel will not suffer from use in salt water. Fixed spool reels are not suitable for bottom fishing from a boat in deep water. Their design is not suited to this type of fishing and it is only asking for trouble to subject them to the strain.

The multiplier is probably the most widely used reel in sea angling today. The freshwater type level wind multiplier is an excellent reel for spinning but requires rather heavier lures than the fixed spool reel to activate it efficiently. The larger multipliers used for surf fishing are first class but require more practice in their use than a fixed spool reel before full proficiency can be achieved. The even bigger boat reels are also excellent, having a large line capacity and a fast retrieve. Most multipliers used today are specifically designed for sea angling and are of rugged construction and made from corrosion resistant materials. Boat fishing reels which have excessively wide spools should be avoided due to their tendency to wobble when reeling in. The range of sizes is very wide and there is a multiplier suitable for every form of angling be it surf fishing or big game fishing.

The centre-pin or Nottingham type reel is mainly for pier or boat fishing. It is possible to make good casts with these reels but they are not as efficient in this respect as either the multiplier or the fixed spool reel. They are excellent boat reels for heavy bottom fish such as big conger or skate. They have a large capacity, recover a large amount of line with each revolution of the drum and possess great "winching" power, which is a big asset when dealing with heavy stubborn fish. They also have the advantage of keeping you in direct touch with the fish which can be played from the reel. This type of reel must, however, be strong and rugged and until very recently it was difficult to obtain a suitable centre-pin in a reasonable price range. Most of these reels had bad weaknesses, usually in the "saddle", which fits into the winch fitting on the rod butt or else in the saddle pillar attached to the back of the reel. These parts were often too weak to stand heavy work and would become twisted or distorted. Recently, however, some good and reasonably priced centre-pins have come on the market and should satisfy a long felt need among sea anglers. There is one other type of reel on the market, i.e. the side cast reel which is a cross between a centre-pin and a fixed spool reel.

It looks like an orthodox centre-pin reel with a shallow arbor and a dished rim similar to the rim of a fixed spool reel. It works like a centre-pin reel on the retrieve but to cast the drum is swiveled through 90 degrees, turning it in effect into a fixed spool reel. Very long casts can be made with this type of reel and it has all the advantages of the centre-pin in playing the fish. It is not, however suitable for heavy boat fishing as its line capacity in the heavier breaking strain is not sufficient and it is best used for shore-fishing.

The check on all sea reels should be strong and positive and the slipping clutch, star drag or brake which is fitted to all good boat reels should be smooth and capable of very fine adjustment. Avoid reels in which there is little scope for adjustment between free running and full brake otherwise you will suffer from breakages and lost fish. All handles on fishing reels should be large, giving a firm comfortable grip.

Reels if they are to give lasting satisfaction require careful maintenance. They should be washed in cold fresh water after *every* fishing trip and should be kept clean and oiled regularly but sparingly They should be taken apart at least once a year and given a thorough cleaning and lubrication. Should sand or grit enter between the spool and the reel or into the gears it should be taken apart immediately and cleaned, otherwise serious damage may result. Stop fishing and attend to this right away and do not wait until you get home to do it.

Lines used in sea angling nowadays are made of either nylon monofilament or twisted or braided synthetics such as Terylene or Dacron. Nylon is cheap and being rounded in section is more streamlined and offers less resistance in the water. It is also less visible and possesses strength and elasticity. This last quality is to a certain extent a disadvantage. Nylon stretches under tension and in stretching loses a certain amount of its original strength. Nylon line which has been subjected to great strain in landing heavy fish or from being caught in the bottom will often part at strains far below its specified breaking strain. This is because each time it is stretched its diameter and strength gets smaller and line originally of 80 lb. breaking strain may break under strains of as little as 50 lb. This same elasticity is a frequent cause of burst or warped reel drums. Nylon when wound on to the reel drum under heavy tension stretches a little and tends to bind in on itself. When the tension is suddenly released, like elastic it tries to expand and the sudden pressure can warp the drum and even burst reels asunder. It is always advisable when using nylon as main line to have a certain amount of soft backing such as cutty hunk to absorb the pressure and give the nylon something to bind on. Nylon deteriorates from exposure to light and in the lighter breaking strains should be discarded after one season's use. Making due allowance for these two factors nylon monofilment is excellent as a main line, for use with fixed spool reels and for traces.

The braided or twisted synthetics although not as streamlined in section or as small in diameter as nylon monofilment possess no spring or elasticity. They may offer slightly more resistance to the water but are much limper in use and do not lose their strength as nylon does. They make excellent and reliable main lines, especially for boat fishing, but are not as good for casting with a fixed-spool reel as some of the softer and more limp brands of nylon. They are unaffected by exposure to light and salt water.

Although modern synthetic lines do not need as much care or maintenance as the old fashioned fibre lines they do need some maintenance. Nylon chafes and cuts easily when abraided by rocks or the tough hides of such fish as tope. They should be examined frequently for damage and any portions showing signs of wear should be discarded. Although unaffected by salt water modern lines should be stripped off the reels occasionally and washed in fresh water. When salt water dries out it leaves behind tiny crystals of salt which do cause a certain amount of wear and tear giving braided lines especially a whiskery or fluffy look.

The terminal tackle is the "business" end of your fishing outfit. The different types of basic terminal rigs will be described in the next chapter but a word on swivels, hooks and wire would not be out of place here. One of the most important items of an angler's equipment is his hooks and unfortunately the one which frequently gets the least attention. He depends on them to hold his bait securely, to hook the fish and to land it. Only the very best hooks should be purchased and the small outlay on good hooks is well worth it. It always amazes me how anglers will willingly spend large sums for rods and reels but are careless about the hooks they buy or begrudge a few extra pence for good hooks.

Sea anglers have not been as well served in the matter of hooks as their freshwater brethren and even today many hooks are far too thick in the wire and more rank in the barb than they should be. I prefer freshwater type hooks where a really big hook is not required. They will, of course, rust but as their cost is small one can afford to discard them frequently.

A good hook should be well tempered, that is, not so soft that it will straighten out under strain or so brittle that it will snap. It should possess a certain amount of spring in it yet retain its shape. It should have a short sharp point and a moderate barb for easy penetration. Long points bend easily and lose their sharpness while a rank barb makes penetration difficult. The point should be inclined slightly towards the shank and there should be ample space between them and also between the point and the bend to allow the hook to take a firm grip. Slices on the shank of the hook, which are supposed to hold the bait securely, weaken the shank and besides tend to mess up fish baits. Hooks with the point inclined outwards tend to scrape along rather than penetrate the fish's mouth as do hooks with a definite brow or hump behind the point. I prefer hooks with a moderate or short shank and only use long shank hooks when fishing for small flatfish.

Hooks should always be kept needle sharp and it's a good investment to buy a small carborundum stone for sharpening hooks. They should be sharpened before commencing to fish and examined frequently afterwards and touched up if necessary. If a hook will not take a good point or if it has become rusty throw it away and use a new one. It is false economy to persevere with it.

Swivels should be strong and free working, made of brass or some non-ferrous metal which will not be liable to corrosion. There are several different types of swivel: barrel swivels, box swivels, ball and socket swivels and link swivels. They are used to join traces to the mainline, to prevent spinning baits from causing line twist and link swivels are used for quick change and attachment of artificial lures to line or trace. They should be no bigger than is necessary for the type of fishing you are doing but the diameter of the wire in the eye of the swivel should always be greater than the diameter of the monofilament used, otherwise it will tend to cut the line. I prefer the ball and socket type of swivel for heavy fishing, and the ordinary barrel swivel for general fishing. Three-way swivels are useful for attaching snoods but I do not trust them for heavy work. Some heavy solid brass cylindrical barrel type swivels have sharp edges around the rim of the eye which will part even wire when subjected to heavy strain. The links on link swivels are usually made of steel, which will rust, and they should be discarded as soon as they show signs of rusting.

Many anglers still use the old fashioned type of brass paternoster or boom and I am afraid that these are a complete anathema to me.

I can see no point in attaching baits to a heap of hardware, especially when it is so easy to make up a very neat and inconspicuous trace from monofilament. The sooner this type of messy and inefficient type of rig disappears from sea angling the better. There is, perhaps, something to be said for using a "spreader" when pier or boat fishing for shoal fish such as whiting but these are best made up from stainless steel wire. When boatfishing using a one hook trace fished on the bottom, a running or detachable boom is sometimes useful as it enables you to search the water for species feeding above the bottom, but many shop bought booms are far too light in the wire and twist and kink very easily. The same applies to the very useful Clements Boom or running leger boom and I prefer to make these up myself from strong coathanger wire. They are not as elegant as the shop bought article but they will support heavy sinkers and will not bend when stuck in the bottom.

Wire is another essential part of terminal tackle when fishing for species with sharp teeth or rough hides. There are two kinds of wire in common use, single strand wire and cable laid wire. Single strand wire is usually of the stainless type or else Alasticum wire. Both are strong and inconspicuous but they are stiff and have a tendency to kink. Once kinked they should be discarded immediately as they then break easily. Alasticum is excellent for short spinning traces and is thinner than monofilament of equivalent breaking strain. Several strands can be twisted together to make a heavy short bottom trace but like the stainless steel wire it is stiff and inflexible.

Cable laid wire, on the other hand, is much limper and makes better traces. Good wire should be thin, flexible and not liable to kink, twist or curl. It should also be stainless or rustproof. Many cable laid wires are covered with plastic. Some of these are excellent but others are dangerous and rust inside the plastic covering, breaking when least expected. Besides the plastic chafes easily on rocks and from the teeth or rough skins of fishes, becoming untidy and unsightly after hard use. If wire becomes rusted, kinked, twisted or has a tendency to curl, throw it away and use new wire.

Leads or sinkers come in all shapes, sizes and weights. One should only use sufficient weight to cast or to get your bait down to the bottom and hold it there. To use more weight than is necessary will detract from your fishing and from your enjoyment. Torpedo or watch shaped leads are best for casting but where there is a lot of surf or tide grip type or spiked leads are best used. Pear shaped or cigar shaped leads are very useful in deep water, especially in strong tides as they help you get your bait to the bottom quickly and offer least resistance to the water. Spiral detachable leads are useful for trolling, driftlining or spinning.

A good stout gaff is an essential part of the sea angler's equipment. A freshwater type gaff is unsuitable for sea work and I prefer to make my own. All that is required is to purchase a gaff hook with a gape of about 3 inches, a good stout broom handle and some copper wire. Drill a hole in the broom handle slightly smaller in diameter than the tang of the gaff hook. Hammer in the tang carefully to avoid splitting the wood and then bind it tightly with copper wire. The result may not be aesthetically pleasing but you have a gaff that you can trust and will cope with tope, conger or very big skate. If purchasing a gaff in a tackle shop do not buy one with a screw-on head as these can easily unscrew, particularly when dealing with conger, and both gaff and fish will be lost.

A landing net is also useful, particularly for such fish as shad, mullet and sea trout but for the larger species a gaff is more suitable. When fishing from a height as one must from piers, harbour walls and bridges a large drop net is nearly always essential. These can be easily made from old bicycle wheel rims to which is attached good stout netting, making a bag about 3 feet deep. Three to four foot lengths of strong rope or handline are tied to three equidistant points on the bicycle rim and brought together and joined to a suitable length of handline or rope. Remember to weight the bag of the net with a few stones, otherwise it will not sink properly when lowered into the water. Such a drop net enables the angler not alone to safely land his fish but also to use lighter and more sporting tackle than would be the case if he had to depend on the strength of his tackle to hoist up his catch.

The angler will, of course, require a bag in which to carry his spare tackle. It should hold such items as spare hooks, swivels, sinkers, split links, artificial lures, wire and monofilment for traces. A sharp knife is a necessity and so is a pair of long nosed pliers and a small screwdriver. In addition, I always carry a "priest" for dispatching the fish I catch, a first-aid set in case of accidents, a roll of insulating tape, some twine and a "fish rag" for keeping my hands clean.   The bag should be large enough to carry all the spare tackle that may be required for the particular type of fishing you intend to do and everything should be stowed neatly away in its proper place.   There is nothing more annoying than a messy tackle bag which is a complete jumble of odds and ends and in which it is impossible to find what you want quickly.   Traces should be kept neatly.   There are many ways of doing this but I prefer to use a length of plywood board notched at both ends and on which the traces can be wound and kept neatly and securely.   Take everything that you are likely to need with you in your tackle bag.   Many a day's fishing has been spoiled through some essential tackle replacement being left at home.

The boat angler and the beach fisherman, too, will find a leather rod butt rest very useful.   It is a necessity in playing heavy fish, as having to support the rod butt on your groin can be painful and even injurious.   It helps you to have greater control over the fish and is restful if the rod must be held for long periods at a time.   A harness is a great aid in playing big fish, particularly large skate, as it enables you to bring your back into play when heavy fish must be raised from the bottom in deep water.

The best advice that I can give to anyone buying new tackle is to purchase the best available.   It may be more expensive at first but in the long run the best is the cheapest and with proper care will last a lifetime.   Second rate tackle is never really satisfactory and if you are a keen angler you will end up by buying the better equipment later anyway.   I cannot overemphasise the necessity for taking the greatest care of your equipment.   Many anglers are very careless in this respect and yet wonder why their tackle does not last or lets them down when they need it most.   Care should be taken also in the use of tackle.   Avoid letting your rod or reel fall or knock against hard objects.   Do not be miserly about your terminal tackle and expect it to last forever.   If it shows any sign of being below par then discard it and use a new trace.   Some anglers seem to be more concerned with conserving their terminal tackle than with catching fish and the few pennies the making of a new trace costs are never worth the loss of a fish.

Clothes are also an important item to be considered.   It is essential to be comfortable and old clothes are the order of the day. Sea angling, especially beach, rock and boat fishing, can be a messy business and to wear good clothes is the height of folly. Besides, one cannot feel comfortable or concentrate properly on fishing if one is worried about keeping one's clothes clean. Your clothes should be warm and big woollen jerseys and windcheaters are very useful. Sea fishing can be cold even on a warm day as there is usually a breeze by the sea and it is better to carry too much clothing with you than too little. You can always shed a garment or two if you are too warm but if you are cold and have no extra clothing you cannot put it on.

Wet weather apparel is an absolute must. In this respect the new P.V.C. type coats and jackets are excellent. The only sure way of keeping dry in a boat on a bad day is to wear a pair of P.V.C. trousers in addition to a coat and sou'wester. The trousers, I admit, are awkward to wear but they are a godsend in heavy weather. I prefer short rubber boots with a pair of these trousers for boat work but when shore fishing long thigh waders are superior. Waterproof trousers, unless they be the new light nylon chest waders, are very cumbersome, tiring and awkward to walk in and besides one is always tempted to wade that little bit extra that means getting soaked no matter whether one is wearing knee boots, thigh waders or trouser waders.

Take good care of your boots for wet feet are most uncomfortable. Mend any punctures or tears in the rubber immediately. Small holes can be easily repaired with vulcanising patches but bigger tears are best left to a garage to mend. The upper part of thigh boots usually go before the portion below the knee. This is mostly caused through folding the lighter top material down or from kneeling in the sand. The exercise of a little care will greatly prolong the life of your boots.

No chapter on tackle would be complete without a reference to knots. Apart from whipping two lengths of line together or a line to hook or swivel there is no way of avoiding knots. In contrast to whipping, which increases the strength of the line at the portion whipped, knots weaken the line and the degree of weakening depends entirely on the knot used, some being more efficient than others. In many instances the way a knot is tied is more important than the type of knot used. A knot that is 80 per cent efficient and is well tied is superior to a poorly tied knot rated 90 per cent efficient. For that reason only a few of the better knots are illustrated here

and the angler would be well advised to practise tying these knots
and these knots only until he is proficient in their use.

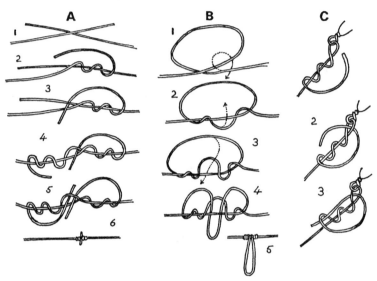

Blood knot " family," basic knots in tackle making

A Blood knot, to join two lengths of monofilament.
B Blood loop, for paternosters, to provide stand-off
attachment for hook link.   C tucked half-blood, to attach
swivel or eyed hook.

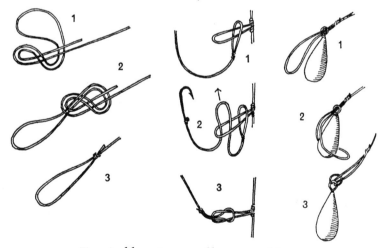

Terminal loop in monofilament, and its uses

CHAPTER 5

TECHNIQUES

IN THIS CHAPTER THE BASIC ANGLING METHODS, I.E. BOTTOM fishing, drifting or fishing on the drift, trolling, driftlining, float fishing and spinning, will be described, together with the tackle appropriate to each type of fishing. Two very simple types of terminal tackle or traces used are illustrated on page 104. It must be remembered that these are basic traces and there are numerous variations on each type of trace to suit different circumstances and, indeed, the angler's fancy.

Bottom fishing or ground fishing is probably the commonest technique used in sea angling and the most productive method for both variety of species and quantity of fish taken. It is used for shore fishing and boat angling alike and in it the bait or baits are fished stationary on or close to the bottom. When fishing from the shore the bait is cast out on to likely ground and allowed to remain there until it is taken by a fish or until the angler feels it should be examined, renewed or cast out to another location. In boat fishing the bait is lowered to the bottom from a boat anchored over a likely or proven fishing spot or mark.

The terminal tackle used in bottom fishing is usually a plain paternoster, paternoster-trot, leger, paternoster-leger, running paternoster or a string of feathers. The paternoster may be a two- or three-hook trace and a point to remember is that the distances between the hook links should be greater than the length of the links, otherwise they will foul each other. The links should also be short, otherwise they will twist around the main line instead of standing out from it. Paternosters are easily made up from nylon monofilment and are far superior to the old fashioned brass wire type of paternoster. A multiplicity of hooks should be avoided. Except in the case of small shoal fish, such as whiting, they are wasteful of bait and no more efficient than a two-hook paternoster.

The paternoster-trot (one or more hooks on a long link attached close above the lead) is a useful rig for pier and boat fishing where the baits are to be fished on the bottom and there is a run of tide or current to swing the longish trace out from the main line. A brass boom is useful on this type of trace to keep the long snood out and to prevent it from fouling the sinker. Two hooks are ample on the flowing trace and a third hook can be used above the sinker if it is desired to fish one bait well off the bottom.

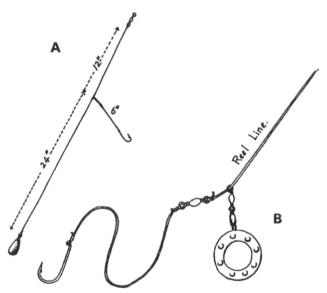

Basic terminal rigs for bottom fishing
A Monofilament paternoster for shore fishing. B Leger tackle.

The leger is a single-hook trace fished on the bottom, and the lead is attached to the line in a manner which allows the line to run freely when a fish takes the bait. The simplest form of leger is a drilled bullet through which the line is threaded or else a link swivel running freely on the line and to which the sinker is attached. The actual trace is usually short, especially for shore casting but can be quite long when used for tope fishing from a boat or when a long flowing trace is required in a tideway. In heavy boat fishing a running boom to which the sinker is attached is used instead of the first two methods described. A "stop", usually half a match, is placed between the running lead or boom and the swivel at the head of the trace. It can be secured on the line by two half hitches and prevents the swivel from running back up the leger. This is a very useful trace for such shy biting fish as tope, conger and flatfish as the fish can take the bait and move away with it without feeling the drag of the sinker.

The paternoster-leger is, as its name implies, an adaptation of two traces and is mainly used in boat fishing. It enables the angler to fish one bait on the bottom leger fashion and another bait well off the bottom. The extent to which the line can run freely through the leger is, of course, dependent on the length of line between the top hook link and the lower swivel. It is a very efficient and useful type of trace for many species of fish.

The running paternoster is an ordinary leger in which the trace is shorter than the link between the free running swivel on the main line, and the sinker. It is used for shore fishing where an ordinary leger may cause difficulties in casting. When casting, the ordinary leger has a tendency to lag behind the bait (particularly if the bait is a heavy one) and runs back up the main line. To overcome this tendency a longer link to the sinker is used so that the bait may be held back by light pressure on the line, allowing the sinker to travel ahead of the bait.

A trace comprising a string of feathers can be used for spinning, drifting, trolling or bottom fishing. In bottom fishing it can be used either as an artificial lure or each hook or feathered lure can be baited with small strips of fish. A string of feathers (which imitate a small shoal of fry) will take most species of fish in the sea, even very big fish such as shark and tope will take them though they are seldom landed. Feathers are usually fished "sink and draw", i.e. by smartly moving the rod up and down, keeping the lures in motion. If there is a good wave on the sea the roll of the boat will give sufficient motion to the lures and obviate the necessity of working them by hand. Fished close to the bottom they will take bottom feeding species and if worked up through different depths will also take pelagic species. Feathers are an essential part of the boat angler's tackle as they are most useful in catching fish bait, such as mackerel.

The foregoing are the basic types of terminal tackle used in ground fishing. There are many variations of these basic types adapted to suit conditions and species of fish sought. The length of the traces and of the different hook links are suggested ones and may be altered as required. I would, however, like to repeat my advice about using too many hooks. They are wasteful of bait, make messy and awkward-to-handle traces and if anything (except in the case of small shoal fish) catch less fish than a one- or two-hook trace. Certainly in deep water fishing for heavy fish one hook and a big bait is quite sufficient. The use of a second hook with a small bait further up the trace only attracts smaller fish and often means that your bait is out of the water while you are unhooking a small fish at the very time a really big fish may come along. Many anglers try to have the best of both worlds but it is far better to decide the type of fish you are going to angle for and to use the tactics and tackle best suited to that particular type of fishing.

SHORE FISHING

The following are suitable outfits for bottom fishing and the tackle used in shore fishing will be described first.

(1) *Light Bottom Fishing.* A light 7/8 foot rod of hollow or solid fibre glass is suitable for heavy spinning or light bottom fishing in estuaries, creeks or on sheltered beaches where light sinkers of up to $1\frac{1}{4}/1\frac{1}{2}$ oz. can be used. It should be used in conjunction with a freshwater type fixed spool reel and 5-15 lb. breaking strain monofilament line.

(2) *Surf Casting.* A long rod of hollow fibre glass approximately 11 feet overall with a 30 inch butt, capable of casting up to 4 oz. sinkers. A big saltwater type fixed spool reel or multiplier with 15 to 25 lb. breaking strain, braided line or nylon monofilment. The actual length of the rod will depend on the angler and his physique and the rod should be light as it must be held in the hands for long periods. A leather rod butt rest is an advantage in holding the rod and in playing the fish and it also helps if the rod weighs no more than 18 oz.

(3) *Heavy Surf Casting.* A rod of similar size to the above but capable of casting 6 to 7 oz. weights. A wide spool multiplier is slightly more suitable than a large fixed spool reel when using this type of rod and the line should be 20 to 27 lb. breaking strain braided line or nylon monofilment. This type of rod is suited for fishing in conditions of heavy surf, for tope fishing from the shore or for fishing over rough bottoms. An adjustable leather rod-butt rest is essential.

(4) *Pier Fishing*.   The type of tackle used will depend on the type of pier and its height above water.   Any of the above outfits may be suitable, but the long surf rods may be awkward to handle on crowded piers.   For conger fishing, however, a shorter, more powerful rod about 7 feet long is advisable and a strong centre-pin reel (Nottingham type) is best.   The line if used for conger should be at least 40 lb. breaking strain and a braided line is preferable.

BOAT FISHING

Boat fishing rods are of necessity more powerful than those used from the shore.   Not only must they be capable of lifting heavy fighting fish from deep water, but must also be able to lift sinkers up to 2 lb. in weight from the bottom without bending too much. They are, therefore, fairly stiff in action as a light flexible rod would acquire such a bend in lifting a heavy sinker thet there would be little or no power left to handle a hooked fish.   As they are not required for casting they are usually short, approximately 7/8 feet in length both for added power and convenience in handling a boat. Either boat-fishing type multiplier reels or sturdy centre-pins can be used with them, but every reel should have a large capacity and an efficient star drag or brake.   Both types are good but the multipliers are better in dealing with fish that run, i.e. tope, while the centre-pin is superior for heavy bottom fish such as conger or big skate.   It is always advisable to use an adjustable leather rod butt rest.

(1) *Light Boat Fishing*.   For boat fishing in shallow water for the smaller species of fish and where light sinkers can be used the tackle suggested for light bottom fishing from the shore is quite suitable and makes for better sport.

(2) *Medium Boat Fishing*.   For use in depths of 10-15 fathoms a 7/8 foot medium action hollow or solid glass fibre rod is suitable.   The reel, either a 6 inch centre-pin or medium sized multiplier, should have a capacity of at least 200 yards of 20/40 lb. braided or nylon monofilment line.   An adjustable leather rod-butt rest is advisable.

(3) *Heavy Boat Fishing*.   A shorter 6/7 foot more powerful type of rod capable of handling sinkers up to 2 lb. is required.   Large centre-pin or multiplier reels with a 300 yard capacity of 60 lbs.

breaking strain braided line if heavy fish are expected. For smaller species 30/40 lb. line is quite suitable but for very heavy fish 80 lb. or 100 lb. line would not be too heavy. A leather rod butt rest is a must for heavy boat fishing and a rod harness is also very useful.

The reel used should balance the rod both for efficiency and comfort. The breaking strain of the terminal tackle used, the weight of the sinker and the hook size should also be balanced to the rod, reel and line. Use the lightest sinker that will take your bait down quickly to the bottom and keep it there. The size of the hook should be matched to the species of fish sought, the size of the bait and type of rod used. A light rod cannot exert enough power to drive a big hook home whilst a heavy powerful rod will straighten out small fine wire hooks. Generally speaking anglers make up their traces from line that is slightly lighter than the reel line. If a breakage occurs it will then be in the trace, thus saving any loss of the reel line. However, knots weaken any line and if a breakage occurs it is usually at or near the knot. For that reason I usually use lines of the same breaking strain or if fishing for fish with rough skins or over rough ground I prefer the trace to be of a heavier breaking strain as it must stand up to a great deal of punishment.

When bottom fishing the angler should always be in contact with his bait and fish a reasonably tight line so that he will be aware of what is happening to it. He should try and keep his bait in the one position on the bottom and not have it wandering all over the place. In doing so he will not only catch more fish but avoid fouling or getting tangled up in the lines of other anglers fishing in the same boat. It is very annoying to fish in a boat with an angler who is not fishing his line properly and is continually fouling your tackle. Another cause of tangles is the incorrect use of weights when a number of anglers are fishing in the same boat and a fair tide is running. This can easily be avoided if the anglers in the stern use light weights which the tide will take well away from the boat and the anglers behind them use progressively heavier weights with the angler nearest the bow using the heaviest sinker. This will ensure that lines are kept well clear of each other.

Fishing in a strong tide or current in deep water calls for a very sensitive touch and many anglers have difficulty in keeping in contact with their sinker. When the sinker is dropped to the bottom

e strength of the tide will lift it off the bottom and sweep it away.
ine must be paid out until the sinker is slanted far enough away
rom the boat for it to hold the bottom. This must be done carefully by feeling for the bottom as you pay out line until the sinker
finally holds. The danger is that if not done properly too much
line is paid out and a big "belly" formed in the line by the strong
tide. If this happens bites may not be felt or if felt the strike is
dissipated in the belly of the line and the fish is not hooked.

Drifting or fishing from a drifting boat can be a very effective
form of angling. It is especially useful when fishing over unknown
ground or when fishing on known marks is poor. The big
advantage it has is that much more ground is covered and when
fish are met with one can always take bearings on the spot where
the fish were caught and then go to an anchor if desired.

DRIFTING

To be effective the drift should be reasonably slow and if conditions of wind and tide are such that the drift is too fast, a heavy
stone or weight attached to the anchor rope and allowed to trail
near the bottom will slow up the drift. There is an art in drifting
which if properly understood would lead to its being practised more.
Many anglers have a rooted objection to this type of fishing because
they lose too much tackle over rough or snaggy bottoms. While
a certain amount of terminal tackle will be lost it need not be much
more than is normally lost in fishing to an anchor and, besides, our
purpose is to catch fish and not to preserve our traces indefinitely.

Ordinary boat fishing tackle is used and the terminal rig can be a
paternoster, paternoster leger, leger with long flowing trace or a
string of feathers. The only adaption I would suggest is that the
lead be suspended about 9 inches below the main trace to which it
should be attached by some weaker line. It is usually the lead or
sinker which fouls in the bottom and if one must break out only the
sinker is lost. The hook will also foul in rough bottoms or heavy
kelps but I find if the point of the hook is embedded in the bait and
covered by it the difficulty will be overcome.

The bait should be lowered over the side and as soon as the
sinker touches the bottom a fathom of line should be wound back
on the reel. The rod should be held all the time and the angler
must be on the qui vive lest his gear get snagged in the bottom.

If the sinker touches an obstruction, line should be reeled in instantly to raise it clear off the bottom. On the other hand, if nothing is felt after a while the sinker should be cautiously lowered to find the bottom again in case the boat is drifting into deeper water or over a hole or gully. The bait should be fished as close to the bottom as possible at all times and this type of fishing calls for alertness, a sensitive touch and quick reactions.

Should the tackle become stuck in the bottom the boat can be brought back up drift of the place where it has become fouled, so that a pull from the opposite direction can be obtained. This stratagem usually frees the bait but if this fails there is nothing else for it except break out and hope for the best. Generally speaking, all bites should be struck quickly and positively as fish strike more definitely at a moving bait than they do at one lying still on the bottom. If they fail to get the bait on the first attempt they frequently don't try a second time.

TROLLING AND DRIFTLINING

Trolling means trailing or towing a natural or artificial bait behind a boat. The strength of the rod used will depend on the size of the fish sought and the depth at which the bait or lure must be fished. A lighter rod may be used for mackerel near the surface whilst a heavier rod must be used for big pollack near the bottom. The bait or lure is fished about 50 to 100 yards behind the boat and the trace should be about 6 feet long and bear at least two swivels. The weight required will depend on the depth at which the bait must be fished; an ounce of lead may suffice for trolling near the surface whilst for deep trolling 8 oz. may be necessary. The rod must be fairly stiff in action, as it not alone has to bear the weight of sinker and line but must set the hooks in the fish when it takes. In trolling, especially single handed trolling, apart from being subject to the heavy strain of line and sinker, it takes a fair amount of hard knocks and needs to be fairly robust.

A nice length for a trolling rod is 7/8 feet and either a fairly large centre-pin or multiplier can be used. The reel must have a strong check or an efficient star drag which will prevent the reel yielding line when the bait is being trolled. The drag or brake, however should not be set too tight but must be finely adjusted so that line is yielded to the hooked fish while the way is being taken off the boat and until the fish can be played by hand. *Never hitch the line around the reel handle under any circumstances to ·prevent line being yielded when trolling or, indeed, in any other form of fishing.* The sudden snatch of a taking fish may not alone snap the line but quite easily knock the rod overboard. This also applies to other forms of fishing both in boats and from the shore. If you must put your rod down *never* hitch the line around the reel handle and make sure also that the line is not accidentally hitched around the top of the rod. I have seen a number of rods disappear from boats and on the shore due to this bad practice and contrary to general belief it does not take a big fish to cause disaster.

Speed and depth play an important part in trolling. Pollack, for example, stay deep during the day but in the evening rise to the surface and it is essential that the bait be trolled at the correct depth to be successful. One must also troll very slowly for pollack but for such species as bass, mackerel and sea trout the troll must be fast. When fish are found shoaling on the surface be careful not to take the boat through the shoal but instead skirt around it for fear of putting the fish down. If the boat is manoeuvered properly as it circles the shoal of fish the lure or bait trailing behind the boat can be drawn right through the shoal.

In a tideway or fast current it is best to steer the boat back and forth across the current. This is a much more productive method than going with or against the current as your bait will cover more fish. Be careful to avoid sharp turns, especially if there is more than one line in the boat, as unless the boat is turned gradually in a wide arc the lines will tangle. Furthermore,, on a sharp turn the speed of the lure through the water decreases and, of course, the lure will sink deeper in the water and perhaps snag in the bottom.

There are special sinkers made for trolling but the handiest type of lead I find is the spiral lead. This type of lead can be attached to or detached from the line in an instant and makes it easy to adjust the weight of the sinker if different depths are to be tried. It can also be easily bent into a half moon shape to form an anti-kink, which is an essential if spinning or revolving baits are used.

Driftlining could in a manner of speaking be described as "stationary trolling". It is a method which can only be used in a fair amount of tide or current. It is used from an anchored boat in a tideway or from some vantage point on the shore, such as a bridge, pier or jetty where the tide is swift. The bait or lure is lowered into the water and line paid out until it is fishing at the desired depth and distance from the angler. Movement is imparted to the bait by the action of the tide and the use of ground bait or rubby dubby to attract fish is an advantage. Natural baits, such as slips of mackerel, sandeels or prawns are better than artificial lures but if the latter are used they should be the kind that wobble or spin well when worked slowly. From time to time a little line can be drawn in through the rings and released again to impart additional movement to the bait.

On the strength of the tide, the depth at which the bait must be fished and the species of fish sought, will depend on the type of rod used. A medium spinning outfit, i.e. 7 foot spinning rod, fixed spool reel and 10 lb. breaking strain monofilment line is suitable for mackerel and bass. Where fair sized pollack are expected a heavier outfit, i.e. a more powerful spinning rod or light trolling rod, a multiplier or centre-pin reel and 10 to 20 lb. breaking strain line would be required. The trace should be about 6 feet long, bear two swivels and a hook size suitable to the species sought.

FLOAT FISHING

Float fishing is an off-the-bottom method in which a float is used to suspend the bait in the water and to regulate the depth at which it is fished. The float should be easily visible and no larger than is necessary to suspend bait, trace and any weights or sinkers used in the water. It may be small and light, i.e. as a quill float used in fishing for mullet or it may be quite big as in shark fishing, where a whole fish and a steel trace must be supported. However, it should be so shaped that it offers little resistance to a taking fish.

Floats come in many different shapes and sizes but there are three main kinds, fixed floats, sliding floats and controller floats. A fixed float is suitable for fishing baits 3 to 4 feet below the surface and as its name implies once fixed in position on the line it remains in that position. Where the bait must be fished at a greater depth a sliding float is used. If, for instance, the bait must be fished 10 feet below the surface, it would not be practicable to cast such a long trace and a fixed float. The sliding float when attached to the line can run freely up and down it. The trace which should be short is attached to the main line by a swivel which will stop the float running below it. The desired depth should be measured off and a "stop" put on the line at this point to limit the upward movement of the float on the line. For casting, a piece of rubber band tied on to the line makes a suitable stop as it will run freely through the rod rings. When boat fishing it is usual to use a match stick secured by two

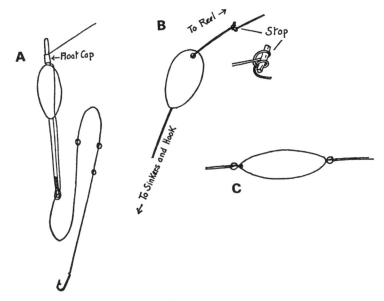

Float Gear

A, Fixed float, for fishing at no great depth. B, Sliding float, for fishing deep. The stop which may be a fragment of rubber, will pass through the rod rings, but not through the float. C, "Controller" float, which floats horizontally. Used with baits which themselves float, its purpose is simply to provide casting weight.

half hitches to the line. When a fish is being played to the boat the match stick will break in the top ring and allow the fish to be brought within reach of the gaff.

The controller float is used with surface floating baits, such as bread crust used in mullet fishing. It is intended for use with a fixed spool reel and its primary purpose is to give casting weight since no weight can be added to the trace which, like the bait, must float.

The trace length will depend on the depth at which the bait must be fished. When fishing deep for bass or pollack the actual trace portion need be no longer than 4 feet and may bear one hook at the end of the trace and if desired another higher up on a short snood. Again I prefer one hook only, especially when big baits are being used. The trace can be weighed with spiral leads, lead wire or split shot depending on the type of fishing but the combined weight of bait, lead and float should be only slightly in excess of the weight necessary to cast. Traces used for float fishing for tope or shark will, of course, be of steel wire and range from 5 to 20 feet in length.

The best type of rod will again depend on the fish sought. A 10 foot trout rod is excellent for mullet and mackerel fishing. It should have stand off rings and be used with a freshwater type fixed spool reel and 5 lb. breaking strain nylon monofilament. For bass and pollack the rod must be more powerful and a light bottom fishing rod, large fixed spool reel and 15/18 lb. breaking strain line would suit. I prefer a long rod for float fishing, as it casts light baits more easily and lifts a large amount of line off the water when striking. This quality is very important in a rod for this type of fishing and it is also important when mullet fishing to treat the main line with a flotant to prevent it sinking. If the line floats and your rod can lift a fair amount of it off the water you will be more successful in striking and hooking the fish. A long powerful rod is very useful in rock fishing for pollack or bass where it may be necessary to cast sizeable baits and to keep the fish out of the weeds and away from snags.

In boat fishing a long rod is not necessary for float fishing and an ordinary medium boat rod will do for tope and indeed blue shark. Blue shark can be taken on light tackle and on the whole anglers tend to use heavier gear than is necessary. Heavy boat tackle is, however, very necessary when fishing for porbeagle or mako sharks.

SPINNING

Spinning is the last method to be described and it is very effective for such species as bass, pollack and sea trout and, beyond doubt, the method which gives the most sport with these fishes. Spinning means casting out a small fish such as a sandeel or sprat or an artificial lure representing a small fish and reeling it back to the rod. The tackle used is light and excellent sport can be had with it both from the shore and from boats.

Two types of spinning outfits are in general use. The most

popular is a 7/8 foot light salmon spinning rod and a freshwater type fixed spool reel, which when fished with 10 lb. breaking strain nylon monofilment is ideal for bass and pollack. A lighter outfit similar to that used for spinning for trout in fresh water is very suitable for mackerel, sea trout and shad.

The main advantages of the fixed spool reel and matching rod is the relative ease with which one can learn to use it and the fact that, as it has an open face spool off which the line spirals freely in casting, there is no initial inertia to overcome and very light lures of ¼ oz. or less can be cast without adding weights to the line. The distance which one can cast depends on the strength of the rod and the thickness of the line used. A light whippy rod with 5 lb. breaking strain line will cast a light lure which would hardly develop any of the action in a stiffer more powerful rod whilst a heavy lure might overpower the lighter rod. The lighter the line used the farther one can cast, but it is important to remember that the spool must be filled almost to the lip with line. If too much line is put on the reel many coils of line will come off the spool together in casting and cause that horrible tangle of nylon known as a "bird's nest". On the other hand, if the spool is not filled sufficiently casting length will be lost through friction and for the same reason it may be difficult to retrieve line from a fish. The spool is deep and if the line is well down in the spool it rubs against the lip of the spool in casting and although there may be ample line left on the spool distance will be lost.

The second type of spinning outfit is a level-wind multiplier reel and a short 5 to 6 foot bait-casting rod. The rod has a crank handle type butt with a trigger grip underneath and the reel mount is inset into the handle on the upper side. In all revolving drum reels there is a certain amount of inertia which must be overcome before the drum begins to revolve freely. It requires a certain amount of force to start the drum revolving and for that reason this type of reel is not suitable for casting light baits. In the heavier weights this reel comes into its own, permitting longer casts and is more pleasant to use as one is in direct contact with the fish and can play it through the reel.

A good outfit is one designed to cast lures ranging from ¼ oz. to ¾ oz. and a 10/12 lb. breaking strain braided line is preferable to monofilment. It takes a good deal more practice and perseverance to become proficient with a multiplier than with a fixed spool reel but it is well worth persevering with it.   A point to remember is not to wind the line back through the line carriage when you are finished fishing.   The line is wound on the spool in synchronisation with the level wind or line carriage and if the line is wound back on to the drum it may throw the whole lot out of "synch" and

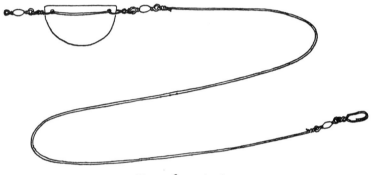

Trace for spinning

With celluloid anti-kink fin or vane and terminal link swivel. Length of trace, 18″. Length of vane, 1″ for little baits, 1½″ for bass-size baits. Swivel between anti-kink and line is important if a fixed-spool reel is used, so that twists put in the line by the action of the slipping clutch can work out of the line.

mean stripping all the line off the drum and re-synchronising it again.

Lures that do not spin or revolve can be attached direct to the main line when spinning if they are provided with a swivel; if not they can be attached by a suitable link swivel.   All spinning baits should be mounted at the end of a short trace which is equipped with an antikink.   When spinning in the sea I always prefer to use a trace about 15 inches long made of Alisticum wire.   This wire is smaller in diameter than the equivalent breaking strain in nylon monofilment and is very useful in fishing over weedy ground.   The wire cuts easily through weed when fouled, whereas nylon will not, and it may mean the difference between losing a lure or recovering it. As artificial lures are so expensive these days this virtue is quite an important one.   There should be two swivels, one on either side of the anti-kink and also a link swivel for attaching the lure at the end of the trace.   Alasticum wire is a single strand wire which kinks easily. It should be examined frequently as it will part under very slight strain where a kink occurs. If kinked, it should be discarded immediately. It is only a minute's work to make up another trace and the wire is cheap.

When casting with a fixed-spool reel it is both wrong and unnecessary to work your arm too much. The action is mainly in the wrist and the flex of the rod should be made to do most of the work. The reel should be mounted underneath and in such a position on the rod butt that it balances the rod and makes it easy to hold. First adjust the tension of the slipping clutch to a pressure well within the breaking strain of the line but not so lightly that a fish can take line off the reel when it strikes, otherwise you will fail to set the hooks. Grasp the rod firmly but not too tightly with the index finger in front of the reel pillar, the other fingers behind the pillar and the thumb extending along the top of the handle. Some anglers may find it more comfortable to place two fingers in front of the reel pillar but if too much of the hand is in front it may foul the pick-up when it is being clicked into position for the retrieve.

Face in the direction you wish to cast with the left foot in advance of the right. Reel in the line until the trace or lure is just clear of the end ring, pick up the line and hold it on the tip of your crooked index finger and then slip the bail arm back into the casting position. You are now ready to cast. Remember that the cast is made mainly by wrist and rod action. The movement is a flicking one not a throwing one and the arm should not be brought into use though the forearm is partly used.

In a right-handed side cast the rod should be held about waist high, the arm bent and the elbow close to the side. Flick the wrist smartly backwards, then quickly forwards again and slightly upwards using the recoil action of the rod to make the forward power cast. The line is released from the finger on the forward cast when the rod bears about 20 degrees off the target. The rod should follow through and the bail arm is clicked over into position by turning the reel handle and the retrieve begun as the lure enters the water.

The distance cast depends on the length of the arc described by the rod when flicked backwards and forwards, the speed at which it is done and the elevation given to the rod tip on the forward cast.

The casting motion should be a fluid easy one allowing the rod to develop its full action and it is not necessary, and indeed it is wrong, to force it. Surprisingly long casts can be made with quite a small flicking movement. With a little practice one can become quite proficient with a fixed-spool reel and overhead and back casts can be made with equal facility. The most accurate casts are made by the overhead method.

The action in casting with a multiplier is similar to that described above but considerable more practice is required in controlling the reel. Although a considerable amount of force is required to overcome the initial inertia in the drum of a multiplier, once it starts to revolve it will continue to do so freely. As the lure or bait passes its maximum velocity and commences to slow down the reel drum tends to run faster than the line is being pulled off, and unless the drum is slowed down an over-run develops and the line gets into a tangled mess on the drum, stopping the flight of the lure in mid-air, sometimes causing the line to snap.

When casting make sure that the check is in the off position and hold the drum stationary by thumb pressure. The drum is released on the forward cast, and as soon as it is revolving freely, should be braked gently with the thumb in case it runs too fast. It should be braked intermittently whenever it shows a tendency to over-run, but persistent pressure on the drum will reduce the length of the cast considerably. The drum should be stopped immediately the lure hits the water and the retrieve can then be started. Proficiency comes with practice and though there is a "knack" in using a multiplier, like riding a bicycle, once it is learned it is never forgotten.

Practice is also the key to accuracy and distance in using both types of spinning gear and after a while becomes automatic.

Before leaving the subject of spinning let us have a brief look at artificial lures. The variety, sizes, types and shapes of artificial lures are legion and, unfortunately, many seem better designed to catch the angler than the fish. It is the action of a lure in the water that is important not its resemblance to a fish or other marine animal and many very effective lures are most unfishlike in appearance. If possible the "casting weight" should be built into the lure itself so that no additional lead is needed on the trace to make casting feasible. The use of uptrace weights with ultra light lures creates difficulties in casting, as the lure lags behind the weight in flight and tends to catch or foul in the main line.

The main types of lures are: (1) spinners (wagtails, devons, etc.); (2) bar spoons, i.e. Vibro, Voblex, Milbro, etc.; (3) wobbling spoons, i.e. Lemax, Toby, etc.; (4) squid type lures, i.e. German Sprat; (5) rubber eels; (6) feathered lures. When using all true spinning lures, an anti-kink is essential, otherwise line twist will be troublesome, but lures that do not revolve can be attached direct to the main line. A spinning lure must be retrieved fast enough to keep it spinning and the speed of the retrieve will also govern the depth at which the lure fishes. If possible choose a lure that spins freely when worked slowly through the water, as many will not spin properly unless the retrieve is very fast. The speed at which the lure will be recovered depends on the species of fish sought and the depth at which it is fished, so that it is important that the lure should spin well at both slow and fast speeds.

Bar spoons are those in which a blade revolves around a central bar which carries the hook flight. They are excellent spinners which work well at very slow speeds. They are very useful for casting upstream in a current, as they will work well when being retrieved with the current, needing very little tension on the line to make the blades spin. In very shallow water they are also very useful, as a fast retrieve will keep them near the surface, clear of the bottom and of weeds or stones.

Wobbling spoons are probably the most effective artificial lures in salt water. They can be worked in many different ways, whereas the spinner can only be fished on a straight retrieve. The wobbling spoon can be fished like a spinner, jigged like a squid type lure, or fished "sink and draw", i.e. allowed to sink through the water for a while before being jerked up again and the action repeated, whilst each time some of the slack is taken up on the reel. In the forward and upward jerked movement the spoon fishes exactly as on a straight retrieve but when allowed to sink it flutters and swoops through the water in a manner very attractive to fish.

On suitable snag-free bottoms it can be fished in the manner of a baited spoon. It is allowed to sink to the bottom and fished sink and draw, being allowed to rest on the bottom momentarily each time.

The baited spoon is not unlike the bar spoon described above, except that the spinning blade should be very light and a long shank single hook is used in place of the usual treble hook. The hook is baited with lugworm or ragworm and proves effective for catching many species of fish especially flatfish.

Squid-type lures are usually heavy, with plenty of built-in casting weight. They have little inherent action on a straight retrieve, and this must be given to them by jigging or jerking the rod tip as you reel in so that the lure fishes in a series of spurts or jerks reminiscent of the squid, which it represents. The action of this type of lure is in its downward wobbling and fluttering flight through the water and it is most effective when fished sink and draw. Due to their weight they are more deep water than shallow water lures and can indeed be used successfully in boat fishing in deep water. They will take almost every species of fish.

The rubber eel is probably the most killing of all pollack lures early in the season, i.e. April/May, but is not quite so efficient as feather lures or spoons later on in the season. They are very light and require an uptrace weight for casting but strangely enough it is the least likely of all light lures to foul the main line. The rubber eel has a wriggling action and it is essential that it works properly when drawn very slowly through the water.

Feather lures can be fished either singly in which case they require a leaded head to give them casting weight and to allow them to be fished "sink and draw" or else several can be fished together, i.e. a "string" of feathers, with the weight attached to the end. Fished sink and draw or on a straight retrieve feathers will take most species of fish but when used on spinning tackle and big fish are expected, a string of three or four feathers is quite enough.

All artificial lures used in the sea should be as corrosion-proof as possible and the swivels and treble hooks should be easily changed. These are best attached by split links and all attachments should be inspected regularly for rust. Split links and hooks will rust and should be replaced when necessary while the swivels should be oiled occasionally to keep them free. It is best to store your lures separately to keep them from getting tangled in one another and never replace a wet lure with other lures even for a short time as the prospects are that all will rust. It is good practice to wash all used lures in fresh water after use and dry them with a rag before storing them away. Hook points should be inspected regularly for sharpness or damage and if necessary touched up or replaced.

When buying lures make sure that the trebles are big enough for sea fishing. A common fault in shop-bought lures is that the trebles provided are too small and many fish are lost for this reason.

SURF CASTING

Surf casting may look difficult but it is not as hard as it seems and with a little practice and patience one can become proficient. It is not a matter of brute strength because one can cast almost as far with half one's power. It is a matter of co-ordination between mind and body which once the fundamentals are grasped leads to a fluid easy casting movement. Once again it is the rod that does most of the work and all the angler has to do is help develop the full power of the rod and give it direction.

The normal casting technique with a multiplier, assuming that you possess the proper surfcasting tackle, is as follows. Stand sideways with your left shoulder facing in the direction in which you wish to cast and your left foot pointing a little to the right of the target. Stand easily with your feet comfortably apart so that you will always be in balance as you shift your weight from one foot to the other. Grasp the rod with your left hand near the end of the butt and your right hand under the reel and your right thumb on the spool of the reel. Put the reel in free spool having first checked that the line is laid evenly on the spool and that the check is off. The best distance at which the sinker should hang below the rod tip will be found by a little experimenting.

You are now ready to cast. Pivot on your hips to face backwards and extend the rod as far back as is comfortably possible by extending the right arm and bending the right knee a little. In this position the rod should be pointing downwards, your right arm almost fully extended and below the level of your left arm. You draw your left arm forward bringing the right arm up to shoulder level with the rod butt still slightly higher than the tip. At this stage you begin to pivot at the waist, at the same time developing the power of the rod by pushing upwards with the right hand and pulling downwards and backwards with the left hand while the weight is shifted from the right to the left foot as the cast progresses. When the rod tip is just beyond the vertical, the thumb is released from the spool and throughout the flight of the sinker only sufficient pressure to prevent an over-run is applied from time to time. At this stage you are facing the target and the rod tip should follow through, pointing in the line of flight of the sinker as you lean forward. As soon as the sinker hits the water stop the drum revolving, put the reel in gear, and take up the slack.

This may sound very difficult but in practice it is quite simple. The main difficulty experienced by beginners is with the reel, where lack of proper control ends in an over-run. At first it is best to watch the reel and ignore the sinker. When loose coils begin to appear on the drum it is a sign that the spool is beginning to run too fast and light thumb pressure is applied until the spoon is running smoothly in time with the sinker again. The less thumb pressure applied to the reel the longer the cast. It is essential that brute force or any jerkiness should not be put into the cast. Try to develop an easy, controlled and fluid casting movement, applying the power to the rod in a gradual and smooth manner. Once this is achieved little braking pressure will be needed on the reel.

Never strive for distance. This will come of its own accord in time. Furthermore, do not be discouraged by over-runs or backlash. Even the most proficient casters get them from time to time.

PLAYING A FISH

The art of playing a fish is one that comes with experience. Playing is the operative word, for when heavy fish are hooked on light tackle one must play the fish as a cat plays with a mouse, letting it run a little, then bringing it back again until the fish tires and can be landed in safety. The mouse has no chance of escaping from the cat but the fish can be very easily lost unless the angler plays it very carefully and any attempt to "horse" the fish is inviting disaster.

In playing a fish the rod has a dual role. It exerts continuous strain on the fish, tiring it out; while at the same time it cushions the line against sudden shocks by yielding to the pull of the fish. It is because of its ability to do this that strong fighting fish such as tope can be landed on line of comparatively low breaking strain. It also, to a degree, prevents the angler from exerting too much strain on the fish and possibly breaking the line.

For example, a tope of 45 lb. is hooked on a rod having a test curve of 2½ lb. and a line with a breaking strain of 20 lb. If the angler were using a handline of the same breaking strain instead and tried to haul in or hold the struggling fish his line would break when the strain reached a pressure of 20 lb. With the rod, however, the angler can only exert a pull of 2½ lb. on the fish (which is well within the capacity of the line) and he can also yield line to the fish when it runs by the controlled release of the reel drum or by the slipping clutch or drag with which most modern reels are provided. The sudden heavy jerks or pulls of the fish which might cause a breakage before line can be released are absorbed by the yielding rod top. It is surprising how a comparatively light though continuous strain will quickly tire even big fish.

The rod, however, must act as a lever and cushion the line from severe shocks throughout the fight and must be held properly to do so. Normally in playing a fish the rod is held at an angle of roughly 60 degrees so that it can exert its maximum safe pressure and still absorb the shocks on the line. If the rod is pulled down or forwards from this position, *line must be yielded* as the rod is no longer able to cushion the line on which the full strain exerted by the fish now rests and a breakage is likely.

Provided you have sufficient line on your reel never be afraid to let a fish run, for the harder and faster it runs the sooner it will tire. However, the line must be given under controlled tension and a steady strain kept on the fish. The tension together with the weight and friction of the line in the water (which can be considerable) puts a great strain on the fish and saps its strength. When the fish stops, try and turn it and recover line, until it makes another run, when you should let it go again. Each successive run will be slower and shorter as the fish tires until eventually it will come easily. Look out, however, for a last desperate bid for freedom which may catch you napping if you try to hold the fish hard. Knowing when to hold a fish and when to let it run is part experience and part intuition. You should be able to almost feel through the rod and anticipate what the fish will do next and so be able to counteract its efforts to escape.

Always set your slipping clutch or drag beforehand as it is not easily adjusted accurately while fighting a fish. It should be set well below the breaking strain of the line for it is not safe to set it only slightly lower. For example, if you are using 10 lb. breaking strain line and set your clutch to slip at a pressure of 9 lb. your line may part if the fish gives a sudden lunge.   This is because it may take a strain of more than 10 lb. to start your clutch slipping although once started it will yield line freely at a strain of 9 lb.   It is an easy matter to set your clutch before you start fishing by pulling line off the reel by hand as you adjust it to the correct strain.   Many reels do not possess a very fine adjustment and it is better not to try and alter the setting while fighting a fish lest you set it too tight or stop it altogether.

A common mistake made by anglers using fixed spool reels or multipliers with a slipping clutch is that they continue to reel in while the fish is taking line off the reel.   This practice serves no purpose at all except to help strip the gears and shorten the life of the reel.   If you want to recover line and the clutch is set too lightly "pump" the fish instead of trying to reel against a slipping clutch.   This is the correct way to recover line anyway when using these types of reels as to try and "winch" a fish in (which can only be done satisfactorily with a centre-pin reel) is imposing a great strain on the gears of the reel.   In order to pump a fish drop the point of the rod and take in what line you can recover in the process.   Stop the spool or reel drum from revolving by finger or thumb pressure and lift the rod to the vertical position; then drop the rod point quickly, at the same time reeling in what line you have recovered by pulling the fish towards you.   Keep on repeating this, but always be ready to release the pressure on the reel immediately the fish shows signs of wanting to run again.

If the fish cannot be stopped and line is getting dangerously low on the reel try increasing the pressure and, if possible, apply side strain in an endeavour to turn the fish.   If it is obvious that the fish cannot be stopped and that you are going to lose all your line then lower your rod and point it at the fish at the same time stopping your reel completely and hold tight.   If you do this your line will probably break at the trace or at a knot and you will only lose a trace.   If, however, you allow the line to go so low on the spool that only a few turns are left it may break at the spool and all is lost.

This is the only time that you should allow the rod tip to drop. If you try to break the line by using the power of the rod you may break the rod itself.   Never allow a fish to pull down your rod. Give it line instead and keep your rod up as in this way you will continue to exert pressure and save the full strain from coming on the line. This is especially important in boat fishing for many a rod has been broken by the angler allowing a powerful fish to pull the rod down on the gunwale of the boat with disastrous results.

When the fish is brought within reach of the gaff put the reel in free spool, the check on, and control the drum by hand. Should the fish make a last desperate lunge or break off the gaff he can take line freely. If the brake is left on the sudden shock of the full weight of the fish falling on the line may cause a breakage. Remember also when bringing a fish alongside not to reel in so much line that the fish cannot be manoeuvered within reach.

When playing a big strong fish from a beach in conditions of heavy surf or from rocks or in an estuary where there are snags or heavy weed close in, do not be afraid to fight it on a long line. Let the fish tire itself out in the deep water behind the surf or away from the snags and when it is beaten it can easily be manoeuvered safely to the shore and landed. If you are sure that your hook has a secure hold do not be in too much of a hurry to land the fish, just keep it on a tight line and play it nice and easily. It is essential that a tight line be kept on the fish at all times. Never allow it slack line otherwise it may throw the hook, especially if it has a poor hold or has worn a hole and is loose in the fish's mouth. Should the fish jump on a short line drop the rod point to avoid the sudden shock on the line which may snap it. However, if there is a lot of line in the water when the fish jumps there is little you can do to cushion the shock.

Many fish when turned or indeed when first hooked run straight towards the angler. It is imperative that line be recovered quickly on the reel in order to keep in touch with the fish and to keep the line tight. This is not always easy in a boat but when beach fishing the angler can often run back up the beach as he recovers line, thus keeping the line tight. If a fish lashes and threshes about on the surface it usually means that it is being held too hard so yield line lest the head shaking throws the hook or the lashing tail part the trace.

Surprisingly enough, many fish can be led by exerting steady even pressure on them while any attempt at pumping or reeling will make them fight desperately. All that is required, provided that you have room to manoeuvre, is to stop the reel by thumb or finger pressure, keep the rod up and walk slowly and steadily backwards.   Do not attempt to use the reel at this stage but line can be recovered by walking forward to the point you started from recovering line as you go, without exerting any additional pressure on the fish other than keeping the line taut.   This is a very useful thing to be able to do when fish must be kept free of snags.

The landing of small fish presents little difficulty as they can usually be lifted out of the water by the simple expedient of catching the trace.   Never use the rod to lift them out as it imposes too great a strain which may break the rod or give it a permanent set. This applies to light tackle but anglers fishing from a height, i.e. from piers or rocks often use powerful rods and heavy line with which it is possible to lift fish up from the water.   However, it is preferable to use a dropnet for this purpose and so enjoy greater sport by being able to use lighter tackle.

All anglers should possess a stout gaff or large landing net for landing their fish.   In sea fishing generally a gaff is far more useful and usually safer than a landing net, especially when the fish are any way sizeable.   Never try to chase a fish with a net.   It is best to first submerge the net and then draw the exhausted fish over it, lifting the net so that the fish falls into it.   If the fish is on the large side try to get it head first into the net by lifting the head a little and then dropping the rod point quickly as the net is lifted over the fish.   This will usually cause the fish to drop head first into the net, obviating the danger of its being able to use its tail to jump out again.

When using a gaff never slash or swipe at the fish.   Draw it within comfortable reach, pick your spot and in one sure swift movement draw the gaff into the fish and lift it out of the water.   I prefer to gaff my fish from below to avoid crossing the trace, which can easily be fouled if you miss your stroke.   If you gaff from above or from the side be sure to do so behind and clear of the trace.   If possible gaff the fish under the lower jaw or in the shoulder, but do not mess about trying to gaff it in the gills lest you lose it.   If you do not have time to pick your spot gaff it wherever you can. Remember that many fish have hard scales, i.e. mullet, and if you try to gaff with the grain the point of the gaff will slide along the scales and not penetrate, so gaff across or against the grain.   The secret of good gaffing is to know what you want to do and to do it smoothly and positively.

A gaff or net is seldom needed on a beach because most fish can be easily beached and lifted out by hand when the sea is calm. Heavy surf presents difficulties, however, to the beginner but the strength of the surf can actually be used to advantage in landing the fish. Make sure that the fish is played out in the deeper, calmer water outside before attempting to draw it into the boiling surf. When you are sure that the fish is ready then draw it towards the shore. Once the fish is in the surf it will come towards you quickly on the incoming wave while the receding undertow will drag it back. As the fish is swept towards you reel in quickly and walk backwards, always keeping the line taut. As soon as the force of the undertow is felt walk forwards, again keeping the line tight and yielding line if necessary, but do not attempt to hold the fish as the pull of the receding wave may break the line or pull the hook out of the fish. The surge of the incoming wave will sweep the fish shorewards again and you repeat the process until the fish is swept up on the beach by the last wave. This may sound difficult but it is really quite easy and will come naturally provided you do not think too much about it.

Very shallow beaches present another problem in as much that big fish will strand themselves in the shallow water some distance from the shore. If you have not anticipated this and are not on the spot quickly with the gaff, the fish's violent struggles may throw the hook and enable it to get back to deeper water. When fishing from rocks and you cannot draw the fish within reach of the gaff it is often possible to manoeuvre a fish on to a ledge by using a suitable wave. You can then climb down and collect the fish but be careful of the following wave lest you get a wetting or worse.

Should you be caught without a gaff (and this should never happen) many fish can be lifted out of the water by inserting your hand in their gills. Take care, however, because many species have quite sharp teeth on their gills which will tear the skin if the hand is incautiously withdrawn. When handling bass in this manner be careful to avoid the sharp spine on the gill cover which can inflict a severe cut. Tope can easily be landed by hand for a secure grip can be taken on the narrow tail column or the dorsal fin.

All fish which are being kept should be killed immediately they are landed. You have had your sport so dispatch them right away and do not leave them to suffer needlessly. To leave them flapping around to die slowly is poor reward for the pleasure they have given you and many anglers I am afraid are very callous and unfeeling in this respect.   Most bony fishes are easily dispatched by a sharp blow on the back of the head with a "priest" or some heavy blunt instrument.   Tope, shark and dogfish are best killed by a heavy blow on the snout rather than on the head while the conger should be struck over its lymph heart, which is situated just behind the vent.

It is pointless and indeed terribly wasteful to kill more fish than you can use or dispose of.   If a fish is injured or damaged and is unlikely to survive then kill it by all means but if it is in good condition and you have no use for it why kill it and leave it there to rot.   You have had your sport so why not return it safely to the water.   The taking and keeping of undersized fish is also needless and is of particularly grave concern in the case of such slow growing species as bass, especially in areas where bass have grown scarce. You cannot expect to have many big fish if you are killing off the small ones and it is nauseating to see anglers keeping numbers of tiny school bass so small as to be hardly fit for cat food.

CHAPTER 6

THE ANGLER AFLOAT

WHEN IT COMES TO LOCATING FISHING GROUNDS YOU MUST
have some idea of what you are looking for. You cannot expect to
get good fishing by sailing off into the blue and dropping your baits
just anywhere. You may get good fishing but you will have a
much better chance if you know what you are doing. Different
species prefer different depths and different types of bottom and the
following table may prove a useful rough guide in this respect.

Species	Depths	Type of Bottom	Season	Remarks
Bass	Inshore	Beaches, estuaries, creeks	April/October	In summer may shoal some distance offshore
Mullet	Inshore	Beaches, estuaries, creeks, harbours	April/October	
Red Sea Bream	3-20 fathoms	On or near rocky ground	June/September	
Black Bream	3-20 fathoms	On or near rocky ground	End of April/ June	Distribution localised
Scad	Pelagic		Mid June/ Mid October	
Mackerel	Pelagic		Mid June/ Mid October	
Wrasse	2-10 fathoms	Rocky ground	May/ November	
Grey Gurnard	1-80 fathoms	Sandy bottoms	May/ September	
Tub Gurnard	5-50 fathoms	Sandy and mixed bottoms	May/October	
Red Gurnard	12 fathoms upwards	Mixed and low rough bottoms	April/October	
Plaice	7-50 fathoms	Sandy-gravelly-shelly ground	April/ November	
Flounder	Inshore	Beaches, estuaries, creeks	May/December	
Dab	1-50 fathoms	Sandy and muddy sand	May/February	
Halibut	20 fathoms upwards	Rough and mixed bottoms	July/December	Scarce
Turbot	3-80 fathoms	Sandy-muddy-gravelly bottoms	July/February	
Brill	3-80 fathoms	Sandy-muddy-gravelly bottoms	July/February	
Cod	15 fathoms upwards	Clean and mixed ground	July/February	Summer ⎫
	Inshore	Clean and mixed ground		Winter ⎭

Species	Depths	Type of Bottom	Season	Remarks
Haddock	15-50 fathoms	Soft bottoms	June/December	
Whiting	15-50 fathoms	Clean bottoms	July/January	Summer
	Inshore	Clean bottoms		Winter
Pouting	10-20 fathoms	Rough ground	May/January	
Pollack	1-20 fathoms	Rough ground	Mid April/ Early October	
Coalfish	10 fathoms upwards	Rough ground	Mid April/ Early October	
Ling	10 fathoms upwards	Rough ground	July/March	
Hake	15 fathoms upwards	Partly pelagic	Summer/ Autumn	Scarce
Garfish	Pelagic		May/ September	
Conger	1-70 fathoms	On or near rocky ground	All year	
Twaite Shad	Anadromous	Ascend rivers to spawn	April/ Early June	
Allis Shad	Anadromous	,,	April/ Early June	
Blue Shark	Pelagic		June/ September	
Porbeagle	Pelagic	Preference for rough ground	June/ September	
Tope	2 fathoms upwards	Mainly clean bottoms	April/October	
Spur Dogfish	2 fathoms upwards	Mainly clean bottoms	April/ November	
Lesser Spotted Dogfish	1 fathom upwards	All bottoms	All year	
Greater Spotted Dogfish		Deeper water and rougher ground than the Lesser Spotted Dogfish		
Thornback Ray	2-20 fathoms	Sandy-muddy-gravelly bottoms	All year	
Blonde Ray	10-40 fathoms	Clean ground	All year	
Common Skate	2 fathoms upwards	Clean and mixed bottoms	All year	

The above is a rough guide to the more common species and it will be appreciated that the arrival and departure of different species will depend on the locality and the season. The beginner may well ask how do you know what type of bottom you are fishing or how do you locate a particular type of bottom? If you are boat fishing in a long established angling centre the boatmen will know their grounds and be able to put you over proven angling marks. However, if you are looking for new ground, run your own boat, or are fishing an unexplored area, the most useful and indeed essential piece of equipment you need is an Admiralty Chart of the area. These are quite cheap, and apart from giving you the type of bottoms they are useful for navigation purposes and are well worth the few shillings they cost.

On the chart will be marked the depths, usually in fathoms (units of 6 feet) but sometimes in feet, at Mean Low Water Springs, i.e. the average height at low water on the spring tides. The depths are marked by numbers, while the type of bottom is marked by abbreviations and other useful information such as wrecks, dangerous reefs, rocks, tide direction and strength, by symbols. A

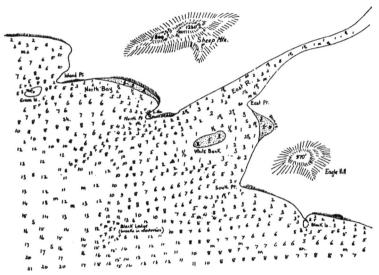

Portion of a Chart

Part of a hypothetical chart, simplified. Soundings in fathoms below mean low water of spring tides. Figures underlined are heights in feet above low water of banks etc. which strip.
m = mud, r = rocks, st = stones, sh = shells, s = sand.

separate sheet giving the full list of signs, abbreviations, etc., is published by the Admiralty and should be purchased with the chart. Quite obviously not every inch of the bottom can be surveyed and shown on these charts and the detail and distance between soundings will vary from chart to chart depending on the importance of the area covered from the point of view of shipping. The closeness of the soundings relative to the scale of the chart will give you an idea of how detailed the survey has been.

Where to expect or look for different types of fish will be dealt with in detail in later chapters under each particular species. It suffices to say here that recognised trawling grounds are usually of

little interest to the angler.   They are hard fished and besides commercial catches are taken on a long sweep of a trawl or net perhaps
hauled over several miles.   The total catch may have been taken in
a very small area on a long haul and it would be very difficult to say
exactly where.   This will not do for the angler who must be able
to locate himself over the exact spot where the fish are or in a place
where the fish will come to him, if he is to be successful.

Mixed or broken ground of alternating rough and clean bottoms
which cannot be trawled are far more productive for the angler
and here the old commercial fishmen who long lined or handlined
for a living can be of great assistance.   They knew their grounds
intimately and if you can get the marks from them it will save you a
lot of exploration.   Unfortunately, in many places the longliner is
a dying breed and if all the intimate knowledge of the fishing
grounds which they possess (often indeed handed down from
father to son over generations) is not obtained from them before
they die it may be lost for ever.   Other things to look for on a
chart are wrecks, submerged reefs, rocks, channels, banks of sand,
gravel or shell, deep holes in an otherwise flat or uniform bottom,
tideways and particular types of bottom suitable to certain species
of fish.

If you have picked out a likely fishing ground and want to find
it when you are out to sea it is not very difficult provided that you
have an elementary knowledge of navigation.   One way of doing
it is to examine your chart and see if a line drawn through and
joining two prominent and easily recognisable landmarks will cross
the ground in which you are interested.   This will give you the
direction and if you sail out to sea with these two landmarks in
line astern of you the boat will pass over the spot you have picked.
To find the exact spot you must have a cross bearing, i.e. two other
landmarks or marks, as they are generally known, in line taken
from a different angle from the first two.   Continue on your course
until the second pair of marks line up (come in line with one
another) and when this happens you should be right over the spot.
The nearer the two sets of marks are to being at right angles to
each other the more accurately you will be able to find the exact
position.   Marks such as described above are known as four point
bearings.

When you find good fishing ground you should always try to

take marks like this so that you may be able to find the same ground
again. Do not trust your memory, write them down and you will
always have them. The importance of accurately finding the exact
place or mark and of fishing directly over it cannot be over-
emphasised. In boat fishing a difference of a few yards can at times
mean the difference between a good bag and no fish at all. It can
be as critical as that. It is not unusual to find two anglers in the
same boat, both fishing exactly the same way and with the same

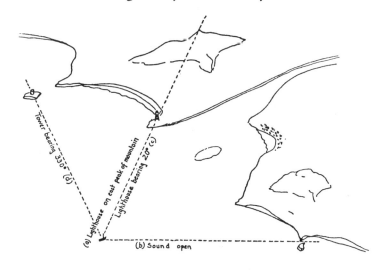

Four point and compass bearings

Locating a " mark " at sea (the " Black Ledge "
shown in the chart, page 131). (a) and (b) are four-
point bearings. In this particular case (b) does not
involve the alignment of a pair of objects as at (a),
since there is only one line of sight along which the
narrow sound is " open." (c) and (d) are compass
bearings, reading clockwise from N as 0°.

baits. One gets all the fish and the other does poorly or gets none
at all. One angler's bait is where the fish are feeding, the others
is not.

When you find your mark, do not drop the anchor on it, for you
must pay out rope for the boat to ride properly to the anchor and
you will end up with the anchor on the mark but with the boat a
considerable distance away from it. It is necessary to judge the
effect of both wind and tide and drop the anchor in such a position

that when sufficient rope has been paid out to hold the boat, that the boat will be directly over the mark. If the tide turns or the wind direction changes, the position of the boat will be altered and it may be necessary to haul up the anchor and relocate it so that the boat is brought back on the mark.

If you cannot find suitable marks on the chart you can quite easily lay a course to the spot you want to reach. For this you will require, in addition to the chart, a pair of parallel rulers and a compass. On every chart you will find a compass rose on which two compass cards are superimposed. One shows the true north whilst the other shows the magnetic north. The latter is the one which concerns us at the moment. Lay the parallel rulers on the line from your starting point to the one you wish to reach, and then work the rulers carefully down to the compass rose and read off the course. Be careful not to allow the rulers to slip as you work them for this will cause an error in the course you will read off.

The scale is also given on the chart and from this you can get the distance you must travel. If you know the speed of your boat you can time your journey fairly accurately. By steering the course by the boat's compass for the proper length of time you should arrive on or near the place you seek. However, there are several other factors which must also be taken into consideration when laying a course. The effect of tide, wind and compass deviation must be allowed for.

If you are travelling with the tide it will increase your speed and if against it your speed will be decreased. This is a point to remember in planning your fishing trips because it is often possible to arrange to be able to travel both to and from your fishing grounds with the tide, thus saving yourself both time and fuel. When the tide is with or against you allowance must be made for the altered time factor but if the tide is running at an angle to your course it will have the effect of pushing the boat off course unless this is allowed for. For example, say you are sailing from north to south at a speed of 7 knots and the tide is flowing from west to east at the rate of 2 knots. At the end of one hour you will have travelled 7 nautical miles but the boat will have been swept 2 miles east of the intended course. To allow for this drift draw a line joining your point of departure A and your destination B. From A draw a line parallel to the direction of the tide and on it measure off 2 nautical miles C. Point C must, of course, be downtide of the line A-B. Using a compass, measure off 7 miles and with C as your base draw an arc to intersect the line A-B at D. By steering the course C-D you will actually travel on the line A-B until you arrive at your

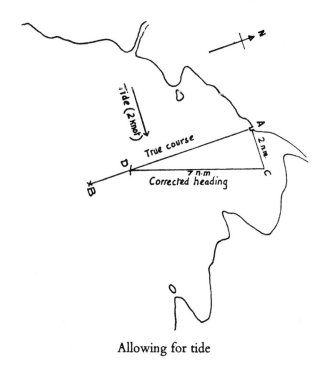

Allowing for tide

destination. You will in fact be "crabbing" across the tide and making good your intended course.

Wind has a similar effect in throwing a boat sideways off course, especially if the boat has a high cabin or a lot of top hamper which acts like a sail and catches the wind. If the wind is on your beam it will tend to blow you down-wind and if you watch the wake of the boat you will know if this is happening. The wake should run exactly opposite to the course you are steering and if it makes an angle to this course you are being blown to leeward. You should alter your course until the wake bears correctly and then you will counteract the effect of the wind.

The needle on your compass should point towards the magnetic north but it is easily deflected by the counter-attraction of any metal objects placed too near to it.   This deflection is known as deviation and the amount of error may vary on different courses.   A professional compass adjuster can make out a deviation card for your boat showing the amount of deviation on each point of the compass and once you know this you can make the necessary adjustments for each course you wish to steer.   However, any additional metal objects placed near the compass will cause further deviation.

It should be noted that the direction of the magnetic pole (to which the compass needle will point) varies slightly from year to year from that shown as the magnetic pole on the chart.   The annual variation will be marked on the chart and allowance must be made for it when plotting the compass course.

Another method is to use two compass cross bearings in the same way as four point bearings.   In this way a compass bearing is worked out from the spot you wish to fish, to two prominent landmarks, i.e. headlands, mountains, church steeples, etc., which are at a fairly wide angle to each other.   You sail out on one bearing and when the second mark bears the correct angle you are over your desired position.   A prismatic compass (one which possesses a sight through which you can line up an object and read off the angle it bears) is a very useful instrument for taking such bearings from the sea.   In using such a compass one must be careful to be far enough away from any metal in the boat, e.g. the engine, anchor, etc., in case the compass needle is affected.

Rocky and very soft bottoms are easily enough recognised by the feel of your sinker as you bounce it off the bottom.   Sandy, gravelly and shelly bottoms are rather more difficult and a sounding lead will be found very useful in this respect.   Any flatbottomed lead of sufficient weight will do provided you can make a hollow in the bottom which you can fill with tallow or heavy grease. When dropped on to the bottom, particles will adhere to the grease giving you a fair idea of the composition of the bottom.   Naturally a length of line should be attached to the lead in order to recover it and if you mark off the line in fathoms, either by a series of knots or different coloured pieces of cloth or string, each denoting a certain depth you will also be able to tell the depth of the water under the boat.   Thus once you arrive on the mark you can check if you are right by comparing the type of bottom and depth with that given on the chart.

In checking the depth you must allow for the rise or fall of the tide. Remember the depths given on the charts are those for mean low water springs and if you are fishing on a neap tide or high water there will be quite a difference in depth. The tide rises about one-twelfth of its total range on the first hour of flood, one-sixth on the second, one-quarter on both the third and fourth hours, one-sixth on the fifth and one-twelfth on the last hour, while the progression on the ebb is exactly the same, i.e. one-twelfth, one-sixth, one-quarter, one-quarter, one-sixth, one-twelfth. Your tide table (every sea angler should have one) usually gives the height of each tide at high water above M.L.W.S. and from this you can calculate what depth should be over the mark after allowance has been made for the stage the tide has actually reached when you are over the mark.

Of course if you are fortunate enough to have an echo sounder on board you will find it a wonderful aid. The most useful type of echo sounder is the one which traces a picture of the bottom on a graph. It will show the exact depths accurately and with practice you can read the type of bottom over which you are travelling. It will show reefs, rocks, holes, gullies, rough and clean ground, shoals of fish and even individual large fish. With intelligent use it will enable you to pinpoint productive fishing ground.

When it comes to locating fish near the surface, sea birds are far more adept than the angler. The sight of "fowl working" on the water is a sure sign of the presence of fish and is always worth investigation. Diving gannets are a familiar sight and a clue to the location of sprat, herring, or mackerel, while the height from which they dive will give you an idea as to how deep the fish are swimming. Concentration of "divers" in deep water, such as shags, cormorants, razor bills and guillemots, should not be ignored either. They will be feeding on small shoal fish and where small bait fishes are present in numbers they are usually being preyed upon by larger species.

When small bait fishes, such as sprat, herring and mackerel, fry, etc., are being driven to the surface by predatory fish large concentrations of fowl are attracted to the sight to join in the slaughter.

A large area may be covered with screaming excited gulls, terns, gannets and divers and a spinner, a feather jig or bait, fished around the edge of the general melee will usually result in fish. Tope, shark, bass, mackerel, pollack and cod may be taken in these circumstances and your bait is best fished near the edge of the shoal where it has a better chance of being seen and taken rather than in the centre where the fry are so thickly bunched that your bait or lure may not be noticed. Frequently, too, the angler will meet with patches of oil and tiny scales, sure evidence that a shoal of fish has been attacked by larger species. It is always worthwhile fishing the area for a while in case the odd fish is still around.

With so many people taking up sea angling nowadays and hiring out boats or buying their own for fishing a few words of general advice on the suitability of boats and boat handling in general may not be out of place. Newcomers to boating are often foolhardy and indeed many seasoned anglers who should know better take unnecessary risks. One should have a proper respect for the sea for at times it can be very treacherous and the first chance you take could very well be your last.

A boat for sea angling should have a fair draught that will give her a good grip in the water so that she may ride comfortably to an anchor and not roll too much in a sea. Ideally her beam should be about one-third of her length, she should have a reasonable amount of freeboard and a good deep well. Flatbottomed boats or those with a planing hull are not really suitable for angling. No doubt they are much faster and perhaps quite stable under way but when stopped they are not the safest boats from which to fish. If the boat is a large one, say 20 to 40 feet, with an inboard engine a certain amount of shelter in the form of a cabin is desirable. Do not go overboard, however, in this respect as one-third or one-half of the boat decked is quite enough otherwise there will be little room from which to fish.

Boats with excessive top hamper, i.e. those with high built up sides and cabins, should be avoided like a plague. They will catch too much wind when drifting, for the high superstructure will act like a sail. Besides, they are often poor sea boats and very difficult to manage in a wind even under power. The cabin deck should be flat, not curved or cambered, as they are dangerous to move about on, especially in a rough sea when one may have to get up on the cabin to haul the anchor. Flush decked boats, i.e. trawlers, are not suitable either for the angler is usually too high above the water to fight and gaff a heavy fish comfortably and in a rough sea these boats can be quite dangerous to fish from, as there is only a very low gunwale between the angler and the water.

Your first consideration in purchasing a boat is that she should be a good safe boat designed for sea work. Such a boat may be slow in comparison with fast speed boats but you are going angling and not water skiing, so settle for safety, comfort and a boat that will get you back to port safely if conditions are bad. The same applies to the smaller 14 to 18 foot craft usually powered by outboard engines. Car top dinghies and many of the light modern type boats may be all right for fresh water but in the sea you need a boat that can take rough work, ride out a sea and is not skittish when you have to move about in her. The older type of small boat on whose gunwales you could literally stand may have been heavy but they were safe.

Good engines are just as important as a good hull. Your engine must get you out and *back* and it is extremely foolhardy to put to sea with a faulty engine. Like the hull, the engine should preferably be a marine type specially designed for sea work and not a conversion. Normally the only faults in an engine which can be remedied at sea are those which occur in the ignition and fuel systems. Get to know your engine thoroughly whether it be an inboard or outboard and carry the necessary spare parts. If your engine is water-cooled always make sure that both the oil and water are circulating properly and check it from time to time.

A certain amount of basic equipment should always be carried. Every boat, big or small, should carry a compass even if it is only a small pocket compass which can be had for a few shillings. You should always have an anchor and sufficient sound rope to anchor the boat in any depth you are likely to fish in. If you intend to fish in 20 fathoms the same length of rope is not enough. No anchor will hold on too short a rope and you will need at least two and a half times the length of rope to give it a chance to get a proper purchase. Apart from fishing, should your engine break down, you will need the anchor, otherwise you are at the mercy of wind and tide and if you have no anchor or your anchor does not hold you may drift a long way before the engine can be fixed, or help arrive; or even worse, you may be wrecked on the shore.

When fishing over a rough or dirty bottom, a kedge is used to hold the boat, because the anchor could very easily foul in the bottom and be lost. The simplest type of kedge is a heavy stone; but as this frequently fails to hold securely in the bottom a grapnel is much more efficient. The grapnel should be made out of mild steel and must be strong enough to hold the boat but not so strong that if it fouls badly in the bottom that the prongs cannot be straightened out allowing the grapnel to be pulled free. When anchoring, head the boat into the tide or wind so that when the anchor is put over the side the boat drifts away from it. This will prevent the rope or chain from falling on top of the anchor, possibly fouling it and causing it to drag. Make sure that the anchor is properly secured to the rope before putting it out. Never throw the anchor out lest the rope foul in something causing the anchor to swing back and hit the boat or if the obstruction happens to be your leg, taking you with it.

Small boats should always carry at least three oars and three rowlocks in case one should be inadvertently lost over the side. Outboard engines must be secured to the boat by a length of rope in case of accidents. Bailers are also an essential item even in boats that are equipped with pumps, in case they fail. The bailers should be big enough to empty the boat quickly. With the modern synthetic materials now available it is possible to build in positive buoyancy in your boat, so that if the worst happens and she fills with water she will still float. If this happens your best plan is to stay with the boat and if you have had the foresight to fix hand rails to the keel you will be able to do so even if she capsizes.

There is nothing worse than fire at sea. The possibility of it happening to you may seem remote but it is always there, so you should have a fire extinguisher placed in a strategic and easily accessible position on board. Never throw water on a petrol or oil fire for instead of putting it out it only helps to spread the flames. If you do not have a fire extinguisher use wet sacks to try and smother the blaze. A fire in an outboard engine usually is easier to handle. The engine can always be dumped overboard.

The provision of proper life saving gear on a boat is one that is often sadly neglected. Unfortunately many anglers tend to sneer at those who use life jackets, insinuating that there is something cowardly about it. Nothing could be more stupid. I always carry a lifejacket and so should every other angler who fishes from a boat. You may never need it but if you do you will need it badly and in the meantime it is more comfortable than a hard thwart to sit on. It is quite easy to supply an amount of flotation gear in a boat and it need not be expensive. A couple of empty sealed petrol tins tied together will support a man in the water, so will kapok filled cushions, an oar and a number of other things that are handy in a boat at any time. Distress signals or flares are also a necessity or at least some means of summoning assistance when in danger. Remember that a white cloth attached to an oar held upright in a boat is a recognised signal of distress, while a powerful torch can be used to attract attention after dark.

When fishing from a boat, be it your own or someone else's, always keep it clean and tidy. Secure all loose gear and rods and stow them where they will not be in the way. In the excitement of fishing or if the boat is rolling it is quite easy to trip over a rod which has been carelessly left lying around or indeed a fishing bag, gaff or any other loose gear. Apart from causing injury, it is quite easy to break a rod in this way. Slippery decks are another hazard. If the fishing is good the decks can become very slimy or greasy and definitely dangerous in a rolling or pitching boat. Bring a box or sack in which to put your fish and wash the deck down occasionally. Do not leave pieces of bait lying around and cut up your bait on a board and not on the gunwale or a thwart. Always leave a boat as you would like to find it and it is not much trouble to clean her down on your way in after a day's fishing.

Nowadays one can hire a boat in many places in the same way as one can hire a car and often people who have little or no experience of boats are tempted to hire one out for a day's fishing. Those who intend to do a lot of this or who intend to purchase a boat of their own should get some knowledgeable seaman to show them the ropes, so to speak, or should read some good books on the subject. There is no room in a book of this nature to go into detail on seamanship but a few elementary facts on boat handling may be useful to some readers.

A car is steered by its front wheels but a boat in contrast is steered by its stern. When the rudder is turned either to left (port) or right (starboard) the force of the water acting on it slews the stern to one side and the bow to the other, causing the boat to turn. Thus, if the rudder is turned to starboard the bow will turn in the same direction while the stern is being slewed around to port. If the boat has a steering wheel it can be steered in the same way as a car, i.e. you turn the wheel to the left to turn the boat to the left. If the steering is by means of a tiller you must remember that if you want to turn to port you must put the tiller to starboard so that the rudder will be turned to port. Another point to remember is that due to propeller torque a boat will turn more easily and more readily in one direction than in the other. A propeller which turns anticlockwise will give the bow a tendency to go to starboard when the boat is moving ahead but to port when it is going astern. The reverse is true of a propeller which turns in a clockwise direction. A few minutes at the tiller will show you which way she tends to turn and full advantage should be taken of this tendency in manoeuvering the boat.

When approaching a moorings or a quay the approach should be made against the tide or if there is little or no tide but a strong wind is blowing then approach against the wind. Slow down in good time, judge your distance, put the engine into neutral and let the way of the boat take her in. There are no brakes on a boat and when the engine is stopped the forward motion or "way" of the boat will still carry her forward for a while. The tide or wind will act as a brake slowing the boat down and so will putting the engine in reverse. If you approach with the tide or wind behind you they will help carry you on and as once the engine is stopped you will have lost "way," the rudder will not steer the boat properly.

You should always make your approach in such a manner that should you come in too fast or overshoot your mark, that you can sheer away in safety and try again. Leaving a quay or moorings is usually much easier than approaching them but care should be taken that your mooring ropes do not trail under the stern lest they foul your propeller. Remember, too, when tying up alongside to make allowance for the rise and fall of the tide, and adjust your ropes accordingly.

If you do get caught in a bad sea, keep a cool head and do not panic. Beginners should not attempt to run before a big sea because a big following wave can make the steering of the boat very difficult and at times unmanageable. There is the danger of the boat then broaching to (turning broadside to the waves) or of being pooped or flooded by a breaking following wave. If conditions get too bad turn the boat and head her into the waves, slowing down the engine so that the boat rides the waves comfortably and is not being driven hard into them. Even in a storm the wave pattern is not uniform and usually after a few dangerous waves pass you will get a few smaller waves which will give you a chance to turn the boat. Wait for a lull, watch your opportunity and act positively.

If your course takes you across the waves at an angle it may be wiser to travel against the waves until you are far enough up wind of your destination that you can turn and run downwind to it in safety. A bad sea on your beam can be very dangerous. With experience you will get to know what waves are dangerous and what are not. You can keep your course on the smaller waves but alter your course to take the bad ones dead astern or dead ahead. Make sure that your boat is properly trimmed. If you have passengers aboard they may all go into the cabin forward to avoid getting wet and their combined weight may put her down by the head, causing her to plunge heavily into the sea and take water. It will also lift the rudder and propeller up or perhaps partly out of the water, making the boat difficult to steer or even unmanageable. If too much weight is concentrated in the stern the bow will be raised out of the water where it will catch the wind and make steering difficult. Distribute the weight evenly, even though it may mean that some of your passengers get a bit of a drenching. In a small boat when things seem bad, sit down low in the boat, on the floor boards, to lower the centre of gravity and distribute the weight evenly.

See that everything is secure in the boat and that there is nothing loose or rolling about, especially your mooring ropes or anchor, for if they are swept overboard they may foul in your propeller with disastrous results. Do not drive the boat so hard that she will ship green water over the bow, and take advantage of every bit of shelter that you can, even if it means going the long way round.

Give yourself plenty of sea room and avoid a lee shore because should something go wrong you may find yourself quickly blown on to it. Avoid fast tideways, narrow channels and overfalls where the sea can be very nasty and dangerous when the wind is against the tide, even in a fresh wind. Submerged reefs or rocks are usually easy enough to see in bad weather as the sea will break over them, whilst in calm conditions the darker colour of the water will give you a clue as to their location. The same applies to shallow sandbanks or bars, the sea will break over them when it is rough, whilst the lighter colour of the water betrays their position when it is calm. If things get very bad seek shelter and ride it out until conditions improve. Always play for safety. You may find that when the tide slackens or changes and runs with the wind that the seas will moderate and passages that were too dangerous to negotiate a few hours before are now passable.

Beginners are often inclined to run an engine flat out to gain more speed. Except in the case of boats with planing hulls this is a false notion. A boat's speed through the water is more or less limited by her design and if she is designed to do 7 knots she may do that on three-quarter throttle and giving her full throttle will make her go no faster. With the engine going like mad you may get the impression that you are going faster but all you are doing is burning more fuel and perhaps harming the engine.

Before we leave the subject of boats there may be no harm in mentioning the "Rules of the Road". All boats under power must give way to those under sail except when a sailing boat is overtaking as the boat overtaking must always keep clear of the boat in front. All boats, whether approaching from ahead, from one side or other or from astern must be passed "port to port", i.e. left side to left side. Thus, if a boat is approaching from dead ahead you keep to the right so that she passes you on your left. If a boat is converging on you from the starboard or right side you must keep clear and alter your course to starboard to pass behind her stern. If a boat is converging on you from the port side you have the right of way and it is her duty to keep clear of you.

If you remember that at night vessels should carry a red light on the port side and a green light on the starboard side the following rhymes will help you memorise the rules of the road.

"If on your starboard red appear,
'Tis your duty to keep clear,
to act as judgement says is proper,
To port or starboard, back or stop her.

But when upon your port is seen
a power boat's starboard light of green,
there is not much for you to do,
for green to port keeps clear of you."

The starboard and port lights should show an unbroken light over 10 points of the compass (112½ degrees) from dead ahead to 2 points (22½ degrees) abaft the beam. Thus, the following rhyme will do for two power craft meeting or passing:—

"When both sidelights appear ahead,
Starboard your wheel and show your red.
Green to green and red to red
Perfect safety, go ahead."

Always keep a good look out when at sea and do not depend on the other fellow to do so. When in doubt keep well clear or slow down and whatever action you intend to take, do it in good time so that the other skipper will know what you intend to do.

"Both in danger and in doubt,
Always keep a good look out,
In danger with no room to turn,
Ease her, stop her, go astern."

Weather plays a very important part in fishing and a little weather wisdom is a very useful thing. Weather forecasts these days are usually very reliable and certainly no boat angler should put to sea without having some idea of the kind of weather he can expect. They are also a big help to the shore angler and will give him a hint as to what conditions on the shore will be and enable him to choose his fishing ground accordingly.

Weather forecasts must of necessity cover large areas and cannot cover purely local conditions. Weather in these islands can be very local and conditions in two places not very far apart can differ radically although the forecast for the whole area may hold good. Through experience and observation we may become quite good in anticipating the kind of weather we can expect by reading the signs in the ever changing pageant of the clouds, and from the strength and direction of the wind.

Roughly speaking, there are three types of clouds, fine weather clouds, storm clouds and the inbetween type that give us showery weather. One of the lowest cloud formations is the *nimbus cloud*, which covers the sky in dense dark monotonous sheets during periods of continuous heavy rain. If you notice numerous high thin clouds which shoot out in different directions above the nimbus as it approaches you may be sure that the rain will be heavy and .lasting. If, however, there are not many of these clouds the rain will be lighter and soon pass over. As the nimbus clears it is usually followed by an ugly ragged cloud (*rag cloud*) accompanied by strong winds and if these grow smaller the weather is about to clear, but if they should increase then you can expect a gale.

Banks of soft white downy clouds which drift across the summer sky often disappearing towards evening are known as *fair weather cumulus*. Sharp or hard-edged cumulus, which rears up majestically from a broad flat base, is known as *shower cumulus* and it tends to increase and cover the greater part of the sky towards evening. Sometimes this type of cloud may form quickly in an absolutely clear sky, catching you unawares and leaving you soaked to the skin. It is a turbulent type of cloud, often standing a mile high, and may bring a sudden squall in its wake which could be dangerous for small boats. Cumulus clouds, which come up in the middle of the day with the wind, are usually the fair weather kind but should they increase in density towards evening, unsettled weather may be expected.

An easily recognised type of cumulus is the *thunder cloud*, which rears up in dense turbulent masses splashed with silver or copper. It has hard sharp edges and is often seen travelling against the wind.

The coming of wind and unsettled weather may often be foretold by the higher type of cloud. *Cirro-cumulus*, small dappled clouds seen high in the sky during a fine spell, foretell a change for the worse but the immediate weather will be the unsettled type that is neither wet nor fine for long. This is the "mackerel sky" of the old sailors and is remembered in the rhyme "Mackerel sky and mares' tails make tall ships carry low sails".

The mares' tails refer to the feather-like tufts or threads of the highest type of cloud, *cirrus*. It is a very thin cloud very high in the sky and its feathery appearance is caused by high winds. A lot can be learned from watching this cloud. If it loses alititude quickly and develops into sheets of cloud the rain is not far away and the wind will blow in the direction the clouds are travelling in. If the feather-like streamers are pointing upwards it means that the cloud is falling and that rain is on the way but if the fingers are pointing downwards then the cloud is still rising and the opposite holds good.

If the delicate streamers are brushed backwards at the tips it indicates that the wind will eventually change its direction to that of the cloud. If that direction is south-west or south-east then rain and high winds can be expected.

Slow moving clouds indicate fine weather but fast moving clouds mean unsettled weather. If the small clouds which come up in late afternoon increase and fill the sky, expect rain, but if they decrease towards evening the fine weather will continue. Clouds which form very high in the sky after a fine spell foretell a gradual change to wet weather but gradual changes are more certain and the rain more prolonged when it comes. Clouds with hard sharply defined edges mean stormy weather whilst soft fluffy clouds mean fine weather.

Many old sayings have a lot of truth in them and are basically sound. "Rain before seven fine before eleven" is a good example, as a wet morning often clears up as a front passes through. However, if it starts to rain at around 8 to 9 a.m. or 8 to 9 p.m. the outlook is poor and a wet day is ahead. Another bad time is around 2 o'clock in the afternoon, as the weather usually does not clear before evening. "Red in the morning shepherd's warning, red at night shepherd's delight" is also a fair guide, but a pale watery sunset usually means rain.

There are other signs too. Watch the sea birds. When they take to the beach and the ground you may be sure that bad weather is on the way. Smoke, too, is worth watching. When it rises straight up the weather will be calm and clear but if it drifts downwards the outlook is poor. You will often notice during a period of fine calm weather that a big heave or swell rises on the sea making white water all along the shore. These high long swells are an indication of strong winds on the way.

If you possess a barometer learn to use it properly. It is a very reliable guide to the weather but remember that it is not the position of the needle that counts so much as whether it is stationary, rising or falling and, of course, the rate at which it rises or falls. If you learn to use a barometer correctly you will seldom be caught napping by the weather.

In boat fishing it never pays to take chances with the weather. If the forecast is bad and the outlook poor do not go afloat. When you are at sea keep a watchful eye on the weather and watch for the signs. A moderate wind can freshen to a hard blow in a remarkably short time. If you have any doubts, up anchor and come in out of it in good time. Do not be foolish and hang on for that extra half hour or more. It is never worth it.

Weather affects the actual fishing in many ways. Heavy gales scatter ground feeding species in water affected by heavy wave action and fishing may not pick up again until conditions are settled. Rough seas and strong winds scatter the shoals of small fry and the larger fish that prey on them seek their food on the bottom once again. Small fry tend to swim against the wind so that onshore breezes tend to take the shoals out to sea whilst offshore winds bring them close to the land. They tend to seek shelter out of the wind so that they may be found on one side of a bay, harbour or headland today and on the other tomorrow if the wind should change its direction.

Flatfish prefer calm conditions while bass like a fair amount of movement on the water. On beaches they take best in a nice surf but a very heavy pounding surf is not good. In very calm conditions they may keep to deeper water, moving into the shallows after dark. The direction from which the wind is blowing may make one beach good for fishing while another one would fish poorly. Fish often feed better before an impending blow or after a gale when the water is beginning to clear.

You must learn how the weather affects the fishing in your own area and this is where keeping a fishing diary is a big advantage. If you conscientiously note down everything after a day's fishing, what at the end of the year or over the years you will be amazed at you can learn by studying your diary. If you rely on your memory however, there is a lot you will forget or you will fail to draw the correct conclusions because some salient facts have slipped your mind. Enter down the type of weather, wind direction and force, condition of the sea and stage of tide, the presence or absence of drifting weed, which often makes fishing a nightmare or quite impossible. It may take a little time to enter all the pertinent facts but it is well worth the trouble. Besides, it makes you think about the things that affect your fishing, and that alone is something accomplished.

CHAPTER 7

DO'S AND DONT'S

IN ANGLING, AS IN ANY OTHER SPORT, THERE ARE CERTAIN codes of behaviour and methods of fishing that the sportsman is expected to conform to. The rules of angling are much more elastic and less rigid than those governing other sports and though they are unwritten rules they are nevertheless there. In competition fishing the rules are quite rigid but in general fishing an angler's conscience must be to a great extent his guide as to what is fair and sporting.

Fair angling is generally held to mean fishing with rod, reel and line as distinct from nets and handlines. The fish is offered a bait or lure which it is free to accept or reject and if accepted it should be hooked in the mouth. To purposely allow a fish to gorge a bait so that when struck it is hooked in the stomach is not sporting. No fish hooked in this manner can put up much of a fight and to do this deliberately is something which should be abhorrent to any real angler. Strokehauling, snatching or the use of tackles calculated to foul-hook a fish is not considered fair angling but the accidental foul hooking of a fish is a different matter.

The angler should hook, play and bring the fish to the gaff unaided. He can obtain assistance in gaffing the fish but no angler can take pride in claiming a fish which has been played or handlined in for him by another. Tackle should be sporting and matched to the strength and speed of the fish being sought. The use of tackle which is too powerful gives the fish no chance and the angler little pleasure but the other extreme of fishing too light should also be avoided. Many anglers who fish with extremely light tackle consider it reflects creditably on their skill; but to fish so light that the fish is more likely to be lost than landed or landed after an unreasonably long period can hardly be considered sporting.

When fishing in the company of other anglers, show them the courtesy you would expect to be shown to you. On the shore, do not encroach on another angler's space but fish at a reasonable distance from him.   If you had got to the spot first you would resent being crowded out.   If you must fish near him or are fishing in a boat, be sure to fish in such a manner that your gear does not foul his.   In boat fishing, lines can usually be kept clear of each other by the simple expedient of using sinkers of different weights, those fishing near the bow using more lead than those in the stern so that their terminal tackle is not swept down to foul the other angler's gear. Whether fishing from the shore or from a boat, always hold your rod so that you will know if your gear is wandering.   Besides, you will catch more fish that way.   If you must put your rod down in a boat, be sure to secure it with a rope to a thwart or a staunchion lest it disappear over the side when your back is turned.   You should also check that the line is not caught around the end ring.

When another angler hooks a big fish, especially one which runs, do not wait to be asked to take your gear in, but do so at once.   Not only will you give him room to "work" the fish but you will save a lot of time on tangled traces and the consequent frayed tempers. Be quick to lend assistance when asked, especially in gaffing or landing a fish.

Due care should be taken when casting.   A 4 oz. sinker can be as lethal as a bullet, so be sure that hook or sinker is not likely to hit anyone before you make your cast.   Avoid damage to other people's property.   Leave a boat as you would like to find it.   Do not leave litter on the shore; burn it or bury it; and if you must cross private property, be sure not to damage crops or leave gates open behind you.   Others may suffer on account of your careless-ness or thoughtlessness.

Some anglers find themselves unpopular because they are chronic borrowers, never having enough tackle or bait of their own.   No angler will see another stuck for bait or tackle unless he is short himself.   Those who make a habit of borrowing, however, will soon find themselves left severely alone.   You should always take good care of your tackle but if you do borrow some item of equip-ment, such as a rod or reel, be sure to take even better care of it and return it in the same condition as you received it.

There are many dangers attached to fishing and occasionally a nasty accident occurs through carelessness or failure to take a few simple precautions.   I have already mentioned the dangers in casting and of slippery decks, especially in a rolling boat.   Care should also be taken in small boats when shifting position or standing up, lest the boat capsizes. It is very easy to get a hook stuck in your hand or finger, especially if you are using a feather jig. Do not try to pull the hook out if the barb is in the flesh. Cut off the eye of the hook with pliers and push the hook right through and out again. A basic first aid kit, consisting of a disinfectant or iodine, bandages and plasters, will take up little room in your tackle bag and should always be carried.

Nylon monofilment, because of its thinness and elasticity, can be very dangerous. If your trace fouls the bottom be careful as you try to break clear. Never look towards the spot where you are stuck lest the lead suddenly break free and come rocketing back at you. A friend of mine lost an eye when struck in this way. Nylon can also slice through wet hands like a knife through butter, if you endeavour to handline your tackle free or try to break your line. Grasp the line with a thick cloth or else wind it around your arm provided that you have covered it with a heavy garment.

A number of tragedies have occurred in rock fishing when anglers have been swept off their perches by an unexpected big wave. Take no chances and leave if conditions get too rough or chancy. If you are caught by a big wave, it is best to cling like a limpet to the rock, pressing yourself closely to it, rather than to grasp hold of it. This way you minimise the danger of the receding wave sucking you off. Remember, too, that wet rocks can be very slippery, especially where covered with Enteromorpha, and never go down into a place that you are unlikely to be able to climb out of, no matter how tempting the fishing may be. Quick-sands are another danger, but usually their location is well known locally and sometimes they are posted with danger signs. What is not often appreciated, however, is that mud can be equally dangerous. A few inches of mud with firm ground underneath is one thing, but deep soft mud where a man can sink to his thighs or worse is an entirely different kettle of fish, as anyone who has been stuck helplessly in it will vouch for. The best solution when stuck badly in mud like this is to lie flat on it, repugnant though the thought may be. It will support your weight if it is spread over a large area.

Some species of fish are very dangerous to handle, as they possess poisonous stings, i.e. the Greater and Lesser Weever, while the Sting Ray can inflict a bad wound with the jagged and poisonous spine attached to its whip-like tail. Many fish have dangerous teeth. The conger is high on this list and as it is so tenacious of life it should be placed in a sack or lidded box, because if left on deck it will slither around and someone may be unfortunate enough to put his foot in its mouth. A rubber boot offers little protection against its sharp teeth. All sharks possess sharp teeth and I make it a practice, as I do with conger, to carry spare traces which dispense with the necessity of having to retrieve the hook before the fish is truly dead.

Ling and hake also have sharp teeth, whilst large skate have

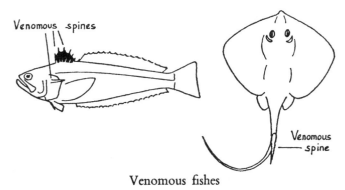

Venomous fishes

Left : Lesser Weever, *Trachinus vipera.*
Right : Sting Ray, *Trygon pastinaca.*

tremendous crushing power in their jaws. Be careful when handling a spurdog, for the sharp and poisonous spines in front of the two dorsal fins can inflict a nasty wound. I always make a practice of breaking off the spurs with pliers before endeavouring to unhook the fish. The two spotted dogfishes, with their rough rasping skins, can inflict a painful "burn" on the unwary and one which takes a long time to heal. Many species which have spiny fins or gill covers, such as bass, mullet and gurnards, should be handled carefully and anglers are inclined to forget that fish like cod and pollack have tiny teeth in the gills. These can give your fingers a rasping if you are careless in withdrawing them.

As in everything else you do at sea, be sensible and careful. If you catch a fish that you are not familiar with, handle it with care just in case it is one of the dangerous ones.

CHAPTER 8

BASS

NO OTHER SPECIES, APART FROM THE POWERFUL TOPE, EXCITES the imagination of the shore angler to the same extent as the bass. A strong, lusty fighting fish, it is a game and a worthy foe and the most sought after of all our inshore species. Unfortunately, it is not distributed all around our coasts, being most plentiful in the south and south-west. A warm water species, it is nearing the northerly limit of its range around these islands and with the exception of the far south, it is a summer visitor to our waters.

Bass are plentiful along the south coasts of Britain and Ireland but as one travels northwards they become less numerous, and north of Anglesey in Wales and the estuaries of the rivers Boyne and Moy in Ireland they have become scarce. Bass have been taken as far north as Donegal and Derry but in Scotland they have been recorded on only a few occasions and they are rare.

The arrival of bass inshore in the spring varies greatly and depends on the locality and the weather. In the far south, i.e. in Cornwall and Kerry, especially in mild winters, they may never leave the shore and provide fishing all through the year. Along the south and south-west coasts they have been taken as early as February but generally speaking they are not taken by anglers in numbers until mid or late April. They arrive progressively later the further north you go and in the colder waters of the Irish sea around the latitude of Dublin it is seldom worthwhile fishing for them before the end of May and they are gone again by the end of September. On the south coast the bigger bass begin to disappear about the end of October or early November but small school bass probably stay close inshore in river mouths and estuaries in the south through the winter, but they tend to frequent deeper water than was their habit in the summer.

It has not yet been established where bass go in winter but it is probable that their autumn migration is partly southerly and into deeper water. (Numbers of large bass have been taken in trawls during November in depths of 60 fathoms west of the Blasket Islands off the coast of Co. Kerry.) When they return in spring they are usually found in shoals off river mouths and estuaries, such as Youghal in Co. Cork, where large concentrations of bass are often seen about mid April. These shoals break up later and the bass start foraging for themselves. By nature bass are solitary fish except as young fish when they remain in shoals and are known as "school bass". The older fish, however, are more or less solitary although large numbers of them may be present on a beach or in an estuary and they remain this way except when small bait fishes are plentiful (as happens in July and August) when bass may be drawn from a large area to combine in shoals some distance from the shore to harry the small fry.

Bass spawn over a protracted period, usually from the middle of or late April to the end of June. How or where they spawn in these islands has not yet been definitely established but it is almost certain to take place in our inshore waters. The males are ripe over a long period but only a portion of the eggs in the ovaries of the females ripen together and spawning must take place on several different occasions. This no doubt has evolved to suit the more or less solitary habits of bass and the female sheds the ripe portion of her eggs whenever and wherever she meets a suitable mate. This protracted spawning also accounts for the fact that, unlike the cod or herring which shed all their spawn together, the bass is never spent in the same sense as these fishes and even during spawning time is in reasonably good condition. Bass are usually mature and able to spawn when they are five or six years old but there is some evidence that the males may mature a year or two earlier than the females. The females live much longer and grow much bigger than the males, few males over 5 lb. are taken and all the really big bass are almost certain to be females.

Bass are very active foragers and voracious feeders yet they are a surprisingly slow growing species. The following table of weights and ages taken from a cross-section of bass caught in different areas may be of interest to readers:—

Inches	Weight	Sex	Age in Years	Month
9.1	6 oz.	F.	3 plus	September
11.1	11½ ,,	F.	3 ,,	,,
11.9	12 ,,	F.	3 ,,	,,
11.4	12½ ,,	M.	3 ,,	,,
16.9	1 lb. 15¾ ,,	F.	7 ,,	,,
	3 ,, 6 ,,	F.	11 ,,	July
19.9	3 ,, 8 ,,	M.	11 ,,	September
20.0	3 ,, 8 ,,	F.	9 years	May
20.75	3 ,, 12 ,,	F.	11 ,,	,,
21.5	4 ,, 0 ,,	F.	10 years	,,
19.4	4 ,, 0 ,,	F.	7 plus	September
20.75	4 ,, 8 ,,	F.	11 years	,,
20.6	4 ,, 8 ,,	M.	13 plus	,,
21.6	5 ,, 0 ,,	F.	13 ,,	,,
22.4	5 ,, 2 ,,	F.	12 ,,	,,
24.7	6 ,, 2 ,,	F.	11 years	June
24.9	6 ,, 12 ,,	F.	14 ,,	,,
26.25	7 ,, 8 ,,	F.	12 ,,	May
25.4	8 ,, 2 ,,	F.	13-14 plus	September
26.05	9 ,, 5½ ,,	F.	13 ,,	,,
29.75	10 ,, 8 ,,	F.	16 ,,	
	10 ,, 9 ,,	F.	18 ,,	August
31.00	12 ,, 6 ,,	F.	17 ,,	September

The reader will notice a great disparity in age between fish of almost the same weight and this can partly be explained by the month in which they were caught. A fish taken in September that has had a chance to feed up during the summer will weigh considerably more than it would have in May or June shortly after it had spawned. However, it is more difficult to explain the age range of 7 to 13 years between fish of 4 lb. to 5 lb. 2 oz. taken in September, that a 3½ lb. fish taken in the same month was over 11 years of age while one of 4 lb. was only 7 years old. A fish's growth potential is greatest in its earlier years and the amount of growth it can make depends on the amount of food available in the locality in which it finds itself and on how successful it is in obtaining this food.

One thing, however, is abundantly clear and that is the folly of unnecessarily killing small school bass. The average run of decent sized bass is from 2½ to 6 lb. and only a small proportion of these will live to grow to 10 lb. or more. If the small fish under 2 lb. are indiscriminately killed the potential number of takeable fish is considerably reduced and the possibility of a few really big specimens almost eliminated. Due to their slow growth, bass are a species whose numbers could be seriously reduced or even fished out, and if anglers only appreciated this fact, the painful sight of small immature fish taken from beach or pier would disappear.

The bass is a fish of the shallow inshore waters and travels far on the tide in search of food. At times the bass may be found in a foot of water right up on the shore, or again combining with other bass a mile or two offshore to prey on shoals of small bait fishes. Favourite haunts are mixed beaches of sand and rock, the broad mud flats of estuaries, tideways, channels and steeply shelving beaches of coarse sand. The bass can tolerate a certain amount of fresh water and will travel far up estuaries and river mouths on the tide but will not go quite as far as the mullet. The larger and more solitary bass seem to have a liking for a rocky coast, the type of coast which when the tide strips reveals rock pools and gullies rich in food.

Bass are voracious feeders and their diet is very varied. The most common item found in the stomachs of bottom feeding bass is the common shore crab although I have also found small specimens of the edible crab as well as swimming crabs and masked crabs. The sand shrimp is an important food of bass foraging over shallow sandy beaches and prawns are also commonly found in them. Fish are a very important item in the diet of bass, especially when such small bait fishes as herring and pilchard fry, sprats and sandeels are present in quantity. Sandeels are a favourite food and so are baby flatfish. Indeed any small fish, i.e. the young of mullet, pollack, coalfish, whiting or gobies, wrasse, sea scorpions, butterfish, blennies, are fair prey to a hungry bass. In river mouths the larger bass sometimes prey on migrating salmon and sea trout smolts. The smaller fish (school bass) feed largely on small crustaceans, shrimps, amphipods, slaters and small fishes. Worms, shellfish and a variety of organisms turn up in bass stomachs from time to time but do not form an important part of their diet.

Indeed many organisms which make excellent baits are not very frequently found in bass. Lugworm is an excellent example and so are razorfish, clams, ragworms, squid, hermit crabs and piddocks. Bass can be taken on a large variety of natural baits but soft or peeler crab is about the best all round bait, especially when used in the vicinity of rocks. It has the added advantage of suffering less from the ravages of crabs where these are plentiful and where a fish or worm bait would be torn to shreds in a matter of minutes.

A very useful bait where it can be obtained is the Hermit Crab. Lugworm and ragworm are also first class baits in estuaries and on beaches but for night fishing the lugworm in my opinion is the better of the two. Prawns are also excellent and razorfish, clams, piddock and even mussel and large cockles will be taken readily. The most attractive fish baits are sandeels (fished alive they are far more effective than when dead), a lash of herring, mackerel or squid, and such small fishes as sprats, small flatfish, and butterfish.

Beach fishing is one of the most rewarding forms of bass fishing but it is also the one which poses the biggest problem to the beginner. Confronted with a beach perhaps half a mile long or maybe stretching away into the distance for several miles it is no wonder that he should feel at a loss and not know where to start. Some beaches are very productive, others very poor, while even on a good beach only certain parts may provide good fishing.

Beaches vary greatly in their nature and extent and before tackling the problem we should know something about the different types of beaches. In general they can be broken down into three main types: shingle beaches, surf beaches of small gravel and coarse sand, and flat firm beaches of muddy sand. These are not arbitrary divisions as many beaches are a mixture of the three main types but the predominant feature of a mixed beach determines the kind of fishing one can expect on it.

The shingle beach is usually a very exposed one on which heavy surf or wave action builds up the steep banks of shingle. It is usually found on a rugged exposed coast or it may be formed as a spit in estuaries, bays or near headlands where strong tidal currents build it up. It is the most unstable of beaches and for that reason holds little or no fish food. It usually shelves steeply into deep water or is washed by fast tides or strong currents. It is on the whole the least productive type of beach but at times when small fry or sandeels are plentiful it can provide good fishing. The strong tides or fast currents may channel the small fish along this type of beach or continuous offshore winds may bring the shoals right in on the shore. In these conditions good bass fishing can be enjoyed.

The second type of beach is usually an exposed one facing into the prevailing winds and open to the surging sea. The sand is usually coarse in texture, often gravelly and when a big sea is running or in bad weather, heavy surf breaks all along its length. Near low water mark the beach is shallow, sloping gradually upwards towards high water mark where it rises quite steeply and is often backed by sand dunes. This type of beach also looks unstable and barren of food except below low water mark where the coarse sand may give way to a finer and more productive bottom. However, this type of surf beach has a fascination for bass and provides the best and most interesting beach fishing for them. The loose coarse sand is often the home of sandeels, which can be very plentiful locally, and in the more sheltered parts of the beach lugworm may be present. Atherines may be present on this type of beach while higher up on the shore the sand may contain amphipods and in some places Idotea (a long slater-like animal) and small flatfish may be numerous. At times small fry can be plentiful and I have seen bass shoal after them on this type of beach.

The first two types of beaches mentioned are *storm beaches* but the last type is only found in sheltered situations which are not exposed to heavy wave action. It is usually flat or gently sloping and composed of firm muddy sand corrugated and rippled by gentle wave action. It is a most stable beach, very rich in fish food. Its surface will be speckled by the castings of extensive beds of lugworm whilst cockles are usually plentiful and down near the low water mark razorfish may be present. In the pools and channels left by the receding tide will be found shrimps, gobies, baby flatfishes, mullet fry, small crabs and other aquatic creatures. Because of its very richness it is the most difficult of all beaches to fish. Food is so plentiful that bass can be scattered anywhere on it and it is often difficult to locate them or to find a spot where they are present in numbers.

These are the three main types of beaches but of course it is only a general classification. No two beaches are alike and often a beach is a combination of two or even three types and even a portion of a very sheltered beach may in certain weather conditions become a surf beach. Anglers must get to know the characteristics of each type of beach and learn to read a beach in the same way as a trout angler learns to read a stretch of river. Fish will be taken all along a beach occasionally but some places fish better than others or may only fish well at a certain stage of the tide. Some stretches may be very unproductive and a waste of time to fish You must learn to recognise the likely spots and the times at which they should be productive. Never fish blindly but think about your fishing before you start and you will find that you will be more successful.

Make a practice of studying the beach you intend to fish at low water and try to sum it up. Look for the places that would attract bass, where food is plentiful and which they are likely to visit on the coming tide. Look also for snags such as rock and weed or anything that is likely to foul your gear. Note these places carefully and if their situation is critical pace off distances so that you will know how far you must cast. Remember that a beach will look entirely different when the tide is in and you may not be able to locate the spots you have picked unless you have lined them up with some prominent object *above high water mark*. This is especially important when night fishing, as even familiar objects look different after dark and it is essential to know that one is fishing in the right place.

On steep shingle beaches there is a point where the slope of the beach suddenly drops off into deeper water. When the tide is in, it is along this shelf that the fish will forage and that is where your bait should be placed. In moderate or light surf such beaches may be fished with light bottom gear, for long casts are not essential as the bass may be no more than a few yards from the edge. The same applies to spinning. Do not cast straight out but rather cast at a tangent so that your bait will fish along the shelf and just behind the surf where the bass are feeding. Fish places where the tide or current sets in against the beach or is set off by some projection. Food will be swept along and concentrated in these places and you can also use the run of water to trot a float to places you cannot fish on the bottom or reach by casting.

In beach fishing, as in any other form of fishing, look for places where the fish will come to you, rather than go searching for them. Bass will forage along the length of a beach so that both ends are obvious places to try. There is a sweep of tide along most surf beaches and as bass tend to swim with the tide this narrows down your choice. One end of a beach may be better on the flood, the other on the ebb or perhaps at half flood or half ebb. By fishing these places consistently up and down the tide you will soon get to know the times during which they fish best.

Bass have a definite liking for fresh water and any place on a beach where a stream or seepage empties on to it is always a likely spot for bass.   Rocks or rocky reefs, patches of weed on a stony or pebbly bottom or anything that breaks up the monotony of an otherwise featureless beach is a place to try.   Patches where sandeels are plentiful are likely fishing spots, as are points on the beach where the surf penetrates a little farther or tends to be a little rougher than elsewhere in moderate or calm conditions.

Fishing on surf beaches normally calls for surf casting tackle, as conditions of surf, depth or sweep of tide may call for long casts or the use of heavy sinkers to hold the bottom.   The distance one must cast varies considerably and depends on many factors.   Food swept out of the sand by the action of the surf is sucked seawards by the undertow until its progress is halted by the opposing force of the oncoming waves, when it is deposited on the bottom.   This usually takes place just behind the last "breaker" and it is here you can expect the bass to be feeding.   They will be found just behind the breaker in a line parallel to the shore and you must get your bait out to them.   On very shallow beaches at low water or in heavy surf the waves may be breaking a considerable distance out and very long casts are essential if you are to get among the fish.   When the tide is well up on the beach near high water and there is good depth close in, the line of breakers may only be 20 to 30 yards away or less and short casts are then the answer.

Do not get into the habit of making long casts just for the sake of doing so because you will find that your bait is often far beyond where the fish are feeding.   Granted there are occasions when you must be able to cast 100 yards or more to reach the fish but these conditions are more the exception than the rule and normally with a nice surf running (three nice breakers are ideal) casts of 50 to 80 yards are all that is necessary.   On some beaches where the surf breaks a long way out you will find a "table" of water.   Here the bass will be inside the line of breakers and you must search the water to find out where they are feeding.   These conditions seem to be ideal for flounders, which can make a perfect nuisance of themselves to anglers fishing for bass.

In calm conditions with light surf or near high water in moderate surf, bass will feed right in on the shore and I have seen them run right up a beach and down again on a wave.   In these conditions and also at night when bass come much closer to the shore it is very easy to overcast as the fish may be no more than 10 to 20 yards out.   It is wise to search the water if after some time has elapsed there is no sign of fish where you expect them.   By this I mean to cast well out and at intervals slowly move the bait in towards the shore, letting it rest again for a while until you find where the fish are.   This is a very useful gambit in calm water with no surf at all when bass are hard to locate or are hard to tempt. You may in this manner bring your bait to the notice of a fish that would have otherwise missed it and, besides, a bass which at times will leave a still bait strictly alone will find a moving bait irresistable and be goaded into taking it.

A fallacy oft repeated among beach anglers is that it is hopeless to fish for bass in conditions of flat calm and crystal clear water. True enough, conditions of moderate surf and coloured water are more conducive to good fishing but calm clear conditions can also be good.   Some of my best bass and indeed best catches of bass have been taken on warm sunny days when the water was crystal clear and the surface as smooth as a sheet of glass.   Frequently in such conditions bass fishing is slow and the fish may not come on the feed properly until the sun has sunk beneath the horizon but at times they also can be very active and feeding eagerly.   It is then a question of finding out where they are.   Longer casts than usual may be called for, as the bass may remain further out in deeper water but they can also be very close in and right in the shallows. The next time we are enjoying a spell of anticyclonic weather do not write off bass fishing during daylight as you may be missing some wonderful sport.

If you are fishing a good spot on a beach and are not getting the bites, do not be in too much of a hurry to change even if you see that anglers farther up the beach are getting fish.   Bass often sweep down a beach in numbers so that after a long blank period you may for a while take fish after fish.   The bass may be on their way down to you and should you move at the wrong time you may miss them altogether.

Beach fishing at night can be very productive and has a charm all its own.   Most fish swim closer to the shore after dark and are less cautious and wary than during daylight.   They hunt more by scent than by sight and for that reason I prefer a bait like lugworm which has a good scent for night fishing.   I have found over the

years that there is little point in fishing all night and now prefer to
fish up to about 2 a.m. or rise early and start about 5 a.m.   I have
found the middle hours of the night generally unproductive and by
the time the fish come on the take again about dawn, that I am
tired and have lost the keenness and alertness so necessary in bass
fishing.   You must know your beach intimately for night fishing
and it is essential that you have a good torch and be warmly
clothed.

When night fishing you will find a large fixed-spool reel more
trouble free than a multiplier, for in the dark when you cannot
watch the flight of your sinker it is easy to get an overrun, which
can cause a bad enough tangle in daylight but at night when you are
unable to see it can be even a greater nuisance.   Sinkers or leads
play an important part in surf fishing.   They should be streamlined
to assist in obtaining distance when casting and the torpedo or
pear-shaped leads are excellent in this respect.   I do not mind my
bait being moved around a little by the surf as a moving bait is
attractive to bass, but when there is heavy surf or a strong current
or run of tide along the beach, the bait and sinker is swept along
too fast, making it quite impossible to fish properly, a grip lead
equipped with wire prongs is essential in these conditions.

Grip leads are efficient and will hold in all except the worst conditions but for all that I am no lover of them and if possible fish
without them.   They suffer from two distinct disadvantages:
firstly, it is difficult to set the hook in a bass when using an ordinary
paternoster trace until the grips have been pulled out of the sand
and this at times requires a fair amount of force;   secondly, the fish
does not battle so well when it must also fight the pull of the grip
lead as it catches in the bottom.

The sheltered beach is a more difficult problem to fish than either
of the storm beaches.   Food is so plentiful that bass can be scattered
over a wide area and there is no focal point at which they will
congregate.   Again you should study the beach at low water,
noting where food is plentiful and where the channels, sandbanks,
and deep pools lie.   Bass are wary of crossing shallow banks until
they are covered with sufficient depth of water and the channels and
gullies between sandbanks and deeper pools are the places to fish.
When casting make sure that your bait does not land on top of a
sand bank but in the gullies on either side.   When the tide is in the

water is often deeper along the shore by sea walls or banks and bass will nose in among the weeds searching for crabs or prawns.

As on the more exposed beaches, places where rock and sand meet are always rich in food. Fish as close to the rock as possible without actually fishing on it and on mixed bottoms of rock and sand place your bait on the clean patches amongst the rough. Where fresh water enters the sea is always worthy of attention as are weed covered outcrops of rock. Crabs can be an absolute pest on this kind of beach but if soft or peeler crab is used your bait is likely to last longer. As surf will not be a problem on a sheltered beach, light bottom fishing tackle and light sinkers can be used instead of surfcasting tackle.

The type of tackle used in shore fishing has been described in an earlier chapter but a few points are worth mentioning about terminal tackles. Two types of traces are generally used in beach fishing, i.e. an ordinary one or two hook paternoster and a running leger. Hook sizes range from 1/0 to 4/0 but if the fish are small or biting very shyly a No. 1 may be used. When using small baits or worms I prefer to use the smaller sizes but for fish baits or large crabs I use a 3/0 or 4/0 hook. The larger hook gives a better purchase and is less likely to tear out of the fish's mouth on the strike, but of course it is not as easy to drive home. When fishing crab or fish bait I use one hook only but when using lugworm or ragworm I often use two hooks. Not that a two-hook trace catches any more fish than a one-hook trace, but when using soft baits which can be torn off the hook in casting, there is a good chance of one bait remaining on if you are using two hooks. This is especially comforting when night fishing when you cannot see if your bait has flown off the hook or not. The use of more than two hooks is absolutely unnecessary and only succeeds in wasting bait.

Indeed I would use two hooks only on clean surf beaches; and where rock and weed constitute a hazard I would use a one-hook trace. I have lost good bass in weedy places when the second hook fouled in the weed, but on clean beaches this danger does not arise.

A running leger is very useful when bass are biting shy, as the fish can take the bait and move away without feeling the weight of the sinker but at the same time a fish can often mouth and reject a bait fished on a running leger without the angler being aware of it. When using a paternoster I prefer to have the hook link nearer the main line than the sinker because if it is too near the sinker the fish will feel the weight of the lead before the angler can strike.

Striking a fish properly is something which comes with experience though at times it is not always easy to know what is the right thing to do. Normally a bass gives a distinctive and unmistakeable "knock" and if you lower the rod point and take in the slack line until you feel the weight of the fish before striking there should be no difficulty in hooking the fish. The strike should be positive and if there is any dithering about it the fish will probably be lost. I prefer to hold my rod low and at right angles to the direction of the line when striking because if the strike is made upwards part of the force required to send the hook home (and remember the hook may be 80 yards away from the rod tip) is lost in lifting line off the water.

Bass at times can be very temperamental and bite very shyly. Big bass, especially, often take very gently in direct contrast to the vigorous "thump" of the small school bass. One could be deceived into thinking that a very small flatfish was mouthing the bait or at other times the only warning you get is a slight twitch on the line or perhaps a gentle tightening. I usually strike these bites quickly and decisively as I have found to my sorrow that leaving the bait to the fish more often than not results in the fish losing interest and departing. Frequently a bass will pick up the bait and run inshore with it, the angler's only warning being a sudden slack line, but fortunately in this case the fish usually hooks itself. However, the slack line must be taken up at once and the fish tightened on and struck. If it is possible to run back up the beach slack line can be taken up more quickly than by staying in the same position and reeling in the line.

Many bass bites, indeed many bites from all types of fish, and this applies to boat fishing as well, would not be noticed if the rod and line are not held in the hand. It may be more tedious and tiring to hold your rod for hours on end than to prop it up on a rod rest or against a pier wall and stick a bell on it, but it will certainly result in more fish being landed. Apart from the failure to notice some bites when the rod is left down there is also the temptation to wander away from the rod perhaps to chat with other anglers, and when a bite is registered the rod cannot be reached in time to strike the fish. The same applies to those foolish enough to try and fish two rods at the same time. They fall between two stools and instead of catching more fish they catch less.

I have seen this proved time and time again by watching one angler who held his rod outfish several others who were too lazy to do the same. *Always hold your rod* and you will find that it pays off handsomely.

Weather and tides have a great effect on beach fishing. Stormy weather and heavy seas make fishing impossible and often leave masses of floating and decomposing weed in the shallows which makes fishing a nightmare for days after the storm has abated. A heavy ground swell which heaves itself up on the beach with a crashing roar in calm weather is also detrimental to fishing. However, a day or two after a storm when the sea has calmed down and the water is beginning to clear is an excellent time to fish, and so, too, is the first day an onshore breeze blows after a period of calm weather or offshore winds. Moderate surf provides ideal conditions but if these are prolonged, bottom feeding bass may become satiated and difficult to tempt.

The direction of the wind is also important. An offshore wind on one beach may be an onshore wind on another and may make all the difference to fishing on that beach. A change in wind may make a normally good beach fish poorly whilst another usually unproductive beach may fish well in the same wind while a wind may make one beach unfishable and another just right. Get to know your beaches and the conditions under which they fish best. This knowledge will enable you to ring the changes on different beaches or save you spending fruitless hours fishing when conditions are wrong.

Get to know how the tide affects fishing on your beach. It is wrong to think that only the flood tide is fruitful for in many places the ebb tide can be better. Some portions of the beach may only produce fish on the first of the flood, others may fish at high water, half ebb or perhaps low water. If you get to know how your beach fishes you can fish on productive ground right up and down the tide by moving to each place as the best stage of tide for that particular spot is reached.

While beach fishing has a fascination all its own, estuary fishing provides some of the most rewarding and enjoyable bass fishing available to the angler. Normally he can use much lighter tackle than on a surf beach and it is in an estuary that spinning, the most sporting of all methods of taking bass, comes into its own. Taken on medium spinning tackle the bass has few equals as a game fighting fish in either fresh or salt water and I must confess that this is my favourite method of fishing for bass.

Estuaries, like beaches, vary greatly in size and extent but the fundamental features of an estuary are very much the same irrespective of its size or situation. Big estuaries, such as are found at the mouths of major rivers, provide very similar fishing conditions, as do the smaller estuaries except that there is considerably more fresh or brackish water, extensive areas of mudflats, side creeks, lagoons, sheltered beaches and even storm beaches, while in addition there may also be very good boat fishing. In the smaller estuaries there is less silt and consequently the bottom is usually of firm muddy sand and the water is mostly salt. At the mouth of a small estuary there is frequently a shallow "bar" of sand or gravel built up by the scouring action of the tides.

Common to all estuaries is the movement of the tides, which to a great extent regulate the movements of fish and your fishing. Fish travel up an estuary with the tide, at first staying in the main channel, but as the force of the flood strengthens and pushes the water up the subsidiary channels and spreads it out over the flats, so too, do the fish. As the tide turns and begins to ebb the fish gradually fall back with it until at low water the cycle is complete and commences again on the next tide. It is important to appreciate this movement of fish with the tides if you are to successfully fish an estuary.

Examine an estuary at low water and you will notice how rich in food it is. Crabs are plentiful, indeed too plentiful at times for the bottom angler, wherever there are rocks and weed, sea walls or submerged ledges. Lugworm castings speckle the sand flats and in the muddier places ragworm will be found. The pools and channels will hold shrimp, prawn and baby flatfish and many small fishes, such as young of mullet and pollack, gobies, butterfish and freshwater eels. In places where conditions are suitable sandeels will be numerous. In some large estuaries at certain times of the year migrating salmon and sea trout smolts will be an added attraction while in summer small fry are often plentiful. Is it any wonder with such a richness of food that bass are so fond of estuaries?

Even in July and August when many bass forsake the open beaches to shoal offshore after small fry, estuary fishing will still be rewarding.

Bass run up an estuary as soon as the tide starts to flow strongly and pushes back the water in the main channel. In small estuaries with a "bar" at its mouth they will congregate outside the bar until there is sufficient depth over it for them to cross. Although they are strong swimmers they like to keep in the fast water of the main current so that they will be taken to the feeding grounds with a minimum of effort. Where the tideway is deflected by a projecting spur of rock or other obstacle bass, instead of working the quieter water of the shoreline tend to stay in the main current until it fetches up on the shore again perhaps a considerable distance downstream. Where, however, there is broken ground of out-jutting reaches of rock and weed split by sandy shallows they will quarter this ground thoroughly.

Early on the tide bass stick to the main channel until there is sufficient depth in the subsidiary channels and finally near high water they will have spread out over the flats. They will nose into side creeks and lagoons, along weedy harbour walls. They ascend a long way up an estuary but do not go as far as the mullet and do not linger as long. As soon as the tide turns they start to drop back, pausing to explore some of the quieter corners or back eddies on their way down. At low water, except for small school bass which may remain in the deeper parts of the channel, most of the bass will have dropped back to the sea. In the very big estuaries bass will remain in the lower reaches but in small estuaries the big bass will drop all the way down, though the next tide will bring a fresh supply of fish.

Once you understand the movements of bass in an estuary and know where the food is and the likely spots to attract the fish you will have no problem. Stop and think before you start. This will save you many fruitless hours of flogging unproductive water and by moving about the estuary you can enjoy fishing right through the whole ebb and flood.

In a small estuary start at the mouth at low water. If there is a bar, fish on to the seaward side of it because that is where the bass will be congregating, waiting to run up. Remember that the tide may be flowing for hours outside an estuary mouth before it has risen high enough to cross the bar and push back the outflowing water.

As soon as the tide starts running back hard up the estuary the bass will come with it and the mouth of the channel will fish well at this stage. It will also fish well on the last of the ebb when you can catch the fish on their way down. As the tide grows stronger and the main shoals move farther up you should retreat back up the channel fishing each vantage point as you go.

Pick your spots so that the fish will come to you rather than you go looking for them. Fish where the main current comes close to the shore or where projecting reefs or rocky spurs enable you to cover the main flow or where there are narrows or necks in the main channel. In fact any place where fish must pass on either the flood or ebb, and remember that the current may strike in one spot on the flood and on another on the ebb. Bass will quarter thoroughly shores of mixed rock, sand and weed, the sandy bays and gullies between out thrusting reefs of rock and the mouths of tidal creeks and lagoons off the main estuary. These are the places to try when the tide has risen sufficiently and the fish are no longer confined to the main channel. On the ebb, some of the eddies or back corners off the main current would be worth a try.

You can spin or bottom fish in the channel but remember that each part of the channel may only fish well for a certain length of time and that it pays to move with the fish. When bottom fishing, do not be afraid to let your bait be trundled along by the tide as long, of course, as the current is not too strong, in which case your bait would not be fishing at all. A moving bait has a great attraction for bass, who will snatch at it eagerly. Remember that in a strong tide a bass will snatch at a bait on the run and must be struck immediately. If it misses the first time it will keep moving on and you will seldom get a second chance. In slack water it may take more gently and can be given more time.

With the lighter tackle which can be used, hook sizes can be smaller and sizes 1/0 to 2/0 will cover most of your needs. In weedy or rocky places a one-hook trace is sufficient and only use enough lead to enable you to cast and hold the bottom or else let your bait move slowly along. Crab, lugworm, ragworm are excellent baits in an estuary, and prawn or crab if you can find a vantage point, such as a bridge, from which you can driftline or

float fish.   Fish baits and razorfish or squid are also good baits and
the usual spinning lures will do.   I have a preference for spoons
but freely revolving bar spoons such as a Voblex or Mepps are
also useful for casting upstream and working down with the
current.   In places bass like to take up station on the ebb tide just
like trout in a river, knocking off anything that is swept down to
them in the current and in such conditions this type of spoon can
be deadly.

Make the best use of cover and do not display yourself to fish in
an estuary.   This may not be important on a surf beach but in an
estuary *it is*, as bass will be found right in the shallows nosing around
weeds and rocks.   Fish in shallow water are easily scared and a
frightened fish will not take.   The fish you see arrowing out of the
shallows when you make an incautious approach, you know you
have frightened, but how many others have seen you and slipped
quietly away without you being aware of it?   If I seem to labour
this point it is because it is important.   Avoid displaying yourself
against the skyline, standing out on prominent rocks or crashing
through the shallows.   If the fish are close in, cast beyond them
to avoid disturbing them and then reel your bait back into position.

Bass in estuaries are usually very close in and it is easy to overcast
and be out beyond the fish.   Casts of 10 to 15 yards or less may be
all that is necessary at times.   For the same reason, when spinning,
fish each cast out carefully as bass may be right in under your feet in
shallow water or may follow the bait right into the shore.   If you
intend moving to another spot, cover it with your lure before you
move to it, lest your arrival disturb a fish you did not know was
there.

Weather affects estuary fishing in a number of ways.   Continuous
heavy rain is detrimental, especially in the larger estuaries which are
the mouths of big rivers, for heavy floods mean too much fresh
water, which tends to drive bass out.   A heavy blow may make
fishing impossible due to large amounts of drifting or rotting weed,
which is carried up and down the estuaries with the tides.   Steady
offshore winds will draw fry into estuaries and harbours in summer
and fishing in these conditions will be described later in the chapter
under boat fishing.   The day after a storm when the water is calm
but still thick can be excellent and so can fishing when an onshore
breeze stirs up the shallows.   Early in the season when **salmon and**

sea trout smolts are migrating seawards very heavy bass can be found in estuaries preying on them.

Just as in beach fishing, you should get to know your estuary. There are many places from which to fish and although some may only be productive for a short period of the tide perhaps only for half an hour or an hour, by ringing the changes you can fish on productive ground all through the tide.

Remember, pick the places where fish will come to you and don't just fish on a "chuck it and chance it" basis. Think about your fishing and do not fish by rule of thumb. Choose the most suitable method for any given place or time and do not be afraid to experiment. It is to the versatile and intelligent angler that an estuary will yield its richest rewards.

Rock fishing for bass may not be as rewarding in the numbers of fish caught as beach or estuary fishing but it does yield a run of consistently heavy fish. The bigger bass are likely to be more solitary in habit and fish probably figure to a greater extent in their diet. A big fish likes large mouthfuls and nowhere is this type of food more plentiful than on a rocky coast, particularly the type of coast which at low water reveals extensive rock pools, gullies and ravines in which small fish such as pollack, wrasse, butterfish, blennies as well as crab and prawn are plentiful. The same applies to low rough ground but unfortunately this type of bottom is difficult to fish and hard on tackle so that too few anglers venture to try it.

The conventional methods used are either float fishing or spinning. For float fishing, prawns, soft or peeler crab, sandeels or other fish baits are excellent and the hook size used should suit the size of the bait. Reasonably heavy tackle is called for, 12-15 lb. line and a longish rod, as the fish may have to be kept clear of obstacles. Before starting to fish look for suitable places to land your fish. I prefer to use a long handled net as it is surer in emergencies. Bass love to nose up gullies and ravines and these should be searched thoroughly. Let the waves and tide wash your float about, as your bait will all the time be searching the water. Bass are as likely to be right in on the rock under your feet, prowling along the weed, as they are to be 50 to 80 yards out. Where there is a run of tide (a likely spot to meet a bass) your float can be trotted a long way and so search a big area, but do not overlook the quiet coves or submerged reefs or platforms of rock in off the tide. The float should be no larger than is necessary, otherwise the fish will feel the resistance when it takes. It should, however, be big enough to support your bait and be clearly visible to you.

When spinning, search the water in depth as well as in area, for bass may be down on the bottom in one place but quite near the surface in others. The speed of the retrieve should also be varied and do not be too lazy to change your lures from time to time if you are not having success. When searching near the bottom there is, of course, the danger of fouling in the weed or kelp, but if a short trace of Alasticum wire is used you will find that you will pull free more frequently when you do get hung up, as the fine wire tends to slice its way through the weed.

When bottom fishing, one must consider the sinker as being expendable, because it will inevitably foul in the bottom. The best terminal rig to use is a running paternoster. The line from the free running swivel to the sinker should be much lighter than the main line, i.e. about 5 to 8 lb. breaking strain, so that when you break only the sinker will be sacrificed and a new sinker can be attached in a matter of seconds to the broken line. Lead sinkers are expensive and for this kind of fishing any object of suitable weight will do, e.g. a piece of old iron, a nut or bolt or even a small stone or piece of rock. The line to the sinker should be strong enough to recover the sinker unless it gets badly stuck but light enough to break easily if it has fouled when a fish is hooked.

The best baits to use in bottom fishing are fish or crab. If you are using a whole fish do not use too big a bait but cut it up. The head and guts of a small wrasse or pollack will make good baits but make sure that the hook point is not covered by tough flesh or bone or it will be impossible to drive home when a fish takes. There is no difficulty in striking a fish when float fishing or spinning, but when bottom fishing over rocky ground they take gently and must be given time. Let the fish run until you are sure it has the bait, then hit it hard. Do not try to hold it but let it head for deeper water. It can be fought out in safety there without the danger of snagging in weed or cutting the line on projecting rocks It is bad policy to hold any strong fish hard in the early stages as it only brings it to the surface where it thrashes about and may part the line with its tail or knock the hook out of its mouth.

One should never forget the inherent dangers in rock fishing. It should never be attempted in rough weather, while even in moderate conditions a sharp lookout should be kept for that occasional "sneak wave" that could easily wash you off your perch. Wet rocks are always dangerous and the danger of slipping and injuring oneself badly is never absent so take care. Do not take chances. It is never worth it.

My earlier remarks on estuary fishing about not displaying yourself to the fish and of making the best use of cover apply with equal force to rock fishing. Again I stress that cover is important and one is never more prominent than when sitting or standing on a promontory or ledge. Do your best to stay back from the edge and merge with the background and above all stay off the skyline and do not move about too much.

So far we have dealt with shore fishing for bass and now we will deal with boat fishing. Without a doubt the most exciting form of bass fishing is spinning for shoaling bass from a small boat. The tackle is light, the fish are in deep water and each fight is long, hard and the result uncertain until the fish is in the boat. One does not fully appreciate the gameness, strength and power of a bass until one has taken a bass on spinning tackle in deep water where it has room to fight and manoeuvere.

Small fry tend to swim against the wind and in summer when they are plentiful (usually in July and August) offshore winds draw them inshore into bays, harbours and estuary mouths. They are drifted up and down the coast and in and out of estuaries by the tides and become concentrated in strong tidal currents, where tidal currents meet or in tidal eddies.

When large numbers of fry are concentrated in an area, bass in common with many other predatory sea fish may congregate and combine to prey on the small fry. In places, under favourable weather and tide conditions, shoaling bass are met with fair regularity, while in others they occur sporadically when conditions are suitable. When strong winds and rough seas scatter the fry or persistent onshore winds take them far out to sea, the shoals of bass break up and return to foraging on the shore and do not come together again until the fry are plentiful once more.

In some places, for example over the famous Splaugh Rock near Rosslare, Co. Wexford or in Dungarvan Bay, Co. Waterford, due to very favourable local conditions bass shoal consistently on the tide from June right through to September and anglers come from far and wide to enjoy this wonderful sport. It is incredible that such large numbers of bass running into tens of thousands at a time can be concentrated in a small area and catches of over a hundred good bass per boat have been made.

The angler's guide to shoaling fish is of course the sea birds. They are experts at the job. One minute the sky is clear and not a bird in sight. The next hundreds, even thousands, of birds, gulls, gannets, terns, etc., suddenly appear from nowhere and form a fluttering, diving, shrieking mass as they join in the feast. It is not difficult to tell whether they are working over bass or some other species. When working over mackerel or pollack the fowl are usually in one big mass but with bass you will notice large numbers of birds resting on the water whilst periodically sections of them will start working in one place and then others in another. The reason for this is that bass do not attack *en masse* as do mackerel but small shoals of bass attack the fry independently and in different places.

Bass make a distinctive swirl in the water, sometimes breaking the surface as they chase their prey. This will give you an idea of the direction the shoal is moving in and the idea is to get above them and drift back down by them with the engine stopped. Do not drift *through* the shoal or you will put them down, and give them a wide berth when motoring up past them as they can easily be disturbed.

Spinning is the most sporting and effective method and 10 lb. breaking strain line is quite strong enough. I have seen anglers use 15 to 30 lb. breaking strain line and just simply haul fish to the boat. That is all very well if its slaughter you want, but for sport, fish reasonably light, and besides if the bass are anyway finicky you will do better with the lighter line. It is hard and tiring work when the fish are taking well and by the time you have fought half a dozen 5/7 lb. bass to the side of the boat your arms and shoulders will be aching in a way you would not have believed possible.

Cast your lure towards the edge of the shoal rather than into the middle of it. It has a far better chance of being seen and taken there. When a bass takes a lure it feels just like coming up against a stone wall—your lure just stops—so strike hard to set the hooks.

Sometimes they will take anything you care to throw at them—at other times they can be very choosy. One or even several of them will follow a lure without taking until they see the boat and sheer off. If you try reeling quickly they will follow, keeping the same distance from the lure; if you slow down they will fall back and never close the gap. This often happens on an afternoon tide and I suspect that the fish may be satiated from the mornings feeding.

I have experienced this frequently when shore fishing, too. A bass will be interested enough to follow the bait but makes no effort to take it. Yet half an hour later the same lure will be taken eagerly. There is nothing more frustrating than to be in the middle of thousands of bass which are churning the water to foam yet will not take your lure. There are two courses of action which you can take. The bass may be feeding on very tiny brit and you should try a much smaller lure. If this fails try something really big or with a crazy action that will startle or goad the fish into taking. If this fails, rise at 4.30 a.m. and fish from dawn onwards. You will find the fish much more obliging in the early morning.

Long, slightly dished spoons are usually the best lures, for, besides being effective on a straight retrieve, they are often taken as they flutter down through the water after landing and before you can take in the slack line and start the retrieve. However, other lures work well, too, and there are too many on the market to enumerate them here. A heavy quick sinking lure such as a German Sprat is very useful, too, for frequently you will find bass under mackerel and the difficulty is to get your lure down to the bass without its being taken by a mackerel.

In these days of bass conservation, a landing net is preferable to a gaff, but make sure it is wide enough to accommodate a hefty bass. As I said, this form of fishing can be very exciting but do not lose your head. *Be careful* how you cast in a boat lest you injure a companion. If you follow the practice of letting the bowman cast first followed in turn by everyone right down to the stern man you will avoid trouble, and if you are fishing from a small boat do not in your excitement stand up lest you capsize it.

When bass have stopped shoaling, especially over reefs or shoal ground in tideways, they may still be hanging around or near the bottom and it is worth while trolling for them. I have found it best to fish the bait a long way astern of the boat, a hundred yards or more and all depths should be searched. Artificial lures, i.e. a large spoon or fish baits, i.e. a long lash of mackerel, can be used and a spiral lead attached to the line will help take the bait down to the right depth. Fish your rod out to one side of the boat to keep it clear of the wake and watch out when the boat makes a turn lest your lure sink to the bottom or foul in another's line.

This method can be used over any ground on which bass are plentiful or in estuaries, channels or tideways. It is better to row back and forth across the tide than to go against it or run with it. You will cover and catch more fish by doing this and remember, unlike trolling for pollack which is a slow leisurely business, you cannot row too fast for bass. Search the different depths until you find the right level. This can be done quite simply by adjusting your speed. The faster you go the higher the bait will travel, the slower you go the deeper it will sink.

Driftlining is another very effective method that is not unlike trolling, except that you fish from an anchored boat and use natural baits. The boat should be anchored in a place that bass are likely to pass and where there is sufficient current to work the bait, i.e. in an estuary channel, fast tideway or over the bar at the mouth of an estuary. Bait your hook with long strips of mackerel, sandeel, small fish, prawns or even ragworm and lower it over the side. Six feet from the hook attach a spiral lead of suitable weight and continue paying out the line until the bait is a sufficient distance from the boat. The water should be searched through all depths until the level at which the fish are travelling is found. This is done by the simple expedient of shortening the amount of line out or by paying out more line. The use of "rubby dubby" or ground bait is a great help in attracting fish but do not overdo it. Remember, your aim is to attract the fish not to feed them.

Bass are a slow growing and relatively long lived species in which the males are slower growing than the females and do not live nearly as long. They can be caught on a variety of baits, by a variety of methods and in a variety of places, each with its own special fascination. Some anglers like to catch them in the creaming surf of an ocean beach, others in the quiet reaches of an estuary while still more prefer the heady excitement of shoaling bass. Whatever your preference bass provide some of the most satisfying and rewarding fishing to be found in the sea.

CHAPTER 9

MULLET

MULLET ARE THE MOST FASCINATING FISH IN THE SEA AND fishing for them provides the sea angler with his greatest challenge. Legends have grown up about their intelligence, wariness and the virtual impossibility of catching them short of using a seine net, a stroke haul or shooting them with a .22 rifle, none of which is exactly a sporting method. Let me state here and now that mullet *can be caught* and *are being caught regularly* but it takes a persistent and intelligent angler to catch them. In places they are relatively easy to catch but on the whole it is difficult fishing, requiring patience and long-term planning. They present a real challenge to the angler as their habits and reactions differ from place to place. A method or bait which is successful in one spot may be entirely useless with mullet a mile or two away. Mullet fishing is no game for the angler who fishes for the "pan" but rather for the man who wants sport and a really strong fighting fish.

Mullet are essentially an inshore species and are found all around our coasts. No other species appears to be so numerous but that is probably because we can see them so often. They are gregarious in habit and it is unusual to see a lone mullet as they normally swim in shoals. They may appear in small shoals of two or three fish or larger ones of ten, twenty or even hundreds and literally thousands. They abound in bays, estuaries, harbours, creeks, pills, lagoons, along beaches, in rocky coves and slobland pools. They will ascend estuaries and rivers a long way, even above the limit of the tide and may live in fresh water for a time.

Mullet are frequently mistaken for bass. Indeed the two species are often found together but there is a marked difference in their swimming habits. The bass is always purposeful and looks as if he has somewhere to go and something to do. The mullet, on the other hand, looks lazy and indolent as if he had nothing to do and all day to do it. On calm summer days mullet will be seen outlined like grey shadows in the lazy roll of a wave in the shallows of a beach or may betray their presence in a river or estuary by the typical arrow-shaped wake they create as they glide along with the tide near the surface. They may be seen hanging motionless in the water, their dorsal fins and sometimes their backs breaking the surface as they sun themselves. For that again they will be seen playing and cavorting, chasing one another around and leaping from the water, for all the world like a crowd of children playing "tip and tig". They are no lovers of wind or ruffled water and will sink deep under these conditions. When swimming some distance under the surface they are not easy to see even when the water is clear on account of their slow, leisurely progress and their presence may only be revealed by a sudden golden flash or gleam as a fish rolls.

A hooked mullet is an entirely different proposition altogether, displaying an amazing turn of speed and possessing incredible strength and staying power. It will jump frequently and when a good fish wants to go, it goes and there is little you can do about it. At times in the early stages of a battle with a 4 or 5 lb. mullet I have wondered whether I was playing the fish or the fish was playing me. The fight goes on for an incredibly long time for a fish of that size, as the mullet gets its fourth and fifth wind and never seems to tire. The result is never certain and by the time it slides safely into the net your wrist and arm are aching badly and you are glad that it is all over.

Mullet, despite their apparent indolence, are very shy and wary fish, doubly so since they frequent shallow water. They possess excellent eyesight and are very easily frightened, especially by sudden movements or shadows. The shadow of a bird flying over the water is enough to make a whole shoal of surface-swimming mullet erupt in panic and even single mullet feeding in very shallow water will frequently take fright at nothing at all as if it suddenly realised that it was in a vulnerable position. It is uncanny how the reaction of one fish in a shoal is instantly communicated to the others and the whole shoal of fish reacts as one. Strangely enough, at times nothing seems to frighten them and of course mullet in harbours and around seaside resorts become accustomed to people and movement and are less easily scared. However, more than with any other species, caution and the best use of available cover are essential if one is to be successful in catching them.

Although a warm-water species, mullet have a more northerly range than bass and are found all around our coasts. Their arrival inshore in spring varies with the season and the locality and they will appear earlier in the south than in the north. They arrive earlier and leave later than bass and there is some evidence that their winter migration is partly southerly as well as into deeper water. In the south and west they may not disappear entirely but lay up for the winter in some sheltered inshore positions in bays and harbours where they can be present in very large numbers.

Spawning takes place after the spring inshore migration. From the condition of the gonads of captured mullet it is inferred that May is the principal spawning month, but beyond that little is known of their spawning habits in our waters. The young fry are plentiful in July and August in harbours and estuaries where they are preyed upon by small bass, sea trout, small pollack and sandeels. The yearling and two-year-old mullet are often seen in small shoals in shallow tidal channels or stranded in sea pools in estuaries and bays. A feature that I have often noted is that shoals of small mullet ($\frac{1}{4}$ to $\frac{1}{2}$ lb. fish or over) are often accompanied or led by one or two large mullet for all the world like a class of school children in the charge of a teacher. Shoals of larger mullet usually seem to be of around the same year class and same approximate size but frequently small shoals of big mullet are accompanied by one or two considerably smaller fish as if the latter had graduated into a higher class.

Mullet are a slow growing and relatively long lived species. Their growth rate is even slower than the bass, being approximately half in terms of weight for age. The following list (see overleaf) of rod caught mullet will provide an interesting comparison.

While bass are voracious feeders, they work hard for their food and burn up most of their nourishment as energy. The mullet, on the other hand, seems to find its food with little effort but though its bulk may at times be great, its food value is low and its conversion factor is poor. The natural food of mullet is on the whole microscopic consisting of diatoms and other tiny organisms which, of course, are of no use to the angler as bait.

They sift sand or mud from the bottom, sucking it in and blowing it out again as they separate their food from the useless matter. In clear water they can often be seen dredging the bottom, stopping now and again to suck and blow, leaving little scours on the bottom similar to those left by the keel of a boat. Their upper lip is equipped with sensitive little papillae which seem to enable them to find their food and which they also seem to use as organs of taste. They will often be seen in the shallows of beaches in gentle surf which disturbs the sand and washes out the tiny animals and microscopic plants on which they live.

Weight	Length in Inches	Date	Sex	Age
1 lb. 2½ oz.	13¼	14/9/58	M.	8 plus
1 ,, 6 ,,	14	13/8/61	?	6 ,,
1 ,, 12½ ,,	15¼	14/9/58	M.	11 ,,
2 ,, 0½ ,,	15¾	14/9/58	F.	10 ,,
2 ,, 5½ ,,	17	14/9/58	F.	10 ,,
2 ,, 8 ,,	16	13/8/61	M.	9 ,,
2 ,, 12½ ,,	17½	14/9/58	M.	10 ,,
3 ,, 4½ ,,	18½	14/9/58	M.	15 ,,
3 ,, 7½ ,,	19½	14/9/58	F.	13 ,,
3 ,, 9 ,,	19½	15/6/54	M.	10 ,,
3 ,, 12 ,,	20	16/6/58	M.	13 or 14 ,,
3 ,, 15½ ,,	19¾	28/5/61	F.	12 ,,
4 ,, 0½ ,,	19¾	15/6/54	F.	14 ,,
4 ,, 3¼ ,,	20	2/9/60	?	16 ,,
4 ,, 4 ,,	19¾	13/8/61	M.	12 ,,
4 ,, 4 ,,	19½	13/8/61	F.	13/14 ,,
4 ,, 13 ,,	21½	19/9/63	F.	16 ,,
4 ,, 5¼ ,,	20½	14/9/58	F.	17 ,,
5 ,, 0½ ,,	21	15/10/62	?	14/15 ,,
5 ,, 1¾ ,,	21½	15/10/62	?	16 ,,
5 ,, 7 ,,	21¼	15/10/62	?	15 ,,
5 ,, 14 ,,	22	23/9/62		17 ,,

Apart from diatoms, fragments of weed, usually Enteromorpha, silk weed or filamentous algae are found in their stomachs but this does not seem to be eaten so much for its own sake as for the minute life on the weed, or to be swallowed inadvertently as they browse on the organisms on the weed in the same way as mud and sand finds its way into their stomachs. A variety of small animals are also found in their stomachs, mainly Hydrobia snails, tiny burrowing amphipods, insect larvae, worms and sea weed maggots. This is the food of the "wild" mullet of beaches, bays and estuaries although a large variety of other organisms appear in their stomachs from time to time. This is the result of their dredging or seemingly casual browsing and in general their food is both minute and soft. Strangely enough, however, they have from time to time been taken by anglers using large hooks and lugworm or ragworm as bait. I have also on a few occasions seen mullet fair hooked in the mouth after taking an artificial lure meant for bass.

Their mode of feeding though seemingly not very nourishing has many advantages. Food is readily available nearly everywhere, there is little competition, if any, from other species and as they frequent shallow water, once they live through the early stages they are in little danger from predators. There is, however, little in their natural food that the angler can use or put on a hook for bait but do not be disheartened for they can still be caught as we will see later.

"Urban" mullet, as we shall call them, are a different proposition. These are the mullet of harbours, towns and seaside resorts which develop a taste for other than their natural food. In such places a considerable amount of offal or waste is dumped into the sea and if the quantities are big enough and the supply regular enough mullet will change their feeding habits. In fishing harbours they will be found feeding on the filleted carcasses and guts of fish, in towns at sewer outlets, and rubbish dumps. If there is a fish canning factory they will browse happily on the waste products or where trippers, picnickers or hotels and cafes dump sandwiches or food they will feed on the edible bits and pieces. Mullet are not fussy once they become accustomed to such waste food, as long as it is soft.

An amazing variety of stuff has been found in the stomachs of "urban" mullet—bread, currants, pieces of soft fish and fish guts, bacon or ham fat, bacon rinds, peas, bits of cabbage stalks, milk waste, cheese, and even pieces of newspaper, tree leaves and milk bottle tops. It is in these conditions that the angler comes into his own, as he now has something that he can use as bait and entice the fish to feed on.

Ground baiting is the secret of mullet fishing. In the case of urban mullet (and it is with these that I have had most experience) they may already have been ground baited and conditioned to feeding on something that you can use as bait, i.e. where they are grubbing on fish carcasses in a fishing port, and it is then a matter of introducing your bait quietly without frightening the fish. If they are not feeding you must introduce ground bait (preferably something which they are accustomed to in the particular locality) to bring them on the feed. With wild mullet, however, the problem is a more difficult one, as you must get them used to and to accept something to which they are not accustomed. This takes time and persistent ground baiting over several days until the mullet come to accept and expect the food and lose some of their natural caution.

Alan Mitchell, in his excellent book *Grey Mullet* ("How to catch them" series, Herbert Jenkins, London, 1961), maintains that pilchard mashed up and pounded into a "soup" makes the best ground bait of all. Not all of us are fortunate enough to be situated where pilchards are easily obtainable but any of the oily fishes, e.g. herring or mackerel will also do quite well. Indeed the finest ground bait I ever used consisted of about three dozen herrings wrapped in a cellophane bag and left in my old Commer station wagon for three days during a heatwave. The old wagon used to heat up like a furnace on a warm day and the resultant brew of highly odoriferous juices mixed with crushed barley meal made an attractive "cloud" ground bait the mullet could not resist and yielded a wonderful day's sport. I must confess, however, that the old Commer never smelt the same afterwards!

One must, of course, know where to place the ground bait. Mullet are in many ways creatures of habit, frequenting the same places on the same stage of the tide. Not always, of course, for weather and other factors may affect their habits; but they frequent certain places consistently enough for them to be known as recognised mullet holes or lies. At low water they will be found waiting for the tide in certain bays or pools and as the tide flows they will travel with it up estuaries or along beaches, usually by a recognisable route, dropping in to visit favourite places. On the ebb the pattern is repeated and by careful observation one can get to know the routes they take and the places in which they lie up or feed. Once you have this information the serious business of ground baiting can be undertaken.

Mullet can be very erratic in their feeding habits. You may fish for hours and watch them cruise or cavort around, ignoring both ground bait and hook bait. Then suddenly one will show an interest and then the whole shoal will start feeding for about half an hour before stopping abruptly and it may be hours before they will feed again. Then again while a large shoal of mullet may ignore every offer the odd fish may take occasionally. Mullet love to cruise around even when feeding so that it is difficult to hold their interest and keep them in one place. For that reason it is worthwhile ground baiting several spots within your fishing zone so that the fish have a choice and can move around yet can be covered by casting without it being necessary for you to move. This problem of holding the fish in your fishing zone is a very real one and "cloud" ground bait (so familiar to coarse fishermen) is very useful in keeping the fish interested without actually feeding them. It should be remembered that when fishing the purpose of ground bait is to interest them and start them feeding so that they may take your hook bait. You must be careful not to overdo it lest they become satiated and stop feeding. It is quite easy to overfeed them, especially if the shoal is a small one and particularly if you are using bread which swells when wet and soon fills their stomachs.

Ground baiting for wild mullet is usually a long term proposition lasting for three or four days before you can fish for them with confidence. Do not be in any hurry to fish as the mullet require time to become accustomed to the new food and if you are patient your chances of catching them will be improved. Ground bait the places in which the mullet feed or remain for some time and in picking these places the question of suitable cover and of being able to land a hooked fish safely must be taken into consideration.

A thick "soup" of crushed and pounded fish makes about the most useful ground bait. Pilchard is superior to any other fish on account of its oiliness, followed by herring or mackerel but most any soft fish will do and the addition of fish oil will greatly help to attract the mullet to the bait. Pilchard oil is the best for this job but even a quantity of veterinary cod liver oil which can be obtained quite cheaply will prove useful. The paste should be smeared over rocks which are exposed by the tide at low water where the flood tide will gradually wash off the scent and little bits and pieces. Where the water is deep the ground bait can be placed "rubby dubby" fashion in a wide mesh bag such as an onion bag or one made of small gauge chicken wire, through which both scent and little particles of fish can escape. The bag if necessary should be weighed with stones to keep it from being swept away. Mashed up crabs, shrimps, prawns and mussel make a very useful addition to the "rubby dubby".

On beaches which do not strip too much and where there is a

suitable incline a good plan to adopt is to bury ground bait in a
very shallow trench running up towards high water mark.   The
incoming tide and light surf will disturb the sand, uncover the bait
and release the oil, providing a steady supply of ground bait to
keep the fish interested and enabling you to fish up the tide.   Sand
releases oil slowly and in little bursts and a small tin of pilchard-oil-
soaked sand placed close to the ground bait is a very useful addition
at any time.

Fillets of fish or the filleted carcasses of fish to which soft shreds
of flesh are attached can also be used.   The fillets can be anchored
by tying them to a small stone or the lid of a tin which is then buried
in the sand.   They can be smeared thickly with fish oil or a tin of
sand soaked with oil can be placed close by.   Remember to give
the fish a choice so use a number of fillets located in an area about
15 yards wide.

Bread is another useful ground bait and has many applications.
When kneaded into tiny balls it will sink to the bottom and nice
patterns of ground bait can be laid with these bread "bullets".   If
the bread is thoroughly soaked and then squeezed dry it can be
moulded into balls which can be cast out to where you want the
bread to be distributed.   It will break up and disintegrate slowly,
spreading the ground bait through the water and over the bottom
as it sinks.   Bread crusts and pieces of stale bread which float on the
surface of the water will bring mullet (particularly urban mullet)
on the feed.   Unfortunately it frequently also brings sea gulls and
swans which can be a dreadful nuisance and in addition as the bread
is floating both wind and tide can waft the bread away from your
fishing area.   There is nothing more frustrating than the sight of
mullet making great holes in the water as they suck down surface
floating bread just outside casting range.

When at last you see that the mullet have come to accept your
ground bait and are feeding confidently on it you can start thinking
about fishing for them.   You should commence by ground
baiting with small particles to bring them on the feed and gradually
increase the size of the particles until they are large enough to be
used on a hook.   It is fatal to introduce one big hook bait in the
midst of small pieces of ground bait for it will be viewed with deep
suspicion and be studiously ignored.   Get them used to the bigger
pieces first and remember to keep up the supply of pieces as you

fish, without overfeeding the shoal. As I said earlier, mullet like a choice and if the only piece of food around is the bit on your hook it will be left strictly alone.

Where the ground is already prebaited, as frequently happens in harbours, towns and seaside resorts by local dumping, it is usually a matter of waiting for the tide to cover the ground bait and for the mullet to arrive and feed. In others it will be necessary to bring them on the feed as described in the last paragraph. Where suitable waste is discharged at regular or irregular times, such as at sewer, factory, cannery or creamery outlets, it may be necessary to wait for this discharge and fish in it if you have no suitable ground bait with which to entice them in between. Sometimes in these conditions a cloud ground bait made up of crushed barley meal mixed with fish oil and thoroughly soaked with water, makes a very attractive cloud in the water and not alone gets but keeps the fish interested in feeding for a considerable length of time.

The ideal mullet rod has yet to be designed. I use an old 10 foot three-piece split cane trout rod with stand off rings for use with a fixed spool reel and it answers very well. The nearest I have seen to the ideal rod is an old 10½ foot Castleconnel type spliced greenheart fly rod in which the action is felt right down to the butt and which yields to every movement of the fish yet has sufficient backbone to tire it out quickly. A mullet rod should be long, light, supple and yet strong. It must be long to enable you to cast very light floats and baits and to lift a lot of line off the water quickly when striking. It must be supple and take on a nice even curve when under tension so that it will iron out the sudden tugs and jerks of the fish without tearing the hook from its notoriously soft mouth. It must be strong to enable you to keep continuous pressure on the fish to tire it out and as striking is probably the most difficult part of mullet fishing the tip of the rod must be "fast" and react instantly on the strike.

I find the ordinary freshwater type fixed-spool reel loaded with 5 lb. breaking strain monofilament the most suitable for mullet fishing. With the light line and a long rod it will cast light floats and baits further than is possible with any other type of reel. The tension or slipping clutch should be preset and not interfered with during the course of the fight as it is very difficult to set the clutch of a fixed spool reel with any degree of sensitivity when you are

in a fish and any attempt to do so is usually disastrous.   Mullet
will tear away suddenly at a terrific rate from time to time during
the fight and the unexpected shock may part the line before the
clutch can start slipping freely.   For that reason I prefer to set the
clutch lightly and apply the additional braking power necessary by
finger pressure on the spool.   In recovery the fish can be "pumped"
by applying similar pressure to the spool, stopping it altogether on
the upward stroke and releasing the spool as the line is recovered on
the downward stroke.

Nylon monofilment of 5/6 lb. breaking strain is about right and
there should be plenty of it on the reel for mullet are very strong
fish and will strip a lot of line off the reel.   Anything lighter is too
light and anything heavier is too coarse.   Line of this breaking
strain has its disadvantages when there is wind as it tends to be blown
about but if you strike in the direction of the curve in the belly of
the line you will not go far wrong.   When float fishing I like to
dress the line with a dry fly flotant to prevent it from sinking as a
sunken line makes striking difficult.

Swivels should be the smallest possible and the hooks needle
sharp.   I find size 6 or 8 suitable for average size baits but with
small or fragile baits drop down to size 10.   Buy hooks of the very
best quality.   It is foolish to economise on this point as soft or
brittle hooks are useless in mullet fishing or indeed in any form of
fishing.   I prefer short shanked hooks as they are easier to cover
and seem to penetrate and hold better than long shanked hooks.
Floats should be as light and inconspicuous as possible, and offer
little resistance to the fish when it takes.   Where long casts are
essential heavier floats must be used but avoid those which have
too much positive buoyancy as the mullet will feel the drag of the
float as it takes the bait.   Sinkers like floats should be no heavier
than is necessary to cast the bait and keep it on the bottom.   The
Arsley Bomb type sinker I find very useful as it can be used either
for legering or paternostering and does not roll about too much
in a current.   Finally you should always carry a supply of split
shot in assorted sizes both for use as stops on leger tackle and for
shotting floats properly.

Never try to gaff a mullet as it has strong and closely overlapping scales which will turn aside the point of the gaff and cause it
to slide along the side of the fish without penetrating.   Use a

landing net instead and make sure it is big and that it has a very wide mouth. A mullet's body is not as flexible as other fishes and when the rim of the net is lifted it does not fold or collapse into the net but tends to lie stiffly across it. Hence the need for a wide landing net. When fishing from a height a drop net is essential. With the light line used the fish cannot be lifted out of the water and even if the line was strong enough the hook would tear out once the weight of the fish came on it.

Mullet can be taken by a variety of methods—floatfishing, paternostering, legering and driftlining. Each technique has its advantages and definite application. Floatfishing is suitable when mullet are feeding on or near the bottom in shallow or not too deep water or when they are up through the water or near the surface. It is also useful for trotting a bait along in a current to a fish feeding in a downstream location.

The floats should be light, quill floats are excellent and the shotting is important. Each float should be tested beforehand to ascertain how much shot it will carry and to minimise drag it should be shotted until it has the minimum of positive buoyance while still being visible to you in the water conditions apertaining during fishing. The distribution of the shot is also important as on it will depend the manner in which your bait will fish and bites are registered. When fishing a surface bait such as bread crust, a controller float which lies flat on the water and is in fact no more than an aid to casting, since your bait is visible to you, should be used. The length of your rod will determine the maximum depth you can float fish, for if the distance from float to hook is longer than the rod you will not be able to reel the fish within reach of the net. Very long traces are also difficult to cast, particularly in windy conditions.

Paternostering comes into its own in deep water, especially when the fish are under the rod or when feeding halfway down a rock face or pier. In the latter case a long hook link, i.e. 2 feet approximately, should be used instead of the normal 4 to 6 inches. The bait will flow and move around more naturally on the flowing trace and this is particularly useful in gullies where there is a backwash and where due to the movement of the water a float would not be a reliable indicator of bites. The orthodox paternoster should be lowered to the bottom and the slack taken in until the weight just pulls the rod tip down. Any bite will then be registered immediately.

On beaches the leger is the most useful technique. The fish is free to sample the bait and take it without feeling any resistance. It is advisable when fishing a leger to leave a reasonable amount of slack line so that the fish can mouth the bait without having its suspicions aroused.

Driftlining for mullet differs from orthodox driftlining in that it is chiefly used in still water rather than where there is a current. If the bait can be cast out it is allowed to sink through the water naturally and all depths can be searched slowly.

The list of baits on which mullet are taken is long and varied so a word or two about them will not be out of place at this point. Fish is high on the list and again the oily fishes—pilchard, herring and mackerel take pride of place. The rolls of flesh from the back of the fish make the most durable baits but I have also had excellent fishing using the guts as well. The roe of the fish seems particularly attractive and so does the liver but it is difficult to keep on the hook. I find that if the liver is wrapped in a piece of fishnet nylon stocking (old nylon stockings if you wish to keep peace in the home) it can be kept securely on the hook.

Bread can be used in many ways and Procea or starch-reduced rolls are most suitable as they are soft and fluff out when wet. If these are not available use a fresh pan or loaf. It must really be fresh and preferably still warm. A piece from the inside of the pan can be kneaded to a doughy consistency with the fingers and it will stay on the hook securely. Usually I like to cover my hook completely but when using bread this way I leave the point exposed. I find that though the piece of bread fluffs out on the outside in the water the inside becomes very hard and if the hook point is blanketed by the bread it will not pull free on the strike and hook the fish. When mullet are taking bread from the surface or just underneath I prefer to use bread crust. The hook should be inserted from the outer side of the crust, turned and the point brought out again. The bait will cast further this way but even at that you will be lucky if you can cast it twice as it becomes very soft when wet.

The small red ragworm is a favourite bait in many areas for wild mullet. They are easily obtained and a fistful or two of mud will usually provide sufficient for bait. It is a soft fragile worm when fresh and there are many different methods used to mount them on the hook. One is to thread one up the hook and on to the trace and two or three others are then hooked through the head and let dangle. The general idea is that the mullet can take the dangling worms quite easily without feeling the hook and with suspicions allayed will come back for the worm threaded partly on the hook and partly on the trace. Another is to mount two worms in tandem fashion, the first partly threaded up above the hook and the exposed bend inserted in the other worm.

Cheese is another successful bait particularly when used where there is milk waste. It can be cut in cubes and impaled on the hook or else if it is very soft it should be mixed with cotton wool. I used the latter method at a creamery outlet in a pool on the estuary at Dungarvan, Co. Waterford, and found that when the fish were really feeding in the outflow from the waste pipe that the cheese was unnecessary. The mullet were quite content to take the cotton wool on its own. Ham fat is also a good bait at times and as it is durable it can be cast with confidence and fish after fish can be landed on the same piece of bait. It should be hooked in the same way as bread, i.e. in through the tough skin and back out again on the same side. Mussels, crab flesh, macaroni, spaghetti, earthworms, banana, boiled cabbage stumps, maggots and a number of other baits account for mullet also and occasionally they are taken on artificial lures.

This is an aspect of mullet fishing that has not been gone into as much in our waters as on the Continent and though the Thin Lipped Mullet, which is reputed to be more obliging to the angler than the Thick Lipped Mullet, may be taken more often in this way on the Continent, I have seen several of the latter species fair hooked in the mouth on small artificial lures in Irish waters. Angling friends in Britain tell me that they have been quite successful in taking mullet with small fly spoons, or tiny golden Mepps and of course they are occasionally taken by anglers fishing wet flies for trout and sea trout in tidal water.

A successful and interesting method used in France is worthy of note. The bait used is a small worm or red ragworm mounted on an 18 inch trace. Above the swivel, the line is threaded through a small perspex "button" about the size of a halfpenny. This is spun or driftlined in a current and gives a crazy "wibble wobble" action to the worm, which from all reports the mullet cannot resist.

When casting to a feeding shoal it is best to cast beyond them and then to reel the bait back carefully into the desired position. To cast into the shoal is to risk frightening them and putting them down. Mind you, there are times when you can throw bricks at them and they will hardly notice it but that is very seldom so take no chances and be careful. When trotting a bait down with the current to mullet feeding below you, remember to delay your float from time to time so that your bait swims down naturally ahead of the float and is not dragged along by it.

Knowing when to strike a mullet is an art that I think is never quite mastered and one which is part instinctive and part painful experience. What a mullet can do to the bait has to be seen to be believed and unfortunately for one's nerves it can frequently be observed. They will move over to your bait and suck it in and blow it out again almost instantly without making your float even quiver. For that again they will do a Stanley Matthews act with the bait, dribbling it about like a football or pushing it with their snouts and making your float dip and dither, causing you to strike when there is no chance of hooking the fish. If the water is clear and you can see the mullet, you can strike when you see the bait in its mouth; but if you cannot see, you will strike when you should not and you will not strike when you should. The crazy action of the float and a succession of missed strikes will in a short while reduce the newcomer to mullet fishing, and indeed the seasoned campaigner, to a bundle of nerves in which state he cannot do anything right.

Part of this dribbling act I think is due to the thick upper lip of the mullet which protrudes some distance beyond the lower. The papillae on the thick upper lip are taste buds which enable the fish to recognise its food. When a mullet takes the bait from below there is little difficulty in striking it but if it takes from above or on the same level as the bait, its thick upper lip encounters the nylon trace. In many instances I believe that the mullet in fact is trying to take the bait but as it swims forward the nylon rides up on the upper lip and the bait is pushed forward until the drag of the float comes into operation and it is then swept up and over the fish's snout. The fish in fact may not be able to get the bait into its mouth due to the protruding upper lip and the trace.

If the float sinks down steadily or runs off steadily on the surface or just below, or if it dips or rises a little and is held steady you should strike. If your float rises and falls over flat on the water it means that the mullet has taken the bait and is swimming upwards thus taking the weight off the float and giving it back its buoyancy. When striking this bite remember that the slack line between the float and the fish must be first recovered otherwise the strength of the strike will be dissipated. When bottom fishing always hold your rod (you should hold it when float fishing, too) and by keeping your finger on the tight line you will feel the fish at the bait and know when to strike. In legering, of course, you will see the line begin to move away when the mullet has taken the bait.

It is hard to say what bites not to strike because I have hooked many a good fish on bites I was sure were not serious. One bite, however, you should not strike and this is when the fish is swimming towards you, for you will only succeed in pulling the bait out of its mouth. Be patient and wait for a better offer. In general, strike when you think the fish is really serious and has the bait but not otherwise. If you find that your judgement was wrong— well, that is the way you learn. I prefer to strike with a smooth motion rather than by a sharp snatch, by pulling down on the line with my free hand as I raise the rod, more or less leaning into the fish. If you can see the fish, strike by sight as soon as you see the bait disappear and always try to strike back over the fish, pulling the hook into it.

When you hook a mullet, do not try to horse or hold it too tight. The mullet has a notoriously soft mouth out of which a hook will tear easily. Its thick upper lip gives the hook an excellent purchase but as it is separated from the rest of the head by a thin membrane a heavy hand can easily tear it off. Generally speaking there is no need to be nervous about it or to hold the fish too lightly as this is almost as bad. Be firm but light-handed, keeping up a steady pressure all the time.

If the mullet wants to run, let it run. You will not be able to stop it anyway and the harder it runs the quicker it will tire. Keep it clear of obstacles such as rocks, boats, mooring ropes, lobster boxes and barnacle encrusted piles. Side strain will help change its direction and in sticky situations try "walking" the fish away from trouble. Hold the fish, stop the reel drum with your hand

and walk slowly and steadily backwards.   You will find the mullet will come quietly with you, but any effort to reel it in will cause it to explode into action.   If you want to recover line walk slowly forward, all the time keeping a steady strain on the fish as you take in the line gained.

Play the fish out fully before bringing it near the net and even then watch out for that last frantic effort to escape.   You will be surprised how long it takes to subdue a mullet for they are amazingly strong.   The longer the fight lasts, especially with a big fish, the smaller your chances become because the hook will be wearing a hole large enough for it to fall out if the fish gets any slack line. Try to lead your fish away from the shoal to avoid frightening the rest of them and if you are returning it to the water do so some distance from the shoal because believe it or not and this is not superstition they do seem to be able to warn one another of danger and carelessness in this respect may cause your shoal to disappear.

Mullet are in many ways more a coarse fisherman's fish than the sea angler's, for the former's technique, i.e. ground baiting, float fishing, legering and fine tackle, are ideally suited to this form of angling.   They are, as I have stated, difficult to catch but they are far from being impossible.   Do not believe all the legends you hear about them or about their wonderful intelligence.   They are no more intelligent than other species but due to their environment they are far more wary and cautious than others and this allied to their feeding habits and the fact that their natural food is not something that you can use as bait makes them a difficult fish to catch.

Not always though, for occasionally mullet seem to fling caution to the winds and become very easy prey.   Generally, however, they provide a wonderful challenge as they present a different problem in each place you fish for them.   What will succeed in one place will not in another and one must continually be thinking about how to outwit them.   That is the danger in mullet fishing because you stand a good chance of becoming one of those strange people "the confirmed mullet angler" who thinks eats and sleeps mullet.   It's a fever for which there is no cure.   I know, for I succumbed to the malady many years ago.   You will find that once you have cracked the way to catch mullet in one place you soon lose interest and would prefer to fish where they apparently cannot be caught and return empty handed.   It is the lure of new fields to conquer, new battles to be won that drives you on and you will only return to fish where you find them easy to catch in order to restore your confidence in your own ability after a series of failures elsewhere.

One final word. If you do not want the mullet for the table why not return them alive to the water to fight another day. They are a worthy foe. Strong game fish that do not give in until they have given their all and lie belly up, exhausted. They have brought out the best in you and made you work hard for your success. You have had your sport and there is no finer. Why leave them on the pier or on the rubbish heap to rot?

CHAPTER 10

POLLACK, COALFISH, MACKEREL, GARFISH AND SCAD

THERE ARE MANY SPECIES OF FISH IN THE SEA AND WHILE some are very acceptable on the breakfast table they provide little sport for the angler. Others, however, are very game and sporting fish and the pollack ranks high in this category.

POLLACK

The pollack is distributed all around our coasts but is most plentiful in the south and west of Ireland, in the west country, the Channel, Devon and Cornwall. It has a more southerly range than its near relative, the Coalfish, and in the north of Ireland and in Scotland is not as plentiful as the latter species.

Pollack first begin to appear on the inshore reefs about the middle of April and these are usually spent fish. By the end of the month they are present in greater numbers and they are most numerous close to the rock during the month of May. Pollack are lovers of the high rock and heavy kelps and at this time of the year are found almost entirely on rough ground. They are found over rocks and reefs, off headlands and around islands in depths ranging from a fathom or two up to 20 fathoms. They are plentiful anywhere a rocky shore drops off into deep water and favourite haunts are ridges or reefs of rock rearing up from deep water to within a few fathoms or less of the surface.

Later on in the summer from about the end of June onwards, when small fry become plentiful, the larger pollack tend to become more nomadic in their habits. They will travel a long way from the rock in pursuit of fry though it is mainly over the rough ground that they are taken by anglers. The smaller fish remain on the rocks and reefs until late in the year but in September about the time of the equinoctial gales the bigger fish begin to leave the reefs and migrate to deeper water.

In winter large catches of big pollack (some often ranging from 20 lb. to 30 lb. in weight) have been taken from December to March by trawlers fishing over clean bottoms in depths of 50 to 60 fathoms off Dingle in Co. Kerry and Dungarvan in Co. Waterford. Spawning takes place in similar depths from February to May before the fish arrive inshore. In summer the young pollack are plentiful inshore along the coast in the weeds of harbours, piers and jetties, and along the rocky shore. Here they remain all summer making rapid growth and by September are about 6 inches in length. They remain inshore in shoals until the following spring when they move out into depths of approximately 5 fathoms and in their second winter they migrate into deeper water.

Though the young fish swim in shoals the adult pollack like the bass is by nature a solitary fish. Large numbers of them will be present together on the one reef or along a stretch of rocky shore; and in summer when small fry are plentiful they will combine together in shoals to prey on the small fry and at times will travel a long way from the rough.

The pollack is a voracious fish and eats a variety of marine organisms but small fish, i.e. sandeels, sprat, herring and pilchard fry constitutes the greater part of its diet. Early in the season (May, June) deep water marine ragworms, of which there are many species which swim up through the water to spawn, are, together with crustaceans, the principal food of pollack, but when fry become plentiful they change over almost completely to a fish diet.

Spinning with an artificial lure is probably the most effective method of taking pollack from the shore, but float fishing and driftlining will also produce results. Fishing during the day time is not as productive as evening fishing. Pollack are no lovers of bright light and are almost impossible to tempt from among the heavy kelp on a bright calm sunny day. A dark dull day with a nice wave or ripple on the water is better for fishing, but even then your lure must be fished deep down. On the other hand a calm evening coming on for dusk provides excellent sport and pollack can often be seen "ringing" or "dimpling" on the surface as the light fades and darkness falls.

Though they stay deep during the day, at dawn and dusk pollack swim up to the surface to feed and it is at these times that they take best. When the sun has slipped below the horizon and the light is

fading fast they come on the feed in earnest and the fun is fast and
furious right up to full dark when phosphorescence on both line and
lure often puts an end to sport.   This period as the dusk gathers
and evening imperceptibly merges into night is known as "pollack
light" and provides the finest pollack fishing of all.

Pollack are fast and powerful fish which provide wonderful
sport on spinning tackle.   Where heavy pollack are expected from
the rocks (a 4/5 lb. fish is a good one from the shore) reasonably
strong line, i.e. 10/12 lb. breaking strain is advisable; for when
hooked, pollack make a tremendous and frequently unstoppable
dive for the heavy kelp.   If they reach the weed you are likely to
leave both fish and lure there though sometimes if you give the
fish slack line it may after a while come out of the weed of its own
accord.   It may not, of course, come out the way it went in and
the only solution to the hopeless tangle is to break out.   If you can
stop the first electrifying dive short of the weeds the fish is yours;
for though it will dive again and again each subsequent dive is
weaker until finally the fish is beaten.

Early in the season the familiar rubber eel is the most successful
lure.   It comes in a variety of shapes, sizes and colours but the
most useful colours are probably the amber, green and red.   A black
rubber eel can be killing at times and a white eel is good when the
water is discoloured or dirty after a storm.   The success of the
rubber eel is probably due to the fact that its slow action resembles
the wriggling swimming motion of the spawning ragworm and not
the sandeel as is generally believed.   The "Porosand-eel" also
imitates this action quite well and is a successful lure.

Pollack like a slow moving bait and for that reason the action of
your rubber eel is important.   It should wobble or spin when
drawn *slowly* through the water.   Many rubber eels sold today
will not work properly unless they are drawn quickly through the
water and these are worse than useless.   Your lure must be fished
deep and close to the weed during the day and as the rubber eel is a
very light lure, weight in the shape of a spiral lead should be added
up trace to help get it down deep in the water.   I dislike using an
uptrace weight with light lures as the lure inevitably fouls the trace
but strangely enough the rubber eel is not bad in this respect.   In
the evening, when pollack rise up to the surface to feed, the lure
should be fished high in the water or just under the surface.

The rubber eel is killing early in the season (and the early part of the season, i.e. May/June sees the best of the pollack fishing) but when fry become plentiful in summer and autumn the pollack feed almost entirely on fish and the rubber eel loses much of its effectiveness.   Any bright flashing lure or a feather jig which is suggestive of small fry is then a better lure.   Long narrow wobbling spoons or a squid-like lure, i.e. the German Sprat are excellent and they should be fished slowly—deep during the day and near the surface in the evening.   The Mevagissey eel which does in fact imitate a sandeel is an excellent bait at this time of the year and will take many other species (even tope) besides pollack.

Feather jigs are usually sold containing six or nine feathered lures and this is far too many for rock fishing.   When pollack are taking well you can take a fish on each hook and six or nine pollack at the same time on spinning tackle is inviting disaster.   Three feathers are quite sufficient and besides a very long rod is necessary to handle a trace consisting of more than three or four feathers.   You will catch just as many fish and save a lot of tackle.   The sinker should be streamlined and no heavier than is necessary for casting and for fishing the lure at the desired depth.   It should be attached at the end of the trace, i.e. behind the feathers.   A feather jig can be fished either on a straight retrieve or by sink and draw but with the latter method care should be taken not to let the lures sink too far lest they foul in the weed.   Squid-like lures, i.e. the German Sprat can be fished in the same manner though this particular type of lure is most effective when fished "sink and draw" or in a jigging manner for in this way its action most closely resembles the movements of the squid which it imitates.

Excellent sport can be had on trout tackle, fly fishing for pollack with a single streamer fly.   This, however, is only advisable where small fish are expected as a trout rod does not have enough power to stop a good pollack or pull it out of the weeds.   A single leaded fly which is quite easily made, makes an excellent lure and as it has built-in weight it is easy to cast.   It consists of a straight-eyed long-shank hook to which are whipped a bunch of cock hackles (you can experiment with different colours or mix different coloured hackles).   Attach to the hook a short length of heavy stainless steel or brass wire with eyes twisted at both ends and fold around the wire a piece of flat lead cut so that the folded lead is shaped like an anti-kink. This should be fished "sink and draw" or with a jigging movement which gives it a squid-like action. Keep the lead well cleaned (a rub of emery paper will do the job) for the dull gleam of lead is very attractive to pollack and indeed to many other species of fish. It is not unusual to see pollack going for the lead instead of the feather.

When pollack are right on the surface in the evening a very effective and very exciting way to catch them is by working your lures right on the surface. This is particularly effective with feather jigs which should be retrieved very quickly so that they whip along the surface of the water leaving a wake behind them. This seems to drive the pollack mad and they will leap out of the water in their efforts to catch them. It is exhilarating sport in the half light to see the smooth surface of the water explode as a hefty pollack throws itself 2 feet or more out of the water in an effort to catch the lures.

For float fishing or driftlining—live sandeels are deadly, but long strips of mackerel or herring are also very effective. Fish baits should be cut in long thin strips to resemble fish and a little tide is of great assistance in giving the bait movement because pollack like a moving bait. Ragworm, too, is an excellent bait for pollack, followed by large prawns and though they will take other natural baits as well none are nearly as effective as those mentioned above.

Shore fishing for pollack is not good everywhere. Some places are better than others and where the rock drops off sheer into deep water over rough ground is the type of place to look for. The good pollack spots are usually well known locally and a few enquiries will usually elicit the information you require and save you fishing in unproductive places. Remember that rock fishing can be dangerous so watch for that sneak wave which can catch you napping and do not fish when the sea is rough. It is pointless anyway because rough seas drive the pollack off the shallow rock and fishing for a day or two after a storm or during a heavy ground sea is a waste of time until the sea settles down again.

The best pollack fishing always seems to be in the most inaccessible places and it is often advisable to leave your fishing rock before dark no matter how good the fishing is as otherwise you may have difficulty getting back on level ground again. You may have had little difficulty getting down to your perch in daylight carrying a light rod and a tackle bag but trying to get back up again in the dark with half a sack of fish is a different proposition altogether. If possible never go rock fishing without a companion. Apart from the company—it's safer.

Boat fishing produces more and bigger pollack and calls for more powerful tackle than shore fishing. Spinning is not practicable unless the fish are on a shallow reef or feeding near the surface in the evening. Trolling, driftlining or drift fishing are the usual methods by which pollack are taken in deep water.

The habits of the deep water pollack are the same as those found close to the shore. They will be found over rough ground on reefs and high pinnacles of rock rising from the bottom in deep water; off headlands and around islands. They stay deep during the day and rise up in the water towards dusk. They can be taken close to the bottom during the day even on bright days but these are not so good for fishing and a dark dull day produces better results. When small bait fishes are plentiful they will frequently shoal after them or be found among other predatory species preying on the fry. I have seen a big pollack take an injured pilchard from the glassy surface on a calm sunny August morning in Dingle Bay and to my knowledge we were travelling over a clean bottom and the nearest pollack mark was a good four nautical miles away.

Trolling a rubber eel is the traditional and a favourite method of taking pollack. I prefer to use a single lure (as I like to use light boat tackle for pollack) on a 6 foot trace attached to a Kinsale type trolling lead or with a spiral lead mounted on the main line. If a spiral lead is used it should be bent in a curve to serve as an anti-kink and prevent the line from being twisted. A feather jig (the sinker is usually attached at the end of a jig) or a wobbling spoon are also excellent and frequently (especially later in the season) more effective than the rubber eel. There are many variations of the above types of tackle depending on the angler's fancy. Sometimes, a rubber eel or spinner is mounted behind a feather jig and the sinker attached to the main line or perhaps three rubber eels are mounted on the same trace. If more than one rubber eel is used they should be attached by very short links (an inch or less) other-wise they will foul in the trace. A long narrow lash of mackerel cut with a sharp knife is also an excellent trolling lure.

One must troll very slowly for pollack. Many outboard engines

will not throttle down to a slow enough speed without cutting out
or fouling the plugs.   This slow troll is essential to success but it
has the disadvantage of making it easy to get hung up on the bottom
especially if you are fishing over rising or pinnacly ground.   You
must always be alert otherwise loss of tackle is inevitable if you are
fishing close to the bottom.   When the fish are near the surface this
hazard does not arise.   During "pollack light" when the fish are
often right on the surface excellent sport can be had with spinning
tackle.   It is also a good idea to remove the sinker from a feather jig
and troll the lures right along the surface like a small shoal of fry
breaking the water in their efforts to escape.   Pollack after pollack
will come right out of the water to slash at the lures.

Small strips of mackerel are often attached to the hooks of a
feather jig to make them more attractive but be careful when doing
this with a rubber eel lest it destroy its action.   On one occasion
when fishing on the Ledge in Sligo Bay (an excellent pollack mark)
we were catching fine pollack on rubber eels when one of my
companions decided to bait the lure with a strip of mackerel.   The
pollack left the baited lure strictly alone but it was readily taken by
tope.   We tried a little experiment and found that every time we
baited the lure we got tope and when we left it unbaited we got
pollack but no tope.   We discontinued the experiment when we
found that the tope were proving a little expensive on rubber eels,
as not all of them were boated.

Although large numbers of pollack will be found on the one
reef, they are by nature solitary and fishing to an anchor is not the
best way to catch them.   It is far better to drift, as in doing this
you cover more ground and catch more fish.   When drifting, care
should be taken not to foul in the rocks or weed.   During the day
fish as close to the bottom as possible without actually getting hung
up.   Some of the best pollack reefs rise steeply out of deep water
to within a few fathoms of the surface or may even lie awash.
Fishing this type of rugged and precipitous ground calls for all
your attention and alertness but the rewards in terms of pollack
caught are usually great.   However, some of these shallow reefs
or emergent rocks are dangerous to fish, so do not bring your craft
too close unless you are experienced and know what you are doing.
Do not be too daring for fear that what started out to be a pleasant
day's fishing may end up in a shipwreck.

I like to fish a long lash of mackerel on a fairly long flowing trace for pollack, but an ordinary two-hook paternoster will also take fish. On a long trace the lash can work in a very fishy manner and I find that it takes better pollack on the average than other methods except perhaps when using a large sandeel as bait. Sandeels are deadly and can also be used for trolling and driftlining. A feather jig is also excellent and should be jigged up and down—not too violently but with an easy sweep to give movement to the feathers. If there is a nice sea running the roll of the boat will often impart sufficient movement without the necessity of jigging up and down continuously. The feather jig can be baited with thin strips of mackerel (I find that nearly any fish from pouting to tope or shark and even big skate will take baited feathers) and when fished in this manner it is not necessary to work them up and down very much through the water.

If fishing reasonably light over ground that produces sizeable pollack do not use too many feathers on your jig as you may fill every hook with a fish. One day when fishing the Ling Rocks off Kinsale with that redoubtable angler, Capt. Paddy Saul, we drifted into a good run of pollack. Paddy was using a 12-hook feather jig when he was taken with a terrific bang and he had the devil of a time fighting the fish to the boat. When we got the fish in we found that the bottom three hooks were gone and every other feather held a good pollack—nine in all and not one of them under 8 lb. The tackle was powerful (about 80 lb breaking strain) as we had been fishing for big skate and had decided to have a drift for pollack before we came in. On pollack tackle he would have been smashed, so when fishing light content yourself with three or four feathers.

When fishing on the drift or anchored where there is a run of tide it is possible to driftline. Again I find natural baits best, i.e. sandeels or a long lash of mackerel but it is possible to use a rubber eel, a Mevagissey eel or a wobbling spoon and movement can be imparted to the bait or lure by rod action. Squid-like lures, i.e. "murderers" or a German Sprat and indeed a wobbling spoon can be fished successfully sink and draw or by jigging. As a single bait or lure is used, the tackle can be reasonably light and this will give the angler more sport.

The first powerful dive of a big pollack is a tremendous and thrilling one and when taken near the surface it fights vigorously. When taken, however, in deep water (15 to 20 fathoms) the pollack suffers from the same disadvantage as many other fish which possess swim bladders when they are raised too quickly up through the water. It will put up a great struggle for the first 4 or 5 fathoms and then the altered pressure causes the swim bladder to inflate and the fish to float upwards towards the surface. Once this happens the fish cannot struggle with its full vigour and comes rather easily to the boat. When taken however on light tackle the angler cannot reel in the fish as quickly as he can when using heavy gear, and the pollack has a chance of adjusting itself to the changing pressure and will put up a stiffer fight for most of the way.

THE COALFISH

The coalfish is often mistaken for the pollack which it closely resembles and indeed from the angling point of view the two species can be treated as one since their habits and haunts are very similar. The most prominent differences in appearance are that the coalfish is a more rounded and a less laterally compressed fish than the pollack, that it possesses a rudimentary barbel under the chin (so small that it is unnoticeable unless specially looked for) which is absent in the pollack, and the lateral line differs in that it is an almost straight and well defined white stripe. In small fish it will appear as a narrow seam lighter in colour than the general ground-tint of the fish. The lateral line of a coalfish is unmistakeable and sufficient to distinguish the species from the pollack.

A faster grower than the pollack, it has a more northerly distribution and our north coasts particularly the north of Scotland it outnumbers the former species. The younger coalfish seem to have a more southerly distribution than the adults and are common in the Irish sea and off our south and west coasts. The small fish are known as billet and in the south in spring and summer they keep to rather deeper water (5 to 10 fathoms) but in the Irish Sea and the North Sea they are found right in on the shore, in anything from a depth of a fathom or two upwards. They are more gregarious than pollack and occur in shoals. They like the same type of bottom, and are found on rough ground, rocky reefs, off headlands and islands and in tideways, sounds and tidal eddies. They are, however, more nomadic, feeding over clean and mixed ground as well, and may be met anywhere.

The adults prefer deeper and colder water and in spring and summer big coalfish are seldom encountered within the 15 fathom line. They are almost entirely fish eaters and will travel far after herring, pilchard, sandeels and fry. Shoals of big coalfish are often seen at the surface in deep water working on fry but it is mainly near the bottom over rough ground that they are taken by anglers. In winter they move inshore like the cod and can be taken bottom fishing in relatively shallow water.

Spawning takes place in depths of 50 fathoms upwards from January to May, depending on the locality. The young are found with pollack fry in the weeds of harbours, jetties and along rocky shores where they remain until the following summer. Their second year of growth is rapid and they move out on to the shallower reefs, coming into the shallows once more in the autumn, and work out again into deeper water in their third summer. At the end of their third summer they no longer migrate inshore, and assume the habits of adult coalfish.

It is usually the second and third season coalfish that are taken by inshore anglers. They are found in harbours, around piers, on rough ground, in river mouths and tide rips. They will take the same baits and lures as pollack, and shoals of them will be found frequently feeding on fry in estuary and river mouths, off tide races and in tidal eddies. They break the surface rather like porpoises when feeding on fry and provide exciting fishing on fly tackle. They rise to the surface like pollack in the evening, but after dark they go to the bottom and can be taken bottom fishing with fish baits, ragworm or mussel.

Billet provide excellent sport on light tackle both from the shore and small boats. They are a stronger fighting fish than pollack and where you meet one you may expect many others as they tend to swim in shoals. Indeed where present on shallow reefs just offshore they may be so plentiful and take so greedily that the use of a 6-feather jig is pure slaughter. The adult fish being more nomadic are not as easily come by but are most likely to be taken by boat anglers fishing deep water marks for pollack, as the methods and lures used for the two species are the same.

MACKEREL

The arrival of mackerel in summer is eagerly awaited by anglers, especially boat anglers, not alone for the sport they provide, but also because of their excellence as bait for other fishes. Unfortunately they are in such great demand as bait that their wonderful sporting qualities are often overlooked.

Mackerel are a pelagic species which are found all around our coasts in summer and autumn. They range far and wide feeding mainly in midwater or near the surface on small fry and may be found anywhere. Being a pelagic species they are not "tied" to any particular type of bottom and will be found where small bait fishes are plentiful. They migrate offshore about the middle or end of October to winter in deep water in large shoals on the bottom. During this period they take little or no food but when they begin their spawning migration into deeper water about January they feed on plankton. Spawning is protracted over a long period from April until July as the eggs do not ripen all together but in batches which are shed at intervals. After spawning the immense shoals break up and the mackerel head for the shallow coastal water, feeding as they go.

The first mackerel begin to arrive inshore about mid June if weather conditions are suitable. However, one cannot be really sure of them until July and the months of July, August and September are the mackerel months. They are then feeding almost exclusively on small fish, i.e. herring and pilchard fry, sandeels and sprats but in October the mackerel begin to change their habits, ceasing to feed in the surface layers of the water and sink to the bottom. At this time they are frequently taken on bait by anglers bottom fishing for other species and mackerel taken in this manner are usually good sized fish. This change from pelagic to demersal habit is a prelude to their winter migration and the fish soon start to move out to their winter quarters in deep water.

Locating the shoals of mackerel is not always easy and indeed at times can be very frustrating for the boat angler who is depending on them for bait. If the shoals are scattered or the mackerel scarce half the day may be wasted trying to obtain sufficient numbers of fish for bait while on other occasions they can be so plentiful that a couple of fish boxes can be filled with mackerel in a matter of minutes. For this reason an "iron ration" of frozen fish bait or some other natural bait is very useful and may on occasions save the day.

The presence of mackerel is dependent on the availability of small bait fishes and where they are, so too, will be the mackerel. ' They may shoal anywhere and here again the sea birds are of great help in locating them. When mackerel drive the small fry to the surface, gulls, gannets, terns and divers will suddenly appear, conjured as it were out of nowhere to form a squawking milling mass to share in the free feast. The water will be glintingly full of tiny silver scales from the ravaged shoals of fry and the water may be covered with a slick of oil. Get to the scene of the slaughter as quickly as possible and drop in your lures. You will be sure of mackerel.

The presence of surface divers, i.e. razor bills, guillemots in numbers indicate shoals of fry swimming deep in the water and their presence should never be ignored for mackerel may be working deep on the fry. Gannets are also excellent indicators of the presence of fish and the height from which they dive will give you a clue as to how deep the fish are swimming. Even when no birds are present one frequently comes across patches of oil or scales in the water, sure evidence that shoals of small fish have been attacked by larger predators and these should be given a try in case some of the fish are still hanging around. When a shoal of oily fishes such as herring, pilchards or their fry have been ravaged, the smell of oil in the air can be quite strong and lead you to the scene.

These are the visual signs of the presence of mackerel or other predators but they are not the only way of finding the fish. In most areas there are well known spots where mackerel are to be found consistently during the summer. These may be off a certain headland, inside a certain bay, rock or tide race and they are traditionally known to local fishermen as good mackerel drops. They should be always tried for when there is no evidence of them elsewhere they may be found in these places. Mackerel are a very active fish which move about a lot and even if they are absent from a mark when you try it, do not write it off for the next tide may fill the place with fish.

When fishing mackerel for bait a feather jig is the quickest and most efficient way of catching them. The feathers can be baited or unbaited and the water should be searched through all levels until the depth at which the fish are swimming is found. It is best to use a heavy streamlined torpedo-like sinker to take your lures quickly to the bottom. The faster your jig descends through the water the better, for mackerel like a fast moving lure and indeed pollack also will often take feathers moving quickly through the water. The reel must be, of course, in free spool as the lures are travelling downwards but the spool should be controlled by the thumb to prevent an overrun. This can quite easily happen if the mackerel are in mid water or above the bottom for when they take, the downward progress of the sinker is stopped or slowed down but the spool unless controlled still continues to revolve at speed.

If you do not encounter fish on the way down work the lures by jigging them up and down, near the bottom for a while. If the mackerel are not on the bottom then recover the lures, stopping every few fathoms on the way up to jig for a while and thus search all levels. When the feathers reach the surface the process is repeated. Once the shoals are located, then everyone can fish at the same depth. Be careful when unhooking mackerel from a feather jig. They are active, ceaselessly moving fish full of vibrant life and when swung inboard it is very easy to get a hook accidentally stuck in one as the trace is pulled and jerked by their vigorous movements. It is also a simple matter to hook oneself or a companion when lowering a string of feathers over the side so be careful how you handle the trace especially in the excitement of fishing a shoal of ravenous mackerel.

Pound for pound, there is nothing to equal the fighting qualities of mackerel. They are strong, vigorous, tearaway fighters that never give up and are still fighting hard when landed. Unfortunately most boat anglers seeking them for bait fish with the same heavy boat tackle that they use for larger and heavier fish. Their main concern is not sport but to get sufficient bait for the day's fishing. When taken on appropriate light tackle, however, the mackerel can show its true worth and is unexcelled as a true game fish.

On a light spinning rod or a trout fly rod mackerel provide wonderful sport. They take with a bang and tear through the water first in one direction, then in another, showing a tremendous turn of speed and never seeming to tire. In deep water even on bass spinning tackle you could be excused for thinking that you had hooked a much larger and heavier fish but its speed and quick-silver changes of direction are a dead give away. Mackerel will take most of the ordinary artificial lures in a very eager and obliging fashion but feather jigs, spoon baits, spinners and German Sprats are the most effective. The familiar mackerel spinner is not really suitable for casting owing to its light weight, and is best used as a trolling lure. Small to medium sized lures are best but it is surprising how big an artificial bait even a small mackerel will tackle.

When boat fishing with light tackle, spinning provides the best sport when the fish are on the surface. If they are swimming fairly deep the same tackle can be used with a feather jig (three hooks are quite enough) or a German Sprat which, due to its built-in weight, will sink quickly and can be jigged up and down. If the mackerel are not too far down a longish narrow spoon is excellent and can be fished sink and draw. Its fluttering action (rather like a falling leaf) as it descends through the water is particularly attractive to many species of fish besides mackerel. Trolling is an effective method particularly when the shoals are hard to locate but calls for more powerful tackle.

In late summer, particularly during August, mackerel come within reach of the shore angler. Spinning is far and away the best method of catching them, though they will take fish baits, sandeels and sprats either float fished or driftlined. I have never taken mackerel on such baits as lugworm, ragworm or crab and indeed the only natural bait of this type that they have displayed any interest in is the small white ragworm or Herringbone which they seem to have no hesitation in taking when it is float fished.

As in pollack fishing, there are usually locally well known places which have a reputation for being good for mackerel. It may be a certain rocky promontory or headland, or a certain rock or rocky platform in a bay or cove. I do not know what attraction these places have for mackerel, perhaps there is a set of tide or tidal eddy, which concentrates the fry or perhaps the set of the prevailing wind on a certain part of the shore has something to do with it. Whatever the reason if mackerel are to be found they will be found in these places and it is important that you know where they are, otherwise you may be wasting your time fishing for them elsewhere.

At certain times mackerel "hit the beaches" and it is then the real excitement begins. In settled weather when fry are plentiful light offshore breezes draw the tiny fish in close to the shore. At times every harbour, estuary mouth and beach will be thick with fry. They will be seen flickering and glinting along harbour and pier walls as they swim along or huddle in the slack water off the main tide. The water takes on a dark colour, and the bottom is obscured so dense are the shoals. The darkness will be shot through with a myriad of little silver lights as tiny fry flash and turn, their silvery sides catching and glinting in the sun. They are never still, swimming first one way then the whole shoal turns as one and goes the other direction. Here and there tiny fry will leap out of the water spattering the surface like light rain as small pollack and coalfish (fry of the year) dart out from the weeds and seize an unfortunate victim.

The mackerel of course follow them in and evening tides (high water 7 to 10 p.m.) provide the most spectacular sights. All will be quiet until suddenly the mackerel arrive and the sea erupts in a welter of spray as they plough through the frantic and panic stricken fry. With a sound like a heavy hail shower rattling on the water the patch of spray which is the mackerel shoal travels with dramatic speed over the surface and the water is full of speeding dark green shapes which plough lanes through the helpless fry. Mackerel are very fast fish and the savagery with which they attack the fry is incredible. They behave with a wild and senseless abandon and in their eagerness will often chase fry up on the shore and strand themselves in numbers out of the water.

My earliest recollections of fishing is as a boy caught with the feverish excitement of taking mackerel in these conditions from a jetty. I was armed with a length of picture cord, a hook and a short gut trace. My casting weight was a rusty bolt attached to the main line and my bait tiny fry captured by my equally youthful companion in a bucket which he lowered into the water by a length of rope. The idea was to cast the baited hook out by whirling the rusty bolt around the head, letting go at the critical moment and then hauling the line back through the shoal. Somewhere along the retrieve a mackerel took and was hauled ashore with the utmost dispatch and little ceremony. With this crude gear we did well, perhaps because of it for the whirling bolt kept a fair space free around us from the hordes of anglers both young and old which packed the jetty on either side.

This type of fishing still fills me with a heady excitement reminiscent of my youthful introduction to sea angling though nowadays my tackle is more sophisticated.   When the mackerel hit the shore you will find the young boys still there with their buckets, handlines, bent pins and bits of milk bottle tops or silver paper.   Among them you will find the not so young boys like myself with rod and reel, caught with the same mad excitement that takes many of us back for a while to the days of our youth and leaves us with a feeling of sweet sadness as we make our way home in the dark.

GARFISH

The garfish which looks like a greatly enlarged sandeel except for its long-toothed bill, is a nomadic and pelagic species which visits our coasts in summer.   It arrives inshore earlier than the mackerel, usually in May and stays until October.   Spawning takes place in the inshore shallows over weedy ground from May to July and the fish appear in shoals in some places whilst in others they are solitary or are found among the shoals of mackerel.

As a species the garfish is not fished for specially and is usually taken by anglers spinning or feathering for mackerel.   Its main food would seem to be small fry and it is frequently met with among shoals of bass, mackerel and other predators which are harrying small fry near the surface.   On account of its long narrow beak or bill it is a difficult fish to hook.   Although it will attack a lure savagely it finds it difficult to seize the bait in its narrow jaws and will often make repeated efforts to take, not infrequently succeeding in getting foul hooked in the process.

The garfish is a very fast and active fish and when fair hooked in the mouth on light tackle puts up a spectacular fight.   It shows tremendous pace through the water, leaping repeatedly and often succeeding in throwing the hooks.   Like the mackerel it may be encountered anywhere and can often be seen jumping gracefully out of the water as it swims along.   It makes a fair bait for bottom fishing and is quite good eating.   Unfortunately its distinctive green bones rather prejudice most people against its qualities as a food.

SCAD

The scad is at first sight rather mackerel-like in appearance but the resemblance is only superficial and the two species do not even belong to the same family. It belongs to the *Carangidae* (the Horse Mackerels) and is the only representative of this family common in our waters. It is easily distinguished from the mackerel by its two dorsal fins which are set close together and by its very distinctive lateral line. This drops steeply downwards below the second dorsal before continuing straight on to the tail and it is covered by a series of plate-like scales. The combination of scales and lateral line gives the impression that the actual backbone of the fish is on the outside. Two sharp spines (to be avoided) are present in front of the anal fin and there is a dark blotch on the gill cover.

The scad migrates inshore in late spring or early summer and spawning takes place from June to August. It is common off our south and south-west coasts but farther north it is not plentiful. Scad are scarce in the North Sea north of Norfolk and are not common in the Irish Sea. In the south large shoals of scad are sometimes met and at times they will enter estuaries and harbours. Their main food seems to be small bait fishes and they are taken by the same methods as mackerel. They are sometimes caught in deep water by anglers bottom fishing with small fish baits or mussel.

Scad are not fished for specially by anglers except where occasionally they are encountered preying on fry in harbours or off piers. They take best at dusk or after dark; when it is too late for spinning they can be caught by float fishing a small slip of fish, or on mussel.

CHAPTER II

COD, LING, HAKE

AN OLD FISHERMAN FRIEND OF MINE ONCE DESCRIBED A COD as being "all head and gut" and I must admit that it is a pretty fair description both of its external appearance and its voracious feeding habits. For all its lack of grace it is not an unlovely fish and is indeed a very acceptable one to the angler.

A cold water fish, the cod is found all around our coasts but is more plentiful in the Irish Sea and in the North Sea than it is along our south coasts where it tends to keep in deeper water. A demersal fish, it feeds mainly on the bottom but at times when herring, sprats or other shoal fish are plentiful it will swim up from the bottom to prey on them and occasionally will be taken quite near the surface. At such times fish forms an important part of its diet but usually its stomach is full of bottom living creatures among which crustaceans predominate. Various kinds of crabs, Norway Lobsters (Dublin Bay Prawns), whelks, marine worms and starfish are all grist to its evergrinding mill. The stomach of one 16 lb. cod which I caught was a hard distended mass of brittle stars. There were literally hundreds of these creatures and I remember thinking at the time that they could not be very nourishing. This apparently does not worry the cod for the most amazing things ranging from lumps of coal to a complete book have been found in cod stomachs. Anything edible on the bottom will find its way into a cod's stomach—it is not fussy and small bottom living fishes as well as squids, octopi and cuttlefish are fair game.

Cod range widely over the bottom in shoals and are found on clean bottoms of sand and mud as well as on mixed ground. They are most plentiful where food is abundant and in some places may live on entirely rough ground for a time. These "Rock Cod" are very red in colour in marked contrast to the olive or greyish green hue of those taken on clean ground.

In summer, adult cod are rarely taken in less than 10 fathoms and good fish are usually found in depths of 15 fathoms upwards. In

late autumn or early winter—usually about November—as the
inshore shallows lose their summer heat and become colder than
the deeper water outside the shoals of cod begin to migrate into
shallower water and come within the reach of the shore and inshore
angler.   At this time of the year they provide excellent sport in
places (particularly on the east coast of England) on steeply shelving
beaches or from piers and are plentiful in bays and some large
estuaries.   They remain inshore until January when the urge to
spawn takes them out once more into deeper water.   Spawning
takes place over the period January to June but in our waters is·
mainly concentrated in the months of March and April.   The spent
cod spread out from the spawning grounds and once again become
distributed in shoals in depths of 15 fathoms upwards and generally
speaking the fish have not fully recovered before the end of June
when they are once again fit to take.

The young fry are at first pelagic and do not assume their demersal
habits for two to three months after hatching by which time they
will have reached the shore and inshore shallows in numbers and
are found among the young of pollack, coalfish and whiting.   Not
all are fortunate enough to reach the shore and go to the bottom
in deeper water where they do not thrive as well.   The cod grows
quickly and the fish that remain in shoals in the shallows all summer
and autumn may be 7 to 8 inches long at the end of their first year.
In their first winter they seek deeper water showing a preference
for localities where there are strong tides or tidal currents.   They
will be found in the channels of large estuaries, in sounds between
islands and the mainland, in bays, over bottoms of mud or sand,
near the edge of rough ground or on mixed bottoms of rock,
gravel, sand or mud, showing a liking for any place where there is
a good scour of tide.

At this stage they are known as "Pickers" in many places and
they remain on this type of ground throughout their second summer,
growing fast, and by their second winter when they once again
work out into deeper water, they are big enough to be called
codling or tamblin (as they are known in some places).   The codling remain in deeper water until the following winter (their third)
or late autumn when they start their first inshore migration and by
the following January many of them are mature and they assume
the habits of adult cod in their fourth year.

Codling can be taken all through the year, but are best in autumn and winter. In summer, like cod, they feed intermittently during the day and feed best in the evening and early morning, i.e. for an hour before and approximately two hours after darkness descends. In winter they feed freely during the day but are more active after dark especially on a flowing tide. Where tides are strong (and codling like to swim against the tide) they take best near low water and on the early flood. In large estuaries they are often found in deep holes in the main channel a surprisingly long distance from the sea.

As codling are usually taken in depths of less than 10 fathoms, light tackle can be frequently used and on suitable tackle their fighting qualities are not to be despised. In some localities where tides are strong and heavy sinkers must be used or where anglers fish on the drift over rough and weedy bottoms, heavier tackle cannot be avoided and naturally the fish will not show to the same advantage. Where the marks are not known, drifting over likely ground is a good method and when "pay dirt" is struck marks can be taken and the spot then fished to an anchor. When fishing to an anchor for codling it is essential that you be right on the marks if you are to be among the fish. Time and again I have seen this point proved. The length of a boat may make all the difference, sometimes even a yard or two will decide who will be among the codling and who will not.

Ordinary paternoster tackle will do for codling fishing, but I prefer to have one bait on the bottom so I usually fish one hook down leger fashion and another hook up the trace on a short link. There is little difficulty in striking because codling usually mean business and can be struck as soon as you feel the weight of the fish. The most useful baits are lugworm, mussel and crab but slices of mackerel, herring or squid will be taken readily as will such baits as razorfish, hermit crab and sprats. Strangely enough ragworm, so successful for other species, is a very indifferent bait for codling or cod. Hook sizes can be large as codling have big mouths. I use 1/0 to 2/0 but if cod are expected I would go up to 4/0. The size of the bait used will dictate the hook size and a large bait is usually more effective than small ones.

I have taken codling on artificial lures particularly when fishing a German Sprat or a long wobbling spoon on or very near to the bottom. Feather jigs will also take both codling and cod but I have found them more successful when the feathers were baited with slips of fish or mussel.

Cod in deep water during summer are seldom fished for specially, but are taken in the course of general bottom fishing. They range far and wide in search of food and may be encountered on every type of ground including very rough ground. They will take the same baits as mentioned earlier for codling but usually it is on a large fish bait that they are caught. Mussel is always a good bait for cod and crab, especially a soft or peeler edible crab, is excellent. Whelk though extensively used by long line fishermen is an indifferent bait for angling and clam or razorfish are infinitely superior to it.

During the summer months large cod are usually found in depths of 15 fathoms upwards and are taken fishing to an anchor or on the drift. Looking back over the years I find that I caught more big cod in summer fishing on the drift than I did when fishing to an anchor and mostly on fish baits (usually a big lash of mackerel). The bait used may not be significant because when deep sea fishing I usually use fish baits anyway except when specifically angling for smaller species such as bream, but I do think that cod are more scattered in deep water in summer than when they come inshore in winter and are concentrated in larger numbers. For this reason drifting over likely ground is likely to be more remunerative in numbers of cod taken than fishing to an anchor. I also think that big baits are more likely to be taken than small ones though feather jigs account for their usual quota of fish.

Feather jigs as I mentioned in a previous chapter will take most species of fish but I must confess to a prejudice where they are concerned. They are excellent for obtaining quantities of mackerel as bait and a one, two or three feather jig used in conjunction with a spinning outfit or light boat rod when pollack fishing gives wonderful sport. However, the use of six, nine or even twelve feather jigs in pollack or general fishing leaves me cold and I cannot bring myself to call it *fishing*. Admittedly it can be a deadly method, but to me it is not an acceptable alternative to either spinning or fishing with bait and I cannot bring myself to spend a day jigging a string of feathers up and down in the water. I have noticed especially where pollack and coalfish are concerned that they take an inordinate number of small fish, but perhaps this is only an excuse to bolster up my dislike of jigging. As I said before I am prejudiced and my prejudice may not be shared by many other anglers.

Big cod in deep water are strong heavy fish that fight well on reasonably light tackle. However when taken on heavy tackle which allows them to be fought up quickly through several fathoms, cod like other species which possess swim bladders cannot adjust quickly enough to the rapidly changing pressure and come easily and quickly to the surface. In winter when the cod is inshore in shallow water this trouble does not arise and when taken either from a boat or from the shore puts up a strong stubborn resistance.

The cod begin to migrate inshore in late autumn or early winter (usually about November) and are preceded by the third season codling which are by now quite sizeable. When a codling becomes a cod has long been a source of argument and differs widely from place to place. In most areas anything under 6 to 8 lb. is classed as a codling or tamblin while in others nothing under 10 to 11 lb. would be deemed worthy of being called a cod. It usually takes an onshore gale to first bring the cod into the shallows in numbers. Indeed they seem to revel in windy conditions which stir up the bottom and are most active inshore in breezy weather. The first fine day after a storm when the water is still dirty is the best time of all and near the shore they feed best at dawn and dusk. They come closer to the shore after dark and are often taken from beaches in very shallow water.

Boat fishing opportunities for cod are rather limited in winter by the weather but when conditions are calm those hardy enough to brave the cold are well rewarded by good catches of sizeable cod. In winter cod feed extensively on herring and sprats and their movements are to a great extent influenced by the presence and location of concentrations of these fish. Fishing with rod and line from a herring drifter can be a most rewarding experience but nowadays, unfortunately, this kind of opportunity is limited as trawling has ousted the traditional drift netting. Even when conditions are not too good certain bays and large estuaries provide good fishing in reasonable shelter. Estuaries on the whole offer smaller cod than the open sea but some like the estuary of the Munster Blackwater at Youghal, Co. Cork have a run of big cod which in the shallow water provide exciting sport. Big baits are a must for big cod either from a boat or from the shore in winter and it is hard to beat the humble lugworm though soft or peeler crab, mussel and fish bait are also excellent.

Do not be afraid to put on plenty of bait. Four or five lugworms on a big hook are not too much. Once when winter fishing in an estuary with a commercial fisherman who was using two handlines, one on either side of the boat, I complained to him that crabs tearing at the lugworm on my hooks were a terrible nuisance. He smiled condescendingly and said that he was happiest when his hookful of lugworms was festooned with crabs as it made a grand mouthful for a big cod. He was right for shortly afterwards a cod with a mouth like an excavator came along and took crabs, lugworm, hook and all in its stride. I mention this story in passing so that you will not be afraid to use really big baits (with correspondingly big hooks) for cod. Usually I like to mount my baits neatly (especially fish baits, cutting them and mounting them in a manner suggestive of a small fish) but with cod it does not seem to matter. When stuck for bait I have put mussel, lugworm and frozen herring all in one horrible messy lump on a hook to have it taken with a resounding thump. Cod are not usually fussy though there are occasions when they will take one bait in preference to another or may seem to leave one type of bait severely alone.

Again I would mention the importance of being exactly on your mark when fishing for cod. Your bait must be in the right spot if you are to catch them in numbers. The same applies to shore fishing as some stretches of beach or rock are better than others. This is well demonstrated at Dungeness where the cod are feeding in a trough scoured out by tidal action and long casts from the shingle beach are essential to place the bait in the right place.

The east coast of England gets a good winter run of cod and from certain beaches and piers from Dungeness northwards excellent shore fishing is to be had. The beaches are usually steep and backed by shingle and surf casting tackle as used in surf fishing for bass is the most suitable gear. Heavier weights up to 6 and 8 oz. (spiked) may be necessary in places due to strong tides and heavy wave action. A leger or running trace is probably superior to an ordinary paternoster when beach fishing for cod but where distance is essential it cannot be cast as far and the use of a paternoster may give that (at times so necessary) extra 30 to 40 yards. The running paternoster described in an earlier chapter is easier to cast than the orthodox leger. A useful tip is to use a length of heavy monofilment as a leader. It should be long enough to reel back on the spool to absorb the shock of casting and for pulling fish clear of the surf. It is best attached by whipping to the main line or by a double blood knot. The hook links should be of the usual breaking strain. This leader is very useful in all types of surf fishing as it saves wear and tear on the main line and obviates the necessity of breaking off lengths of weakened or doubtful line before starting to fish.

Piers, apart from a few isolated instances, are not noted for their good fishing and the angler would be better occupied on a beach, in an estuary or fishing from the rocks. Winter cod fishing is, however, the exception and there are many piers which are excellent for cod. Paternostering is as good a method as any for pier fishing but again I would prefer one bait on the bottom. If there is a run of tide to swim out the bait a paternoster trot tackle will place the bait on the bottom.

Unless one has a dropnet or can get down to water level by means of a flight of steps, fairly strong tackle must be used from a pier. It may be necessary to winch up a heavy fish a considerable height to the fishing platform and this calls for a shortish stiffish rod and strong line. Naturally you will not have as much sport from the fish but in the conditions it cannot be avoided and it is well worth while making up a drop net and so be able to use more sporting tackle.

The end of the pier is not always the best place from which to fish though it seems to have a magnetic attraction for many anglers. The type of pier, i.e. whether it is solid or constructed on piles or threstles, the nature of the sea bed and the set and strength of the tide all have an effect on the location of fish and as on the shore certain parts of the pier will be better than others or will fish well in certain conditions or stages of tide. In one spot it may be best to fish close to the piles, in another a longish cast may be necessary to reach productive ground. In pier fishing as in any other form of fishing you must think and not just slavishly walk to the end of the pier and cast seawards as far as possible. The angler who lowers his bait down to the bottom on the inner end of the pier may quite easily fill his bag while you go home empty handed. The fact that you are fishing in deeper water is no guarantee that the fish are out there too.   The reverse is very often the case.

Beach and pier fishing is relatively luxurious in comparison to the shore fishing for cod on parts of the Yorkshire coast.   There, anglers must fish over extensive areas of low rough ground covered by an absolute jungle of tangled kelps and weed.   The cod fishing is good but difficult and I have often heard anglers from the south, where conditions permit the use of sporting tackle, decry the heavy gear used on this part of the coast.   I am all in favour of the use of sporting tackle but, of course, within reason and conditions often dictate the type of gear one must use if one is to fish at all.   The tackle must be powerful to pull a fish through the dense clutching weed.   The rod must have plenty of backbone yet be long enough to cast a respectable distance, the line must be strong and a centre-pin reel is standard as it gives a quick recovery and enables the angler to "winch in" the fish when the going gets tough.   Needless to remark one hook only is used and sinkers must be expendable and attached to the trace by some "rotten bottom" so that only the sinker is lost when the weed is fouled.

The anglers who fish in and overcome these conditions have my admiration and I often feel that their more fortunate fellow anglers who can enjoy fishing with lighter tackle are frequently too quick to run down their methods and tackle without fully understanding the obstacles with which they are faced.

LING

The ling (*Molva molva (Linn)*) should not be confused with its smaller relations, the rocklings.   It is a deep water species attaining a length of 5/6 feet and weights of 60/70 lb though the average size in our waters is 12 to 30 lb. or thereabouts.   It is found all around our coasts, sometimes on clean ground but it is essentially a fish of rough and rocky bottoms.

The ling is a demersal species and almost entirely a fish-eater and its favourite haunts are the high reefs and rocky ledges found in deep water.   While ling have been taken in depths of 10 fathoms the adult ling are usually caught in depths of 15 fathoms upwards and are more plentiful in depths of 20 to 60 fathoms.   Small or baby ling are sometimes taken over rough ground in shallow water during the summer but they migrate into deeper water in winter. It is more or less solitary in habit though large numbers of ling may be present in an area or on the same reef or wreck. Divers working on the wreck of the *Lusitania*, lying some eleven miles off the Old Head of Kinsale in 45 fathoms report great banks of very big ling on the wreck and excellent catches of heavy fish have been made by anglers fishing over it.

The ling is a strong and very powerful fish, rather eel-like in appearance and with a mouth filled with sharp teeth. Although I have taken good fish on heavy monofilment the hook links have usually been so badly frayed that I prefer to use a short length of wire to the hook when fishing over ground where sizeable ling are expected. A large hook (size 6/0 or bigger) and a big lash of mackerel or herring, or even a whole herring, fished on or close to the bottom on an ordinary paternoster will answer quite well. As ling are taken on ground where you would expect large conger I usually use a leger with at least 18 inches between the weight and the lower hook and find it very effective. Ling are frequently taken while fishing for conger or cod on rough ground and although they are strong and stubborn fighters, like the cod they come easier after they have been lifted through several fathoms of water and the tackle used need not be as heavy as that used for conger fishing.

Where ling are known to be plentiful I prefer to fish for them specifically with light boat tackle and have found that even when taken in depths of 40 to 50 fathoms they will fight very strongly and vigorously all the way up to the boat. This would not be the case if heavy boat tackle is used, for when raised quickly from the depths they suffer from swim bladder trouble after a while and come easily to the surface. If you miss a fish when you strike, drop the bait quickly down to it again. Ling are fierce fish that seemingly become annoyed when a tasty morsel is snatched from their jaws and if the bait is dropped back to them immediately they will take it savagely.

Ling spawn from April to June and are usually well recovered by July. They are not fished for specially by anglers except in the case of a particular ground where they are very plentiful, i.e. the *Lusitania* wreck off Kinsale, and are usually taken in the course of general bottom fishing for such species as cod, conger, etc., over rough ground.

HAKE

The hake is not unlike a ling in general outline but its body is less rounded and it has no barbel under the chin.   Its dorsal and anal fins are similar to those of the ling but differ in that they are more erect, the first dorsal being triangular in shape and the extremities of the second dorsal and the anal fin are wider than the anterior portions.   The tail fin is squarish while the lateral line is black as is the inside of the mouth.   The hake is a smaller species running to a little over 20 lb. in weight and is much fiercer in appearance possessing a large mouth and very sharp teeth.   The hake is very much a deep water species being found mainly in depths of over 20 fathoms and even as deep as 500/600 fathoms.   It was once plentiful around our coasts but has suffered badly from commercial fishing.   Towards the end of the last World War and for a few years afterwards hake in common with many other species of sea fish became plentiful again around our shores but with the coming of peace intensive commercial fishing was once again resumed and the stocks of hake were quickly thinned out and reduced.   Being a deep water species (the bulk of the commercial catch is taken in depths of over 50 fathoms) what was coming within the reach of the angler was the overflow of the large numbers of hake in deep water and also the smaller fish which tend to frequent shallower water than the bigger hake.

As the commercial fishermen decimated the shoals in deep water the overflow into coastal waters ceased and the hake has now become very scarce inshore and is unlikely to figure in the catches of many anglers.   The hake is a slow growing and slow maturing species (the females may not be mature until their tenth year) and because of this are particularly vulnerable to overfishing.   A heavily fished, slow growing and slow maturing species does not get time to replenish its stocks and I shudder to think what would happen to the bass if it ever became the subject of intensive commercial fishing.

Spawning takes place over a long period from January to November but usually in our waters April to September is the main period.   Hake keep to deep water during the winter but there is a seasonal movement into shallower water during summer and autumn.   They feed entirely on smaller fishes and are nocturnal

in their habits.   They lie on the bottom during the day, rising up to
feed on shoal fish in mid water or in the surface layers.   At times
they will be found right on the surface.   Angling for hake entails
mainly night fishing although they have been taken occasionally
on the bottom during the day.

In our inshore waters in summer and autumn they prey mainly
on shoals of mackerel, pilchard, herring, garfish and scad.   The
most successful way to catch hake is to fish at night from a herring,
mackerel or pilchard drifter but, unfortunately, this type of commercial fishing is a dying trade and the opportunities that come the
angler's way to avail of it are now few and far between.   A whole
fish (mackerel, herring or pilchard) mounted on a large single hook
is the best bait.   The hook should be fished below the lead and a
wire trace is essential as the sharp teeth of the hake will cut easily
through the line.   The top 10 or 15 fathoms should be searched
to find the level at which the fish are feeding.   At dusk the fish
are likely to be swimming fairly deep near mid water but after
dark may come right up to the surface.   The middle reaches of
the night are usually fairly slack and from dusk to midnight and
again just before dawn are the best times.   Remember that the
hake has very sharp teeth and a link swivel from which the wire
trace can be detached and a new one mounted may save accidents
in the dark.

CHAPTER 12

WHITING, HADDOCK, POUTING AND POOR COD

IN MANY AREAS THE WHITING IS THE MAINSTAY OF THE inshore and pier angler's winter fishing and as such is welcome. A member of the cod family, it may attain a weight of up to 8 lb. but the main run of fish is very considerably smaller (1 to 2 lb.) and a 3 lb. whiting is generally considered a specimen.

The whiting is found all around our coasts but is more plentiful in the south particularly in the Irish Sea, the south and west of Ireland, in the Channel and the North Sea. Whiting swim in shoals, feeding over clean bottoms of sand or mud, although I have often caught them in deep water on little patches of clean ground amongst the rough. It is almost entirely a bottom feeder and is taken usually within a fathom of the bottom though it will sometimes follow small fry, e.g. herring fry, and sandeels up right to the surface.

It is almost entirely a fish-eater, feeding extensively on small herrings, sprats, sandeels and any small fry including the young whiting on which it preys heavily. Crustaceans and marine worms are also eaten and may be important locally. Spawning time is from February to June, the precise time depending on the locality and usually takes place in depths of 20 fathoms upwards. A fast growing species in its early years, the young whiting which is found in the shallow inshore waters all summer and autumn may attain a length of 6 inches by November when it starts to move out into deeper water for the winter. In its second summer it may be found among shoals of small whiting in depths of 5 to 30 fathoms, moving closer to the shore in its second winter. The whiting usually matures in its third year and assumes the habits of adult whiting.

Whiting fishing may be considered under two heads—summer fishing in deep water and winter fishing inshore or from the shore.

The whiting like the cod is a cold water species and during the summer months is found in deep water. At spawning time, during the spring and early summer it is usually out of reach of the angler but from July onwards shoals of adult whiting will be found in depths of 15 fathoms or more on clean ground. Marks are important in whiting fishing but they are usually easy enough to obtain in most places as whiting formed an important part of the old commercial hand-line fishermen's catch and the "whiting grounds" were well known to them.

To enjoy whiting fishing one must use light tackle. There is no sport in hauling in one, or two pound whiting, maybe three at a time on heavy tackle such as used for skate or conger. In fact they can at times be a perfect nuisance when one is angling for larger fish. Once when fishing in 35 fathoms over a clean patch in the middle of some very foul ground off Dingle we hit a shoal of whiting. As soon as one hit the bottom—bang, bang, bang—three whiting at a time, all good fish around the 2½ lb. mark but 35 fathoms is a long way to come up time after time for whiting so I changed to one big bait on the bottom and awaited the arrival of something bigger. My companions became so tired after a while that when the whiting took they left them there in the hope that something big should take them in turn.

That is one of the drawbacks to fishing a two or three hook trace when large bottom feeding species are the quarry. Usually the large bait is on the bottom with one or two smaller baits up the trace. This only invites the attentions of smaller fishes such as whiting or pouting which take the small baits and frequently your terminal tackle is out of the water at the very time a big fish comes along. Be single-minded about your fishing. If you want big fish, then fish for them, and if you want small fish adapt your tackle to suit.

On light boat tackle, whiting can be good fun, fighting quite well and usually when they are present they are present in quantity so that one is kept busy. An ordinary three hook paternoster is the usual terminal rig but some anglers when fishing specifically for whiting use "spreaders" that is stainless steel or brass booms to spread the baits far enough apart and to carry two hooks on the same level. There is a standard size whiting hook but at times one can be pestered with really small whiting tearing the bait to rags with their very sharp teeth and when this happens a smaller hook is indicated.

The best bait for whiting is a fish bait, e.g., a small strip of mackerel, herring, pilchard or a whole sprat, while a fresh mussel is also good. They will, of course, take a feather jig either baited or unbaited, and fished close to the bottom. They will also take lugworm or ragworm but these are poor in comparison to fish baits. When there are no known whiting marks it is best to fish "on the hull", i.e. drifting until one encounters a shoal, and then one can anchor.

In summer, deep water whiting feed on and off during the day and take best at dawn and dusk. They are most active around the first two hours after dark and again just before dawn. Bad weather can scatter the shoals in relatively shallow water and fishing may be poor for a few days after a storm. While whiting prey extensively on other fishes (they are particularly partial to their own young) they are in turn preyed upon by larger species. Packs of spurdogs are often found on whiting ground and tope and shark too. Indeed a whole whiting makes an excellent bait for tope and a lash of whiting is a good bait for conger.

In late autumn whiting begin to migrate inshore like the cod but do so much earlier. The first whiting begin to appear in late October or early November usually after the first period of sharp hard frost. Their arrival may be advanced or delayed by the presence and the location of the shoals of sprat, small herring and fry on which they feed. The smaller whiting arrive first followed by the larger fish later. The larger whiting are now in relatively shallow water (10-12 fathoms) and provide excellent sport for the inshore boat angler. This early run of whiting often delays the offshore migration of tope which follow them in to prey on them and excellent tope fishing can be enjoyed for a while before the tope finally depart.

Winter whiting take well during the day but feed even better after dark. Some of my earliest fishing as a youth was for whiting and I have clear memories of cycling 7 miles to the nearest pier in the evening or rising early to catch that very productive hour before dawn. Winter whiting fishing is always associated in my mind with clear crisp starry frosty nights as these seemed to be the best of all. If I arrived early, fishing would be quiet for a while and then suddenly the whiting would be there tugging at the baits, their silvery flanks glistening in the lighthouse beam as I handlined them up on the pier.

The small whiting would come first and after a while they would disappear. Then I knew the larger fish had arrived for big and small whiting do not seem to mix, the smaller fish having a healthy respect for the appetite of their larger brethren. We caught our biggest whiting after a period of offshore winds which drew the sprats and fry inshore right into the pier and harbour. The big whiting followed them and great were the bags of nice well filled fish which we took when conditions were right. Sometimes the whiting were followed in by dogfish and we would catch no fish until they were gone. At that early stage I learned to dislike dogfish and since then I have had no reason to change my opinion.

The whiting remain inshore until about the middle of February when they start migrating out into deeper water for spawning. The bigger fish are the first to go followed later by the smaller whiting. Their departure marks the end of the winter shore fishing for there is a lean period ahead until the flounder, bass and pollack bring the summer cycle into full swing once again.

Winter provides the best of the whiting fishing. Apart from concentrating the shoals in the inshore waters, the fact that the fish are then found in relatively shallow water means that the boat angler can use lighter and more sporting tackle. The pier angler of necessity must usually use more powerful tackle than the size of the fish warrants. Apart from having to reel the fish up on the pier, a procedure calling for a short and stiffish rod (not rigid, for there is no need to use a pole) and strong line, there are other difficulties. Piers are often crowded with anglers, there are overhead wires and other obstructions which preclude the use of a long flexible rod. A three hook paternoster is the most effective terminal rig for whiting fishing from the shore and the baits used are the same as those described for boat fishing.

The table qualities of the whiting are much maligned. Granted that shop-bought whiting are tasteless and insipid, but a whiting straight from the sea has a delicate flavour all its own and it is not for nothing that it has been called "the chicken of the sea". Like the mackerel, the whiting does not keep well and must be eaten fresh. Even in less than a day it will deteriorate and its flesh becomes soft and tasteless.

HADDOCK

The haddock is another species which has suffered badly from intensive commercial fishing. It was once plentiful all around our coasts but overfishing has rendered it scarce in most places and apart from the west coast of Scotland it is unlikely to be taken in any numbers by anglers. Anglers fishing in Belfast Lough on the north-east coast of Ireland take some good haddock from time to time. The Irish record haddock, a magnificent fish weighing 10 lb. 13½ oz., however, was taken in the south at Kinsale in 1963, but the average size of haddock in our waters is very much less, averaging 2/4 lb. in weight.

Strangely enough during the 1964 season haddock seem to be making a comeback on the south coast of Ireland particularly in the Kinsale, Cobh, and Ballycotton areas and are once again featuring in the catches of anglers fishing at those centres.

Like the whiting, the haddock swims in shoals over clean and soft bottoms and while other fish do figure in its diet it feeds mainly on crustaceans, molluscs, marine worms and in places small starfish such as brittle stars and sand stars. A cold water species, the summer haddock will be found feeding in depths of 15 fathoms upwards, but in early winter (usually in November) it migrates into shallower water and in our more northerly areas particularly in Scotland will be found close inshore. In February it begins to migrate again into deeper water to spawn and spawning takes place from as early as January in some places until June in depths ranging from 30 to 80 fathoms.

Haddock are not fished for specially by anglers (except in the far north) and are usually encountered when fishing for cod or whiting. Mussel is an excellent haddock bait and so is lugworm, but small pieces of mackerel, herring, pilchard, squid or sprat will also be taken. Hook sizes should be smaller than for cod and whiting tackle is most suitable.

POUTING

The pouting, so familiar to pier anglers, is another member of the cod family that is found all around our coasts. It is more plentiful on our southern coasts, being more a warm water fish than the other gadoids. The 3 to 5 inch specimens so common on piers and rocks may delight the younger fraternity with their eagerness to take a bait but they are of no interest to the experienced angler and provide no sport.

The pouting is a fish of rough ground and when it is taken on clean bottoms it is never far from the rough. The adult pouting are found in shoals on rocky bottoms and on wrecks in deep water, usually in 15 or more fathoms. The younger fish frequent shallower water and may be found in large shoals over rough ground, around rocks and piers. They take a bait freely, indeed too freely, at a very young stage and will tear a bait, meant for better fish, to shreds in no time at all.

Deep-water pouting run to a fair size and attain a weight of approximately 5 lb. but the average run of fish is about 2 lb. and a 3 pounder is reckoned a good one. On very light tackle they can provide brisk sport, taking mussel and small fish baits eagerly. They swim in fairly large groups and when one makes contact with a shoal they can be reeled in three at a time. As the shoals are rather localised one must fish right on the marks as even a boat length may make all the difference between catching them or not contacting them at all.

As a species they are seldom fished for seriously by anglers but are taken in the course of general bottom fishing over rough ground. When pouting are nibbling at baits meant for their betters it is a fairly safe bet that there are no big fish about. A quick change to smaller baits, smaller hooks and quick striking will save both bait and your temper, and as the shoals of big pouting are usually not too large their eagerness to take will help you thin them out considerably in a short time. However, should pouting suddenly stop pestering you, be on the alert, for it is usually a sign that some big fish are in the vicinity and the pouting have decided that it is healthier elsewhere. I have often noticed this and have landed good ling, conger and tope shortly after pouting have stopped taking.

To enjoy pouting fishing, the lightest tackle possible in the conditions prevailing should be used, a 3 hook paternoster, small hooks and only sufficient weight to hold the bottom. Small fish baits (even slips of other pouting will be taken eagerly) and mussel will be taken readily and remember the strike must be quick. Pouting make fair baits for tope and a small pouting will be taken readily enough by conger. Fresh caught pouting are fair eating but spoil quickly. Spawning takes place from January to April in depths of 25/30 fathoms approximately.

THE POOR COD

The Poor Cod is often mistaken by anglers for the pouting and indeed both species are often taken together on the same ground. It is a smaller species than the pouting. It possesses no dark spot at the base of the pectoral fin and the origin of the first anal fin is farther back than in the pouting and is located level with or slightly in advance of the rear edge of the first dorsal. The pectoral fins do not reach as far back as the origin of the first anal fin whereas in the pouting they overlap.

Poor cod frequent the same type of ground as pouting and are found together with them on rough ground, reefs and wrecks. Unlike the pouting they also feed widely over clean bottoms and will be found a long way from the rock. Spawning takes place from March to June and fishing methods are the same as for pouting.

CHAPTER 13

CONGER

THE CONGER IS A VERY STRONG AND TENACIOUS FISH FOUND all around our coasts and provides fishing for both the shore angler and the boat angler all through the year though the summer and early autumn are the best periods. It is found from low water mark out to depths of 70 or more fathoms and is on the whole a fish of the rough and rocky bottoms. Wherever there is rock you will generally find congers, but in deep water they frequently range widely and live for a time over clean bottoms of sand or mud. These "clean ground" congers are very light in colour, a sort of greyish blue on the back in contrast to the very dark coloration of those found over rocky bottoms.

The conger, like the freshwater eel, spawns only once and does not survive spawning. There seems to be no definite spawning time, the fish migrating when they are ready and spawning takes place in the Atlantic at the incredible depths of over 2 miles. The male is the smaller of the species, seldom exceeding 3 feet in length but the female can grow to be a very large fish and the largest recorded specimen weighed 160 lb. and reached a length of 9 feet. It feeds mainly on other fishes especially those found on or in the vicinity of rocks, whilst on clean bottoms flatfish figure largely in its diet. Squid and cuttlefish are often found in the stomachs of conger as well as crustaceans, i.e. crabs and even an occasional lobster. As a youngster fishing for conger with a handline from the Poolbeg Lighthouse at the entrance to the port of Dublin, I once witnessed a battle between a conger of about 12 lb. and a large lobster. The lobster was in a hole in the rock and the conger was endeavouring to get it out but was kept at bay and finally driven off by the formidable pincers of the lobster. However, if it had caught the lobster out in the open the ending might have been different.

Although a lot of water has passed under the bridge since my youthful days with a handline before I could afford a rod, the handline (though I no longer use it) is to my mind much more efficient for dealing with big conger than rod and reel. What the conger lacks in speed it more than makes up in sheer brute strength and power and an encounter with a large conger usually degenerates into a tug of war and a contest of strength between the fish and the angler. When hooked the conger tries desperately to get back to its hole or to the bottom and if it succeeds and can get a purchase with its powerful tail on some rock or other obstacle, victory may well go to the fish, for its hold is extremely difficult to break. The angler must lift the fish clear of the bottom and keep it coming, giving not an inch when the fish struggles and if there are obstacles or snags present (as there usually are when pier fishing) the conger must be held away from them. There is nothing superior to a stout handline for this kind of work. I am not advocating that anglers use handlines when fishing for conger but illustrating that the tackle must of necessity be very strong where big fish are expected.

Conger taken over clean bottoms in deep water can be played on reasonably light tackle and landed like any other fish, but when taken over bottoms where they can obtain a purchase, the strongest tackle is called for. The conger fights like no other fish. It twists, writhes, revolves and shakes its head from side to side in its efforts to break the hook hold. It corkscrews its long sinuous body through the water as it backs away, rather like the propeller of a boat in reverse, obtaining a tremendous grip and traction in the water which is murderous on tackle and will soon expose any weakness. The fish will, of course, weaken as the fight progresses but in the early stages a big conger will test the strength and skill of any angler.

When fishing specially for big conger, heavy boat tackle is recommended. A strong boat rod, 60/80 lb. braided synthetic line, a large capacity centre-pin reel, short steel trace and hook sizes 9/0 to 12/0. Monofilament line, due to its elasticity, is not entirely suitable for conger fishing as under the tremendous strain it will stretch and weaken so that one cannot be sure of the breaking strain. A large centre-pin reel is more suitable than a multiplier type reel as it gives "winching power" together with a good recovery with each full turn of the reel. A short wire trace is essential, for the conger has very sharp teeth which will sever any nylon line. Some anglers use long wire traces but they are not really necessary and 6 to 9 inches of wire will suffice. Hooks should be needle sharp and there is a lot to be said for the standard conger hook with the revolving eye which allows the fish to twist without putting a twist in the line. I like to use at least two swivels on the trace for the very same reason.

The tackle I have just described is in fact heavy skate tackle. Indeed big conger and big skate are the only two species in our waters (with the exception of some of the sharks, tunny and halibut) for which really heavy tackle is required. I have taken conger of over 30 lb. on a very light boat rod and 20 lb. breaking strain line but where really big conger are expected, heavy tackle is a must.

When one thinks of shore fishing for conger one inevitably thinks of piers and harbour walls for these places commonly hold conger and sometimes very large ones running to 40 lb. or more in weight. Conger are (in shallow water anyway) mainly nocturnal in habit, coming out from the holes and crevices in the harbour or pier walls, as darkness falls, to feed. During the day they remain in their niches or homes in the walls though they may be tempted out during daylight if trawlers are gutting a lot of fish in the harbour or if offal has been dumped in the harbour. They feed mainly by scent and are quick to locate such windfalls over quite considerable distances. Normally, however, they will stay put until dark, but if one knows where the holes are, a bait can be lowered down to the right spot and the fish tempted to take the bait. If possible try and lure the conger out of its lair before letting it have the bait, for if it takes whilst still in the hole the chances of hauling the fish out are slim. Success does not always attend one's efforts to lure the conger out and I have spent many an hour dangling a succulent bait in front of a conger's nose and see it follow the bait out for 6 inches or so but no farther.

As darkness falls the conger come out to feed. They will swim along the pier or harbour wall often near or on the surface seeking the small fish living in the weeds. Conger fishing is best at night, especially on warm still nights in summer and early autumn. The tackle used should be the same as described for boat fishing for apart from the chance of connecting with a very large conger, piers and harbours are usually strewn with hazards. There may be piles and girders around which the fish may take the line or may itself obtain a purchase on. There are usually boats, mooring ropes, anchor cables and even lobster boxes in harbours, all difficult enough to keep a heaving struggling conger from in daylight, but in the darkness these hazards become doubly difficult. A good torch is essential and before commencing to fish the angler should note carefully the location of anything likely to prove a hazard and also locate a suitable place from which the fish may be gaffed or landed in safety. When you are actually in a conger in the dark is no time to start looking for some spot from which to land it.

There is seldom need to cast far from a pier or harbour wall and all that is usually necessary is to lower down the bait to the bottom. A leger is the most suitable terminal tackle as conger bite very shyly and will drop the bait more often than not if they feel any resistance. It is said that they prefer soft baits such as the whole side of a mackerel or herring yet I find that the head of a mackerel is an excellent conger bait and so are whole small pouting. A lash of mackerel is also very good but I doubt that in nature conger find their food so conveniently filleted. Conger seem to mouth the bait before taking and the first indication of a bite is a sort of soft plucking pull. If the strike is made at this stage the fish is often missed as it has not got the bait properly in its mouth. It is better to wait until the fish starts to move away with the bait before striking but do not wait too long or it may swallow the bait and be hooked far back in the gullet or stomach instead of in the mouth.

Should the fish wrap itself around some object there is nothing for it except to hold on and keep up a steady persistent strain. This will tire the fish eventually although it may take some time and the chances are that before you can break its hold the constant head tugging of the conger may work the hook free or even part the gear. In the case of really big fish especially, if it gets back to its hole, the angler may tire before the fish. At times it is worthwhile giving the fish slack line, taking off all pressure for after a while it may let go and move off of its own accord and then the angler can once again join battle. When landing big conger a gaff is essential and avoid the screw-on type of gaff like a plague. The twisting of the conger will unscrew the gaff head from the handle in no time at all and both fish and gaff head will be lost.

The fight is far from being over when the fish is landed for conger are very tenacious of life and difficult to kill. They are best quietened by blows from a heavy instrument on the lymph heart which lies just behind the vent near the tail. This will quieten but not kill the conger and for safety it is best to sever the backbone just behind the head with a sharp knife. The conger has powerful jaws like steel springs and a mouthful of razor sharp teeth and one cannot be too careful in unhooking the fish especially in the dark. It is much safer not to attempt it and instead use a spiral link to join the wire trace to the rest of the line. The short wire trace can be detached in a second or two and another one substituted in its place. This is not alone safer but will save a considerable amount of fishing time. Several traces should be made up in advance and they can, of course, be recovered later at leisure when one is sure that the fish are dead.

Conger may be taken along rocky shores and at times on beaches which are fringed with rock or where there is rough ground at no great distance from the shore. A leger rig is again best, but when fishing over rough ground the sinker should be attached to a free running swivel or sliding boom which forms the leger, by a piece of "rotten bottom" or weak line so that if the sinker fouls in the rock or weed, the weak line will break and only the sinker will be lost. Remember, too, to bury the point of the hook in the bait lest it foul the bottom as well. When fishing from the shore the conger should be kept coming once it is hooked and never given time to catch hold on anything. To give the fish time or slack line is usually fatal.

While night is the time for conger fishing from the shore, in deep water fishing from a boat they can be taken all through the day, although they become more active after dark and night fishing seems to produce the biggest specimens. I have found that during the day they take best on the slack of the tide, i.e. near high water and low water as they seem to move about more at these times.

Conger taken on clean ground are usually caught in the course of general fishing and when specifically seeking conger the rough and rocky ground are the places to try. Another favourite haunt are wrecks and it is over wrecks that some of the best conger fishing can be enjoyed. Exact marks are, of course, essential for this type of fishing as one must fish right over the wreck. The wreck itself presents hazards in fishing and once hooked the conger must be lifted clear as soon as possible so that it cannot fasten on to part of the wreck or indeed take the line into it. The same hazards to a lesser extent apply to fishing over very rough ground and the fish should be raised off the bottom as soon as possible and kept off it. This is often easier said than done and if the conger gets a tail hold on anything a long and punishing battle may be expected.

When a conger does get a hold on the bottom there is nothing for it but to hang on and keep up a steady persistent pressure on the fish. This will eventually tire it unless it is a very heavy fish and when it does let go, it should be kept coming as fast as possible so that the rest of the fight takes place well up in the water where the advantage rests with the angler. A useful tactic at times is to give the fish slack line for a while so that it feels no strain. Sometimes the fish will let go and move off when it feels that it is safe and when this happens the slack should be taken in carefully and the fish lifted suddenly and quickly off the bottom before it realises what is happening.

This stratagem is all right when the conger are roaming over the bottom but when they are resting in their holes it is useless. When fishing over rough bottoms to an anchor during the day the bait may drop on the bottom close enough for a conger to stick its head out of its lair and take the bait or close enough for the fish to get back to its hole before the strike is made. Then the angler may be in real trouble. Frequently, indeed, the angler may not feel the fish take the bait and think that he is fast in the bottom, which in a manner of speaking he is. The same mistake can be made when a big skate takes, but with conger one usually feels some movement on the line as the fish shakes its head in an endeavour to rid itself of the hook.

When this happens, steady persistent pressure may eventually tire the fish and bring it out of its hole, provided that the fish is not a very big one. Many are the dodges which anglers use to try to dislodge stubborn fish and this reminds me of an amusing experience I had in Dingle a few years ago. I was fishing in Dingle Bay with two companions during a northerly gale. As we were on the southern side of the Peninsula we were able to get out and fish right in under the cliffs where there was shelter from the wind. The bottom was very foul and full of conger which we were hooking right in their lairs and had the very devil of a job getting them out. Half the time we could not be sure whether we were in fact in fish or in the bottom.

One of my companions hooked what he thought was a conger and after 15 minutes had failed to move it. He then tried strumming on the line with his fingers a dodge which often seems to irritate a fish and make it move. No success attended his efforts so he decided instead to administer a few sharp blows to the underside of the rod above the handle and after the fourth blow sure enough the fish came free. The rest of us had reeled in long before this to give our friend a chance to play the fish and we waited anxiously, each with a gaff in hand as he sweated and grunted over what was obviously something very heavy. When it finally came into view it proved to be a large piece of rock weighing about a stone which he had actually broken off the bottom for the line of cleavage was clearly evident.

Conger usually take quietly and shyly, sucking and mouthing the bait for a while before gently moving away with it. Unless the rod is held in the hand, finger on the line, the first gentle indications of a bite may be missed. A little slack should be given at first so that the fish may not feel any resistance. Do not be too hasty, give it time to get the bait properly and when it starts to move away strike vigorously and lift the fish as far off the bottom as possible before it realises that it is hooked and really starts to struggle.

The struggle is not over when the fish is brought to the gaff for things can get really hectic once the conger is in the boat, indeed with big fish they can often get out of hand. As I said in the beginning of this chapter, conger are strong and tenacious. In addition they are very slimy and slippery and possess a dangerous mouthful of teeth. They will twist and trash about on deck until quietened by a few heavy blows over the heart and as they are never still it can be difficult to administer the blow in the right place in a heaving or rolling boat. A boat should always be kept tidy with nothing loose or unsecured. If the deck is cluttered up with gear or rods are left lying around things can get in a dangerous mess with an active conger threshing about. Rods can be broken and accidents occur, causing injury to the occupants.

It is always best to use a detachable trace on a spiral link leaving the trace to be recovered later. Trying to get a hook out of a live conger is a messy, dangerous and time wasting business. Have plenty of wire traces made up in advance and leave the used ones in the fish to be recovered later. The slime from conger can make the deck dangerously slippy, so wash it down frequently to avoid accidents. Do not leave apparently dead conger lying around on the deck for even hours afterwards they can come to life and start slithering around, an imminent danger to all on board. Their powerful jaws and sharp teeth can inflict a bad wound and will penetrate even the stoutest of rubber boots. Conger are best kept in sacks which can be tied up and stacked out of the way. In this way the decks can be kept clean and the occupants safe. It is not always easy to get a conger into a sack especially in the dark, but they can be inserted more readily tail first than head first. If you do not have sacks use fish boxes. They will lie more quietly in one than on deck and unless the box is very full of fish, will do their slithering around within the box even if it has no lid.

Night fishing on deep water marks seems to produce the largest congers. Fishing in the dark poses its own problems and calls for careful planning. The decks should be kept absolutely clear of loose gear and a powerful light or lantern should be kept on board so that one may see what one is doing. One should get out before dark to be certain of getting on the marks as it would be difficult and sometimes impossible to find the right ground once night has fallen. Night fishing requires that extra bit of care and when an angler gets into a good fish the others should reel in right away to give him a clear field. Apart from the trouble of sorting out tangled gear in the dark one should always do so without being told as a matter of courtesy at any time. Handling a big conger on board at night calls for a bit of organisation and all hands should know what to do beforehand and not get in one another's way.

Conger are taken on paternoster tackle but a plain leger rig is the best terminal tackle for this shy-biting fish. I have taken conger (good ones too) on baits that have been really "high", but I suppose a hungry fish is not fussy just as an angler who is stuck for bait will use what he has. However, it is generally held that the bait must be really fresh for conger and I find no reason to quibble with this assertion. Indeed bait for all types of fishing should be as fresh as possible. Conger will take any small fish of 6/7 inches in length and a small pouting, whiting or a poor cod make excellent baits. So, too, does the head or lash of mackerel, herring or pilchard while squid is also an acceptable bait.

FRESHWATER EELS

The freshwater eel, though it begins and ends its life in the sea, is not really a sea angler's fish. It spends most of its adult life in fresh water where it gives sport to the coarse fisherman. It is, however, met with by sea anglers in estuaries, creeks, lagoons, harbours and around piers and it is often mistaken for young conger eels. The two species can be easily told apart from relative positions of the pectoral and dorsal fins. In the conger, the dorsal fin commences over or very close to the tip of the pectoral fins whilst in the freshwater eel the dorsal commences a considerable distance behind the pectorals. In addition the upper jaw is longer than the lower jaw in the conger whilst in the freshwater eel the reverse is true.

As a species they are of no particular interest to the sea angler but are taken by anglers bottom fishing for mullet or flounders in estuaries, harbours, creeks and from piers. They are very slimy fish, not in the least bit fussy about food, unlike the conger, and can get one's tackle in an abominable mess. The hook will frequently be taken well down, necessitating cutting the trace and the line is usually badly twisted about the fish and covered with a tacky slime which is difficult to clean off. Taken all in all it is an unattractive and undesirable fish which is best left to those freshwater anglers who enjoy catching them. They feed most actively by night but will be very active during the day when the water is thick and dirty after a storm or flood.

Small specimens from 4 to 7 inches long make excellent baits for bass or pollack. They are frequently met with by anglers searching for crabs or butterfish under weed and stones in estuaries, creeks and slobs. Float fished or driftlined alive they will take bass and they make an excellent trolling bait for pollack. Like the conger they are most tenacious of life and will live a long time out of water if kept in damp weed.

CHAPTER 14

THE FLATFISHES

THE FLOUNDER

THE FLOUNDER IS THE FLATFISH MOST COMMONLY TAKEN BY SHORE anglers. It is essentially an inshore species, frequenting bottoms of sand or mud along beaches, in harbours, creeks and estuaries and often ascends right into freshwater far above the influence of the tide. It is a right handed flatfish, i.e. the eyes and colour are on the right side but "reversed" specimens with the eyes and colour on the left side are frequently taken. The colour is variable, ranging from dark brown (almost black) to a sort of greenish grey and some specimens may be covered with orange spots when captured. Spotted examples are often mistaken by anglers for plaice, but the species are easily distinguished if one remembers that the flounders have on the coloured side a line of rough scales along the margins of the dorsal and anal fins as well as patches of rough scales on the head (behind the eyes) and on the beginning of the lateral line. These are absent in the plaice which possesses a smooth skin and has a line of hard knobs or tubercles on the head ridge.

The flounder is a shallow water fish and is most plentiful in estuaries, creeks and along flat beaches. It will be found on storm beaches as well but has a definite preference for quieter and less disturbed water. It is most plentiful from the second half of April to October and the early part of the season, i.e. May and June are the best months. In early winter the offshore spawning migration of the flounder begins. This is a gradual process as the fish first moves out into the deeper water in the channels of estuaries and bays but by February it will be found offshore in depths of up to 30 fathoms. Spawning takes place from February to May but by the middle of April the first flounders begin to appear in the shallows. Fish taken early in the season are often very thin and in poor condition but they are not long in recovering and soon begin to thicken and fatten up.

The flounder's diet is varied and it can be taken on a variety of baits, but crab, lugworm, ragworm, mussel and fish baits (small pieces of mackerel, herring, sandeels and sprat) are the most successful. It feeds mainly on crustaceans such as shore crabs and sand shrimps but marine worms and fish also bulk largely in its diet. While it obtains most of its food on the bottom it will swim up through the water in pursuit of sandeels, small sprats and herring fry, and I have often seen flounders follow large spoons meant for bass.

Flounder fishing is usually best near high and low water and the middle reaches of the tide are not very productive. At low water flounders will be found in very shallow water on beaches and in estuaries and channels. When walking through the shallows at times in no more than 2 or 3 inches of water you will often disturb them and send them scuttling away in a puff of sand or mud. This is the best time to fish for them in channels for at low water they are concentrated there, while later on the tide they can spread out over the sand and mudflats and will be thinner over the ground. They feed freely through the day and can be taken on either paternoster or leger tackle, and it is best to use long shank hooks no bigger than size 1. It is surprising just how big a hook a flounder can get its small mouth around for I have taken them while bass fishing using a large peeler crab on a size 4/0 hook.

Indeed where they are plentiful they can be a perfect nuisance to anglers fishing for bass, attacking and stripping the baits off the hooks before the bass can see them. The familiar "tug-tug" as the flounder plucks at the bait and backs away with it can be very frustrating to the bass angler, as hooking a flounder on a large hook is difficult and usually results in loss of bait and frayed tempers. The only thing to do at times is to change to smaller hooks and fish for flounders. Most anglers recommend leger tackle, but I find an ordinary paternoster quite satisfactory provided that the fish is given a little slack line when the first "tug-tug" is felt and the strike is made when the line straightens out again.

At low water it is a mistake to make long casts, for the flounders are right in the shallows. On surf beaches, however, it will be necessary to get out beyond the breakers as they prefer quiet water. On some beaches where the surf starts breaking a long way out and a "table of water" (flounder surf) is created, the flounders will be found quite close in, as on this type of beach the depth remains constant over a large area and the undertow is not too strong. Flounders swim with the tide, moving in over the newly covered ground to feed. They do not, however, move in as quickly as bass and mullet, preferring a greater depth of water once the tide has started to flood, and it is half tide before the fishing improves again. Longer casts are necessary than at low water and fishing is usually good from half tide to an hour after high water but they take best on the top of the tide.

I prefer to do my flounder fishing in estuaries, because I can use much lighter tackle than on a beach. Flounders cannot put up even a token resistance against surfcasting tackle and if they are to be enjoyed at all very light tackle must be used. In estuaries and channels I find a spinning rod, freshwater type fixed-spool reel and a 1 oz. Arsley Bomb quite adequate and the same tackle does me for boat fishing. Actually boat fishing for flounders can be excellent fun for, with a reasonable depth of water over them they can put up a fair fight against light tackle. When taken from the shore their very shape is a handicap and allows them to be pulled through the water with little resistance.

Boat fishing for flounders is mainly estuary and channel fishing at low water, whilst the sand and mudflats can be fished when the tide is in. I prefer to fish them on a slow drift with the tackle described above. The flounder shows an amazing amount of curiosity and will follow a moving object on the bottom or anything bright or fluttering. It is for this reason that a *baited spoon* is so effective for flounder fishing. The spoon (it can be either a wobbling or a spinning spoon) is baited with lugworm or ragworm and it should be retrieved either just fast enough to make the spoon work or else in a series of jerks or twitches which causes the spoon to rise from the bottom and then flutter back down again. It must, of course, be fished close to the bottom.

The action of the spoon arouses the curiosity of the flounder which will swim over to investigate and will then see the bait and turn its attention to it. When the fish tugs at the bait, keep on retrieving until the weight of the fish is felt and then strike smartly. Flounders will in fact take an unbaited spoon and I have caught them on large bass spoons which I was fishing slowly near the bottom. They seem to prefer a wobbling to a revolving type spoon, though the bar type baited spoon is very effective. The same principle of arousing the flounder's curiosity is behind another type of rig used by anglers. It consists of a three hook trace, two hooks fished above the lead and a third on a flowing trace attached just above the lead. The upper hooks are rigged paternoster fashion on two white plastic booms and the flowing trace hook link is about 12 to 16 inches long. The lead is dragged slowly across the bottom sending up a little cloud of sand or mud, attracting the fish over to investigate and the purpose of the white booms is also to attract. It is not unusual where flounders are very plentiful to get two and occasionally three fish at a time on this type of tackle.

The above remarks apply to shore fishing as well as boat fishing as the same principles apply. Even when fishing an ordinary paternoster from the shore, if the lead is slowly drawn through the water, flounders will investigate the puff of sand or mud it sends up and then transfer their attention to the bait. If a hook of suitable size is used they can be struck immediately, as they take a moving bait with determination and usually manage to get it down. Both of the tackles described above can be used from the shore as well as from a boat.

Flounders are curious enough to follow a hooked fish right up the side of the boat before sheering away. I have often seen this when drifting slowly in no more than 6 feet of clear water in the estuary at Youghal, Co. Cork. My method is to cast out and let the lead trail along the bottom behind the slowly drifting boat or if there is no drift to retrieve the bait or lure slowly along the bottom. A lot of ground can be covered in this manner, and as I said before, flounders caught in 6 to 10 feet of water on light spinning tackle from a boat will give more sport than anglers who have only taken them from the shore will give them credit for.

I have always found clear water and calm conditions best for flounder fishing. They do not like rough seas or dirty water and after a blow do not take well until the sea is settled again.

THE PLAICE

The plaice is a larger species than the flounder and one that frequents deeper water. It is taken generally by anglers on sandy and gravelly or shelly bottoms, over mussel beds in depths of 10 to

15 fathoms, and while good fish may be caught in depths of 6 or 7 fathoms, those caught from the shore are usually small fish that have not yet worked out into deeper water. It feeds mainly on shellfish, razorfish, marine worms and small crustaceans but unlike the flounder does not feed on fish to any great extent.

In winter, plaice migrate offshore into deeper water (20-30 fathoms) for spawning and this takes place over the period January to March. Their return to shallower water varies with the locality, it may be as early as April in some places but generally speaking the months from May to October see the best of the fishing. As the plaice is a bottom feeder, a leger or paternoster trot is the most suitable terminal tackle, though an ordinary paternoster will answer when fishing from the shore. Not infrequently they have taken an uptrace hook in preference to one lying on the bottom but not frequently enough to alter my belief that the bait should always be on the bottom.

The plaice is a commercially desirable fish and, unfortunately, it lives on clean ground that is easily trawled. The angler is likely to catch greater numbers if he can find suitable ground among the rough, i.e. clean patches of sand or gravel alternating with rough or rocky ground. This mixed type of bottom is often too rough for fishing boats to trawl and offers better fishing to the angler. Small hooks, light nylon monofilament traces and soft baits are best in fishing for plaice. Lugworm, razorfish, mussel, cockle and rag-worm are the most useful baits. Plaice tend to drift with the tide and take best when the tide is slack, i.e. near high and low water. Like the flounder, it takes best in calm conditions when the sea is placid and the water clear.

The plaice is a surprisingly strong and active fish when hooked and specimens of over 7 lb. have been taken on rod and line. Reasonably sized plaice, when taken on suitable tackle, especially when caught from a boat, put up a strong exciting fight and the species could be classed as a sporting one.

THE DAB

The dab is a smaller species than either the flounder or the plaice and a good fish would weigh in the region of 1 lb. It more closely resembles the plaice but possesses a thinner and more rounded body and can be distinguished by the fact that it possesses no tubercles, bony knobs or patches of rough scales on the head. The scales on the upper side are rough when rubbed against the grain and the lateral line is very distinctively curved almost in a half circle over the pectoral fin.

Its food is similar to that of plaice except that in addition to molluscs, crustaceans and marine worms it will also eat small fish such as sandeels and herring fry. The dab is found on the same type of ground and in the company of plaice, but has a preference for soft bottoms of sand and mud where there is a good run of tide It can be taken from the shore or in depths as great as 50 fathoms but the main run of good dabs is in depths under 20 fathoms and mainly in 5 to 10 fathoms of water.

It is often plentiful on sandy bottoms just at the edge of the main run of tide in the mouths of large estuaries, in sandy bays, sand banks or on clean ground just off tideways. Its habits are similar to the plaice, migrating into deeper water in winter but it spawns later, usually between February and July. The first fish arrive back on the grounds about May and the dab continues to provide fishing until October. Tackle, methods and baits are the same as those described for plaice but hooks should be smaller.

THE SOLE

The sole is not likely to be taken very often by anglers fishing during the day as it is essentially nocturnal in habit. It lives on soft bottoms of sand or mud, feeding on worms, small molluscs and crustaceans, but it will occasionally take small fishes. During the day it is believed that it buries itself deeply in the mud or sand and does not become active again until darkness falls.

The sole frequents shallower water during the summer than in winter and is found in bays and estuaries. It has a preference for soft bottoms on mixed ground or in the vicinity of rocks or ledges. While its range extends out to about the 60 fathom line it is most plentiful in depths ranging from 5 to 15 fathoms.

Spawning time is over the period February to August and the species is more plentiful in the southern than in the northern half of the British Isles and tends to be rather localised in distribution.

Like the plaice and dab it may be taken in places by anglers

fishing from steeply shelving beaches or from piers or harbour walls.
The best baits are ragworm, razorfish and lugworm. Tackle for
boat and shore fishing as described for plaice and dabs.

TURBOT AND BRILL

From the angling point of view turbot and brill may be considered more or less as the same species, for their habits, haunts,
foods and fishing methods are almost identical and the two species
are taken on the same type of ground. The turbot is a large flatfish
attaining a weight of up to 40 lb., but the average weight ranges
from 10 to 18 lb. and fish of 15 lb. and upwards are considered
specimens. The brill is a smaller species, attaining about half the
weight of the turbot, and while I have seen trawl-caught fish
weighing 15 or 16 lb., a 10 lb. fish is usually considered a very good
one.

They are very similar in appearance, both being "left handed"
flatfish, i.e. with the eyes and colour on the left side; but whereas
the brill is more or less oval in shape, the turbot is a broader fish
and more angular in appearance. They can be easily told apart
by the fact that the coloured side of the turbot is liberally covered
with blunt, bony tubercles while the brill presents a smooth surface
to the touch.

While they have been taken in 50/60 fathoms of water they
are essentially shallow water fishes and are most plentiful in depths
ranging from 10 to 15 fathoms. They are found on bottoms of
sand, gravel or mud particularly at the mouths of rivers or on
shallow sand or gravel banks in deep water. Most of the noted
turbot marks such as the Varne Bank in the English Channel or the
Race off the Old Head of Kinsale have one thing in common and
that is strong tides. It is on this type of ground that their favourite
food, the sandeel is most plentiful and the turbot lie in ambush on
the bottom or just off the shelf of the bank ready to pounce on any
small fish which is swept along by the fast tides.

Both species possess large mouths and sharp teeth and are almost
entirely fish eaters. Their chief food is sandeels and sprats, but
any small fish such as herring, pilchard, whiting, pouting and flatfish
that come within their reach is fair game to them. They may travel
about a bit for I have taken them over muddy bottoms, usually

where there is a good run of tide as in the channel of an estuary and they seem to go in small groups. Where you take one turbot you are nearly always sure to meet one or two more.

The turbot spawns offshore during the period April to July and the brill spawns over a more extended period from March to August. They have a more southerly distribution than either the plaice or flounder and are found chiefly around the southern half of these islands, i.e. in the Channel, the southern part of the North Sea, on the south and west coasts of Ireland and in the Irish Sea. Fishing usually picks up around July, and August to late autumn is generally considered the best time, with August being one of the best months.

As in the case with plaice, dabs and soles, small specimens (young fish) may be taken from the shore in places, but in order to catch decent sized turbot one must fish from a boat. The strong tide-ways which seem to go hand in hand with good turbot fishing create certain difficulties. Due to the strong run of water it is difficult at times to hold the bottom even with heavy sinkers and at times only a portion of the tide may be fished and in places where the tides are very strong it may be impossible to fish the marks at all except on the weakest of the neap tides. Turbot take best when there is movement on the tide and at slack water, i.e. high and low water they seem to rest. When the tide turns, they commence to feed actively, and the first of the flood or first of the ebb usually provide excellent fishing. If anything, the early ebb seems better than the early flood tide, and the fishing in late afternoon superior to that earlier in the day. Like most other flatfish, they take better in settled weather and clear water.

Turbot, despite their size, are not very vigorous fighters and were it not for the strong tides very light tackle could be used. However, when hooked in heavy water they bring their broad bodies into play like the skates, using the great pressure exerted by the rush of tide against the angler. For this reason and also because it may be necessary to use heavy sinkers, at times reasonably strong tackle is called for. A medium boat rod, a centre-pin or multiplier type reel and 30 to 40 lb. breaking strain line will answer nicely. Turbot have very sharp teeth that will cut through light monofilment and although a short wire trace will obviate this danger, wire is not very flexible and does not "work" as nicely as monofilment in the water.   For this reason it is preferable to use heavy monofilment in the 60/70 lb. breaking strain for the trace, but be sure to examine it frequently and change it when it becomes frayed.

The terminal tackle may be either a leger with a long flowing trace (6 to 10 feet long) or a paternoster.   Those who use a running leger on a long flowing trace and hold that there must be plenty of movement in the bait, may wonder at the paternoster, but turbot rise from the bottom to snatch small fish being swept along in the tide and baits mounted on a paternoster present no problem to them.   Even though the bait should be fished on or very near the bottom I do feel that a certain amount of movement is necessary and this probably explains why fishing is better when there is a nice wave or "hump" on the sea than in a flat calm for the roll of the boat imparts some movement to the bait.

Hook sizes need not be big.   Jim Sheehan of Cork, one of the most successful turbot anglers I know, with a long list of really big turbot to his credit, is a great believer in using small hooks.   Turbot are taken by anglers using very big hooks and baits when fishing for heavy skate and this allied to the fact that the turbot has a big mouth may have given rise to the idea that only big hooks should be used.   Turbot suck and mouth a bait gently and a small hook is more readily taken, easier to drive home and quite strong enough to land the fish.   Hook sizes 4/0 to 6/0 are usually quite adequate but it must be remembered—and this applies to fishing generally— that it is the size of the bait that usually dictates the size of the hook. Thus one would use a larger hook when baiting up with a big lask of mackerel than would be necessary when the bait is a small sandeel. The deciding factor, however, will be the size of the bait used and a larger hook will be necessary for a big bait than for a small one.

When it comes to bait there is no doubt that the Greater Sandeel or Sand Launce has no equal as a turbot bait. It is, however, difficult to obtain. It is not unusual when jigging for mackerel near the bottom with feathers over suitable ground to foul hook sandeels and if a feather jig (herring type) mounted with freshwater type hooks is used they can be taken easily. They are usually very plentiful on turbot marks and this method of catching them should be tried.   Sandeels are very plentiful on the shore in some areas, on beaches, in estuaries and channels.   In these places they can be procured alive quite easily but unless one has a courge which can be towed behind the boat, it is very difficult to transport them to the grounds alive.

Freshly caught mackerel is also an excellent bait. This is usually cut in long narrow strips to represent a small fish or sandeel. Take a long lash (the whole side of a mackerel) and cut it lengthways down the middle. This will provide two long strips and I prefer to insert the hook in the narrow end as the bait will work much better in the tide than if it were inserted in the wide end. I have also found that turbot like a nice big chunky bait fished right on the bottom. I cut a lash from the whole side of the mackerel and cut the lash between a third of the way and half way from the narrow end. I mount the larger portion on the hook and while it looks in no way fish-like it does produce results.

Most turbot fishing is done to an anchor and it is essential to be right on the grounds. Usually when you catch one turbot you can expect one or two more in a short time as they seem to go in little groups and then business is slack again for a while. It is as if that little group was cleaned out and nothing happens again until a new group moves in. For this reason I like to use a light sinker so that I can trot my bait along the bottom with the tide and in this way cover a larger area in search of fish. Turbot can also be taken on the drift but although a large area of ground can be searched in this manner, it presents its own difficulties. It entails motoring back time and again to get on the marks when one has drifted off productive ground and also the drift is frequently too fast when wind and tide do not suit.

The whole secret in turbot fishing is to give the fish plenty of time to get the bait into its mouth. The turbot seldom "knocks" but takes very gently as it sucks and mouths the bait. The first indication the angler gets is a "lean" on the line and if struck at this stage the fish will not be hooked. If the fish is missed do not be disheartened but leave it the bait, for turbot frequently come back to take the bait again. When the fish is first felt it should be given a little slack and let take the bait. Give the fish plenty of time until *it hooks itself.*

Those who have not fished turbot may raise their eyebrows at this remark but a common mistake among experienced anglers is striking turbot too soon. An inexperienced angler will not usually feel or recognise a turbot bite as such and the fish will have hooked itself before the angler realises that it is there at all. The experienced angler (but not one experienced in turbot fishing) is more sensitive, and alert to anything playing with his bait and will strike as soon as he feels the fish and inevitably loses it.

When fishing on turbot ground, to be successful one must be singleminded and fish for turbot and turbot only. There is no point in messing around using baits for other species as well, for you may find yourself unhooking a small whiting at the very time a companion gets stuck in a turbot that could have been yours if your bait was on the bottom where it should be. Remember, too, to give the fish plenty of time to take the bait and do not strike until you are sure that the turbot has it.

The flatfishes generally are not game fish or noted for their sporting qualities. They are, however, very acceptable on the breakfast table and a nice big fat turbot will always ensure a warm welcome in the home when one returns from a day's fishing.

CHAPTER 15

THE WRASSES, GURNARDS AND SEA BREAMS

The wrasses are a large and colourful family represented in our waters by seven species. Four of these species are rare or scarce and only three—the Ballan Wrasse, the Cuckoo Wrasse and the Corkwing Wrasse are taken by or are of any interest to the angler. All of the wrasse family are fishes of rocky and weedy bottoms and in summer are found in shallow or moderate depths around our coasts.

THE WRASSES

The BALLAN WRASSE is the largest of the three species and the only one of real angling interest. It attains a weight of 10 lb. or more but the average size is approximately 2-3 lb. A fairly deep, thick set and heavily-scaled fish, it is usually brownish on the back, shading to a lighter brown on the sides and orange on the throat and belly. The lips are thick and protrusible, exposing the very powerful teeth common to all the wrasses. There is a single row of conical, canine like teeth in each jaw, and beds of rounded molars in the throat near the entrance to the gullet—two beds above and one below. It feeds mainly on crustaceans (various types of crab) and molluscs such as mussels and winkles which it finds among the weeds and rocks. Its powerful teeth and strong jaws are admirably suited to such a diet and it will also take ragworms and small fishes though they do not form an important part of its food.

The Ballan Wrasse is common all around our coasts on rough and weedy ground but is more plentiful and seems to attain a larger size in the south. It is a fish of moderate depths (usually under 10 fathoms) and may be found right in on the shore along a rocky coast as well as over shallow reefs in deep water several miles off-shore. During spawning time (May to July) large wrasse may be taken right in on the shore; but normally the bigger fish keep to deeper water (5-10 fathoms) and the smaller fish stay closer to the shore. In common with the Cuckoo Wrasse and the Corkwing Wrasse, it is a nest builder, depositing its eggs in nests made of seaweed stuck in crevices among the rocks in very shallow water. This species is very plentiful inshore from May to November but winters offshore in deeper water.

Those of us who started rock fishing at a tender age will always have a soft spot for the wrasse, for it is probably the first fish we caught and provided us with full bags on what would be otherwise blank days. It is easily caught, feeding freely throughout the day even on those hot bright calm days when it is impossible to move a pollack. I have whiled away many a pleasant hour on such a day fishing for wrasse whilst I awaited the coming of the "pollack light" and the more exciting pollack. Bait is seldom a problem and is usually to hand in the shape of mussel, crab, limpet and winkles. It takes freely and on light gear puts up a sturdy and frequently tackle-breaking fight.

Its home is among the tangled kelps and weeds along a rocky shore. The deeper the water close in, the bigger the fish which can be expected. You must fish as close to the weed as possible and with tackle which is light this is a problem as the wrasse will fight desperately to get into the weed and if it succeeds you can usually say goodbye to the trace. If wrasse fishing is to be enjoyed one must be prepared to fish light and accept a certain amount of lost traces. I usually use a medium spinning rod, 10 lb. breaking strain line and a fixed-spool reel, but a longer rod and a light centre-pin reel would probably answer better especially for driftlining (hook sizes should be small, size 1 or 2 and the hook must be strong in the wire and needle sharp). Where a run of big wrasse can be expected, heavier tackle than the above should be used. The usual terminal tackle is a sliding float or driftline with the bait fished just above the waving weeds, otherwise it will foul in the heavy kelp. A paternoster can be used either from a pier or from a ledge of rock overhanging deep water and the sinker held just clear of the weeds. It is also the best terminal tackle to use where it is possible to fish on to a hard but weed-free bottom such as a submerged ledge of rock. A paternoster or leger fished on a clean bottom close to rocky ground will also take wrasse but they are not specially fished for in this manner.

Soft or peeler crab is undoubtedly the best bait but prawn, ragworm or lugworm will also be taken. The "works", i.e. the inside of the large edible crab often found in crevices among the rocks at low water, is also excellent, as is the meat found in its claws. This is very difficult to keep on the hook and it is best to bind it on with wool or elastic thread. Mussel is also a first class bait for wrasse and they will take limpets, winkles and small pieces of fish as well. While wrasse do not swim in shoals, large numbers of them will be found on the one reef or stretch of shore and ground-baiting is a definite aid to fishing for them.

Crushed-up crabs, mussel or a very fine rubby dubby made from fish and cast into the water will usually bring them round and start them feeding. Do not overdo it. Just give them enough to keep them interested. In many places small seed mussel will be found on the rocks and can be used to advantage. They can easily be crushed by the boot and kicked into the water as ground bait. Keep your finger on the line and as soon as you feel the fish has the bait, strike upwards and keep it coming as fast as you can. Hold it well clear of the weed (this is not always easy for sizeable wrasse can be very strong) for if it once succeeds in getting down it will knit a fancy stitch with your monofilament trace among the kelps. Sometimes if given slack line it will come out again of its own accord but usually it goes deeper into the tangle and there is nothing for it but to break out.

Wrasse suffer more than most other species of fish from abrupt changes of pressure and depths and even when taken in very moderate depths the swim bladder will be found protruding. It is often useless returning the fish to the water as it will usually float on the surface and fall prey to some passing sea gull. The best time to fish for wrasse is on the flood tide though I have taken them at all stages of the tide. They love the rough white water in reason-ably settled weather, but a very heavy surf or swell is bad for fishing, and after a gale they may not be found close in until the sea has settled down once again. Strangely enough wrasse seem to sleep at night and have been observed in aquaria lying on their sides after dark.

As in all rockfishing it is essential to exercise care. There is always that unexpected treacherous wave which may sweep you off your perch and as the very best fishing always seems to be in the most inaccessible places accidents can easily happen.

The largest wrasse are usually taken by anglers boat fishing for pollack over shallow reefs offshore. They frequently take baits and lures meant for pollack, but if they are to be fished for specially it is best to paternoster or driftline close to the bottom from an anchored boat using crab, prawn, mussel, ragworm or small fish baits. Not many boat anglers fish specially for them, preferring to tackle the larger and more attractive pollack.

The remaining two species are of no real angling interest. The CUCKOO WRASSE is a small species taken by anglers bait fishing over rough and mixed bottoms. It is a very strikingly coloured fish and the coloration differs between the sexes. The male has five or six blue bands radiating tailwards from the eye on both sides over a background of orange, red or yellow. The female is less vividly coloured and possesses no blue bands but has a number of dark spots under and just behind the soft rayed port on of the dorsal fin. The ground tint is more or less reddish, becoming pale on the belly. The male is the larger of the two and seldom exceeds a foot in length. This species prefers deeper water than the Ballan Wrasse though it is often taken from the shore and is found on mixed bottoms as well as on the rough. It will also be taken on clean ground but never very far from the rough.

The CORKWING WRASSE is another small species seldom exceeding 10 inches in length and it is very plentiful in summer on rocky and weedy ground in shallow water. A short, thick set wrasse, it is variable in colour but can be easily distinguished from the other two species by the serrated edge of the preopercular bone situated on the gill cover. It is almost as common as the Ballan Wrasse in our waters. Both the Corkwing and the Cuckoo Wrasse are also nest builders.

GURNARDS

The gurnards are a very distinctive and easily recognised family possessing large bony heads completely devoid of both scales and skin, a feature which readily separates them from most other species taken in our waters. Their short thin bodies taper quickly to the forked tail fin and the very long and large pectoral fins carry modified fleshy fin rays not unlike fingers, and which are used by the fish in seeking out food on the bottom. The head, gill covers, dorsal fins, and in some species the groove in which the dorsals are set, are armed with sharp spines which makes the unhooking of a gurnard a tricky and sometimes "bloody business".

The Grey Gurnard, the Tub Gurnard and the Red Gurnard are the three species common in our waters. The former is easy enough to recognise, for it is usually greyish in colour with a liberal sprinkling of white spots on the back and sides. The lateral line is composed of prickly, backward-facing scales and the groove in which the dorsal fins are set, though prickly, is not armed with spiny plates as in the other two species. It also differs in that the pectoral fins are shorter than the pelvics and do not reach as far as the vent whereas in both the Tub and Red Gurnards they are long and extend beyond the vent.

While the Red Gurnard is a very brilliant red in colour, the Tub Gurnard can also be very red in colour and anglers often confuse the two species. They are easily separated, however, if one remembers that the lateral line in the Tub Gurnard is a smooth raised seam whereas in the Red Gurnard it is crossed by narrow vertical plates giving a sort of backwards facing "arrowed" effect when held at an angle to the light. The Tub Gurnard also has a very vivid bright blue border to the tip of the large pectoral fins which is not present in the Red Gurnard.

The GREY GURNARD is the most common of the three species and is found on clean sandy bottoms all around our shores. A bottom feeder it is particularly fond of shrimps and other small crustaceans as well as the young of flatfish, herring and such small fishes as sandeels, gobies and the like. It is taken in a great range of depths running from the shallows of a flat sandy beach out to depths of 80 fathoms or more. It swims in over beaches of flat muddy sand with the tide and like the flounder does not come within reach of the angler until about half tide and fishing is best from half flood to the first hour of the ebb. It is also caught from piers extending out over clean sandy bottoms but I have never encountered it in an estuary though I have taken Tub Gurnards in the mouths of large estuaries.

It will take ragworm, crab and small pieces of mackerel or herring and seems very partial to a small piece of gurnard flesh. The bait can be fished either paternoster or leger fashion from the shore or from a boat and if the bait is moved slowly along the bottom it seems to attract the gurnard. Indeed a moving bait or lure such as a small spoon, particularly a baited spoon, is very effective. The spoon must, however, be spun slowly near the bottom in the same way as in baited spoon fishing for flounders and should be allowed to touch the bottom from time to time. If it is retrieved too quickly the gurnard will not be able to swim fast enough to catch it. In clear water I have seen gurnards literally "panting" after a spoon that was moving just a little too quickly for them.

Where you take one gurnard you may expect to catch others, for while they do not swim in shoals, numbers of them will be found on the same ground. The Grey Gurnard is a small species and a fish of 1½ lb. is a good one. It is plentiful inshore from May to September and spawning takes place over the period from April to August.

The TUB GURNARD is the largest of our three common species, attaining a weight of 10 lb. or more. The average size, however, is from 2-4 lb. and really large fish should be examined carefully lest they prove to be specimens of a larger though much rarer species of gurnards, i.e. the Piper. The Tub Gurnard is not as plentiful as the other two species and although found in very shallow water, like the Grey Gurnard it prefers deeper water and is more abundant in depths of 15 fathoms upwards. It is essentially a bottom feeder, preying on crustaceans, molluscs and small fish, and though a fish of clean sandy bottoms it also ranges over mixed bottoms of rock and sand. Though found all around our coasts it is less plentiful in the northern part of the North Sea. It is one of the latest spawning of marine fishes and the spawning period extends into October.

In relatively shallow water it will swim up from the bottom to prey on small bait fishes which are being harried by other predators. I have taken Tub Gurnards on artificial lures while spinning for shoaling bass in the mouths of large estuaries and in relatively shallow water offshore. Generally, however, it is caught on bottom tackle by anglers using pieces of fish such as mackerel or herring as bait but will also take mussel, ragworm, crab or lugworm. It is often encountered on the same ground as dabs and plaice and can also be caught on feather jigs, especially if the hooks are baited with a small slip of fish.

When hooked, the Tub Gurnard puts up a surprisingly strong, head-shaking fight giving the angler the impression that it is a

much bigger and heavier fish.   No doubt its large and very beautiful
pectoral fins, which are usually fully spread out when the fish is
being landed, help it to create greater resistance in the water than its
actual size would seem to warrant.

The RED GURNARD is next to the Grey Gurnard in abundance and is found all around our coasts.   It is, however, of more
localised distribution and is a fish of deeper water, being found
generally in depths of 15 fathoms upwards.   It is a larger species
than the Grey Gurnard but much smaller than the Tub Gurnard.
It is difficult to give an average weight because in some areas where
conditions are very suitable the general run of fish will be bigger
than in other places.   This is particularly true of Moville in Co.
Donegal where anglers take large numbers of big Red Gurnard but
even there a 2 lb. fish is a good one.

At Moville the gurnards are taken over low rough corally ground
where deepwater shrimps and crustaceans are plentiful.   They are
taken on paternoster and paternoster leger tackle, baited with small
lashes of mackerel, herring or gurnard.   They will also take feather
jigs either baited or unbaited as well as mussel.   Elsewhere they
are taken mainly on rocky and mixed bottoms but will also be
found on clean bottoms of sand or mud.   Like the Grey Gurnard
it is gregarious and though not a shoal fish numbers of them will
be found in the same area.   It is common on the Irish coasts and in
the Irish Sea but appears to be scarce in the North Sea.   Spawning
takes place between April and June.

THE SEA BREAMS

The Sea Breams belong to a very large group of fishes and ten
different species have been recorded from the waters around these
islands.   Most of them, however, are either scarce or rare and only
two species, i.e. the RED SEA BREAM and the BLACK BREAM,
are commonly taken by anglers.

All of the sea breams are very handsome fishes, easily recognised
as a group, but the individual species are often difficult to tell apart.
Their dentition is highly specialised and is an important diagnostic
character but the two species of interest to the angler can be readily
differentiated from each other without going into much detail.

The Red Sea Bream is a deeper bodied, laterally compressed

perch-like fish with high shoulders sloping steeply to the snout giving it a rather humpy appearance. It is red or orange red in colour, darker on the back, becoming lighter on the sides and with golden (sometimes silvery) reflections. It possesses a conspicuous black spot on the shoulder on and at the origin of the lateral line.

The Black Bream is very similar in general outline but is more compressed laterally and does not have the diagnostic black spot at the origin of the lateral line as in the Red Sea Bream. The "black" in its name is rather misleading for though the colour is variable it is frequently a silvery grey and may be a combination of several colours. There may be dark vertical bands on the sides and there are dark spots in bands on the dusky coloured dorsal and anal fins.

Both species are summer migrants from the more southerly and warmer seas and are fishes of the rough and rocky ground. At one time the Red Sea Bream was very plentiful around our shores particularly around the Irish coast and the south and west coasts of Britain but was not so plentiful in the eastern end of the Channel and in the North Sea. For some reason it gradually became very scarce and in many places non existent about thirty to forty years ago probably through commercial overfishing in deep water. When I first started boat fishing I was always puzzled by the number of well known marks all around the Irish coast known locally as the "Bream Rocks" and on which I could never catch any bream. According to the old fishermen they were extremely plentiful at one time but gradually disappeared though the name lingered on.

In recent years, however, they have started to come back on the Irish coast and are now quite plentiful in the south and south-west and are gradually extending their range northwards. They are not specially fished for by Irish anglers and are usually taken in the course of general fishing on rough ground. Indeed they can be a veritable nuisance at times to anglers seeking bigger fish, stripping their baits time after time. However, when fished for specially with light tackle they provide excellent fun though their sporting qualities are not held in such high esteem as those of the Black Bream.

The Red Sea Bream arrive on our coasts about the middle or end of June depending on the season and they remain inshore until September, before once again moving out into deeper and warmer water. They are found over rocky and weedy ground in depths of as little as 5 fathoms, but these are usually small fish and the best fishing is in depths of 15 fathoms or more. They swim in shoals and are easily caught provided the shoals can be located. Marks are very important and are usually known to local fishermen. Though they swim up through the water to feed they are generally taken on or near the bottom and can be caught on a variety of baits. Small pieces of mackerel, herring or squid, sandeels, mussels, ragworm, lugworm and limpets are taken readily and they should be fished on a small hook (size 1/6) depending on the size of fish encountered.

The Red Sea Bream is a small species averaging 1 to 3 lb. in weight so tackle should be light if the maximum amount of sport is to be enjoyed. A medium fibre glass spinning rod, light centre-pin reel, 8 to 10 lb. breaking strain line and an ordinary 2 or 3 hook paternotser is a suitable outfit, enabling one to use light sinkers even in deep water. It takes readily during the day in deep water but feeds best in the early morning or late evening where the water is shallow and clear, though if the water is dirty or coloured it will feed readily enough throughout the day. Ground bait is a great help in keeping the shoals interested, and as bream are omnivorous feeders almost anything will do—crushed mussel, crabs, minced up fish or even boiled rice, but remember a little goes a long way and your purpose is to keep the fish interested and not to feed them.

The Black Bream has a reputation of being a very tough and scrappy little fighter when taken on freshwater type tackle and is much sought after by anglers in the Channel. It is also a small species, indeed slightly smaller than the Red Sea Bream. A 3 lb. fish is reckoned a good one whereas a good Red Sea Bream would run 1 lb. heavier. It is another summer migrant from the warmer south and seems to be most plentiful in the eastern part of the English Channel.

The main shoals arrive about the middle or end of April though after mild winters anglers may catch some of the "advance guard" as early as March while hard winters may delay their arrival until early May. The first Black Bream are caught by boat anglers on offshore marks and it is not until June that they come within reach of the shore angler who has to be content with small or medium size fish as large bream are rarely taken from the shore. The early run of fish is to the eastern end of the Channel off the Sussex, Kent and Hampshire coasts but the best of it is over by the end of June whilst farther down the Channel they continue to give good sport into August and sometimes into September on the outer grounds.

Their distribution is very localised and an exact knowledge of the marks is essential to success. Like the Red Sea Bream they are fish of the rough ground, preferring rocky and weedy bottoms in 5 to 12 fathoms. The Ditches and the Kingsmere Rocks at Littlehampton are famous grounds for Black Bream and other well known centres are Shoreham, Worthing, Eastbourne, Brighton and Bognor. Elsewhere around these islands they seem to be scarce or non-existent. They are of rare occurrence on the Irish coast. As bream are not specially fished for in Ireland they could well be present in some areas without anglers being aware of it.

In Black Bream fishing the first essential is to find the shoals and although they are bottom feeders and usually found within a fathom or two of the bottom, they will swim up through the water to feed and at times may be found right on the surface. This means that the angler must search the water (as in mackerel fishing) to find the level at which the fish are feeding and then fish at that depth. The bait should be lowered to the bottom and if the fish are not there it should be retrieved slowly until the proper level is ascertained When found, the judicious use of ground bait will serve to keep the shoals within your fishing area.

The same light tackle as described in fishing for Red Sea Bream will suit very well and though anglers take their share of fish on paternoster and leger tackle, driftlining is the most popular method used. A certain amount of tide is necessary for successful drift-lining and the weight of lead used will depend on the strength of the tide. A 6 to 8 foot trace of 5 to 7 lb. breaking strain monofilment is ample and it is advisable to use only one hook. The hook size will vary with the size of bait used but should not be bigger than a No. 1 (long shank) and sizes 4 to 6 are about usual. A pat-ernostor with a 6 foot flowing trace is also a suitable terminal tackle but if an ordinary paternoster is used the hook links should be long and flowing and well spaced apart.

The Black Sea Bream will take the same baits as Red Sea Bream but lugworm, ragworm, mussel and small strips of herring or mackerel (about ½ inch long) seem to be the most successful. Both species can at times be very shy biters and it is best to let the fish take the bait a little way and then strike by lifting the rod and tightening the line.   When using light tackle it is advisable to take a landing net, for bream are small and difficult to gaff.   Besides it would be a pity to disfigure such handsome fish with a gaff mark.

Little is known about the spawning habits of either the Black or the Red Sea Bream and it is a strange fact that both species are hermaphrodites, i.e. each fish combines the two sexes.   Whether they change sexes from time to time or are self fertilising or capable of cross fertilising another is not known for certain.   The inference is, however, that they do spawn in our waters for the young fish (known as chad) swarm inshore in summer and can make a nuisance of themselves to the shore angler.

CHAPTER 16

THE SHADS AND THE SEA TROUT

THE SHADS

THERE ARE TWO DISTINCT SPECIES OF SHAD, THE ALLIS Shad and the Twaite Shad. They are anadromous fishes which, like the salmon and sea trout, ascend our rivers to spawn. They belong to the herring family and indeed closely resemble the herring but grow to a very much larger size. Though resembling the herring in general outline they have very much deeper bodies and like the sprat their bellies are saw edged and can in the Twaite Shad at least be very sharp.

The Twaite Shad is the smaller and in our waters the more plentiful of the two species. Fresh out of the water it is a beautiful fish to behold. Its large glistening opalescent scales have a wonderful sheen, rather like good french polishing, giving one the impression of being able to see right into the fish. Dusky on the back, it has silvery sides and radiating streaks across the gill covers. A row of dark spots run along the upper side and the very forked tail has dark tips with a V shaped bar near the base of the tail fin. The row of dark spots along the upper sides may be partly or entirely concealed save for the shoulder spot by the silvering of the scales but become clearly visible once the easily detached scales are removed. It attains a length of approximately 18-19 inches and a weight of about 3½ lb. but the usual size is about ¾ lb. to 2 lb.

The Allis Shad has a smaller head and is less "chunky" in appearance. The adults possess a dark blotch on the shoulder but there is no line of dark spots or blotches as in the Twaite Shad though a series of dark spots occurs in very young fish. The principal diagnostic character is the number of gill rakers on the lower limb of the first gill arch. There are 60 or more of these on the lower limb of the gill arch of the Allis Shad while in an adult Twaite Shad there are no more than 30 and these are neither as long, as fine or as closely spaced as those of the former. The Allis Shad is the larger of the two species attaining a weight of 8 lb. or more.

The distribution and habits of the Allis Shad in our waters are something of a mystery which the fact that the two species closely resemble each other does not help solve. It is reported to ascend the Severn and the Avon to spawn and has been taken amongst shoals of Twaite Shad in the Solent. In Ireland specimens have

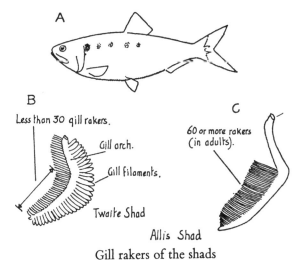

Gill rakers of the shads

A. Twaite Shad. B. first gill arch of Twaite Shad. C. first gill arch of Allis Shad. In the young of both species, the gill rakers are much fewer—e.g. a 4″ Twaite has only about 18 or 19 rakers on the lower limb of the first gill arch while an Allis of the same size has as few as 30.

been taken by salmon fishermen netting in the estuary of the River Ilen in West Cork and I have seen one fish of 2 lb. 7½ oz. taken there in 1960. One specimen was found dead on the shore of the Upper Lake in Killarney in 1958 but these are the only authentic examples received from fresh water in Ireland. In the sea they have been taken by trawlers at Baltimore (mouth of the River Ilen), Dunmanus Bay, Bantry Bay, Dingle Bay and Galway Bay.

On the Continent it "runs" a number of rivers notably the Rhine, Elbe, Seine and Loire to spawn between April and June. It ascends rivers almost as far as the salmon and is reputed to travel as far as Basle on the Rhine and nearly to the source of the Seine and Loire. It used to run the Thames but pollution there like in many other rivers has driven it away. It is noteworthy that though numerous specimens were taken in Dingle Bay between February and April and again in July and August, i.e. before and after the spawning period, only one was taken in both May and June. This would suggest that spawning does in fact take place in some of the rivers in the south-west area; many of the specimens taken were empty but those which did have food in their stomachs were feeding on plankton (mainly Euphausids) while a lesser number were feeding on small fish. Their gill rakers are admirably adapted to capturing plankton and like the mackerel it is probable that they feed on both plankton and small fishes.

The Twaite Shad is the common species in our waters though its distribution in fresh water is somewhat localised. In Ireland it ascends the Rivers Barrow, Nore and Suir and Blackwater, to spawn and a landlocked form is found in the Killarney Lakes. In Britain it ascends a number of rivers in the southern half of the country notably the Avon and Severn, but as in the case of the Allis Shad, pollution has closed many rivers to it that formerly it used to run. Little is known about its habits in the sea. I have taken shad on spinning tackle in Youghal Harbour in June but these could possibly have been fish which were dropping down to sea after spawning in the River Blackwater. I have also taken a few while fishing shoaling bass over the famous Splaugh Rock near Rosslare, Co. Wexford. In July and August it is sometimes found among the mackerel shoals in Youghal Harbour, and in August, too, numbers of shad are encountered in Baltimore Harbour, at the mouth of the River Ilen. It has also been taken by commercial fishermen in Dingle Bay, at the mouth of the River Moy on the west coast, and also at the mouths of the Rivers Boyne and Liffey on the east coast.

In Britain, Twaite Shad are taken by anglers in the late summer and early autumn in the Solent and off Southend in the Thames Estuary. They are present in the Thames Estuary for most of the summer, but in early autumn they are found in shoals in the creeks and over the mudflats near Southend and Leigh-on-Sea and they begin to move out again as soon as the first frost comes. The shoals of shad are easily spotted by their characteristic "ringing" on the surface and local anglers use a lot of ground bait to hold the shoals once they are located. The shad no longer breed in the

Thames, due to pollution in the upper reaches of the estuary and it is thought that the fish come in to feed on the large shoals of shrimp present in the river in early autumn.   Very light tackle is used, not alone for the sake of greater sport but also because the shad will leave medium or heavy tackle well alone.   Strangely enough, spinning does not prove very successful for them there but this may be due to their preoccupation with bottom food at the time.

While I have caught Twaite Shad in the open sea it has mostly been unintentional and it is only when they ascend into fresh water that I fish specifically for them.   It enters rivers in May and June, somewhat later than the Allis Shad but does not penetrate as far into the fresh water.   It only travels as far as the upper tidal reaches and spawns chiefly at night at the very limit of the influence of the tide.   That is, in the fresh water which is backed up upon itself by the pressure of the tides down river.   It ascends as far as St. Mullins on the River Barrow, Carrick on Suir (30 miles from the sea) on the River Suir, and Cappoquin on the Munster Blackwater.

Their arrival in a river is sudden and varies with the season—sometimes they will come in late April and at other times early May.   The weather, state of the river and the tides all seem to influence their arrival.   There may be no sign of them in the morning, yet the next tide, and this is especially true of spring tides, may literally fill the river so large are the shoals.   Their characteristic "ringing" and clumsy rises to a fly betray their presence and shoal will succeed shoal right into early June.   They take best in bright calm sunny weather when the river is low and they do not like too much fresh water.   A heavy flood will drive them out of the river and they will not return in numbers until the level has dropped and the water has cleared.

Although not big as sea fish go, they are lively and exciting fighters when taken on suitable tackle.   When hooked they usually dash downstream, "planeing" with the current and using the water pressure on their broad flanks to full effect.   Suddenly they will jump Tarpon-like out of the water, upwards and backwards with gills extended, and send the lure flying with a vigorous shake of their heads.

I find a very light spinning rod (the type used for trout), a fixed spool reel and 5 lb. breaking strain monofilment very suitable. They will take any small bright spinner eagerly, and fine line is essential if the very light lures are to be cast any distance. Shad seem to take a lure from behind, frequently following the bait from some distance and many fish seem to swim over the lure and get hooked in the gills. As the gills and the thin membrane of the mouth are very fragile and tear easily, very many fish will be lost when they jump. Hooking a shad is one thing but landing it is another and often one is lucky to land 4 out of 10 fish hooked, so effective are their head shaking leaps.

At low water the shoals congregate in the deeper pools and holes in the river. In fine sunny weather they will be seen ringing on the surface but if conditions are bad they may stay deep and it will then be necessary to spin your lure slowly and near the bottom. When the level of the river rises as the tides push the fresh water back on itself, the shad travel with it and often take freely as they go.

Most of the fish I have caught proved to be empty on examination but a number of them had small flies, nymphs and (on the River Barrow) mayflies in their stomachs, and two were full of shad spawn. They rise freely if clumsily to a fly and can be taken on the dry fly. If the dry fly is allowed to "drag" on the surface of the water it is more effective than if fished in the orthodox manner, for the dragging fly seems to be irresistible to shad. They also take wet flies eagerly, so eagerly indeed that local anglers fishing for the more edible trout consider them a perfect nuisance. On fly fishing tackle, however, they put up a terrific fight and give first class sport. Less fish are lost when fly fishing as the small fly hook gives a much more secure hold than the coarse treble hook on a spinning lure.

Like the herring, they are very bony fish and as the bones are strong they are not considered very edible and are not sought often by local anglers in the rivers in which they occur. This is also one of the difficulties in obtaining information about shad for they may run a river in their thousands, yet no one save the local anglers will be aware of it. In Ireland they would never think of mentioning their presence to anyone, as shad are held in such low esteem and only prove a nuisance to those seeking the much tastier and more desirable trout. Thus for years I passed rivers by without being aware of the tremendous runs of shad that filled them in May and June. It is a great pity really, for from the sporting point of view shad have a lot to offer to the angler who is prepared to fish light and prefers sport to the delights of the table.

SEA TROUT

So much has been written and said about sea trout fishing in fresh water that the fact that they can be caught in the sea is generally overlooked by anglers. The sea trout spends the greater part of its life living and feeding in the sea and only ascends into fresh water to spawn. It can be and is being caught on rod and line in salt water. The sea lough fishing for sea trout in the Orkney and Shetland Islands is famous but this species is also plentiful on other parts of our coasts.

Unlike the salmon, the sea trout does not wander far from the coast and is essentially a fish of the shallow inshore waters. It will be found feeding in estuaries, off river mouths, along the weedy shallows of sheltered beaches, or off a steeply shelving beach, in tideways, off rocky headlands and shingle spits. The spawning run of fish is into the acid rather than alkaline waters and the sea trout is most plentiful in the short spatey rivers running off mountainous or hilly country. It is most plentiful in the sea off this type of coast and abounds on the south-west, west and north-west coasts of Ireland, in Scotland, and the north-west of England, and in the south-west around Devon. It is also very plentiful in the south-east corner of Ireland off the Wexford Coast. Generally speaking it runs into fresh water from the middle or end of June onwards, though in some river systems the run may start as early as April. The spawning run is not a massive one as with shad but continuous over a long period, and while some fish are upriver others are still feeding in the sea and provide fishing all summer and autumn.

The Sea Trout and the Brown Trout are different forms of a single species, the Brown Trout having lost its migratory tendencies and now lives entirely in fresh water. They closely resemble each other but the question of identification is unlikely to bother the sea angler unless he is fishing in the middle or upper reaches of a large estuary where he may encounter slob trout. The colour contrast between the two trout is great and there is little risk of making a mistake. The sea trout is a very silvery fish covered with X shaped black spots while the Brown Trout is much darker in colour and has round spots. The head of the Sea Trout is smaller and the flesh red or orange as against white or pale pink in the Brown Trout.

Salmon are occasionally taken by anglers spinning or trolling in the sea and as large Sea Trout look very like salmon it may be of interest to mention a few rough and usually reliable diagnostic points at this juncture. The position of the eye in the Sea Trout is above the level of a line drawn from the tip of the snout to the farthest extremity of the gill cover, while the eye of the salmon is below the level of this line or else is intersected by it. The first ray of the anal fin of a Sea Trout extends beyond the last or inner ray when the fin is folded back but does not in the salmon. The juncture of the tail column and tail fin in the salmon is "waisted" enabling one to hold a wet fish up without difficulty but this "wrist", as it is known to salmon anglers, is not present in the Sea Trout.

My first encounter with Sea Trout in salt water was when spinning for bass. I have hooked Sea Trout on large spoons and on German Sprats but found more often than not that they followed these large lures or "knocked" at them without being hooked. When hooked they frequently threw the lure after a few spectacular jumps and it did not take me long to realise that Sea Trout possess much smaller and softer mouths than most sea fish. A change to very small lures like a Brown and Gold Mepps or 1 inch Blue and Silver Devon and the much lighter spinning rod and lines (5 lb. breaking strain monofilament) needed to cast such lures any distance resulted in a greater measure of success. I also found that they are just as shy in salt water as they are in rivers and that the full use of available cover and careful casting were essential to success.

Local knowledge of their haunts is also very important, for though they will betray their presence in river mouths and outside the bars of tidal inlets and estuaries by jumping, they have regular haunts where small shoals or even large numbers of fish are known to be present. Like bass and mullet they ascend estuaries (both large and small), tidal inlets and creeks with the tide. While I have found bass right under my feet in the shallows of estuaries, the Sea Trout seem to stay a little farther out than bass and are very wary of sudden movements or shadows, hence the necessity to avoid showing oneself and for making full use of any cover available. Standing up in full view on rocks or rocky promontories, splashing through the shallows or careless casting should be avoided like a plague.

Places to look for them in channels are where the current is set off by projecting rocks, or by banks of sand or shingle, in the narrows where the tide runs fast, in the eddies at the edge of fast water, in slack water at bends or at the mouths of little side streams flowing into the channel. These situations provide admirable conditions for fly fishing, using small streamer type flies. When fishing blind it is best to fish in the same way as in fishing wet flies on a river. Cast down and across working the flies with both rod tip and hand action. Fish will often take as the flies swing around in an arc at the end of the cast and any swirl or flash in the vicinity of the flies should be struck immediately. When the flies hang directly downstream work them for a while by raising and dropping the rod or by recovering and releasing line by hand. Work your way slowly downstream, a few steps at a time fishing and searching each piece of water thoroughly as you go. If you can actually see your fish it is often best to get behind it and cast up to it dry fly fashion.

Spinning calls for small lures fished very fast and just below the surface. I do not think that you can spin *too* fast for sea trout, for many fish have taken my lure as I was recovering line furiously after making a bad cast to a feeding fish. The same applies to boat fishing. More sea trout are taken when the outboard motor is driving the boat at a fair clip (much faster than for mackerel or bass) and especially when making an outside turn and the lure is swinging around after the boat. When trolling from a boat a very long line should be used—80 yards is not too much. In a tide race it is best to go to an anchor and spin. Fly fishing from a boat, however, is best done under oars, casting in towards the weeds on a rocky shore or being worked in the fast water of a tide way.

Sea Trout will be found in fast tideways or where projecting promontories, headlands or shingle spits set off the tidal stream. They will also be found outside estuary mouths or bars waiting to travel in when the flowing tide is high enough. On rocky shores they will be close in searching the weed, rock pools and gullies for prawns and small fishes. Their chief food is small fish, sandeels, herring fry and sprats where these are plentiful or the young gadoids, i.e. pollack, coalfish and whiting, found among the waving weeds along a rocky shoreline. They also eat prawns, shrimps, mysids, and other small creatures. I have never taken Sea Trout on bait except when using sandeels but I believe that small prawns are excellent and that the ordinary earthworm will also kill.

Steeply shelving beaches of shingle or coarse sand are also good places for Sea Trout, for there is usually a run of tide which channels small fry along them. When periods of offshore winds draw fry close in along these beaches sea trout can be very plentiful indeed. I have never had any success with them on storm beaches, but Sea Trout can be very numerous on flat sheltered beaches, especially those with a fair amount of weed or pebbly bottoms. Small shrimp are plentiful in these conditions and are very attractive to Sea Trout. On one such beach on pebbly ground near the mouth of a stream (where fresh water flows on to the beach is a good place for bass as well as Sea Trout), I have literally stood in water not quite up to my knees and found shoals of Sea Trout all around me. In such conditions a small spoon or tiny rubber eel is killing and so also is a small sandeel legered on the bottom.

It may seem strange to think in terms of bottom fishing for Sea Trout but they obtain a large amount of their food on the bottom, especially when small fry are scarce. A slip of mackerel fished on the bottom is a favourite method used by boat anglers in Killala Bay, Co. Mayo. The mackerel is cut in thin strips about 3 inches long and mounted on a size 8 hook. As the slip of mackerel is fairly long, many anglers prefer two hooks mounted pennel fashion. The bait is leger fished on the bottom from an anchored boat though a similar bait driftlined or trolled is also effective.

When hooked, Sea Trout should be played carefully. They have soft mouths from which the hook can be easily torn and most sea anglers may tend to be a bit heavy handed with them. Sea Trout fishing in salt water is a branch of the sport which requires further investigation and if more anglers fished for them better techniques would be evolved. The sea is where Sea Trout feed and grow and once located they are very catchable. They are quicksilver on light tackle, putting up a most exciting battle, more often in the air than in the water so frequently and spectacularly do they jump.

CHAPTER 17

TOPE

THE TOPE IS A SMALL, SLIM-BODIED SHARK OF GREAT strength and "staying power" that lends itself to light tackle fishing. In recent years there has been a growing awareness of its great sporting qualities among anglers which is reflected in the number of "tope specialists" to be found in these islands today. It is often referred to as the "poor man's big game fish" on account of its speed, strength and exhilarating runs, a title which I must confess rather irritates me as the tope is a game fish in its own right.

The tope is found all around our coasts and some areas are noted for their tope fishing. It is particularly plentiful in the Wash, the Thames Estuary, the Solent, the south Wexford coast at Kilmore Quay, in Sligo Bay, Tralee Bay, Ballybunion, and in Lough Swilly on the Donegal coast. Elsewhere it may be more numerous than is generally thought, for tope fishing is a rather specialised form of angling and unless specifically fished for one cannot be sure as to whether it is plentiful in an area or not.

In winter the tope is in deep water, usually out of reach of the angler, but in late spring, usually towards the end of April or early May, depending on the season, it migrates into shallower water. It is most plentiful inshore from May to October and in places may be taken as late as December. Usually, however, it begins to seek deeper water by early winter but its departure may be delayed by the presence of large numbers of shoal fish especially whiting in the inshore waters. The tope brings forth its young alive, and the baby tope (up to fifty in number) are born in the inshore waters during the summer months. Fertilisation is internal and the males (which do not grow as big as the females) are equipped with claspers.

In summer I have caught tope in water as shallow as a fathom or two off a beach and out to depths of 45 fathoms; but it is in depths of 5 to 20 fathoms that the tope is most plentiful. The fact that it

is on the whole taken in relatively shallow water and also that most
tope angling is done over clean bottoms, allows the use of light
tackle and light sinkers and makes tope fishing a very sporting
proposition indeed.

Although a true shark ranging widely over the bottom and
through all levels of the water it feeds mainly on demersal fishes
particularly those found on clean ground. Flatfishes and such shoal
fishes as whiting and other members of the cod family form its
main diet but such typical rock species as pollack, pouting and
sea breams are also eaten. It is almost entirely a fish eater though
crabs and starfish have also been found in its stomach. One of the
difficulties in ascertaining the food of tope is that so often on
examination its stomach proves to be empty but this is possibly
due to regurgitation during the course of playing the fish. It takes
squid and cuttlefish and octopus very readily and I have also hooked
tope when using large sandeels as bait. It does not confine itself
to feeding entirely on and near the bottom and I have frequently
taken tope on feathers when jigging for mackerel near the surface.
It will harry and drive to the surface shoals of mackerel, herring,
pilchard, sprat and even small fry. Anglers may be surprised that
a large species like the tope will feed on small fry but I have seen
tope working on the surface on small herring fry when no other
predators were present (possibly because the tope were there). It is
not uncommon to hook tope on feather jigs and though many of
them will be foul hooked on examination it will frequently be
found that the tope actually has one feather lure in its mouth though
the nylon line may be bitten through and the fish held by other
hooks in the back, tail or belly.

It is not, however, only over sandy and gravelly bottoms that
the tope is found. It ranges widely over mixed bottoms and even
over very foul ground. It is frequently found on pollack reefs and
ledges and in the vicinity of wrecks. Once when fishing the Ledge
in the middle of Sligo Bay (a famous reef for pollack) we were
taking good pollack on rubber eels when someone got the idea
that a slip of mackerel added to the rubber eel might be effective.
It was, for every time we baited the rubber eel we caught tope
while the unbaited lure took only pollack. The tope were so
numerous that we had to give up as it was proving rather expensive
on rubber eels. Tope were very plentiful on the ledge on this

occasion and this is a feature of tope fishing, for while certain areas always hold a good population of tope, in others they may be temporarily very plentiful. It is probably a question of the abundance of suitable food and where the food is to be found so will the tope.

The tope will enter shallow water no more than a fathom or two in depth. It can be caught along fairly steeply shelving beaches, in the coves and little bays along a rocky coast and in the channels of large estuaries or tidal inlets. It provides very exciting fishing when taken from the shore, often leaping dramatically in its efforts to escape. Other favourite haunts are the mouths of estuaries where it lies in ambush feeding on the fish that swim out or are swept out with the ebb tide. It has a liking for fast water and tideways where small fish are channeled and concentrated and will be found in the sounds between islands and between islands and the mainland, or lying just at the edge of fast currents or in the slack water off a promontory that sets off a tidal stream, waiting for food to be brought to it by the run of water.

In some areas smallish tope which for convenience we may call "Pack Tope" though they do not swim in packs in the same sense as, say, Spur Dogs, may be very numerous. Kilmore Quay on the south Wexford coast is a good example. Here anglers fishing for bass with lugworm from the beaches often have to give up fishing for bass so frequently are they broken by tope that will even take hooks baited with lugworm. These fish are in the 20/25 lb. range and although they do not swim in shoals they are so thick over the ground that they may well be called Pack Tope. Three companions and myself have taken as many as twenty-seven tope in a few hours fishing at Kilmore Quay while drifting in a boat over the clean sand no more than 150 yards from the beach. Boat fishing in Sligo Bay in equally shallow water (no more than 2/3 fathoms) with two other rods equally large catches were boated but the fish were larger, averaging 28 lb.

Areas in which tope are as plentiful as this are exceptional, though in places, while they cannot be classed as pack tope, they are very numerous over the ground. On the Irish Coast they can be taken in numbers at Ballybunnion, the mouth of the Shannon, Tralee Bay, Lough Swilly and in the area extending from the Tuskar Rock to Hook Head on the south coast of Wexford. Conditions must be very suitable for tope in these areas and food plentiful. As the depths are relatively shallow light tackle can be used and the very best in sport is obtained. Large tope (specimens of over 80 lb. have been recorded) are more solitary in habit and fish of 40 lb. and upwards are regarded as specimens. Strangely enough, quite a lot of really big tope have been taken by anglers shore-fishing from a rocky coast, and it may be that the habits and haunts of really big tope, like large bass, differ from those of their smaller brethren. When I say that big tope are more solitary in their habits I mean that they do not hunt in packs but it is quite common to find two or three fish hunting together. For that reason when a tope is landed it is important to get a fresh bait back in the water as soon as possible as there is an excellent chance of catching another fish.

Until quite recently in Ireland there has been little specialised fishing done for tope and while large numbers of tope are caught each year, they are taken by anglers during the course of general bottom fishing, using 2 or 3 hook paternosters as terminal tackle. Light monofilment traces are useless for tope fishing, as the sharp teeth of the tope will part them near the hook or else the rough skin on back and tail will cut through the nylon. Either way, light traces will be snapped like thread. Irish deep sea anglers generally use heavy nylon monofilment traces of about 80 lb. breaking strain with 6 to 9 inches of wire to the lower hook which is fished on the bottom for big fish. The steel wire prevents the tope from cutting the trace with its teeth and the very heavy nylon will land the tope though it becomes badly frayed and abraided in the process. I have on occasion actually boated two tope in succession on the one heavy nylon trace but would never chance it for a third fish. After the second tope the monofilment is unsightly, badly weakened and chafed and must be discarded.

It is best to use an all wire trace though I find that tope take baits mounted on monofilment more freely. Frequently a tope will take a small bait fished on the upper hook of a paternoster in preference to the larger bait on the bottom and this I am convinced is because of the wire to which the bottom hook is attached. The quality of the wire used is important, for it must be both flexible and supple to be most effective. The wire that I use is a 5 strand twisted wire of 40 lb. breaking strain, so limp that knots can be tied with it as easily as with nylon. It does not kink or twist, and curls left by coiling will straighten out with a slight pull. It has a smaller diameter than monofilment of equal breaking strength, but unfortunately it is no longer manufactured. I do not like stiff wires or those liable to kink. The former do not allow the bait to be presented in a natural manner while the latter once kinked snap very easily. Kinked wire should be discarded at once and traces should be frequently examined for faults.

There are some very light flexible plastic covered steel wires of small diameter available at present for making traces. They are excellent for tope traces but one should not try to make them last too long. The wire tends to rust quickly inside the plastic covering, particularly if the cover is cut in any place, and it may part unexpectedly. Secondly the rough hide of a tope chafes the plastic, and after a few tope have been landed the trace becomes unsightly and I believe this militates against its effectiveness. Never be stingy about your terminal tackle. This is most important for your trace should be the very best if the bait is to be presented properly. There is little point in having the finest available in rods, reels and lines if you are going to be careless about your terminal tackle. *Good enough will not do*, so be quick to discard anything that is not up to the mark.

I use a light boat rod (test curve $2\frac{1}{2}$ lb.) and a 2/0 multiplier reel loaded with 27 lb. breaking strain braided Dacron line and find it ideal for tope fishing. There is no need to fish any heavier and while I have landed tope on spinning tackle it is foolish to fish too light. I prefer a multiplier type reel for tope, as they are ideal for a fish that runs, and the tope certainly can run. A rod harness is not necessary when fishing for tope, but a rod butt rest is of great assistance both in boat fishing and shore fishing. The classical tope trace is a running leger but anglers have their preferences as to how it should be fished. The actual business end is usually all wire from 5 to 7 feet long. Where large tope are expected it is safer to use 7 feet of wire, as the tope will roll on the trace, winding it around its body, and if the trace is short the fish's tail may come in contact with the main line and sever it. At least two swivels should be used and it is a good idea to mount several hooks on a short wire trace (6/9 inches) for attachment to the main trace by means of a spiral clip or strong link swivel. This saves messing around trying to get the hook out of a fish, as the hook link can be easily detached to be recovered later and a new one mounted in its place. Hook sizes will depend on the size of the bait used and the power of the rod. With very light tackle and small soft baits I would use a 4/0 or 5/0 hook but with large baits 6/0 to 9/0. The hook points should be kept needle sharp and touched up with a stone when necessary. My own preference is a short wire trace 18 inches to 2 feet in length joined to approximately 5 feet of heavy monofilament (60/80 lb. breaking strain). I find this more successful than an all wire trace, and though the nylon portion will get chafed after a few tope have been boated, it is only a few minutes' work to replace it.

When fishing to an anchor over clean ground where there is sufficient run of tide to swim the bait away from the boat and make it work, I prefer to fish the bait a long way from the lead on a long flowing trace. The trace is lowered over the side and the tide allowed to take it away as about 8 yards of main line is measured off by a span of the arms and paid out. A "stop" is put on the line to prevent the lead running down towards the trace. The "stop" can be either the conventional split matchstick attached to the line by two half hitches, or what is better, a piece of rubber band tied on the line. A Clements Boom is the most suitable attachment for the sinker but if one is stuck a large link swivel will do. The rubber band should be just thick enough to pass through the eye of the sliding boom under pressure, thus permitting the boom to slide down to the trace when the fish is being brought to the gaff. I like to fish my bait well away from the boat and only use sufficient lead to take it down to the bottom gradually. As the slant of the line is gradual there is less slack to be taken up on the strike and the hook can be driven home more effectively.

While I have caught tope on bait that was really "high", there is no doubt that freshly caught fish is the best bait. Most small fish will be taken, i.e. whiting, dabs, pouting, small pollack, sea breams, pieces of squid or even octopus, but I have a preference for the oily fishes, i.e. mackerel, herring or pilchard. They seem to be more easily "scented" by the tope and I have found them more successful than the other baits mentioned. Whether to use a whole fish or a part of one as bait is a matter of choice. Where there is a chance of large tope I would use a whole fish and a big hook with slightly more powerful tackle to drive the hook home. For the average run of tope, however, a large lash of mackerel or herring, i.e. the whole side of the fish is quite sufficient and of course a smaller hook and consequently lighter tackle can be used. The use of rubby dubby is a great help in attracting tope, for they can scent food over a long distance, particularly if there is a fair run of tide, and the rubby dubby bag will greatly increase your catches.

Tope fishing is often a waiting game. You may get the odd "run" over a long period or perhaps several blank hours followed by a period when a number of fish are met in quick succession. I have recommended that when fishing the angler should *always* hold his rod in his hands lest a bite be missed, but where tope or indeed sharks are concerned, there is no need for this and the rod can be left down, but be sure that it is well secured and that the line is not caught around the rod tip or the reel lest it be whipped over the side when a fish takes. Put the check on and the reel in free spool or if the run of tide is too strong and the line still runs off the spool when the check is on, put the reel in gear and adjust the drag lightly so that the line no longer runs off but so that the fish will feel as little resistance as possible. When a tope takes, throw the check off and the reel out of gear and allow the fish to take line freely, meanwhile controlling the spool with light thumb pressure to prevent an over-run.

An orthodox tope run never fails to thrill me. Typically the reel suddenly starts to scream as line is torn off the spool, an electrifying sound that galvanises one into instant action. The tope usually seizes the bait in its jaws, runs with it for a while, then stops and turns the bait in its mouth to swallow it and then runs again. When large baits are being used, i.e. whole fish, the tope must be given time to turn the bait in its mouth and commence to swallow it before the strike is made. If struck on the first run, the fish is invariably lost, for it is only holding the bait between its teeth and a strike at this stage will tear the bait out of its mouth and scare the fish off. It is not easy to suppress the instinctive urge to strike and one must be patient and await the second run before driving the hook home. Do not wait too long on the second run, however, otherwise the fish will have swallowed the bait and be hooked in the stomach. There is little pleasure in playing a fish that is hooked in the stomach and to do this deliberately is not sport.

The strike is made by stopping the revolving spool by thumb pressure and "leaning back" into the fish as the line tightens. This pulls the hook into the fish and the strike should be smooth and positive. Remember, of course, to release the thumb pressure on the spool before the strain becomes such that it would cause a breakage. I like to throw the reel into gear before striking and if the clutch has been set very lightly to prevent the tide stripping line of the reel it should be gradually tightened up once the hook has been set. It is difficult to adjust the tension delicately when actually playing a fish and I prefer where possible to have it pre-set. Many reels do not have a fine adjustment and great care must be exercised lest the clutch be set too tightly in the excitement of playing a fish. It is better to err on the light side because additional braking power can always be applied by hand to the revolving spool and line recovered by "pumping". If the clutch is set too tight it may not be possible to ease the tension in time as the fish plunges for freedom. When small baits are used, i.e. a lash, half the side of a mackerel, the tope should be struck immediately it takes as it has no difficulty in swallowing a small soft bait. If the strike is delayed too long the fish may drop the bait altogether. Occasionally a tope will take the bait and run towards you. Your first indication of a bite will be slack line and the slack must be taken in quickly and contact made with the fish before striking. I find it best to wait until the fish starts to run away from me before setting the hook.

The tope runs hard and fast when hooked and it is for this reason that the old fashioned type of centre-pin reel in which the handles revolve is dangerous. The whirling handles can skin knuckles or even break fingers if the reel is incautiously handled, and if a brake is not fitted to the reel, the use of hand pressure on the drum to prevent an overrun may result in a bad burn. The harder and faster a fish runs the sooner it will tire itself and many anglers let the fish take line without putting on any pressure at all allowing the fish to expend its energy and using the weight and friction of the line in the water to sap its strength. This calls for a large amount of line on the reel—220 yards would not be too much as there is no harm in having a safety margin, for some tope make very long runs. Personally I prefer to put on light strain, making the fish work for the line it takes off the reel. To put on too much strain is bad policy for apart from the risk of breakage when the fish makes a sudden plunge, it also, especially in shallow water, tends to bring the tope on to the surface where it thrashes and plunges about when held too hard.

In shallow water tope often come to the surface and jump or half jump in their efforts to escape. The thrashing about on the surface which results from holding a fish too hard (and this applies to bass and other species as well) is dangerous; for heavy blows on the trace from the fish's tail may knock the hook out of its mouth. There is the added danger with tope, which have a tendency to roll the trace around their bodies, thus bringing the main line within reach of their rough hides or thrashing tails. The sudden plunge of a struggling fish often proves fatal if the tension is set too tight. While the slipping clutch or drag on the reel will continue to slip smoothly when the pressure for which it has been set has been reached, it will not do so initially and usually a strain in excess of the setting is needed to overcome inertia and start the clutch slipping. If the clutch is set too close to the breaking strain of the line, the strain required to start the clutch slipping may be in excess of the strength of the line, thus causing the line to part and the sudden plunge of a fish is just the thing to cause this to happen.

After the first long run the tope may double back on its tracks and line must be recovered as quickly as possible and the fish kept in contact. If it runs under the boat (a frequent occurrence) keep the line clear of the keel of the boat lest it be cut. It may be necessary to manoeuvre the line around the bow or stern to play the fish from the other side, a manoeuvre not always easy to accomplish. Whatever happens make sure that the line does not get tangled around the propeller for if this happens serious trouble may result. Another hazard with such a fast moving, far running fish like the tope is the anchor rope. A few turns of your line around the rope and the tope is usually away and heading at full speed for safer pastures. Many anglers avoid this danger by casting off the anchor rope (previously buoyed) and play the fish from a drifting boat. Once the fish is landed the buoy and rope can be picked up again and the boat anchored on the same mark.

The fish should be fully played out before being brought to the gaff for a tope still full of fight is difficult to gaff as it turns the water white with its struggles beside the boat. It is best gaffed towards the tail, for once the tail is lifted out of the water the fish is powerless but if this is not possible go for the thickest and most accessible part of the fish. If fishing in company in a boat where the gunwale is not too high above the water, a gaff is not really necessary for a good grip can be got on the "wrist" of the tail and on the dorsal fin and the fish can be lifted undamaged out of the water, by hand. Personally I prefer to use this method where possible, as I prefer to release my fish unharmed. When landed a tope is quickly quietened by a few blows with a heavy blunt instrument *on the nose* and not on the head as is usual with other species.

When an angler hooks a tope, every other rod in the boat should reel in immediately and take their tackle out of the water until the fish has been landed. Apart from the question of common courtesy, by so doing the other anglers will avoid the mess of tangled lines which inevitably occurs when lines are left in the water for the tope to pick up as it tears around. It should not be necessary to stress this point but unfortunately it is, for too many anglers in this respect are lacking in courtesy and common sense. It should also be unnecessary to say that every assistance should be rendered to the angler in a fish when *he needs it*. "Do unto others" should be the motto of every angler.

When not fishing on known tope marks or when fishing over ground where tope are widely scattered, drifting is often a very productive method. On clean ground the leger is still the best terminal rig and again I like to fish it a long way from the boat. I use no "stop" on the line, letting the sliding boom run down to the swivel where the main line and trace are joined. Even on clean bottoms there is the odd snaggy bit of ground and I like to feel it as soon as possible so that I can lift sinker and bait clear in time. Needless to say when fishing on the drift the rod should be held in the hands at all times.

Ground baiting is again a big help, when drifting, though I have never had really great success with tope using a rubby dubby bag hanging over the side as is done in shark fishing. I prefer to use chopped up chunks of fish (preferably mackerel, herring or pilchard) dropping the pieces over the side and laying a trail on the bottom. It is surprising how tope will pick up the trail and follow it. This I have proved to my own satisfaction repeatedly by examining stomach contents.

When drifting over rough ground I like to keep as close to the bottom as possible without getting stuck in it. Generally I do not bother to rig a special trace but suspend the lead from the Clements Boom by a few feet of weaker line. In this way I can feel for the bottom occasionally to ascertain if the water has deepened or if the rock is rising I am aware of it before the hook gets fouled on the bottom. If I do get stuck only the sinker is lost and it is much easier to replace it than a whole trace. When fishing over the shallow rough ground that pollack love, a float can be used to fish the bait clear off the bottom. This allows the angler to relax as there is no need to hold the rod, but, except in shallow water, float fishing in the upper surface layers for tope I have not found to be very productive.

Where tope can be caught from the shore they provide some of the most exciting fishing that comes the way of the shore angler. Shore fishing for tope is a rather new and specialised form of angling, attracting a growing number of enthusiasts. To be successful one must be single minded about it and fish only for tope and not be distracted or tempted into angling for other species at the same time. One can do a little light spinning for mackerel or pollack for bait but to fish a second bottom rod is only inviting trouble and trouble usually obliges. Stick to the one job for you will find a sizeable tope from the shore a difficult enough proposition to land without having to worry about it fouling in your second line and maybe whipping the other rod into the sea. Besides you will find that you will miss less bites and catch far more fish by concentrating on the job in hand.

In some places tope are taken regularly from the shore. Kilmore Quay, Fenit Pier, Ballybunion and parts of the Welsh coast are noted for their tope fishing, but tope are found all around our coasts and must be catchable in many other areas from the shore, only no one has tried fishing for them or even suspects that they are present. They frequent beaches, especially those on which flatfish are plentiful and which are steep-to, and have a fair depth of water close in, though they have also been taken on very shallow flat beaches. They run up tidal channels and estuaries a long way and are best fished for right in the channel at low water. They are not found in every estuary, for they have no great tolerance of fresh water and the more saline the conditions the better the prospects.

The channels between islands (a short distance offshore) and the mainland are also favourite haunts, for the fast tides forced through the narrowed water, channels and concentrates food. Tope will run through these "necks" feeding as they go or will indulge in their favourite habit of lying in ambush on the downtide end, waiting for food to be swept down to them. On a rocky coast, try the slack water at the edge of tidal streams set off by projecting headlands or the coves and bays between projecting headlands. Fry and other small fish often seek shelter from fast currents in these places and the slacks and eddies off the tide make ideal places for tope to lie comfortably in wait for anything being swept by with the tide. They will quarter little coves and bays along the coast, often at the same stage of tide, and the best time to fish can often be found out by persistent fishing in the one spot. The knowledge gained will save fruitless hours of fishing afterwards.

When shore fishing for tope I find that ordinary surf casting tackle answers very well but I prefer to use a rod capable of casting up to 6 oz. rather than one designed for 3½ to 4 oz. Not so much because the fish are stronger and heavier but because a sinker plus the weight of the bait (often a whole fish) may overload the less powerful rod. I use 19 lb. breaking strain line and find it quite adequate but when fishing in channels or tideways where drifting weed is a hazard it may be necessary to use line of 30 lb. breaking strain or heavier. When weed is plentiful it is amazing how much weed the line can collect especially if there is a rampaging tope at the other end of it. Only strong line will give the angler a chance of landing a tope in these conditions.

A leger once again is the most suitable trace but it presents difficulty in casting except when fishing on to clean bottoms in deep water from rocks. In these circumstances it may only be necessary to drop the bait down the rock face or only a short cast need be made. On beaches, however, long casting may be called for and a long wire trace of 5/7 feet makes this difficult or even impossible. Furthermore, when the cast is made the free running leger tends to lag far behind the bait, with a consequent loss of distance. The tide or wave action may move the bait about considerably on the bottom and while this may be good in one way it does make it extremely difficult to contact a fish when it takes, for one has no idea where the fish actually is and may strike ineffectively against the big belly in the line, causing the tope to drop the bait.

A straightforward paternoster would eliminate these difficulties but I do not care for this type of trace for tope and after experimenting with different types of terminal rigs I find the following quite satisfactory. I use only 4/4½ feet of steel wire with a swivel at one end and a strong link swivel about 6/9 inches from the hook. This enables the hook link to be quickly detached when a tope is landed and replaced by another thus allowing me to get another bait out quickly as tope tend to come in pairs or more. The short wire trace makes casting easy and while tope will roll on the line I have yet to find the short trace inadequate when fishing from the shore. To join the reel line and the wire trace I use a length of heavy monofilment line (60/80 lb.) long enough to enable me to get a few turns of the heavy line on the reel when casting. The length of heavy line has many advantages and is equally useful in surf fishing for bass or cod. Should the tope roll up on to the line it will not part like the lighter main line and it also absorbs the shock of casting heavy baits which might snap the main line. It is also useful in landing a fish in surf or from rocks as once a few turns of the heavy line is on the reel you can manipulate or haul the fish in with much more confidence.

I mount the sinker by placing on the longer part of the wire trace a swivel which runs freely up and down it and attach the sinker to a length of light monofilment so that when the trace is held up the sinker hangs below the bait. Thus in casting the weight travels ahead of the bait but when on the bottom acts as a restricted leger which gives the tope a chance to mouth the bait without feeling any resistance. As I only use the minimum amount of lead necessary to give sufficient casting weight when the weight of the bait is included, I find that it does not frighten the tope when it starts its run. This method suffers from the drawback that the sinker is usually lost by the time the fish is landed, for sometime during the struggle the nylon to which the weight is attached will find its way into the tope's mouth or else be cut by its rough skin. However, if one uses old nuts and bolts instead of lead weights the question of expense will not enter into it.

On the question of scaring the fish I do not find tope in the least bit shy on beaches, though Clive Gammon, who is a very able and experienced angler with a long list of specimen rock caught tope to his credit, maintains that tope taken on a rocky shore are extremely shy fish. Not only must they feel no resistance when they take the bait but neither must they feel the hook and this should be buried in the bait. Naturally unless the bait is soft like a frozen herring a considerable amount of power is necessary on the strike to pull the point of the hook through the bait and into the tope. A free running leger as used in boat fishing is also advisable and as very long casts are seldom necessary when fishing from rocks on to clean sand, it is not a drawback in casting.

Again the oily fishes, mackerel, herring or pilchard are to be preferred for bait though small flatfishes (and on a rocky shore small pollack) are also good. When baiting with flatfish it is best to bind the fish with twine around the widest part so that the blind or opaque side is upwards otherwise the natural camouflage of the coloured side may conceal the bait from the tope. Any of the baits recommended for boat fishing will also kill and the hook size will depend on the size of the bait used and the power of the rod. Size 4/0 to 5/0 is big enough for small baits but I prefer 6/0 or 7/0 when using whole fish.

Once again ground baiting is important. Where there is a run of tide or a channel emptying out on to a beach, a bag of rubby dubby weighed with stones and dumped where the run of water will take out the scent is effective. The addition of blood or fish oil to the rubby dubby is a big asset in attracting tope to where you are fishing. It is not always easy to get a large amount of material for rubby dubby or to carry it to your fishing spot and I usually ground bait by hand. I cut up some of the bait into small chunks and throw it into the water in places where I think it will do most good. The set of the tide, a likely spot to meet a tope, the suitability of the bottom for placing your bait (there is no point in ground baiting where you cannot fish) must all be taken into consideration. Properly done, however, it can be amazingly effective. On one occasion I counted the number of pieces of mackerel I used to ground bait and in the only tope caught that day I found sixteen of the eighteen pieces of ground bait. Time after time I have proved the effectiveness of ground baiting. It will produce fish on a day that would otherwise be blank and will turn a good day into a better one.

The stage of the tide has an important bearing on shore fishing for tope. Some beaches fish well only on the top of the tide; while creeks, lagoons and estuaries emptying into the sea may fish best on the ebb when the tope come in to feed on the fish moving out with the tide; or they may nose into coves and bays on a rocky coast only on a certain stage of the tide. This information can only be found out by persistently fishing up and down the tide at any given place until a recognisable pattern appears. Once you have established this feeding pattern you will not only save yourself wasting time fishing when there are no fish present but it may enable you to ring the changes among a number of fishing places, travelling from place to place as the right stage for fishing each particular spot comes around. The effect of the weather and sea conditions should also be studied for they can rule out fishing altogether or may make fishing in one place not worthwhile but turn an otherwise poor fishing station into a good one while the conditions last.

Rock fishing creates its own difficulties, for frequently due to the nature of the terrain there is little room to swing the rod in making a long cast. Where the bottom is clean close in, an orthodox boatfishing type of trace for tope is best for they are often very shy and a free running leger is advisable. In these circumstances it is not necessary to cast far; but where the foul ground extends for a considerable distance a long cast is essential, the type of trace mentioned for beach fishing is best, provided you have room in which to cast. Where the bottom is all foul, float tackle must be used and the depth at which the bait is fished can be regulated by a sliding float. While I always prefer the oily fishes as hook bait, when fishing over rough ground pollack makes a very good bait. I do not care for it very much when boat fishing but at Ballybunnion in Co. Kerry where tope are plentiful local anglers use nothing else either from the shore or from a boat, and find it very successful.

Tope fishing from the shore is a waiting game. You will have many blank days and for that again very good days. As you may have to wait a long time between bites there is no need to hold the rod and it can be placed on a suitable rock when rock fishing or on a tripod or rod rest when on the beach. The check should be put on and the reel left in free spool but it is essential that the rod be watched closely all the time.

Tope do not always take with the classical reel-screaming run and on occasions a sudden slackening of the line is the only indication that a fish has picked up the bait and swum in towards the shore. If you are not watching you will miss this and the fish may drop the bait before you are aware of its presence. On a rocky coast tope may take very gently, mouthing the bait and dropping it if they are suspicious, without you knowing. At times your first indication of a tope's presence may be a spectacular jump as it tries to throw the hook. Only once have I seen this happen on a beach where normally tope are not so suspicious. Another good reason for watching the rod is that in places crabs and dogfish can be an absolute pest. Dogfish are an abomination, destructive of bait and you may find yourself unhooking a dogfish at the very time a tope comes along. This is particularly galling when rockfishing, for tope hunting along a rocky coast quarter a bay or cove quickly and do not linger. Crabs, too, are destructive and may rob your bait in a very short time, and it is difficult to decide whether to reel in and inspect your bait in case the crabs have wholly demolished it or to take a chance that your bait is all right. Whatever your decision you will usually find that you are wrong. As tope taken from the rocks are often so cautious it is advisable to treat every bite be it from dogfish or marauding crabs as a possible tope bite. Sometimes it is difficult to tell them apart.

In the usual tope run, the fish picks up the bait and moves off with it as the ratchet on the reel sings out its exhilarating tune. When using a small bait and hook the tope can be struck immediately but when a whole fish is used the tope should not be struck until it commences its second run. As soon as the tope takes, the rod should be picked up, the ratchet released and the line allowed to pay off smoothly so that the fish feels no resistance. Light thumb pressure on the spool will prevent any danger of an overrun. If you do not get to the rod in time the jerkiness arising out of the combination of ratchet and rod tip action may cause the tope to drop the bait.

The strike is made by stopping the revolving spool completely with the thumb and as the line tightens, set the hook smoothly by lying back into the fish. If the spool is kept "frozen" the line may part under the strain and it must of course be allowed to start revolving again under controlled tension as the fish drives out for deeper water. The amount of strain to apply and the timing, i.e. the critical moment at which to release the pressure from the spool, comes with experience and with a little practice this method will be found to be more effective than the normal upsweep or sideswipe of the rod which may dissipate most of its force in taking up the bend in the line and consequently fail to set the hook properly. When tope run in towards you with the bait, i.e. give a slack line bite, the line must be recovered as quickly as possible until contact is made with the fish. I prefer to delay this strike until the fish is running away from me again and so avoid the risk of pulling the bait out of its mouth.

Again many anglers when the hook has been set like to allow the tope to make its first long run under little or no tension, so that it may tire itself out more quickly. As some tope make incredibly long runs this calls for a very large amount of line on the spool (an essential in tope fishing anyway) and 300 yards is not too much. I prefer to keep a little pressure on the fish and to apply side strain, to keep the fish off balance. Full use should be made of the beach and with a little smart footwork the fish can be turned or made swim parallel to the shore. Do not hold the tope too hard otherwise it will be forced to the surface where it will thrash about and possibly break free.

Should the fish run inshore, the slack line must be recovered quickly and again by quick legwork and by making use of the beach by backing up it as you continue to reel in, direct contact can be kept with the fish. Where you have room to manoeuvre do not be afraid to move about and play the fish with your body as well as from the reel. When the tope is a long way out and resists strenuously any effort to reel it in, line can often be recovered by "walking" the fish. Clamp down on the reel keeping a steady even strain on the fish as you walk slowly and steadily back up the beach. The tope will usually follow quite docilely while any effort to use the reel would cause it to explode into furious action. Line is recovered by walking slowly back down the beach again reeling in as you go taking care to keep the same even strain on as you shorten the line. Do not try to reel in the fish but aim at spooling on the line recovered by your forward march.

It is best to play out the fish in deep water before bringing it into the shallows or into the surf. The strong undertow of the waves is a tackle-smashing trap if the tope is still full of vigour, and even when the water is flat calm a tope grounded in the shallows will often thrash about, throw the hook, and make deeper water again before you can reach it. There is no need for a gaff on beaches unless they are very steep-to, as the fish can be easily beached in the shallows and then lifted out by catching hold of the tail and dorsal fins. Watch out for its mouth, however, for its teeth are very sharp.

When fishing from the rocks it is not easy to move about and the fish usually has to be played from where you stand. Space is restricted, footholds treacherous and the rock frequently slippy from spray so the fish must be played from the reel. Again the tope should be played in deep water away from submerged rocks around which the line may get caught with disastrous results. This is seldom a danger early in the fight for the tope makes instinctively for the depths but later as the fish is fought into the shore it may attempt to bore deep in an effort to escape and sunken rocks are then a hazard.

Another danger when fishing in coves or bays is that the first long run of the tope may take it out past a headland or rocky point and that's the last you will see of it. You have two courses of action. Either you continue to let the tope run in the hope that it will stop before it reaches the danger point or you can put on as much strain as possible hoping that your tackle will hold and that the fish will turn. Either way when the danger point is reached all you can do is clamp down on the reel altogether and hope for the best.

Landing a tope from the rocks is often a tricky business for seldom is there a convenient shallow ledge that you can get down to or on which you can strand the fish. Usually a gaff is essential and your first task before commencing to fish should be to pick out likely places from which to land the fish and note them carefully. When you have your hands full of fighting fury is no time to have to start looking for a suitable place from which the tope can be gaffed.

CHAPTER 18

THE DOGFISHES, THE MONKFISH AND THE ANGLER FISH

THE DOGFISHES BELONG TO THE SHARK FAMILY AND ARE VERY WIDELY distributed around our coasts, indeed too widely for the many anglers, to whom the word dogfish is an anathema.

THE SPURDOG

One of the livelier members of the group is the Spurdog which in general appearance resembles a tope. It is, however, a much smaller species than the tope, seldom exceeding 14 or 15 lb. in weight and a 10 lb. fish is considered a very good one. It is readily distinguished by the presence of two sharp spines (from which it derives its name), one in front of each of the two dorsal fins and its tail fin is not deeply notched as in the tope though the lower lobe has a very definite curve. The colour is usually blue, blue-grey or brownish on the back and some small pale spots may also be present.

The spines in front of the dorsal fins are dangerous, for apart from the actual physical injury they can inflict, they are also poisonous making the wound a slow and difficult one to heal. When boated the spurdog will twist and squirm, lashing about with its tail and it should be handled carefully for the sharp spines will penetrate even the stoutest rubber boot. I make it a practice to pin the fish's tail to the deck and to remove the spines with pliers (every boat angler should carry one in his fishing bag) before killing the fish with a few blows on the snout. The hook can then be removed in safety and this practice also obviates the danger of an angler inadvertently injuring himself later by standing or falling on one of the spines.

The spurdog winters in deep water, migrating inshore in early summer to spawn. It is viviparous (fertilisation is internal and the males are equipped with claspers) and the young are born alive in the shallow coastal waters usually over the period August to about November, when the adults once again seek deeper water. A large number of young are produced over this period and it is a common sight when numbers of female spurdog are boated to see the deck littered with young as the mothers give birth. The young are perfect miniature little spurdogs with an attached yolk sac and if the female is opened the varying stages of reproduction from the embryo in the egg capsules to the almost fully developed baby spurdog can be seen.

The Spurdog feeds almost entirely on small fishes particularly shoal fish such as mackerel, herring, pilchard, whiting and small fry such as sprats and sandeels but any small fish is fair prey to this most voracious species. Unlike the other dogfishes, it is a shoal fish which hunts in packs. The packs may be small, numbering no more than a dozen or two or for that matter again the numbers may run into thousands. At times it can be so numerous as to rule out the possibility of catching any other species. The shoals of spurdogs are usually composed of fish that are all about the same size and at times may be made up of fish of the one sex.

Not alone is it a most voracious fish but it is also a most savage one. It will take almost any bait, tear hooked fish from the anglers' lines and does severe damage to the nets of commercial mackerel and herring driftnet fishermen. Nothing small enough for it to handle is safe from the hungry marauding packs and where it is very plentiful it is a wonder that anything living is left after its departure. Certainly when packs of spurdog arrive on the scene other species depart in a hurry and even if fish too big for them to handle remained the angler would have little chance of catching them, as his baits would be taken immediately by the spurdogs. Its greed is exemplified by one Spurdog which I saw break off a gaff and escape as it was being boated. The gaff in some way had completely torn its underside and as the fish swam away it could be seen that its entrails were protruding from its torn belly. Yet that same fish was fair hooked and landed thirty minutes later by another angler. How it escaped its bloodthirsty brethren I could never understand.

The Spurdog may be encountered anywhere for it roams widely over all types of bottoms and through all depths from the bottom right up to the surface. It feeds on both demersal and pelagic species and may be taken in depths as little as a fathom or two right out to 80 fathoms or more. It may be encountered in small groups or in tremendous packs and may for a time be very plentiful locally remaining in an area until it has been cleaned out before seeking fresh pastures. Some places, particularly large shallow bays and inlets, seem to hold large populations of resident Spurdogs. Where this happens, the packs seem to frequent certain definite areas or use certain routes which are easily discovered. Channels are favourite haunts in these conditions and if you desire to catch other species of fish it is best to stay away from the recognised "runs" of Spurdogs.

When Spurdogs are present there is little difficulty in catching them for they will take almost any bait greedily. Small pieces of fish (almost any fish will do though the oily fishes are best), feather jigs, and even lugworm, ragworm or mussel will be taken greedily. They possess sharp cutting teeth which will sever light nylon and even heavy nylon if they are hooked well inside the mouth. Normally wire traces are not necessary and heavy nylon (60/80 lb.) direct to 1/0 to 4/0 hooks will handle them nicely. The nylon does, however, tend to become very chafed and frayed when numbers of Spurdogs have been taken, for their hides are rough when rubbed against the grain. The type of trace used is not very important but if quantity is required a 3 hook paternoster is best. When a pack of Spurdogs is encountered, 2 or 3 fish can be taken at a time especially if a hooked fish is not reeled in immediately but is left to play around for a little while as is practised in feathering for mackerel. It is not uncommon to see several fish follow a hooked fish right to the surface.

Spurdogs fight quite well on light tackle and can be good fun but where they are very plentiful the sport soon palls for it usually degenerates into wholesale slaughter. Most anglers in these conditions will prefer to up anchor and seek other marks where they can catch perhaps less but more interesting fish.

THE LESSER AND GREATER SPOTTED DOGFISHES

The other two members of the dogfish family found in our waters, i.e. the Lesser Spotted and the Greater Spotted Dogfishes, cause a great deal of confusion among anglers in the matter of identification. There is no difficulty in separating the two species from each other but unfortunately their names tend to lead anglers astray. The spots have no significance in differentiating between the two fishes and it helps if one remembers that the correct titles should be the *Lesser* and the *Greater* of the Spotted Dogfishes.

The principal diagnostic characters are the nostrils and the relative positions of the second dorsal and anal fins. In the Lesser Spotted Dogfish the nostrils are covered by large, simple undivided nasal flaps whose lower margins are in line with the front of the mouth. The end of the *base* of the anal fin is under or slightly in advance of the origin of the second dorsal while in the Greater Spotted the end of the *base* of the anal fin is well behind the origin of the second dorsal, i.e. they overlap. The nasal flaps of the Greater Spotted Dogfish are smaller and divided, i.e. separate from each other and do not reach down to the mouth. In addition there is a small gristly point or spur projecting from the centre of each nasal flap. While examples may be caught in which the position of the fins are not quite true, the nostrils can always be relied upon for identification.

Both species have very rough skins and care should be taken with the Lesser Spotted especially when unhooking a fish. When landed it will squirm and twist about in an effort to rasp its body on your hands and if successful can badly skin or "burn" your hand. Not alone is this very painful but it is also slow to heal. As its name implies the Lesser Spotted is a small species, the average size is 2 to 4 lb. The Greater Spotted attains a weight of over 20 lb. but a fish of 13/14 lb. is usually considered a very good one.

Unlike the Spurdog, the Spotted Dogfishes are not viviparous and produce eggs in tough horny capsules (Mermaid's purses) with adhesive curly tendrils. The egg purses are attached to weeds beyond low water mark by means of the tendrils and the empty capsules are often found washed up on the beach after the young have hatched out.

The Lesser Spotted Dogfish is an abomination and the bane of the sea angler's life. There is no art in catching this pest and if there was an art it would be in the avoidance of it, but the secret of *how not* to catch the Lesser Spotted Dogfish has yet to be discovered. As a species it must be extremely successful for it is found everywhere.   It is taken by shore fishermen in a foot or two of water on shallow beaches, and by deep sea anglers out in the deeps.   It is most plentiful over clean bottoms of mud or sand but will be taken on mixed bottoms and even on really foul ground.   Those taken over rough ground are very black in colour in contrast to the usual light brown of those taken on clean bottoms.   A clumsy swimmer with poor eyesight, it finds its food mainly by smell and this sense is very highly developed in it as it evidenced by the large nostrils.

It is essentially a bottom feeder and its diet consists of easily captured bottom food such as crabs, whelks, worms, shrimps and any small flatfish or sandeels it may find buried in the bottom.   It is not, however, equipped to capture fish unless it comes upon them unawares or finds them dead.   It is a scavenger that will take any fish bait, as anglers know to their cost, and, indeed, will take any natural bait that can be put on a hook.   In places it can be a perfect nuisance, robbing baits both large and small and what is too big for it, it will mouth, tear and generally mess up.   It is a poor fighter which comes in like a dead weight at the end of a line and I can find nothing to commend it.

The Greater Spotted Dogfish is a little better.   It is, of course, a much larger and heavier fish and while I could be uncharitable and say that its greater size is the only thing in its favour, I must confess that some big specimens do put up a fair fight though it could never be classed as a sporting fish.

It is found all around our coasts but is not as plentiful as its near relative and is usually found in deeper water.   On the whole it prefers rougher bottoms and is most plentiful over mixed and foul ground.   While it also feeds on crustaceans and slow moving bottom creatures it is quite a good swimmer and fish forms a fair part of its diet.   It will take any fish bait and I have also caught it on mussels and feather jigs.   It is not fished for specially but is taken in the course of general bottom fishing.

The Smooth Hound is another small bottom living shark taken by anglers during the summer and autumn months.   In appearance it looks like a clumsily built tope but it can easily be distinguished from it by the fact that its teeth are *flat* (skate-like) and arranged in a mosaic pattern while the back and sides are much lighter in colour than in the tope and are sprinkled with white or pale spots. As its teeth would suggest, it feeds mainly on crustaceans and molluscs and prefers harder ground than the other dogfishes. In summer it is found in moderate depths but winters offshore in deep water. Like the Spurdog it brings forth its young alive in our inshore waters. It is not specially fished for and is of little angling interest.

THE MONKFISH

The Monkfish is an ugly and rather extraordinary looking fish which seems to fall half way between the sharks and the skates and rays. It is flattened from above downwards like the latter fishes but its pectoral fins though greatly enlarged do not form a complete disc and are separate from the body. It does in fact possess both pectoral and pelvic fins which are separate and extend out from and along the body and it does not have an anal fin. In general appearance it is not unlike a large base fiddle and derives its name from the rather hooded, monkish appearance given by its spiracles and shape of its head. Unlike the sharks and skates its mouth is situated very far forward and it opens almost at the end of the head. The teeth are sharp and conical and the nostrils which are just in front of the mouth are covered by flaps which have rather frilly looking edges.

As its flattened shape would suggest, it is adapted for life on the bottom and though it will eat crustaceans and molluscs it is mainly a fish eater. It is a clumsily built fish not adapted for speed yet its food consists of fishes that are much faster than it is, i.e. flatfishes, whiting and even mullet. It cruises slowly over the bottom, picking up any half buried flatfish it comes across or it lies or half buries itself on the bottom in channels or tideways where fish will be swept over it only to be pounced upon and end up in its cavernous mouth. It is said also to attract fish towards it by disturbing the mud or sand by movements of its fins as it lies on the bottom, seizing any inquisitive fishes that come within reach of its jaws.

The Monkfish winters in deep water but in summer is found in the shallow inshore waters usually on clean bottoms of mud or sand. It is found all around our coasts but is more plentiful in the south and south-west and well up on the west coast of Ireland in the Clew Bay area. It frequents very shallow water and is particularly fond of large shallow bays and estuaries and in many places can be taken from the shore. Locally it can be very plentiful and noted places in Ireland are Tralee Bay and Clew Bay. It has been taken on rod and line to a weight of 69 lb. and a fish of 50 lb. is considered a specimen. The Monkfish is viviparous, the young being born in shallow water during the summer.

Though not a fast swimmer the monkfish is both heavy and powerful and medium boat tackle should be used when fishing for it. It is not specially fished for from the shore although in many places it comes into such shallow water that it could be taken in numbers by shore anglers. It is indeed quite often hooked by anglers bottom fishing for flounders or bass but usually it is not landed as the tackle used is too light. The very rough skin and sharp teeth will part the line and a short wire trace backed by heavy monofilment at least should be used. The main line should also be fairly strong or if light line is used quite a considerable amount of it is required on the reel for though slow it is both strong and powerful, as the light tackle fishermen will find to his cost when a big Monkfish quietly and steadily swims out to sea with his bait until all the line is stripped from the reel—then " ping " and all is lost.

I always feel a bit ridiculous when boat fishing for Monkfish as usually it means fishing with fairly strong tackle in little more than a fathom of water. I have often when returning from fishing the outer grounds in Clew Bay stopped on the way back to Westport to try for Monkfish and not bothered to change my terminal rig of a two hook paternoster leger for the more efficient single large bait, leger fished on the bottom. On dropping my trace over the side I have frequently been able to see the bait on my top hook and indeed at times when the water is clear it is possible to actually see the monkfish on the bottom, so shallow is the water. Locally Monkfish can be very plentiful and I know of one catch of thirty-seven Monkfish ranging from 40-63 lb. made by a party of four anglers during a few hours fishing in a depth of 10 feet of water off Fenit in Tralee Bay.

When taken in such shallow water on strong tackle the Monkfish can be quickly fought to the surface and indeed is often gaffed and boated before it realises what is happening. Usually it realises that something is wrong when it reaches the surface and suddenly explodes in a fury of spray as it lashes about and can easily break away if held on too tight a line. When hooked on medium tackle the Monkfish should be played out until it is tired before being brought to the gaff and care should be taken that the fish's ponderous runs do not take the line around the anchor rope. I have never met a fish obliging enough to run back the same way around the anchor rope and free itself and if the fish does not break free the only thing to do is to haul in the anchor and do the best you can to free the tangle and land the fish. Fortunately in such shallow water hauling the anchor is no great chore and can be done quickly and easily. In deep water, however, it is another kettle of fish entirely and many anglers unless in a very good fish would prefer to break free rather than haul a heavy anchor from 30 fathoms and run the risk of not being able to drop back again on exactly the same spot.

While long wire traces are recommended for Monkfish, I prefer to use a short wire trace about 9 inches long backed by about 5/6 feet of heavy monofilment which is attached to the main line by a swivel. The bait should be fished right on the bottom and a running leger is preferable to fixed sinkers. Baits should be large, the whole side of a mackerel, the head, or the tail portion and hook sizes will again depend on the strength of the rod and line and the size of the bait used, but I would not go smaller than a 6/0. When using half a mackerel, i.e. the head or tail portion, in conjunction with a small hook make sure that the bait does not mask the hook and prevent it getting a good purchase when the strike is made. When soft bait such as a long lash of mackerel is used this danger does not arise. Any of the oily fishes or small to medium flatfish or whiting make excellent baits.

The Monkfish is not a very exciting fish but it is, however, both big and strong and in shallow water on reasonable tackle can give the angler a share of sport.

THE ANGLER FISH

The Angler Fish is the most extraordinary and most repulsive looking fish likely to be caught by the sea angler. Its appearance is grotesque, seemingly consisting of an enormous head which is broader than it is long while the body and tail are short and tapering.

The lower jaw protrudes beyond the upper, the mouth is very wide and enormous when opened.   There are rows of needle sharp movable conical teeth in the jaws which can be directed backwards to prevent captured prey from escaping.

The pectoral fins are short, fleshy and stumpy, and are situated well back on the body towards the tail column while the stunted pelvic fins seem to function as legs used to lift the fish clear off the bottom where it lies half buried in the sand.   The second dorsal fin is situated on the tail column and the first dorsal has evolved into five or six separate and movable rays the first of which terminates in a long fleshy appendage, coloured dull white on one side and a dull drab indeterminate colour on the other.

The first long ray is in fact a combined fishing rod and lure used by the Angler Fish to attract its prey within reach of its cavernous mouth and terrible teeth.   The rod is flexible and tapered while the lure is both limp and flabby.   The Angler Fish half buries itself in the bottom and as soon as a fish comes within range the rod is erected and the lure waved to and fro.   The fleshy appendage acts on the same principal as many artificial lures such as wobbling spoons which are bright on one side and dull on the other.   The flickering or flashing lure, alternatively bright and dull as it wobbles gives the impression of a small fish in difficulties and proves irresistible to fish.   The Angler Fish's lure must be singularly effective for the species has been recorded to weights in excess of 80 lb.

The adult Angler Fish prefers clean ground though the young fish may be found on rough and weedy bottoms.   In colour it is a dull drab dirty brown but, it can change its coloration to suit the bottom on which it is feeding.   Its camouflage is near perfect as it lies half buried in the sand or mud and the small fleshy flaps which fringe its sides break up the outline of the fish so that it is indistinguishable from its surroundings.

The Angler Fish is, of course, a demersal species and almost entirely a fish eater.   Its food will vary with the locality in which it finds itself and because of its way of life it is not a species which will figure often in the angler's catch.   It is of no angling interest and is not fished for specially.   It is just a matter of luck that the angler's bait drops right into its mouth or close enough to entice it to move and "stalk" the bait.   However, it is an interesting if

repulsive catch and is a very good example of specialisation among
fishes.

Although a bottom dweller it does occasionally swim up in the
water and has been seen by commercial fishermen near the surface
from time to time.   For what reason it is hard to say as it is a poor
swimmer and not adapted to chasing its prey.   Perhaps it may
have eaten some large specimen of a species possessing a swim
bladder which upsets its own pressurisation and causes it to rise in
the water.   One such fish was observed by an angler fishing from
Dunlaoire Pier in 1962 who some time after it was first seen fair
hooked it in the mouth on an artificial lure.   The fish turned the
scales at 62 lb. 9½ oz. and proved very difficult to land on the light
spinning tackle used by the angler.   In June 1964 an even larger
fish weighing 71 lb. 8 ozs. was caught by an angler while bottom
fishing in Cork Harbour.

The Angler Fish is often referred to as the Frog Fish on account
of its crude resemblance to a frog and it is not only in this respect
that they are rather similar.   The Angler Fish lays its eggs in a
mass of spawn rather like the frog.   The eggs are attached to each
other by their sticky adhesive outer surface and as large Angler
Fish lay well over a million eggs the whole mass makes up one
huge sheet of spawn 1 to 3 feet wide and anything from 20 to 50
feet long which floats on the surface of the water.

CHAPTER 19

THE SKATES AND RAYS

FISHING FOR SKATE, THAT IS TO SAY BIG SKATE, HAS A SPECIAL fascination for sea anglers. Perhaps it is the sheer size and bulk of big skate (they attain weights greatly in excess of 200 lb.) that is the attraction and that the angler, in Irish waters at any rate, has an excellent chance of hooking a really big fish. I said hooking rather than catching, for the landing of a heavy skate, especially in deep water, is far from easy, and very many good fish are lost each year. The specimen weight in Ireland is fixed at 120 lb., a figure considered too low by many on account of the large number of fish in excess of this weight taken by fair angling annually; yet any fish of 100 lb. or more is in my opinion a good one, and worth recording.

The skates are a readily recognised group of fishes that superficially at least seem to have more in common with the flatfishes than with their close relatives, the sharks and dogfishes. They are cartalaginous fishes adapted for life on the sea bed, but, unlike the flatfishes, which are flattened laterally and swim on their sides, the skates are depressed, that is flattened from above downwards, and lie on their bellies. The same is true of the rays, for they both belong to the same family, the *Rajidae*, which for convenience is divided into two groups, i.e. the long snouted species (the skates) and the short snouted species (the rays). The most obvious way to differentiate between the two groups is to draw a line from the tip of the snout to the wing tip. If the anterior margin of the disc intersects this line, then the fish is a ray; but if it does not intersect the line, it is a skate.

The species of skate taken by anglers in our waters are: the Common or Grey Skate; the White Skate; and perhaps the Long-nosed Skate. While the differences between the three skates are obvious when seen together, they are not easy to identify when seen singly, and this is true generally of both skates and rays, for within each group there is a close physical resemblance.

The skates possess the characteristic diamond or heart shaped disc and the long attenuated whip-like tail of the *Rajidae*. The disc is formed by the pectoral fins or "wings" which have evolved and developed enormously, extending backwards as far as the tail and merging with the flattened body to form one unbroken surface. The small pelvic fins are situated at the junction of the disc and the tail column while the two dorsal fins have migrated almost to the end of the tail column. The mouth and gill slits are on the underside and the closely set eyes are located on the upper surface in the central portion of the snout. Behind the eyes are situated the large spiracles through which they breathe, for the *Rajidae*, being adapted to lying on the bottom, cannot conveniently take water through the mouth as other fishes do.

Typical also of most of the *Rajidae* are the rows of thornlike spines along the middle of the back and tail, which in large specimens may be flattened or worn away. There are usually patches of small spines on the anterior margin of the disc or snout and the males possess a bed of thornlike spines near the tip of each wing which are absent in the females. The males can also be recognised by their claspers (fertilisation is internal as in all the shark family) and they do not grow as large as the females. The females produce eggs (usually in pairs) enclosed in horny capsules or "purses". The shape and size of the purse varies with the species but typically they are flat, roughly quadrilateral with stiff projections or "horns" projecting from both ends (in some cases the purse is covered with sticky fibrous matter and long adhesive fibres) which help anchor the purse to rocks, weeds or debris on the bottom where the eggs hatch out.

The colour of the dorsal surface in the skates is very variable and while it is usually drab with ill defined and vague markings, it may vary from brownish grey to bluish grey, and on occasion be very colourful and variegated. The following is a list of the most easily checked of the essential differences in the three skates which may assist the angler in correct identification:

The Common or Grey Skate. The length from the tip of the snout to the mouth does not exceed 20 per cent of the total length from the tip of the snout to the end of the tail. The ground tint of the underside is normally grey and is covered with an abundance of dark dots which mark the mucous pores. There may also be dark stipplings or streaks. Fish taken on muddy bottoms may be very black or dirty coloured around the snout and mouth but the central body region is usually clear.

The Long Nosed Skate. Underside as in the Common Skate but the shape of the snout is distinctive. Whereas the leading edges of the wings slope gradually into the snout in the Common Skate, they come in very sharply about level with the mouth in this species giving it a very "long nosed" appearance. The length from the tip of the snout to the mouth is 25 per cent or more of the total length.

The White Skate. The underside is white *without any black dots* (which mark the pores in the other two species) and there may be a tendency towards a greyish border to the hinder margin of the disc. In young fish there is a definite black border to the hinder margins. The snout is prominent and is a parallel-sided projection jutting out from the convergence of the leading edges of the wings for an appreciable length, giving the fish a "bottle nosed" appearance.

It should be noted that large specimens of the Common Skate are taken occasionally in which the ground tint is more or less white or entirely white and may be taken for a White Skate or identified as a Flapper Skate. These are only a colour variety of the Common Skate and the mucous pores which are stippled in black are a diagnostic feature and are never present in the true White Skate.

Of the three species, the Common Skate is by far the commonest in our waters and is found all around our coasts. Large Skate are particularly plentiful on the south, south-west and west coasts of Ireland and very good fish have also been taken on the coasts of Scotland. They are found over clean bottoms of sand, mud and gravel but are more plentiful on mixed bottoms. It may seem strange to find "flatfish" on rough bottoms, but big skate range widely over the sea bed and will be taken on low hard ground while favourite haunts of theirs are near the edge of rough ground, and in the sand or mud filled gullies and ravines that fissure really rough and pinnacly bottoms. They will also be found in tideways and channels where the current or tidal scour will bring food to them and in places can be taken in surprisingly shallow water.

Skate weighing up to 147½ lb. have been actually caught by

anglers fishing from Fenit Pier in Co. Kerry while fish of over 100 lb. have also been taken from the pier at Tarbert on the Shannon Estuary. Numbers of specimen skate (weighing over 120 lb.) have been caught in the shallow waters of Clew Bay, Bantry Bay and Kenmare Bay but the bulk of the rod caught specimen skate are taken in depths of 14 to 40 fathoms and it has been recorded commercially in depths exceeding 200 fathoms.

The Long-Nosed Skate is a fish of deeper water and has been recorded in depths of 500 fathoms but the younger and smaller specimens are found in shallower water than the big fish. Captures by anglers have been reported but require further investigation as some at least of "the Long Nosed Skate" caught on rod and line proved in fact to be White Skate.

The White Skate is also a species of deeper water and though recorded from the far north it is on the whole of more southerly distribution than the other two species. Not a lot is known about its actual distribution, as anglers seldom differentiate it from the Common Skate and many of the big skate taken around our coasts may in fact have been White Skate. Several fish weighing over 100 lb. have been taken by anglers fishing in Clew Bay (Westport) and Galway Bay; and Galway Bay holds the record for this species with a fish weighing 146 lb. 14 oz. These fish were taken in relatively shallow water and young fish are quite common in the shallow coastal waters of the west country. This is the largest of our skates and grows to 500 lb. or more in weight.

All of the skates possess extremely powerful jaws and flat teeth (some have little curved points on their teeth which are often worn flat) designed for crushing their prey and various crustaceans which figure largely in the diet of young fish present no problem. The bigger skate, however, feed mainly on other fish and stomach examinations have yielded a great variety of species including cod, ling, hake, mackerel, pouting, gurnards, dogfish, smaller skate, whiting, flatfish, large crabs and even lobsters.

It will be noted that their food includes some very fast and active swimmers found both over clean and rough bottoms; yet the skates are not adapted for chasing their prey as are the sharks. Though fast and active swimmers when the occasion demands, their shape and position of the eyes and mouth do not fit them for chasing active swimmers. They capture their prey by pouncing on them, pinning them to the bottom with their wings and feeling about until they can bring their powerful jaws to bear. While this may seem easy when the prey is flatfish, whiting or dogfish, it must also be successful with species found on rough ground for I have found sizeable ling (up to 15 lb.) and pollack in large skate.

When considering how to fish for skate there is no need to differentiate between the species; for the methods used are the same in each case. Ordinary medium boat tackle will do for fishing for small skate (fish up to 40 lb.) and the smaller fish are usually much livelier and run harder than their bigger brethren. Hook sizes 4/0 to 6/0 will do but they must be strong in the wire as the crushing power of the skate's jaws are such that if it gets traction on a light wired or badly tempered hook, it will snap. Hooks as in any form of fishing should be needle sharp.

Big skate, that is fish in the 100 lb. class, are, however, an entirely different proposition and while I know of a few fish of over 100 lb. that were landed on line as light as 35 lb. breaking strain, it is an uncertain business at best and it is only sensible to fish with tackle strong enough to give you a chance to land these heavy fish. Big skate are usually taken in fairly deep water and only the strongest of tackle will stand up to the punishment entailed. When hooked, large skate usually cling tenaciously to the bottom, seemingly using their huge wings to gain suction, or by digging their snouts into soft bottoms. Often it is impossible to move them for a considerable length of time and the angler would be forgiven for doubting that he is actually in a fish and not in the bottom. When the hold is broken, the skate may be fought up a fathom or two only to dive down again to gain another purchase on the bottom. This may happen time and time again and only sustained heavy pressure will eventually tire the fish. Allied to the skate's own weight and strength is the not inconsiderable weight and pressure of the tons of water resting on its broad back. Fighting up a heavy skate from deep water is a strenuous, back breaking, punishing business on the angler and tackle alike and both will be tested to the full. Only powerful and well matched tackle will stand up to the strain of fishing for heavy skate and it is essential that there be no weak links; no carelessly or badly tied knots if the fish is to be eventually boated.

A powerful boat rod with plenty of backbone should be used.

It should not be as stiff as a barge pole for that type of rod only
tires the angler and puts little pressure on the fish. Neither should
it be so supple that it bends over in a half circle, exerting no pressure
of its own and allowing all the strain to come on the line. It must
be flexible enough to absorb any sudden shocks on the line yet
have enough backbone to keep a steady pressure on the fish, tiring
it out and lifting it every time it yields.

The reel should be strongly made with a large capacity of 60/80 lbs.,
b.s., line. A large amount of line is desirable, for in strong tides a
heavy fish may take you a long way down tide as it "kites" up in
the water, using the force of the current to full advantage. Size
4/0 to 6/0 multiplier type reels or 6 to 9 inch centre-pin reels will
do but I prefer the larger sizes. As in fishing for large conger, I
prefer a big single action or centre-pin reel for this type of work
as it gives greater leverage and allows one to "winch in" those
precious and hard-earned few feet of line at a time and I feel it
keeps you in more direct contact with the fish. Multiplier type
reels are also good provided the angler recovers line by "pumping"
rather than trying to winch up the fish and this is not always easy
to do if the angler tires. I have seen the gears on multipliers
stripped and the reels rendered useless by anglers trying to recover
line by winching. These reels were never designed for this method
of operation and line should always be recovered by pumping the
fish. A good brake or slipping clutch capable of fine adjustment
is essential and it should not be set too tight lest when the fish
suddenly dives it may part the gear or bring your rod down on the
gunwale of the boat with disastrous results.

Monofilment line is not really suitable for this type of fishing
and a braided line of the non-stretch synthetic type is best. Monofilment has a certain amount of elasticity and stretches under
tension. When the tension on the line is released, as when a fish is
landed, the line tries to attain its original length and thickness and
the sudden expansion on the arbor of the reel may buckle the
metal end plates on multipliers or even burst centre-pin reels
asunder. I have seen this happen and if you must use monofilment
ensure that there is sufficient backing on the reel in the form of hemp
line to give the monofilment something to "bite on". Make it a
practice also to release tension from the line when a heavy fish
has been landed by dropping the sinker over the side and paying

out the line again. It can then be rewound on the reel evenly and smoothly. Nylon in stretching loses some of its original strength especially when strained near its limit and has the undesirable trait of parting later under far less pressure than its supposed breaking strain. In that way it is not reliable and is inferior to the non-stretch braided synthetic lines.

While big skate have on occasion taken small baits fished uptrace off the bottom and even been fair hooked in the mouth on a feather jig there is no doubt that a bait fished right on the bottom is the proper method. In Ireland a popular terminal tackle is a 2 or 3 hook paternoster, the lower hook, leger rigged being fished right on the bottom. A large bait is used and the hook joined to the trace by about 6 to 9 inches of wire. I am prejudiced against this type of skate trace because anglers are trying to combine general fishing for smaller species and at the same time be prepared for any big skate that happens along. It is effective but I feel it causes anglers to fish far too heavy for many species of fish and so sacrifice the sport which they could have with these fish on lighter tackle for the off chance of meeting a heavy skate. Besides the use of a small bait on one or two hooks uptrace leads to the catching of small fish which can at times be a positive nuisance and the chances are that your bait will be out of the water at the very time a big fish comes along.

Anglers who specialise in skate fishing use one hook only and fish a big bait (the whole side of a mackerel or half a mackerel or a whole mackerel, herring or pilchard) right on the bottom. Some use a long flowing trace where there is enough tide to take the bait out, others use a short trace. A size 9/0 hook is about right for big fish, joined to 6 to 9 inches of wire and about 5/6 feet of 80 lb. monofilament on which the leger runs. Two swivels should be used and they must be strong, to withstand the strain.

I prefer to use the shorter type of trace for at times it is not easy to tell whether one is in a fish or in the bottom. Skate often take quietly, especially when a long trace is used and the angler's first indication is that he is in something unyielding. Many good fish are lost by anglers who break their traces on the assumption that they are fast in the bottom but at the other end of the scale are the very many anglers who claim to have hooked skate and were in fact in "rock skate", i.e. the bottom. While skate on occasion take with a "bang" rather like the first run of a tope (it does not last for long and the fish soon enough goes to the bottom) it generally takes quietly and the advantage of the short trace is that the skate's wings should be felt on the main line as it feels around for the bait with its mouth, thus signalling its presence. The fumbling of a skate with a bait is often deceptive and one may think that some small fish is at the bait. When in doubt do not be hasty but await developments.

The fish must be given time to get the bait into its mouth and if struck too soon may be missed altogether or else foul-hooked in the snout or wing. This, apart from being undesirable, gives a poor purchase and the hook frequently tears out. Give the fish plenty of time and wait until it starts to move away before striking hard and lifting the fish at the same time. The fish must be lifted and kept coming before it realises what has happened. In this way you may be able to prevent the fish "glueing" itself to the bottom and thus avoid a long hard fight. Usually, however, the skate goes to ground and can only be shifted by steady sustained pressure which may take a considerable amount of time. When its hold is broken, it should be kept coming nice and steadily, but be prepared for sudden tackle breaking dives. If it does make the bottom again (and a big fish may succeed in doing this several times) you will find that it is less difficult to break its hold each time, for the fish will be tiring.

Take it nice and steady all the time and do not be tempted to bring the fish up too quickly if you feel your strength giving out. Many anglers make the mistake of fighting a heavy skate to the surface too quickly, exhausting themselves in the process only to find that the relatively fresh fish takes fright at the sight of the boat or as frequently happens at the many eager faces hanging over the side for a first glimpse of the fish. The inevitable result is that the skate makes an unstoppable dive for the bottom and the unfortunate angler lacks the strength to bring it back up again.

One of the dangers in skate fishing is that the sudden dive of a heavy fish may pull the rod down on the gunwale of the boat or as the angler tires he may be tempted to rest the rod on the gunwale. This is fatal and usually results in a damaged or broken rod. This danger must be guarded against especially if there is a heavy sea running. The boat must go up and down with the waves but a big skate does not and it may make a sudden dive for the bottom just as the boat is rising to the swell. The result is inevitable and not alone means the fish is lost but frequently results in a set of bruised knuckles and a broken rod. So make sure that your clutch or brake is properly adjusted and is not sticking.

With big skate it is advisable to use two strong gaffs in landing the fish. They should be inserted, one into the leading edge of each of the wings (behind the ridge of cartilage which will prevent the gaffs cutting through the flesh and pulling out of the fish) and the skate can then be slid in over the side. When fishing from small boats the fish should always be taken in over the stern lest its weight overturn the boat or drag the gunwale down near water level. You will find that it will rest more quietly on the deck if it is turned over on its back but beware of its mouth for the crushing power of its jaws is tremendous. A rod butt rest should *always* be used when fishing for big skate for the butt of the rod can quite easily do serious injury to either the stomach or groin; and the use of a rod harness is of great assistance in fighting the fish.

Needless to say, if there are other anglers in the boat they should take their tackle out of the water immediately a skate is hooked and they should be ready to drop fresh baits over the side immediately the fish is landed. Big skate usually travel in pairs (male and female) or sometimes three fish may be together and if baits are got into the water quickly more than one fish may be landed. If a fish is lost do not despair because they are not easily frightened and may not go far away. It has often happened that a fish that smashed one angler, was landed shortly afterwards by an angler in the same boat and the lost trace recovered.

While the bulk of big skate are taken in fairly deep water, numbers of them are taken in Ireland each year in very shallow water, sometimes in depths of 3 to 6 fathoms. Even though shallow water skate may fight more spectacularly they are more easily beaten than those taken in deep water because the angler has not got the tremendous pressure exerted by the water on the broad backs of skate to contend with. They run up channels in harbours and large bays and big skate may be quite common in places without anglers being aware of it. The same applies to many parts of the coast and is only by being single minded and fishing specially for them that their whereabouts will be discovered. While large skate will occasionally take small baits it is a sizeable fish requiring a sizeable bait to interest it, so the old principle of a large bait on one single hook is one that should be adhered to. The use of ground bait is a big asset in attracting fish to the area you are fishing but does at times tend to attract too many dogfish of the lesser spotted variety.

Readers may be interested in some statistics on the number of specimen skate (over 120 lb. in weight) accepted by the Irish Specimen Fish Committee up to the end of the 1964 season. The Committee was formed in 1955 to verify and record the capture of big fish in Irish waters and in its early years its existence was not widely known to anglers. In addition Irish sea anglers were not very "specimen conscious" and very many good fish went unrecorded. The Committee's progress can be gauged from the number of claims it received for all species of fish (both marine and freshwater) which rose from 38 in 1958 to 371 in 1964. It is only in the last three years that its existence has become widely known yet large numbers of specimens still go unrecorded, sometimes because anglers cannot be bothered to submit a claim and sometimes because many anglers are not yet aware that such a Committee exists.

I would like to stress that only fish that can be thoroughly verified as to weight and as having been taken by *fair angling* are accepted by the Irish Specimen Fish Committee. This rules out any fish not taken by sporting methods on rod and line. Instances in which the angler received assistance (very important in skate fishing for many anglers have been physically beaten by big skate that finally had to be handlined up from the bottom) and breakage of rods, etc., rendered many good fish ineligible.

Since the inception of the Committee 197 specimen skate weighing over 120 lb. have been accepted and the bulk of these were caught during the last 4 years, i.e. 27 in 1961, 58 in 1962, 50 in 1963 and 34 in 1964. The distribution of big skate on the Irish Coast may be gauged from the number of places they have been taken, ranging from Strangford Lough on the north-east corner of the Irish Sea right round to Moville on the mouth of the Foyle in the far north and include Bray, Greystones, Wicklow, Ballycotton, Cork Harbour, Kinsale, Bantry, Kenmare, Valentia, Dingle, Fenit Pier, Galway, Westport and Achill. A very wide distribution indeed.

Pride of place must go to Kinsale with 70 skate over 120 lb., a truly remarkable record considering that the first claim for a specimen skate was submitted from this centre in 1956. Ballycotton is next with 31, followed by Valentia with 27, Cork Harbour 12, Westport 11, Kenmare 10 and Fenit 9.

Naturally enough most of the big fish were taken in July (51) and August (55) when the number of anglers fishing would be greatest as these months are the peak of the holiday season. September proved almost as good with 32 followed by June with 30. October accounted for 16, May 10 and April 3. Little is known about catching big skate outside of these months for Irish anglers like to fish in comfort and, with the exception of east coast anglers, pack up about the beginning of October and do not start boat fishing again until early summer. Skate however do not seem to make seasonal migrations like other species of sea fish and are found close to the shore all year round. One big skate weighing 166 lb. was taken on rod and line in Bantry Bay in January 1959.

Size ranges are also interesting. The Irish Record stands at 221 lb. and was taken at Ballycotton, Co. Cork. In all 9 fish of over 200 lb. have been authenticated by the Committee; 10 weighing between 170 and 200 lb., 46 between 150 and 170 lb., 31 between 140 and 150 lb., and 101 between 120 and 140 lb. A formidable list indeed when one considers the short time the Committee has been in existence and that the list does not include all of the big fish taken during the period for the reasons previously stated. While 120 lb. is the specimen weight any skate around 100 lb. is a good one and how many good fish weighing between 80 and 120 lb. have been caught is hard to estimate but the number must be very considerable.

THE RAYS

The rays are the short snouted members of the family *Rajidae* and as a group are readily recognised, but the individual species present some difficulty in identification. The Thornback Ray is familiar to most boat anglers but some of the other rays which are taken on rod and line are not so easy to tell apart. There are eight species of Rays found around our coasts. A brief description of those likely to be taken by the angler is given below.

The Spotted Rays, i.e. the Blonde Ray and the Homelyn Ray, closely resemble each other and cause a certain amount of confusion among anglers. Both are very heavily spotted all over the upper surface of the disc which in the Blonde Ray is fawn coloured and in the Homelyn Ray it is dark brown. The spots in the former species are small and extend right out to the lower edge of the wings, while in the latter they are larger, less numerous and *do not* extend out to the lower margins of the wings. There are usually ten or more small pale patches ringed by small dots on the disc of the Blonde Ray (an equal number on each wing) while those on the disc of the Homelyn Ray are not as obvious and one patch on each wing may be larger than the others. A diagnostic character of the Blonde Ray is the border of small spines along part of the anterior margin of the underside of the disc which is not present in the Homelyn Ray.

Both species are common all around our coasts though not as frequently taken as the Thornback by anglers, and are most plentiful in depths of 10 to 40 fathoms. The Blonde Ray is quite a sizeable fish and has been taken on rod and line up to a weight of 27 lb. 13 oz. in Britain and 32 lb. in Ireland, but the Homelyn Ray is a much smaller species seldom exceeding 30 inches in length.

The Cuckoo Ray and the Sandy Ray are also quite like one another and are similar in outline. While the former is found in shallow or moderate depths the latter is more a deepwater species and is usually found in depths exceeding 40 fathoms. The Sandy Ray is also the larger species, attaining a length of about 4 feet, while the Cuckoo Ray seldom exceeds 2½ feet in length and is one of the smallest rays in our waters.

The Cuckoo Ray is easily distinguished by the large dark spot on each wing. These dark spots are very distinctive as they are covered with yellow, squiggly hieroglyphic-like markings. The Sandy Ray has about twelve to fourteen symmetrically arranged small round spots which are coloured cream or yellow.

The most interesting of the rays from the angling point of view and the one most frequently taken on rod and line is the Thornback Ray. It is easily distinguished from the other rays by the fact that apart from the characteristic spines on the middle of the back and along the tail, the Thornback Ray also possesses rows of large thorn-like hooked spines with swollen bases on each of the wings. The only other ray which has similar spines on the wings is the rare Starry Ray, a species unlikely to be taken by the angler and one which is very spiny indeed. The colour on the dorsal surface of the Thornback is variable but is usually some shade of brown and presents a very mottled appearance. The males apart from possessing claspers differ also from the females in that they have pointed teeth.

The Thornback has been taken on rod and line to a weight of 38 lb. but the average size of this species ranges from 5 to 15 lb. It is an inshore species of shallow or moderate depths and is found mostly over clean bottoms of sand, mud or gravel. It frequents very shallow water and comes close enough to the shore along beaches, in estuaries and off piers to figure in the shore angler's catches. It is taken mostly by inshore boat anglers and has a liking for a good run of tide or a fast current. It is found all around our coasts being the commonest of our rays but tends to be more plentiful in the south than in the north. It is an omnivorous species, feeding freely on crustaceans, i.e. shrimp and various crabs, molluscs and a large variety of small fish such as small whiting, sandeels, plaice and dabs.

Like all the *Rajidae*, fertilisation is internal and the female lays eggs which are enclosed in the characteristic "purse" or egg capsule. The young are born in early summer after the adult's annual migration into the inshore waters.

The Thornback is a much more lively proposition than its much larger cousins, the skates; but it must be taken on reasonably light tackle if its sporting qualities are to be enjoyed to the full. Where the bottom is suitable in bays, large estuaries and channels it will be found in numbers in very shallow water which permits the use of very sporting tackle. I once had a splendid day's sport, fishing for Thornbacks in Dingle Harbour on a day that was too rough to fish the deep water marks outside. The water was not more than 1½ fathoms in depth and I used a strong spinning rod and 15 lb. line on a multiplier reel with a single size 2/0 hook leger rigged on a monofilament trace.

The rays took ragworm and small fish baits and when hooked took off as if they were stung. They made long fast runs before slanting up towards the surface and a few even jumped clear of the water, coming down again with a smack in their efforts to escape.

The sport was both fast and furious and so enjoyable that I feel I would still be there only the supply of bait ran out.

It may not always be feasible to fish them so light, but the inshore boat angler should be able to use light or at the most medium boat tackle and 15-30 lb. breaking strain line. As the fish can quite easily be hooked in the mouth if the angler is holding his rod and minding his business, there is no need for a wire trace and the hook (it need be no larger than a 4/0) can be tied direct to fairly heavy monofilament. It will take most baits and though lashes of mackerel, herring or pilchard are favoured by most anglers, it will also take ragworm, lugworm, razorfish, crab, sandeel and squid readily. The fish should be allowed to move off with the bait and should be struck as soon as the line tightens. In very shallow water I prefer to fish my bait well away from the boat and if there is any current or run of tide it is quite easy to swim your bait away from the boat by using the proper amount of lead.

One other species of ray is worthy of mention, not because of its sporting qualities, but because it is a dangerous fish. This is the STING RAY, which in late summer or early autumn appears on our southern shores in fair numbers. It is a warm water species and one which frequents very shallow water and is often taken by shore anglers on the west coast, in the Channel, the southern part of the North Sea and on the south coast of Ireland.

It has a very short snout and is more rounded in appearance than the other rays. It is usually brownish in colour on the upper surface without any markings and its teeth are small and flat topped. It possesses no dorsal fins and can be immediately recognised by its long whiplike tail which is armed with a jagged spine (sometimes there are two spines) situated some distance from the junction of the tail and disc.

This fish is very dangerous for when beached or landed in a boat it will lash about violently with its whip-like tail and the jagged spine which is its chief weapon of defence against its enemies can penetrate even the toughest rubber boot. Not only can the jagged spine inflict a very serious wound but it secretes a venom which when injected into the wound can cause temporary paralysis. In addition, it seems to prevent the blood from congealing and the flow of blood from the wound is extremely difficult to stop.

Make no mistake about it, this fish *is dangerous* and should be handled with the greatest care. If you are unfortunate enough to be injured by a Sting Ray you should seek medical attention immediately. I for one would not care to take this fish into a small boat and would prefer to cut it free. However, if you do boat or beach a specimen do not take any chances. First pin down its tail with your foot while stunning the fish with a few heavy blows on the head. Still keeping its tail pinned down, cut it off with a sharp knife near its base. Once its tail is removed it can do no damage but if this is not done a seemingly dead fish may suddenly come alive and start lashing about in a boat or on a beach and may do some serious damage before being finally killed.

The Sting Ray is viviparous, giving birth to its young alive. It has been recorded to weights of over 60 lb. in our waters and though a sizeable fish is of no angling interest.

CHAPTER 20

THE SHARKS

Sharks! I doubt if anyone is entirely unmoved by the word, for there is something fascinating and perhaps a little frightening about these fish. They are the legendary destroyers of the sea, the cold merciless killers enshrouded in a legion of myths and legends, some true, some exaggerated. Most of them are indeed highly efficient predators but others, like the plankton-feeding Basking Sharks and Whale Sharks are quite harmless. The fact that we know very little about their life history and habits (for they have not been studied to the same extent as the commercial fishes) adds to their mystery and for most non anglers and indeed many anglers they represent the glamour fishing of the sea on our coasts.

Of the numbers of sharks found in our waters only four, i.e. the Blue Shark, the Porbeagle Shark, the Mako Shark and the Thresher Shark, are of any real angling interest. At this juncture a short description of the four sharks may prove useful in helping anglers to differentiate between the different species.

The Blue Shark is a long, slim, streamlined and very graceful-looking species with long, slender, pointed, sickle-like pectoral fins. The gill slits are small and the raked-back tail has a long shallow notch in it. There is a pit at the root of the tail on the upper surface but there is no lateral keel on either side of the tail column. The teeth are triangular in shape, razor sharp and in the adult fish have a serrated cutting edge. When first landed the colour of the back is a wonderful rich steely blue, shading to pure white underneath but unfortunately the colours fade very quickly after death.

The Porbeagle is a much stouter and more heavily built fish than the Blue Shark. It is inclined to be a bit "portly" looking and weighs much more heavily than a Blue Shark of equal length. The more or less vertical tail is crescentic in shape but the upper lobe is longer than the lower. The origin of the first dorsal fin is well in advance of the upper hind corner of the pectoral fin when the latter is held. The origin of the second dorsal is in the same vertical line as the origin of the anal fin. The two most easily checked diagnostic features are: (1) the small secondary keel on the tail below the main lateral keel which runs along each side of the narrow tail column; (2) the small secondary basal cusps at the base of each tooth present in adults but which may be absent or not noticeable in young fish. The teeth are long, slender and pointed and the eyes are large. The colour is usually a dark bluish grey or brownish above, shading to white underneath.

The Mako Shark is a beautifully formed fish, less heavily built than the Porbeagle, and its tail is more symmetrical, shaped rather like a new moon, while the upper lobe is not very noticeably longer than the lower. The origin of the first dorsal fin is behind the upper hind corner of the pectoral, and the origin of the second dorsal fin is well in advance of the origin of the anal fin. The teeth are long and slender but bear *no* basal cusps, and there is *no* secondary keep on the tail. The colour on the back is blue or bluish grey.

The Thresher Shark is a very distinctive and easily recognised shark on account of its enormous elongated tail, the upper lobe of which represents about half the total length of the fish. This tail is sufficient to distinguish it from the other three species and in addition it possesses a very large first dorsal fin and large pectoral fins. Both the second dorsal and the anal fin are very small and the triangular teeth are also small with a smooth cutting edge. The only other species of shark in our waters with a very elongated tail is the six gilled shark, a bottom feeding species rarely taken by anglers. As its name implies, it possesses six gills while all other species of shark in our waters possess only five gills.

THE BLUE SHARK

The Blue Shark or the Great Blue Shark, to give it its proper title, is a wide ranging species of the warmer seas and of world wide distribution. In the tropics it grows to a very large size, attaining lengths in excess of 20 feet, but the Blue Sharks taken in our waters are very much smaller, averaging in the region of 40/60 lb. in weight and though specimens in excess of 200 lb. have been taken on rod and line, a fish of 100 lb. is usually considered a good one.

A summer visitor to our shores, it has been recorded from all around our coasts but is most plentiful in the south. It is taken in great numbers by anglers off Devon and Cornwall and is plentiful on the south and west coasts of Ireland. Brigadier J. A. L. Caunter, in his book *Shark Angling in Great Britain*, states that off Cornwall Blue Sharks are to be found some forty to fifty miles offshore during May; and in June, as the warm waters of the Gulf Stream push farther into the Channel, they are found fifteen to twenty miles out. In July they are nine to twelve miles offshore and during August and September they are sometimes taken within five miles of the shore in normal summers—provided there is not less than 15 fathoms of water. In October the majority begin to leave the shore and to find them it is necessary to try some twelve to fifteen miles out. By November only a very few, if any, remain inshore. The above theoretical timetable may be upset by abnormal weather conditions.

On the Irish coast they first appear in numbers during June off the Fastnett Rock some eight miles off the west Cork coast. They are encountered by commercial fishermen drift netting for the early run of mackerel and by the end of the month they are so plentiful and the damage they do to the drift nets so great that the fishermen must give up their fishing. Outside of Kinsale, Bally-cotton, Achill and more recently Dungarvan little if any angling for Blue Sharks is carried on, so that not much is known about their movements, or how far offshore they are found early in the season. Certainly they are not encountered in numbers inshore until mackerel are plentiful and then they are found very close to the land. I have taken Blue Sharks within 100 yards of Helvic Head in Dungarvan Bay in July and have seen them from the cliffs quartering the little rocky bays and coves where the water was deep close in. They are more plentiful in warm than cold summers when mackerel and pilchard abound. Once shark fishing "catches on" in Ireland and Irish anglers fish specially for them more will be found out about their habits and distribution.

The Blue Shark is a pelagic species feeding mainly in the upper layers of the sea on such shoal fishes as mackerel and pilchard. When it comes inshore, however, it will also feed on the bottom when mackerel or pilchard become scarce, eating any demersal species that comes its way. It has a preference for shoal fish and is quite common on whiting ground where it preys on the whiting. In the stomach of one 84 lb. Blue Shark I found flatfish up to 3 lb. in weight as well as one sea gull. Whilst I have frequently seen sharks stalk sea gulls resting on the surface in calm weather I have never seen them succeed in catching one and whether this particular bird was taken dead or alive I could not say.

The female of the species attains a greater size than the male and peculiarly enough most of the Blue Sharks taken in our waters prove to be females. The Blue Shark is viviparous and while an occasional female gravid with young is taken it does not seem to breed in our inshore waters. I have only once caught a young Blue Shark (which weighed approximately 8/9 lb.) and any of the male fish I caught were also small fish around 40 lb. Occasionally, however, a big male is captured and the Irish record, a fish weighing 206 lb. taken at Achill was in fact a male blue shark. During July and August small blue sharks ranging from 15 to 40 lb. can be very numerous. These are probably the previous season's fish and the disparity in weight between individual fish may be explained by the relative abundance or scarcity of food available to the young fish. These small blue sharks leave early and fish encountered later in the season (and I have met them up to the last week of October) are usually sizeable fish.

Before the technique of using "rubby dubby" from a drifting boat was introduced into these islands, fishing for Blue Shark was generally carried out from an anchored boat and while the former method is by far the most effective, fishing from an anchor can still be productive. When fishing on whiting or pollack grounds and indeed even when jigging for mackerel it is not unusual at times to have a hooked fish torn from the hook or else chopped in two leaving the angler nothing but the gory head. This is the work of a shark which may, if the anglers are doing well, take up station beneath the boat and avail itself of an easy meal by "knocking off" the hooked fish as they are reeled towards the surface. Tope will often behave in a similar fashion but do not cut as cleanly as the Blue Shark. The work of a tope is more of a tearing cut which leaves torn edges and tendrils. If you are not interested in shark the only thing to do is shift station but even then the shark may follow, being loth to part with an obliging "bread winner". If, however, you want a shark, then bait up with one of the species of fish which is being "chopped" and put your shark gear over the side.

Indeed when fishing to an anchor it is good practice to put out a shark line and fish a big bait near the bottom as some very heavy shark can be taken in this way. Care should be taken, however, to see that your shark line does not interfere with the other anglers bottom fishing from the boat and it must be let swim away with the tide to keep it clear of the other lines. When the tide slackens or changes the shark line will display a tendency to wander and unless carefully watched may foul up several lines to the annoyance of everyone concerned. You can bottom fish with another rod while the shark line is out but first ensure that the line runs freely off the check on the reel and is not twisted around the rod tip or rings. A shark or even a relatively small fish can whip an unattended rod out of the boat in a flash should the line become snagged and for this reason the rod should be secured to a thwart or any other convenient part of the boat by some light rope.

The drawback in shark fishing to an anchor is that you must wait for the sharks to come to the spot where you are fishing. You could hang a bag of "rubby dubby" over the side of the boat to attract the sharks but on the whole this method of shark fishing is one to avail of as an opportunity presents itself during the course of general bottom fishing.

Drifting for Blue Shark using "rubby dubby" is a different and more effective proposition altogether for when using this method a large area is being searched and a trail of oil and pieces of fish is being laid down to attract the fish to the boat. In nature large predators are never as plentiful as their prey, otherwise the prey (in this case smaller shoal fishes) would be wiped out instead of being "cropped". Blue Sharks are therefore thinner over the ground than other species and where sharks are known to be, the more ground that is covered by the angler the better are his chances of success.

Rubby dubby is essentially chopped up or minced up pieces of fish, or fish offal, placed in a fairly loose meshed bag or sack and hung over the side of the boat so that the bag sloshes in and out of the water with the roll of the boat. Oil and pieces of fish are washed out of the bag, laying down a slick of oil and a trail of pieces of fish which will lead the sharks to the boat. Pilchard, herring or mackerel are the best basis for rubby dubby as they possess a high oil content which helps to lay down a good lane of scent in the water. A large mincer is excellent for making fine rubby dubby but a small mincer is useless as it quickly gets clogged up with the skin and fins of the fishes. If you do not possess a mincer the fish can be cut up in small pieces and placed in a bucket where they can be pounded into pulp with a heavy piece of wood or "pounder".

I prefer my rubby dubby to consist of a mixture of fine material and small pieces of fish so that a good trail can be laid down, interspersed with odd pieces of cut fish to interest the sharks. The mesh of the bag should not be so big that the fine material is washed out of the bag too quickly and a few larger holes should be made with a knife to allow the bigger pieces to pass out into the water. I like to use two bags, one for the very fine "mush" and another with a large mesh for the bigger pieces. It is important that a good supply of rubby dubby be made so that the bag may be replenished as soon as it is washed clean of oil and fine material. The trail must not be broken otherwise any shark which may follow it up will come to a dead end and fail to pick up the new trail.

There is more to laying down a rubby dubby trail than just hanging the bag over the side. The way the boat drifts plays a very important part in the operation and this is dependent on the tide, on the wind or a combination of both. Fish can only scent in an uptide direction, i.e. in the direction from which the scent is coming to them and they cannot scent what is downtide of them. If there is no wind the boat will drift with the tide and if the wind is blowing in the same direction as the tide is running the boat will drift much faster, its speed depending on the strength of the wind and tide. If the wind is blowing against the tide it will hold the boat back so that it will drift much slower than the tide while if it is blowing across the tide the boat will travel more or less diagonally across the tide, i.e. downtide and downwind. The effect of the wind varies greatly from boat to boat and a boat with a lot of top hamper or superstructure will take more wind than one with a low silhouette and therefore drift much faster.

Obviously when both wind and tide are moving in the same direction the boat will drift very quickly. In these conditions the rubby dubby will not be very effective as it will only search a short distance downtide or it may be falling beneath the boat or the trail may even be uptide of the boat. The chances of encountering a shark are far from favourable unless the boat can be held against the tide and wind by using the engine so that the rubby dubby trail spreads out downtide of the boat. Slack water with little or no wind is also unsuitable for there is little movement in the tide or boat and an effective trail cannot be laid down.

When the wind holds the boat against the tide a nice lane of oil and pieces of fish is taken out by the tide and in suitable conditions will search the water a long way from the boat. Wind across the tide is even better, for in addition to searching downtide the rubby dubby trail is also being laid across the tide and a much greater area is being covered. Both of the above mentioned conditions are very suitable for sharking and the amount of rubby dubby used will depend on the speed of the drift. On a fast drift I like to lay a fairly heavy trail for fear that the lane of scent be too weak by becoming too dispersed though the greater area of water being searched.

Now a word about tackle. When I first started to fish for Blue Sharks I followed the usual practice of using very heavy gear; a Hardy No. 5 shark rod and 80 lb. line. As it would take a 1000 lb. shark to put a proper bend in the rod it did not take me long to realise that I was fishing far too heavy and that on such tackle the average run of shark would not be able to show their true merit.

Let me state here and now that there has been a lot of misconception about Blue Shark fishing and the idea has grown up that it is difficult, expensive and requires very powerful, elaborate and expensive tackle. Nothing could be further from the truth and the trace apart, the medium to strong tackle possessed by the average boat angler will cope quite satisfactorily with the usual run of Blue Shark. It is a very easy, almost lazy form of fishing (once the rubby dubby technique has been mastered) in which long waits are interspersed with furious bursts of action.

The average run of Blue Sharks in our waters is 40/60 lb. and while powerful tackle would be necessary for a really big shark, such as a big Porbeagle, Mako or Thresher, these very large fish come our way so infrequently that unless one is fishing specifically for them or in an area where there is a good chance of taking a really big fish, powerful tackle is unnecessary, and detrimental to sport with the ordinary run of fish. The other side of the picture is fishing too light and while I know of sharks of over 100 lb. being taken on very light rods and 12 lb. breaking strain line (not a very difficult feat if one has sufficient line on the reel) one has little control over the fish in the early stages, it takes overly long to bring the fish to the gaff and spoils the sport of any other anglers in the boat.

A suitable outfit is a medium strong fibre glass boat rod, 20/50 lb. breaking strain braided synthetic line and a large capacity reel (300 yards of line is not too much) similar in size to a 4/0 or 6/0 multiplier. I prefer a multiplier type reel for any fish which runs and a Blue Shark taken on reasonable tackle can certainly run. Whatever the type of reel used it *must* have an efficient drag or slipping clutch and the handles *must not* revolve when the fish is stripping line off the reel. If the handles do revolve you stand a good chance of splitting your knuckles or breaking your fingers when the shark makes a sudden powerful unstopable run.

The business end of the tackle, i.e. the trace, must be of wire, preferably cable laid stainless steel wire of 120/150 lb. breaking strain, and it should be anything from 17 to 20 feet long. Very heavy wire is not essential and the lighter wire in my opinion is more flexible and less obvious while still being strong enough. I do not like plastic covered wire, for apart from the danger of rust inside the covering, the plastic becomes very scruffy and torn looking after the first fish has been landed. The trace should bear at least two, preferably three, swivels and these should be of the big game type. These swivels are very strong and do *actually* work under severe strain and though more expensive than the ordinary swivel are well worth the extra cost. The first swivel should be placed about 3/4 feet from the hook and this short link may, if you prefer, be of heavier gauge wire. Where there is a chance of very large shark I would advise using heavy wire for this link for the teeth and jaws of a really big shark can fray or cut through light wire. I would also make this lower link detachable by using a patent big game spring link or by making one out of heavy gauge steel spring wire. Sharks have powerful jaws and extremely sharp teeth. Recovery of the hook is best left until you go ashore and are sure that the fish is really dead. The detachable link saves the trouble of trying to recover the hook from a stunned shark and means that the angler can get a fresh bait into the water again in the shortest possible time. The alternative is to have several spare traces.

I like to use a short shank hook about size 10/0. Sharks can exert great leverage on a long shank hook and may even snap it in two. The hook point must be kept needle sharp to ensure perfect hooking. Buy only the very best in hooks for anything short of the best is false economy. Examine your traces frequently for damage and discard a doubtful trace immediately after first salvaging the hook and swivels. It is only a few minutes' work to run up a new trace and swivels apart (hence the need to salvage them) the cost is slight. I buy my wire in 150 feet lengths, it being cheaper that way, and with the aid of a crimping set make all my own traces. A crimping set is a most useful tool for making up any type of trace in which wire must be used. It consists of sets of rust proof sleeves or ferrules of varying diameters to suit different thicknesses of wire and a pincer-like crimping tool for squeezing the ferrules tightly on the wire. The result is a neat, efficient trace in which the wire cannot slip but do cut the wire off close to the ferrule and not leave a sharp end which may draw blood later.

The only other tackle required is a few 4 to 8 oz. spiral leads, a float and a large strong gaff (preferably two gaffs) with a good wide gape. The spiral leads are used to sink the bait and the float to adjust the depth at which the bait fishes. The float need not be elaborate. I have seen balloons, whiskey bottles (the line is put over the top of the cork and then pushed into the bottle), empty detergent bottles, net corks and pieces of foam plastic used as floats. The trouble with the two first mentioned is that you need a good supply of them as the balloon bursts and the cork pulls out of the whiskey bottle on the strike. All that is required is something that will suspend your bait in the water (it should not be so big as to form a drag on a hooked fish), that is visible and that can be rigged so that it will run up and down the main line. This can be done by simply inserting a piece of wire into the float leaving a small loop in the wire for the line to run through or else by tying a small swivel to the float and the main line can run through the eye of the swivel.

It will be obvious from the foregoing that the average boat

angler possesses all or most of the tackle needed for blue sharking and what he does not possess can be easily obtained at a small cost and with a little ingenuity.

Three rods or at the most four in a very large boat are the most than can be fished in comfort without getting into a tangle. Most Blue Sharks are taken near the surface, in the top 10 fathoms, but when starting your drift it is a good practice to fish three baits at different levels until a fish takes, thus searching the depths. One rod can fish, say, 5 or 6 fathoms down, another midwater and a third near the bottom. The bait (usually a whole mackerel, pilchard or herring, though whiting or pollack are also used) is mounted on the hook and dropped over the side followed by the steel trace. Sufficient weight in the shape of a spiral lead has already been mounted on the line and 5 or 6 fathoms of line are roughly measured off by spanning the arms and a "stop" then put on the line to prevent the float running beyond the required distance. The float must, of course, be below the "stop" which can be either a matchstick (with two half hitches of line taken around it) or a stout rubber band tied to the line. All that is required is something which will hold the float in the desired position, yet will run through the rod rings when the fish is being brought to the gaff. Of the two the rubber band is the better.

Line is paid out until the float rides 20 to 30 yards out from the boat in the rubby dubby trail. The rod fished near the bottom does not need a float and can be fished over the side in the orthodox manner. It is essential that the three rods be spaced as far apart as possible so that the floats do not ride close together and the lines tangle.

There are many schools of thought as to how the bait should be mounted, most of them based on the assumption that a shark grasps the bait across the middle and turns it in its mouth before swallowing it head first. I once fed a school of six sharks beside the boat to keep them interested while a companion played out a fish. I was tossing them whole mackerel and they took the fish just as they came to them in the water, head first, tail first or sideways. They just glided towards the mackerel, dropped the trap door which is their lower jaw and literally swam over the fish. The water was calm and crystal clear, the sharks only a foot or two under the surface and as far as I could see no effort was made to turn the baits and swallow them head first.

When using live bait the fish can be hooked lightly through the lips or in the upper part of the back just in front of the dorsal. I have tried various ways of mounting dead bait and hooked shark on all of them so that I find it dificult to recommend any particular method. As I use only one hook it can simply be inserted in the tail, or put in through the mouth and out the gills and the point of the hook then inserted into the side of the fish so that the hook shank lies flat and is an unobtrusive as possible. A baiting needle makes a very neat job of mounting a bait. The needle is inserted through the vent and out the mouth where a short hook link is attached to the split eye of the needle and then pulled back through the fish. Only the point of the hook is left protruding—the shank and part of the trace being concealed inside the bait and the tail can be fastened to the trace by a few turns of elastic crimping thread. Sharks can at times be very finicky or timid in taking a bait and it can be a definite advantage to have the hook concealed in the bait. They will mouth the bait and drop it should they feel the hook. They may even rob you of most of the bait when they are suspicious and the hook is mounted at one end or the other of the bait. I have watched a bait being lowered to a Blue Shark and was amazed at the ease with which it can "chomp" a bait. It just swam over the bait and while closing its mouth it made a scissors like movement with its jaws, cutting through the bait as easily as a fine wire cuts through butter. The reason for the serrated edges on its very sharp teeth was then very obvious.

Once the baits are out there is nothing to do but wait and the rods may be left down. The check should be left on the reel and line pulled off the rod to make sure that it runs freely and is not caught around the rod tip or rings. If the check is not strong enough to prevent line being taken off as the boat rolls or lurches, put the reel into gear and adjust the tension on the star drag so that the line is no longer pulled off. The tension must be very light, just sufficient to hold the line on the reel so that the shark will feel little resistance when it takes the bait. Sharking is the only time I would advocate that the rod be left down and when bottom fishing the angler should always hold the rod in his hands.

Sometimes the shark's fin will be seen cutting through the water as it swims up the rubby dubby trail, then disappears as it sees the hook bait and dives for it. At other times the first indication of the shark's presence is the merry tune of the reel ratchet as the fish runs off with the bait. I like to grab the rod immediately, knock off the ratchet and if the slipping clutch is engaged, throw the reel into freespool so that the shark feels the minimum amount of resistance. Danger of an overrun is guarded against by light thumb pressure on the spool. The shark must not be struck at this stage as it is only holding the bait in its mouth. Wait until it stops put the reel in gear and strike hard as soon as it starts to run a second time. Sharks have tough mouths and it is worthwhile striking a second time to ensure the hook is driven home. I like to preset my slipping clutch if the ratchet alone is strong enough to hold the line when drifting but if not the clutch can be adjusted *gradually* in the early stages of the fight taking care that it is not adjusted too tightly or that it does not seize altogether.

The fish should be allowed to run under pressure and be pumped back towards the boat every time it stops or eases up. It should not be given time to rest but be kept continually on the move so that it is tired out quickly. Even if the fish comes right in beside the boat make no attempt to gaff it until it is fully played out for 8 or 10 feet of shark that is full of vigour is very dangerous in a small boat. Watch out for a run beneath the boat and be ready to take the rod around the bow or the stern lest the main line rub along the keel and be cut. When executing this manoeuvre always put on the ratchet and throw the reel in free spool, otherwise a powerful dive, or run by the shark may take the rod (and possibly the angler if he is wearing harness) out of the boat. Sharks have a habit of trying to roll on the trace, hence the necessity for a long trace and if their tail can reach the main line it will be severed.

When the shark is played out it should be pumped carefully to the boat. The "stop" will run through the rod rings and the float will slide down to the top of the trace. As soon as the trace is within reach the man with the gaff may grasp it (a glove should be worn to prevent the wire from cutting or tearing the hand) and the fish brought within reach of the gaff. If possible the gaff should be driven home near the vent and the shark's tail lifted out of the water. Once the tail is out of the water the shark has lost most of its power. If it is gaffed towards the head instead of the tail it can put up a tremendous struggle. If there is only one gaff in the boat a loop of rope can be thrown over the shark's tail and the fish hauled into the boat.   The shark should be stunned quickly with heavy blows on the snout from a heavy blunt instrument. As soon as it is quiet stick a sharp knife through its vertebrae behind the head as a further precaution as sharks are very tenacious of life.

I should have mentioned that once the fish is gaffed or the trace grasped, the reel should be put out of gear, the ratchet put on and the spool controlled by thumb pressure.   This applies to any other heavy fish besides sharks for should the fish break off the gaff or make a sudden dive the rod can easily be pulled down on the gunwale and smashed and the fish, of course, go free.   The angler should make a practice of doing this until it becomes automatic from force of habit.

When playing a shark a rod butt rest is an absolute must because it is quite easy to do serious injury to one's unprotected groin or stomach if the butt of the rod is rested there.   The shark should also be fought from a seated position, particularly if the boat is rolling.   To stand up in these conditions is dangerous, for the powerful runs of a shark can easily unbalance an angler.   Many shark boats now carry a fighting chair equipped with a rod socket on a gimble arrangement and these are a great convenience when tackling heavy shark.   However, a couple of leather rod butt rests strapped to seats or thwarts in a boat will also serve and if fixed in different positions will allow the angler a certain amount of mobility should the shark circle the boat.   A rod harness is useful in dealing with really big fish but is unnecessary for the average run of fish.

When a shark takes, the other rods should be reeled in immediately to avoid the risk of lines becoming entangled.   As more than one shark may come at a time there is the added danger of hooking two fish together if the rods are not taken in very quickly.   The rods should be stacked away neatly out of the way and the boat checked to see that everything is shipshape and nothing is loose or is left lying about the deck.   This should be done before you actually commence to fish lest in the excitement of playing a fish it be overlooked.   Not alone is a cluttered up deck dangerous and a hazard to the angler fighting the fish but once the shark is landed it is amazing the damage it can do as it lashes about violently with its powerful tail if there are loose objects and rods lying about on deck.   The decks should also be washed down frequently and kept free of blood and slime which makes them slippery.

At times small shoals of shark will swim up to the boat and can be kept interested while another fish is being played, by feeding them pieces of fish and whole fish. If the rubby dubby bag is hung over the side of the boat facing the direction in which you are fishing they may tear at the bag but if it is placed on the far side the trail runs under the boat and the sharks will seldom pass the boat. Once the fish is landed all that is necessary when the shoal is beside the boat is to drop the bait over the side to them and it is even possible to pick out the fish that you want; though not always, for the smaller fish are quicker to the bait than the big ones. Once in these conditions I wanted to get my bait to a really good fish only to find that a smaller fish got there ahead of it. I tried to pull the bait away and actually got it out of the water but the shark came at least 3 feet out of the water and seized it. I landed it in due course and when weighed it scaled 84 lb. A fair fish but very much smaller than the one I wanted.

A word of warning. When dropping baits out to sharks swimming close to the boat, be calm, cool and collected and check that everything is in order first, i.e. that the line is free running and not tangled up in the rod, that the reel is in free spool and the star drag set and everything in the boat is shipshape. Once the shark takes it will be too late.

There is nothing difficult or mysterious about fishing for Blue Sharks. It is easy and relaxed fishing until the action starts. Then it can be hectic. Many anglers like to combine bottom fishing when drifting for shark but personally I prefer to be single minded about it for when a shark takes there is little enough time to get the other shark rods in without the added handicap of bottom rods to worry about. It is different when bottom fishing to an anchor with one shark line out, for the bottom rod can be handed to the boatman to reel in while you take care of the shark rod. When fishing to an anchor there is the danger of the fish taking the line around the anchor rope and as it is not feasible to haul the anchor in the time available the rope is best buoyed and the boat allowed to drift. When the shark is landed the buoyed rope can be picked up and bottom fishing resumed.

I find that Blue Sharks are not as consistently good fighters as tope. Some fight poorly and give the impression that they do not realise that they are hooked and only come to life when gaffed.

Others put up a wonderful struggle, providing all the thrills that an angler could desire. I feel that it is a question of matching the tackle to the fish and not fishing too heavy. Certainly on light tackle one could not ask for a more sporting fish.

PORBEAGLE SHARK

The Porbeagle is a very portly looking shark which weighs far heavier than it looks. A 5 foot specimen with a girth of 3 feet weighed 130 lb. while an 8 foot Blue Shark would weigh about 110/114 lb. It is found all around our coasts and is more plentiful in our waters than is generally believed. It has been taken on rod and line at Achill in Co. Mayo, Killybegs in Co. Donegal, at Dingle in Co. Kerry, on the Clare coast and at Kinsale and Ballycotton in Co. Cork. In Britain it has been caught on the south coast by anglers fishing out of Looe in Cornwall and off the Channel Islands.

Not much is known about its habits and it is thought not to be as plentiful as Blue Shark in season. This is possibly because anglers catch it infrequently and I believe the reason for this is that the techniques used in Blue Shark fishing are not suitable for Porbeagle fishing. Certainly it is plentiful enough to be the subject of a big commercial fishery off these islands. The Danes fish for Porbeagle with floating long lines off the East Anglian coast while on the south and west coast of Ireland a large fleet of Norwegian shark boats using similar methods fish during the summer months. The Norwegians fish within ten to fifty miles of the Irish coast and take the bulk of their catch (which is very considerable) between fifteen and twenty-five miles offshore. Shoals of Porbeagle shark have been reported by commercial fishermen off the Clare coast near Black Head, off Achill and on the Donegal coast.

The Porbeagle is viviparous but little is known about its breeding habits. A number of very small Porbeagle have been taken inshore off the Irish coast and the inference is that some at least breed in our waters. It is more tolerant of cold water than the Blue Shark and of more northerly distribution. It probably remains near our coasts all through the year for it has been reported preying on the winter herring shoals.

Though it is classed as one of the Mackerel Sharks and does prey extensively on the mackerel and herring shoals, it has been taken on rod and line mostly over rough and mixed bottoms. It seems to have a decided liking for good pollack ground and while it will be found where shoal fish, such as mackerel, pilchard and herring are plentiful it seems to feed more extensively through the depths than the Blue Shark. It can be very troublesome to long liners fishing on the bottom and wherever demersal species are plentiful, Porbeagle Sharks are likely to be present too.

The first serious fishing for Porbeagle Shark was done in Achill back in the 1930's by Dr. O'Donnell Browne and the Marquess of Sligo. Despite having to fish with unsuitable tackle and from a small canvas Currach they killed numbers of very big Porbeagle including six fine fish ranging in weight from 300 to 365 lb. The fish were taken towards the end of September and in early October when herring were plentiful off Achill but in the last two years they have been taken on rod and line as early as June on the Clare coast. As there is evidence that they are present off Achill until December the fishing season is an extended one. Since the 1930's little or no angling for Porbeagle has been carried on in Achill but the sharks are still there awaiting the enterprising angler. In Britain since the war some fine fish have been caught, including a 271 lb. specimen taken at Looe by Mrs. Hetty Eathorne and off Jersey in the Channel Islands a fish weighing 367 lb. fell to a Mr. B. Phillips.

Fishing to an anchor on grounds known to be frequented by Porbeagle would appear to be more successful than the drifting technique used for Blue Shark. Porbeagles seem to prefer bigger mouthfuls than the Blue Shark and may be slow to leave fruitful grounds where bottom living species are plentiful or they may hang around a good pollack reef where they do not have to travel far for a meal. A large bait and a much bigger hook (the size of the bait dictates the size of the hook) should be used. When I say a large bait I mean a good sized fish, e.g. a 4 to 6 lb. pollack, and while I consider that the tackle recommended for Blue Shark adequate for all except very heavy fish I would recommend a much stronger trace and 60/70 lb. breaking strain line. The Porbeagle is a strong heavy fish, not perhaps as fast or as lively as the Blue Shark, but it is stubborn and much more difficult to subdue.

In Ireland in recent years there has been a very interesting development in Porbeagle fishing. Mr. Jack Shine, Moy, Lahinch, Co. Clare, has shown that they can be successfully fished for and taken from the shore. In the last three years he has taken over thirteen Porbeagles up to 138 lb. in weight on rod and line from the rocks at Green Island in Co. Clare. Truly remarkable fishing indeed.

He first tried for Porbeagle in 1962 when in company with other shore anglers he found that big fish were repeatedly taking their feather jigs and spinning lures and, of course, smashing their tackle in the process. Mr. Shine is a very intelligent angler who decided to try and catch some of these fish and started to experiment with different methods and tackles. He did succeed in landing three of the many fish encountered (using a 19 lb. breaking strain line) in his first season and they weighed 75 lb., 77 lb. and 91 lb. During 1963 using slightly heavier tackle and longer traces he landed Porbeagle Sharks weighing 90 lb., 101 lb., 106 lb., 130 lb. and 138 lb. He believes that Porbeagle Shark can be taken from the shore in many areas where conditions are suitable and at the time of writing has extended his operations successfully to the north coast of Clare where he has taken fish at Ballyreen near Black Head.

He considers that a likely spot for Porbeagle is where there is deep water close in (at Green Island the rock drops away into 6 fathoms) and deeper water outside where mackerel and sprat shoals are plentiful. He states that Porbeagle definitely feed on sprats and indeed has seen them chase and take his feather lures repeatedly. The tackle he now uses for the sharks is as follows. A 12 foot hollow glass rod; 6½ inch Alvey side cast reel, 300 yards of 32 lb. breaking strain monofilment over 60 yards of braided nylon as backing; and a 7 to 8 foot cable laid steel wire trace with a 10/0 hook. Previously he used an 8 foot solid fibre glass rod and a 5½ inch reel but believes the longer rod and bigger capacity spool a better combination.

The trace bears two swivels, one where the main line is joined and the other 4 feet from the hook. A small float is attached to each of the swivels and a bottle cork is fitted to the trace between the swivels so that this portion floats and the bait, half a fresh mackerel (tail end) fishes not very far below the surface. Mr. Shine believes that the sharks tend to swim near the surface when inshore and his experience seems to bear this out. The reason for buoying up the upper half of the trace is to prevent the shark from getting tangled in the trace as it takes the bait. Should this happen and the fish roll the light main line would be within reach of the tail and a breakage would be inevitable. The trace is unweighted as there is sufficient weight in the bait for it to be cast out 40/60 yards. If the wind is favourable a balloon can be attached to the trace and the bait floated out a considerable distance.

Porbeagle near the shore take very delicately, mouthing and playing with the bait for a considerable length of time. It must be given plenty of time until it definitely takes the bait and runs seawards with it before being struck. It usually hooks itself through "munching" the bait but strike hard sideways to be sure. The fish will run long and hard, hence the necessity for a large capacity reel and the fish should be played out fully before any attempt is made to bring it within reach of the gaff. The further out the fish is played the better for when it comes close to the shore there is the danger of the line being tangled or cut on submerged rocks when the shark bores deep close in. A strong gaff is essential, preferably one with a length of strong rope attached to it and make no attempt to gaff the fish unless you are sure that it is exhausted. Remember, too, that though the fish may not look very big its weight can be deceptive.

Shark fishing from the shore is rather like rock fishing for tope. It requires a great deal of patience and perseverance. There will be very many blank days, perhaps even months when conditions are not suitable but surely the rewards are great. As Jack Shine says, there must be a number of places where really big fish may be taken from the shore. He has pioneered this type of fishing in these islands. If only others follow the example he has set, who knows what may yet be caught.

MAKO SHARK

The Mako Shark is classed as one of the big game species and is sought by anglers all over the world on account of its magnificent fighting qualities. It is a beautifully proportioned fish, streamlined, thick in the body (though not portly in the sense that the Porbeagle Shark is) with the body thickness retained rearwards. It attains a great size and has been taken on rod and line up to 1000 lb. in weight. It is a very strong and fast fish which usually leaps clear of the water when first hooked and jumps several times during the struggle. It is a very fierce shark which has been known when hooked to attack the boat and on occasion has even jumped into the boat.   It should be treated with the greatest respect.

The Mako was considered something of a dream by anglers in these islands but the fact that it is present in our waters during the summer months at least has now been well demonstrated.   Several are boated each season at Looe in Cornwall and some heavy Mako have been taken near the Channel Islands.   It has been hooked but not landed by anglers at Ballycotton and Kinsale in Co. Cork and it is almost certainly the "leaping fish" so frequently reported by commercial fishermen on the west coast of Ireland.

The Mako is one of the Mackerel Sharks which feeds on shoal fishes on or near the surface and though it will also feed on or near the bottom it more closely resembles in habit the Blue Shark than the Porbeagle.   Indeed very little is known about its habits or distribution in our waters and it is another species which may be more plentiful than is generally realised.   It was only in 1955 that the first Mako, a first weighing 352 lb., was recorded on rod and line at Looe.   This fish was at first identified as a Porbeagle and it is possible that a number of big Porbeagle's taken previous to this were in fact Mako and not identified as such.   Since 1955 several big fish of over 400 lb. have been taken by anglers but little specialised angling has been done for this species and most of those taken were by anglers fishing for Blues or else encountered by anglers bottom fishing and who put over a shark line when a hooked fish was "snatched".   When a proper technique and fishing method is devised for this most sporting shark it may prove to be more plentiful and widely distributed around our coasts than it is considered to be at present.

In New Zealand it is normally taken by trolling with a whole fish as bait or deep drifting with live bait.   Brigadier Caunter points out that most of those taken off Looe were caught from boats which were drifting very quickly before very strong or near gale force winds and it is possible that trolling would be the most effective method.   Heavy tackle is a must for these are very strong and fast fish which take a long time to subdue and there is always the chance of encountering a really big specimen.   I would suggest a powerful shark rod, 80/100 lb. breaking strain synthetic line and a 20 foot steel wire trace around 600 lb. breaking strain.   As a really big bait is indicated hook sizes 14/0 to 16/0 would be most suitable.

THRESHER SHARK

The Thresher Shark is another very large and game species of shark which has been recorded from all around our coasts. A surface or sub-surface feeder, it preys on small shoal fish such as mackerel, pilchard, garfish and herring and where shoal fish are plentiful it will probably be present. It has been seen as far north as the Orkneys and is quite plentiful at times off the Kent and Sussex coasts. At times it comes very close to the shore, off beaches, and in estuaries and I have seen one very large specimen jump well up the estuary at Kinsale in Co. Cork.

Little is known about its habits and it is a difficult species to catch and even more difficult to land, most of those hooked breaking free before they can be brought to the gaff. It is a spectacular fighter which jumps repeatedly, making full use of its enormous tail in an effort to cut the line and a longer trace than normally used in shark fishing is advocated.

It is known to round up shoal fish by swimming round and round the shoal (often in company with another Thresher) until the terrified shoal is driven into a tight huddle or "pill" when the Thresher then charges through the huddled mass striking left and right with its terrible tail and picking up the dead and injured fish at leisure. The normal rubby dubby technique and fishing on the drift has not proved very successful, possibly because of this habit of the Thresher of feeding on numbers of shoal fish and a solitary mackerel drifting through the water may not interest it greatly. Most of those hooked have been taken by anglers fishing for other species and it has frequently taken feather jigs and lures being trolled for mackerel or pollack so that it possibly also feeds on sprat. It is more likely to take a trolled bait and as this fish grows to a great size very heavy tackle is recommended.

It has been taken to weights exceeding 900 lb. in warmer waters and though the British record still stands at 280 lb. (taken at Dungeness in 1930) very much larger fish are present in our waters. Heavy tackle, such as is recommended for Mako, is indicated at least until more Thresher are landed and more information on the best methods and tackle to use is discovered.

CHAPTER 21

BIG GAME FISHES

MANY READERS MAY NOW THINK THAT I HAVE REACHED THE stage of wishful thinking and that big game fishing in our waters is a bit of a pipe dream. However, I make no apology for this chapter for I believe that a few at least of the big game species are present in our waters though very little is known about their habits, distribution or the methods by which they can be taken. Apart from a few isolated instances they have not been specially fished for and as this is an expensive form of angling requiring special tackle, techniques and boats, it has not to date been investigated to the extent that I think it merits.

Most of the fishes considered to be game fishes are warm water species which do not reach our latitudes but there are a few notable exceptions. Mako and Thresher Shark are known to frequent our coasts (these have been dealt with in the previous chapter), but tunny are also present, as are the halibut, swordfish, albacore and bonito. It may be argued that they are not present in sufficient numbers or that only in exceptional seasons do some of them reach our coasts, yet it should be remembered that even in the most renowned big game angling centres in the world these ocean giants are not taken every day or even every week.

I believe that the sharks are present in greater numbers and are more widely distributed than we realise. The tunny is a regular visitor, even though in most places it may only be in transit, and to date has only been taken in the North Sea. The Broadbill Swordfish even in tropical waters does not seem to be very "thick over the ground" and is a very difficult fish to catch but it has been reported from points as far apart as the north of Scotland and Cornwall. The halibut, because of its more or less solitary habit and the fact that it is on the whole a deep water demersal species, may never figure largely in anglers' catches yet in places it is within the reach of the deep sea angler and would prove a very welcome bonus in any fishing season. The smaller game fishes, i.e. the albacore and bonitos, are considered as occasional stragglers, but are we sure that they are? We do not really know.

The presence or absence of some of these fish and the distance they are found from our coasts may depend to a great extent on the season. Some of them are pelagic warm water species and the influence of the Gulf Stream or more correctly the North Atlantic Drift has a great bearing on their movements. The effect of the North Atlantic Drift varies with the season and in some years its warm waters penetrate farther north than in others. I have noticed that in years when we had persistent easterly winds in winter and spring the warm waters were held back and our inshore waters never really warmed up with a very detrimental effect on fishing. In years when we experienced strong and persistent westerlies and south-westerlies the waters of the North Atlantic Drift were pushed farther north and closer to our coasts and these were excellent years in which mackerel, pilchard and small bait fishes were plentiful close to our shores. The larger predators would, of course, follow their food and it is in these seasons that most of the unusual fish reported by fishermen have been observed.

They will be closer in during some seasons than in others but we know little or nothing about their presence or how far offshore they stay. Our ignorance is not a valid reason for dismissing them as a pipe dream for there has been very definite evidence of their presence over the years. Granted that our very changeable Atlantic weather is a big stumbling block but it should be possible with a big fast boat to investigate thoroughly our offshore waters and I feel that the effort would be very much worthwhile. Who knows what we might find if we tried?

THE HALIBUT

It may seem strange to start off the list of big game fish with a flatfish; but this is no ordinary flatfish, but a real giant in a family not noted for the great size of its individual species. Not only is it a big fish but it possesses great strength, endurance and a wonderful fighting spirit that makes it compare more than favourably with the most sporting fishes in the sea.

The halibut is a right-handed flatfish, having the eyes and colour on the right side and in general outline it is longer and narrower than most other flatfish. It is also much rounder and thicker in the body and it has a very large mouth and sharp teeth. The body is covered with smooth scales and the dorsal fin commences level with or in advance of the eyes and the lateral line is strongly curved over the pectoral fin. The colour is usually brownish on the upper side and pearly white beneath.

A cold water species abundant off Iceland and in the Arctic, it is most plentiful in our northern waters, particularly off the north of Scotland but is taken in the northern part of the North Sea, off the west and south coasts of Ireland and in the Channel, but is reaching the more southerly limits of its range in the south. It is essentially a deepwater species, attaining a weight in excess of 600 lb., but the larger specimens are unlikely to come within the reach of the angler as they keep to very deep water. While the bulk of really big halibut are taken in deep water (over 100 fathoms) Howell's statistics show that 65 per cent of the commercial catch is taken in depths ranging from 20 to 55 fathoms. This would bring reasonably big halibut within reach of the deep sea angler who is prepared to fish in 30/40 fathoms of water.

The halibut is a very active predator which seems to swim off the bottom, feeding mainly on other fishes. It shows a preference for rough and mixed bottoms and while shoal fishes such as haddock and whiting figure largely in its diet, its food is varied and includes species typical of both rough and clean bottoms. It is rather solitary in habit and for that reason is not likely to be taken in any great numbers by anglers. A big fish, it requires a lot of food and though it ranges widely over the bottom it is likely to linger on good feeding grounds. It is, however, not likely to be found in any great numbers on the same feeding grounds for its appetite is such that numbers of them could not be supported in a small area.

Likely ground is gullies and ravines that fissure and split really rough high ground in deep water; mixed bottoms of rock alternating with sand, mud or gravel where fish are plentiful; the edges of rocky reefs and the gullies between banks where it can wait in ambush for fish that are channeled towards it by the tides. Spawning time is January to May but may even extend into July.

Some very good halibut weighing over 100 lb. have been taken on rod and line at Ballycotton and at Valentia, and the Irish record, a fish weighing 152 lb. 12 oz., was taken at the latter centre.   It is significant that at both of these centres there is deep water and a great deal of rough and mixed bottoms.   Although halibut were specially fished for at Valentia with success in the old days it does not seem plentiful enough over the ground to warrant specialised fishing and a halibut when hooked could be considered an unexpected though very welcome windfall by the angler.

It is most likely to be taken by deep sea anglers using heavy tackle and very large baits for heavy bottom feeding species such as skate and conger, though their tackle may not always be adequate to hold a big specimen when it is hooked.   The halibut is a tearaway fighter of great strength and endurance, which runs fast and hard and may be fought up to the boat several times only to take off again at great speed.   It is certainly a worthy foe and a very game fish.

THE TUNNY

Our tunny, i.e. the Bluefin or Short Finned Tunny, is the big brother of the mackerel family, possessing the same streamlined appearance and all the wonderful fighting qualities typical of this group of fishes.   In general outline it closely resembles the mackerel but is more stoutly built and is deeper in the body.   It is a real giant which may attain a weight of 1500 lb. and a length of 12 feet. It is one of the most sought after of all the game fish and while it does not provide the spectacular and acrobatic thrills of the marlins and sailfishes, for sheer power, strength and speed it has few equals.

Tunny were first observed in the North Sea in the vicinity of herring drifters where they were seen to feed on the herring which fell out of the drift nets when the commercial fishermen made their haul.   North Sea Tunny Angling was pioneered by the late Mitchell Henry and one fish which he took off Whitby in 1933 weighed 851 lb.   For a long time it stood as the world record for this species and still stands as the British record.   Tunny appear in the North Sea about late August and are present during September and October.   They do not appear to penetrate farther south than Flamborough Head and Scarborough is the main base for the sport and also the headquarters of the British Tunny Club.

The usual practice was to hire a small coble or a small drifter at

Scarborough or Whitby and rendezvous with the herring fleet in the North Sea. The actual fishing was done from a small row boat specially brought along for the purpose and not from the "parent ship". Watch was kept for the schools of tunny to show close to the nets and as this could happen at any time either during the day or night the tackle was always kept in readiness. As soon as tunny were observed the angler was quickly put adrift with a boatman in the small boat, for tunny are fast moving fish that may not stay around for long, and the angler had to be quick off the mark if he was to get among them.

The tackle was of necessity heavy, for North Sea Tunny run big, averaging around 600 lb., and took anything from three-quarters of an hour to three hours to land. A typical outfit would be a very powerful rod similar in strength to a Hardy No. 5 or No. 6. Saltwater rod, and a large capacity reel comparable to a 9 inch Fortuna or 12/0 to 16/0 multiplier. Tunny run fast and far and 400 to 800 yards of 100/130 lb. breaking strain braided non stretch synthetic line is advisable. A heavy cable laid steel wire trace, 18-20 feet in length with big game swivels and a 12/0 to 16/0 hook is used. The hook is needle sharp, of finest tempered steel, and the size must suit the bait used, usually herring or mackerel. The rod butt is rested in a swivelling butt socket attached to the boat and a shoulder harness is essential.

While some very heavy fish have been taken in the North Sea the fishing tends to be patchy and in some seasons no tunny at all are caught. The North Sea is not noted for its placidity and the present methods of operating leave a lot to be desired. The schools of tunny may be anything from 40 to 100 miles offshore early in the season though later they may be encountered within five to fifteen miles off the Yorkshire coast. This means long journeys in small slow boats and the cobbles cannot stay out for long though the small drifters which have sleeping accommodation on board can stay at sea for several days. If tunny fishing is to be developed, fast seaworthy fishing launches specially equipped for tunny fishing must be used. The actual fishing can then be done from the boat, a fast trip made to the grounds and should the weather deteriorate a quick return to port can be made. Granted it will make fishing expensive but tunny fishing is an expensive sport anyway and the best is always the most economical in the long run. It would greatly increase the chances of success and surely that is worth paying a little extra for!

The North Sea is not the only place where tunny can be taken on rod and line. Large fish are caught by anglers off Brittany and Denmark. The Danes are fortunate for most of their fishing is done in the Kattegat area at no great distance from the land. Though they have only been angled for off the Yorkshire coast, tunny have been reported from many parts of these islands. They have been seen on the south and west coasts of Ireland, on the north and north-west coasts of Scotland and schools of small fish have been reported from Cornwall, the mouth of Bantry Bay and Achill. A tunny weighing 650 lb. was washed ashore dead on the coasts of Donegal in August, 1960, and I have seen a photograph of one small fish weighing about 60 lb. which was stranded at low water in a tidal pool at Cloghane on the Dingle Peninsula.

The tunny is a far ranging species and a voracious feeder, preying chiefly on pelagic species such as mackerel, herrings, flying fishes, garfish, sandeels and fry. It is found in the Mediterranean, eastern Atlantic and the east coast of America. The Mediterranean tunny spawn off Sicily, Sardinia and Tunis from April to June and although there may be some interchange between the Mediterranean and the Atlantic tunny they seem on the whole to behave as two separate populations. Tunny make extensive migrations and tagging experiments carried out by the Americans show that some tunny at least make transatlantic migration for fish tagged on the coast of America have been recaptured in the Bay of Biscay.

Investigations have shown that our tunny appear to travel in from the Atlantic to spawn off the south coast of Spain and the west coast of Morocco during late May or early June. Ripe fish which are quite empty and not feeding arrive off Cadiz and about two weeks later spent fish are taken on the way out again while others are still arriving. This would indicate that spawning takes place in this area. This is a run of big tunny (which we will call group A) ranging in weight from 400 to 650 lb. and in age from 11 to 14 years.

About the same time a second group (Group B) arrives off the west coast of Morocco to spawn and as no spent fish are taken it would indicate that they strike straight out westwards after spawning. These are smaller fish in the 200/350 lb. class and ranging from 8 to 11 years old. In July another group (Group C) arrive in the Bay of Biscay and mill around for a while before heading off for their spawning grounds which are suspected to be in the vicinity of the Spanish Bank. These are 5 to 8 years old fish running from 80 to 200 lb. in weight.

The spent tunny migrate out into the Atlantic and head for the rich feeding grounds off the Norwegian coast where their weight is estimated to increase at the rate of 11 lb. per week. The fish travel in schools, in which the fish are roughly all of a size. The smaller fish travel in much large schools than the bigger fish and the schools of really big tunny may be quite small. On their northward journey they seem to follow the edge of the Continental Shelf (about the 100 fathom line) and are next observed off the Tampen Bank which lies between the very far north of Scotland and the Norwegian coast. About two weeks later they appear on the Norwegian coast roughly in the area between Tromso and Trondheim. They arrive in July and remain during July and August and these fish are the very big tunny and belong to Group A.

Group B though spawning later than Group A arrive only two weeks later. The largest concentration is in the Alesund-Stavanger area (the run of tunny extends right down to the Kattegat) and they make a quicker passage because the distance between the Tampen Bank and their feeding grounds is considerably shorter than Group A's. The next arrival is Group C which appear in late August or early September and remain until early October. The strange thing about their arrival is that as soon as they appear Group B disappears and is not seen again that season on the Norwegian coast. There is an important commercial seine net fishing for tunny in Norway and the largest concentration of fish seems to be in the Bergen area.

On first arriving in Norwegian waters the tunny behave like plankton feeders and there is a great upwelling of plankton on that coast in late June-July and early August. Later in the season they feed on herring fry and jumping is characteristic of their behaviour during this period. It is interesting to note that the composition of the schools of tunny found on the east coast of England near the Dogger Bank is the same as Group A's. This ties in closely with he late August/September/October tunny fishing out of Scarborough and it is possible that these are Group *A* on its return journey from Norway.

It is also interesting to note that there is a very intensive bait fishery for small tunny on the north coast of Spain. These are mainly 1 to 3 year old fish with the 2 year old class predominating. The season is extensive lasting from May to September and a tremendous number of immature fish are taken. Tunny mature at 3 years of age, at which age they weigh approximately 40 lb. It is significant that the Norwegian commercial tunny fishing suffered a very serious decline shortly after the post-war Spanish fishery for small tunny reached its full efficiency in the late 1950's. Heavy fishing of immature fish of any species will have a very great effect on the numbers of adult fish available, particularly on the numbers of very big adults and in the case of tunny will, of course, have a direct bearing on the angling possibilities in our waters.

What, then, are the possibilities of tunny fishing in our waters apart from those already discovered in the North Sea? I believe that they are good but that a great deal of exploratory work must be undertaken to establish it. The tunny migrating northwards from their spawning grounds are lean and hungry and require a tremendous amount of food. They seem to follow the edge of the Continental Shelf—there is little food for them west of it—around the south and west coasts of Ireland and the north-west and west coasts of Scotland. The Continental Shelf comes in very close to parts of the west coast of Ireland, particularly in the Mayo, Sligo and Donegal areas. Travelling tunny do not seem to feed but it is possible that the schools come in to rest and feed on the way and that part of them remain. Indeed fish which from descriptions appear to be tunny have frequently been seen in these areas and while there would not be sufficient food for the main body of tunny heading for the rich feeding grounds off Norway there should be sufficient to tempt at least some of them. I believe that the possibilities are there and that the fish can be located not too far from the land. The same holds true of the south coast but there it would probably be necessary to seek them farther offshore. The same may be true off the Cornish coast.

What little we know about the movements of tunny indicate that they are there but there are so many questions to be answered. Do the tunny come in and feed on the way? Where do they rest and at what times can they be expected? What route do they take? Are they within reasonable reach of the land? Can they be expected again on their homeward journey in the autumn? What, if any, baits will they take and what are the best methods to use? One could go on speculating forever but the answer will only be found by enterprising anglers prepared to undergo the expense and trouble and perhaps the heartbreaks and disappointments, too, of doing the pioneering work.

THE BROADBILL SWORDFISH

This is the true swordfish in which the upper jaw is prolonged to form a broad flat smooth sword which is not armed with teeth.

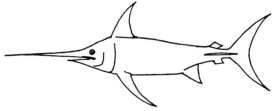

Broadbill Swordfish

The sword is used to stun or kill fish by swiping blows, and is not used to impale prey. The fish once hit can then be picked up by the swordfish at leisure. The first dorsal fin is tall, erect and crescentic, the pectorals are long and set low down while the pelvic fins are absent. There are no scales or lateral line present on the body, the second dorsal is short and low; the first anal fin is broad and the second anal small while there is a single lateral keel on each side of the caudal peduncle. The colour is greyish blue or purplish on the back becoming silvery grey below.

The Broadbill Swordfish is a fast vigorous swimmer found in the Mediterranean, also on the western side of the Atlantic, and has been recorded from many parts of our coasts between June and November, and specimens have been reported from as far north as Scandinavia. Little is known about its habits or distribution but it is an ocean species feeding on the surface and subsurface on any fish of suitable size. I think that it can be considered a little more than just an occasional straggler from warmer seas and it has been reported from the Bristol Channel, the Estuary of the Severn, Yarmouth, Cornwall, and the coasts of Scotland. A swordfish weighing 130 lb. was taken in a salmon net in Bantry Bay in 1950 and it has been observed in the holds of Norwegian shark boats which fish floating long lines on the south and west coasts of Ireland.

I would not say that it is plentiful for even in warmer seas this particular species is not very "thick over the ground". Who knows, however, until we try for them. It is only in very recent years that anglers discovered it was possible to take them off the Portuguese coast by drifting. It is a very difficult fish to catch and is usually taken by slowly trolling a bait (a whole fish) across the path of a swordfish seen finning on the surface. Like the tunny, it does not jump when hooked but is considered to be one of the strongest and most stubborn of the big game fish.

ALBACORE

The albacore is another member of the mackerel family and a scaled down version of the giant Blue Fin Tunny. It is also called the Long Finned Tunny on account of its long curved pectoral fins which extend backwards to beyond the origin of the anal fin. Its habits also are rather similar to the tunny and it travels in quite large shoals, feeding on the surface and subsurface on any smaller fishes and on squid.

It is widely distributed in the Mediterranean, the Bay of Biscay, and the warmer reaches of the Atlantic. It has been reported from a number of places around our coasts, i.e. Devon, Cornwall, Portland, Lancashire, Scotland, Orkneys, Dingle, Clifden (Co. Galway), Wexford and Achill. It has been caught on rod and line to a weight of 66¼ lb. but the average size of fish recorded from our waters is 10 to 12 lb.

A very strong and vigorous swimmer, it takes many types of artificial lures, e.g. feather lures and jigs and spoons trolled fairly fast through the water. Light boat or heavy spinning tackle and a fine short wire trace is the usual tackle and when taken on this gear the albacore can be depended on to put up a terrific and exciting struggle.

This is another species which is present off our southern and western seaboards but how close to the land it comes is not known. It normally does not come as close inshore as the bonito but schools of fish thought to be albacore have been sighted off Kinsale. The French fish albacore commercially off the south and south-west coast of Ireland but they are notoriously tight mouthed about their fishing and information is impossible to obtain. It is likely that the annual penetration of the North Atlantic Drift has a considerable effect on their northern range and albacore may be found nearer the coast in some seasons than others.

THE BONITO

The bonitos also belong to the mackerel family and though smaller than the albacore possess all the wonderful fighting qualities

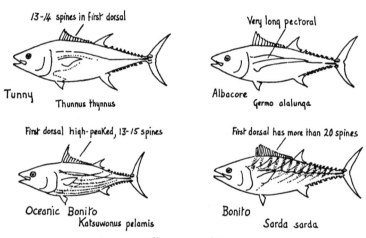

Tunny, Albacore and Bonitos

inherent in this large group of fishes. The Oceanic Bonito is more stoutly built than the mackerel and possesses four, five or six curving parallel bands running laterally along its sides. It attains a length of 3 feet but recorded specimens from our waters average 5/6 lb. in weight. A close relative, the Pelamid or Belted Bonito, also strays into our waters (it has been recorded from Kinsale) but this species has a series of narrow stripes obliquely crossing a series of broad bands on the upper portion of the sides.

The habits and distribution of the bonitos are similar to the

albacore's but they are more active fish which swim in shoals
feeding on small fishes. They are fished for with very light tackle
and are taken on a variety of lures; feather lures and jigs, spoons,
plugs, imitation squid, streamer flies and long strips of cut bait.
Trolling is the usual method and a very fast troll is essential (faster
than for albacore) for the bonito has been known to take a lure
trolled at 18 m.p.h. Little is known of their habits in our waters
but the same remarks probably apply as for albacore.

INDEX

Admiralty Charts, 131
Albacore, 341
Allowing for Tide, 134
Anatomy of Fishes, 25, 26
Anchoring, 133, 140
Angler Fish, 72, 294
Artificial Lures, 116, 118

Baits, 73
Bass, 28, 154
Beaches, 19, 20, 21, 158
Beachfishing
    for Bass, 158
    for Tope, 280
Bearings—compass, 133, 136
Birds, 137
Boats, 138
Boatfishing tackle, 107
Boat handling, 141
Boatfishing for Bass, 173
Bonito, 342
Bony Fishes, 25
Bottom, types of, 17, 18
Bottom fishing, 103, 108
Boots, 101
Bream, Red Sea, 30, 255
Bream, Black, 30, 255
Brill, 49, 244
Butterfish, 83

Carbon dioxide, 3
Cartilaginous Fishes, 25, 60
Casting, 117, 118, 121
Casting with a fixed spool reel, 117
Casting with a multiplier reel, 118
Charts, 131
Chemical elements, 3
Clams, 83

Clothes, 100
Clouds, 146
Coalfish, 54, 202
Cockles, 81
Cod, 49, 50, 211
    Winter Cod, 215
    Summer Cod, 214
Compass, 135
Conger, 57, 229
Courtesy, 150
Crabs, 77, 78
Currents, 4, 9, 11, 12

Dab, 47, 242
Dab Lemon, 47
Dangers, 151
Dangerous fish, 152
Depth, 1, 16, 17, 137
Diary, xx, 148
Dogfish
    Greater Spotted, 61, 289
    Lesser Spotted, 61, 289
    Spur, 62, 287
Driftlining, 111, 188, 198, 201
Drifting, 109, 200

Echo Sounder, 139
Eel, freshwater, 237
Estuaries, 21, 22, 167
Estuary fishing
    for Bass, 167
    for Flounders, 240

Fair angling, 150
Feathering, 197, 201, 206
Feathers, 105, 120
Ferrules, 91
Fish baits, 84

Flatfishes, 43
Floatfishing, 112
Floatfishing
  for bass, 171
  for mullet, 187
  for pollack, 198
  for shark, 321
Flounder, 45, 238
Fundamental principles, xiv

Gaffs, 99
Gaffing, 126
Game Fishes, 332
Garfish, 56, 209
Ground bait, 181, 182
Gulf Stream, 5
Gurnards
  Grey, 40, 41, 252, 253
  Tub, 42, 252, 254
  Red, 42, 252, 255

Haddock, 50, 226
Hake, 56, 220
Halibut, 48, 333
Hermit crab, 86
Herring, 59, 84
Hooks, 96, 97

Irish Specimen Fish Committee, 306

John Dory, 43

Knots, 101, 102
"Know How", xiv

Landing fish, 126
Landing net, 99
Leger, 104, 105
Light, xvi, 5
Limpets, 83
Lines, 95, 96
Ling, 55, 218
Locating fishing grounds, 129, 136
Lugworm, 74

Mackerel, 33, 84, 204

Marks, 132
Monkfish, 62, 292
Mullet
  Red, 32
  Grey, 38, 177
  Thinlipped, 40
  Golden, 40
Mullet fishing, 177
Mussels, 80

Osmosis, 2
Oxygen, 3

Paternoster, 103
Piddocks, 83
Pier fishing, 217, 231
Pilchard, 59, 84
Plaice, 44, 241
Plankton, 6
Playing a fish, 122
Pollack, 53, 54, 194
Pollack from the shore, 196
Pollack from boats, 199
Poor Cod, 51, 53, 228
Pouting, 51, 52, 226
Prawns, 79

Ragworm, 75, 76
Rays, 67, 307
  Blonde Ray, 70, 308
  Cuckoo Ray, 308
  Homelyn Ray, 71 308
  Sandy Ray, 308
  Shagreen Ray, 70
  Sting Ray, 71, 152, 310
  Thornback Ray, 70, 308
Razorfish, 81
Reels, 93, 94, 106, 107
Rods, xix, 88, 89, 90, 106, 107, 110
Rod butt rest, 100
Rod fittings, 91
Rocky shores, 19
Rockfishing
  for bass, 171
  for Pollack, 195
  for Tope, 283

for Wrasse, 250
Rockling, 55
Rubby Dubby, 316

Salinity, 2
Salmon, 58
Sandeels, 82
Sea, 1
Sea Breams, 30, 255
Sea shore, 18, 19, 23
Sea Trout, 58, 265
Seasonal migrations, 14, 15
Selachians, 25
Senses, of fish, 27
Scad, 31, 210
Shads
    Twaite, 59, 200
    Allis, 60
Sharks
    Blue, 63, 312
    Porbeagle, 64, 312, 326
    Mako, 64, 313, 329
    Thresher, 65, 313, 331
Shore Fishing tackle, 106
Skate
    Common, 68, 297, 298
    White, 69, 297, 299
    Longnosed, 69, 297, 299
    Flapper, 69
Sinkers, 98 108
Smooth Hound, 66, 291
Sole, 47, 243
Sounds, xviii
Spinning, 114, 119
Spinning
    for Bass, 169, 172, 173
    for Flounder, 240
    for Mackerel, 206
    for Mullet, 189
    for Pollack, 195

for Sea Trout, 267
Squid, 85
Surf casting, 121
Surf fishing, 161
Swim bladder, 17
Swivels, 97
Swordfish, 35, 340

Tackle, xiv, xix, 87, 106
Technique, xiv, 103
Temperature, xvi, 3, 4
Temperature migration, 15
Test curve, 92
Thermocline, 7
Tides, xviii, 8, 9, 10, 11, 12, 22, 23,
    134, 137
Tides, effect on fish, 12
Tide Tables, 11
Tope, 65, 269
Tope from the shore, 279
Tope from boats, 273
Traces, 103, 116
Trolling, 110, 199, 175
Tunny, 35, 335
Turbot, 48, 244

Weather, xvii, 13, 145, 148, 166
    effects on fish, 13
Weevers, Lesser and Greater, 32, 152
Whiting, 51
Wind, xvii, 13, 14, 135
Wire, 98
Wrasse
    Ballan, 36, 249
    Corkwing, 37, 249, 252
    Cuckoo, 36, 249, 252
    Rainbow, 37

Zonation, 23, 73